Edited by

ROBERT F. GLECKNER
University of California, Riverside

GERALD E. ENSCOE
Franklin and Marshall College

Romanticism
Points of View
SECOND EDITION

PRENTICE-HALL, INC.
Englewood Cliffs, N.J.

PRENTICE-HALL ENGLISH LITERATURE SERIES

Maynard Mack, editor

C–13–782987–6
P–13–782979–5

Library of Congress Catalog Card No.: 77–97922

Current printing (last number):
10   9   8   7   6   5   4   3   2   1

Printed in the United States of America

PRENTICE-HALL INTERNATIONAL, *London*
PRENTICE-HALL OF AUSTRALIA, PTY. LTD., *Sydney*
PRENTICE-HALL OF CANADA, LTD., *Toronto*
PRENTICE-HALL OF INDIA PRIVATE LIMITED, *New Delhi*
PRENTICE-HALL OF JAPAN, INC., *Tokyo*

Preface

Since late 1961 when the manuscript of the first edition of *Romanticism: Points of View* was completed, several important works on the subject have appeared; and, in addition, the inevitable process of revaluation of and second thoughts about the original selections has proceeded apace. All the essays originally labelled, perhaps somewhat pontifically, as "classic statements" on the general subject of romanticism do not seem now to support such a description: some, in the course of classroom use, finally contributed less to the discussion of romanticism than anticipated, and still others were superseded by later statements to the same point.

Accordingly, the present collection represents a revision of about half the original. In addition, each selection retained from the original has been carefully reedited to maintain the continuity and clarity of the writer's argument where it has been necessary to abridge the original in any way. A greater number of editorial footnotes have been added to provide bibliographical cross-reference to other essays in the collection and to pertinent and significant works on romanticism outside this collection. New to this edition, bibliographical notes at the end of each selection provide further assistance to the student. As before, I have excluded a number of good essays that center on individual writers in favor of those that define, evaluate, criticize, defend, or attack the ideology, aesthetic, style, or implications of the Romantic Movement as a whole, in an attempt to provide, as the title suggests, as many varied points of view toward romanticism as the exigencies of space allowed. Necessarily, then, several essays taking the same point of view as others in the collection have been omitted. If those that are included appear to the student or instructor inferior to another in the same vein, but not included, the choice clearly must be chalked up to my own taste and judgment. For advice and counsel in this and other matters, I should like to thank the following, while absolving them entirely of my lapses in judgment and errors of commission and omission. If the present volume approaches more nearly than the first a collection of "classic" essays, they, as well as the authors themselves, of course, should receive considerable credit. It is a pleasure, then, to acknowledge an ample debt to Professor Gerald E. Enscoe, my former co-editor, and to Professors Meyer H. Abrams, Walter J. Bate, Edward E. Bostetter, Richard H. Fogle, Northrop Frye, E. D. Hirsch, Jr., Herbert Lindenberger, the late William H. Marshall, Martin K. Nurmi, Morse Peckham, David Perkins, Jack Stillinger, Earl R. Wasserman, and Carl R. Woodring. My thanks also to my colleague Professor Stanley N. Stewart for invaluable advice and to Nathaniel Teich for his great help in the reediting process. I am grateful to the University of California for assistance in the form of an Intramural Research Grant and to Paul E. O'Connell for continuing advice and encouragement. My greatest debt, of course, is to the authors, publishers, and journal editors of the works here reprinted. Where I have had to make excisions in their material, I trust that I have done so with sufficient care not to misrepresent, distort, or unduly fragment the original. In all such cases the reader is encouraged to consult the original for its fuller footnote and bibliographical reference and, in the case of excerpts from longer works, for the important totality of context in which the essay appears.

A note on the text. Omissions from the original text of the essays are indicated clearly by ellipses. All ellipses in the volume are mine unless otherwise noted. I have also deleted many of the original footnotes to the essays in the interests of space; those that have been retained I have renumbered. All asterisked page notes are mine. I have retained all original spelling and usage with the exception of punctuation of quotations, which I have made consistent with American usage. Passages and phrases in foreign languages have been italicized.

R.F.G.

Grand Terrace, California

iv

Contents

Introduction

In his Nobel Prize acceptance speech William Faulkner said of man "that when the last ding-dong of doom has clanged and faded from the last worthless rock hanging tideless in the last red and dying evening, that even then there will be one more sound: that of his puny inexhaustible voice, still talking." With similar persistence critical and scholarly discussion of romanticism during the last century or so has been remarkably lively and continuous. Indeed, it can be argued that the seemingly inexhaustible dialectic of championship and attack that the romantic idea has provoked testifies to a peculiar and genuine immortality. And the value of that debate is substantial—to the student of literature, the literary critic, the literary historian, and the scholar, all of whom, of course, are in some measure responsible for the body of definition, analysis, commentary, and evaluation from which they gain. If occasionally the critical woods become too dense for clear viewing of the literary trees, the fact remains that most essays on romanticism at once turn us back to the romantic texts lying quietly and unchangeably at the center of the storm; prompt us to reconsider the complex, patterned historical milieu that gave rise to and supported this literary insurgency; continue to reveal to us neglected angles of vision from which to approach the literature and its context; and remind us firmly of the insistent vitality and development of literary criticism through the nineteenth and twentieth centuries.

1

For all these reasons the editors remain convinced of the usefulness of a collection such as this, despite the fact that exigencies of space and an abundance of good essays on British Romanticism precluded even token inclusion of the important body of critical material on Continental Romanticism. If, in addition to this lack of continental material, other apparently awkward omissions may be noted, it is because the choice of essays has been limited to those that seem to develop critical approaches, stances, and points of view which involve central issues—literary, critical, social, political, psychological, and philosophical—of major concern to the twentieth as well as to the nineteenth century.

II

A good example of critical aestheticism as well as basic historical sense is Walter Pater's Postscript to *Appreciations*. He sees the "addition of curiosity" to "the desire of beauty," that "fixed element in every artistic organization," as constituting "the romantic temper." With typical emphasis on the particular "charm" and "exquisiteness" of a literary work, Pater's essay gracefully poses one aspect at least of the continuing quarrel over the now familiar antithesis of classical and romantic. H. J. C. Grierson's Leslie Stephen Lecture of 1923 speaks of romanticism as a "recurring tendency" rather than a quality, and attempts to establish three major historical "romantic" ages—in contrast to those "classical" ages which in their confident maturity and stability enabled man to "look round on life with a sense of its wholeness." Unlike Pater's insistence upon "a spirit" that can appear at any time "in individual workmen and their work," Grierson's concentration is upon the characteristics of an historical age that gives rise to literary work reflecting those characteristics. Despite this, the areas of general agreement between these two critics should not be ignored—that romanticism is not limited to a single age; that, as Grierson puts it, "the great romantic knows that he lives by faith and not by reason"; that their conceptions of classical art—Pater's via Sainte-Beuve and Stendhal, Grierson's via Brunetière—neatly overlap;

and that perhaps in all great art ("perfect art" as Pater says) the two "tendencies" merge, even if not in absolute balance.

Writing in 1919, somewhat earlier than Grierson, Irving Babbitt rejects the established practice of contrasting romanticism to classicism solely on the grounds of a supposed conflict of imagination and reason, and launches a famous attack on romanticism in the name of the "ethical imagination." Laying the blame largely at Rousseau's door, Babbitt charges most romantic "imaginative activity" with a "confusion of values" productive of recreative illusion and delusion rather than of wisdom. The "Rousseauist wants unity without reality," and the romantic, following him, turns his "emotional romanticism" into "a vast system of sham spirituality." The "faith" that Grierson and several of his predecessors claimed for the romantic poet is here ridiculed and relegated to the young. Babbitt's exhaustive and exhausting onslaught bore abundant fruit, both in collaborators as well as defendants, and it is not surprising to find his voice still heard, though perhaps less stridently, in certain quarters today. Far less eloquent but often equally pungent is T. E. Hulme's *Speculations*. Hulme echoes Babbitt's claim that Rousseau was the romantics' spiritual forefather, but he turns the accusation of sham spirituality into "spilt religion," the inevitable result of that sort of thinking (or, better, feeling) which insists on "dragging in the infinite." With less emphasis on the ethical center of art than Babbitt, Hulme proposes a revival of a "dry and hard" classical poetry, whose great aim is to be "accurate, precise, and definite." Imagination, which deals with emotions, is to be replaced by fancy, which is exhibited "in the contemplation of finite things." Withal, Hulme curiously aligns himself with Grierson's view that conventions or traditions in art, classical or romantic, inevitably grow old and decay, while at the same time he conceives of the "new" literature not as emerging out of or reflecting the qualities of the new age but rather as being produced quite deliberately by "a new technique, a new convention," that will purge art of its previous excesses and excrescences.

In the same year as Hulme's *Speculations* (1924) Arthur O. Lovejoy complicated future discussion of romanticism by recognizing not one coherent movement but rather several romanti-

cisms. Implicitly condemning previous definitions and evalua-
tions, as an historian of ideas Lovejoy makes it clear that moral
judgments such as Babbitt's are impossible prior to analysis and
detailed comparison of the "exceedingly diverse and often conflicting" strains of romanticism. From his own discrimination
of several romanticisms, he concludes that "any attempt at a
general appraisal even of a single chronologically determinate
romanticism—still more, of 'romanticism' as a whole—is a
fatuity." Thus stepping aside from the several controversies
already current in 1924, Lovejoy, perhaps unwittingly (but for
those who knew him probably quite deliberately) initiated his
own.

Somewhat similar historical assumptions are discernible in
Mario Praz's *The Romantic Agony* (1933), though finally his
emphasis is quite un-Lovejovian, one that gives impetus to an
enduringly uncomplimentary approach to romanticism. Praz
insists early that terms such as "baroque," "romantic," and
"decadent" must be considered approximate rather than defini-
tive, and he attacks those critical tendencies that detach the
terms from "their historical foundations and apply them generously to artists of varied types, according to . . . more or less
extravagant whims." These descriptive approximations instead
have "their origins in definite revolutions of sensibility." "The
legitimate use" of the term "romantic," then, depends not upon
the mere interpretation or response of the reader but "upon the
deliberate method of the artist." Praz next advances his notion
that "one of the most characteristic aspects" of romantic literature was "erotic sensibility"—"certain states of mind and peculiarities of behavior, which are given a definite direction by various
types and themes that recur as insistently as myths engendered
in the ferment of the blood"—a sensibility that leads inevitably
to the decadence of late nineteenth-century literature. Despite
important disclaimers that his book deliberately examines only
the crack in the House of Usher "without troubling about its
general architecture," the total impact of Praz's study tends to
represent romanticism as characteristically depicting "the mysterious bond between pleasure and suffering." As such, it opens
the doors wider for future exploration of Goethe's judgment that
"Classisch ist das Gesunde, Romantisch das Kranke."

Herbert Read's position is, in a sense, the opposite side of the coin. In his introduction to *Surrealism* (1936), his intention clearly is to establish romanticism as the only health—indeed to "liquidate" classicism "by showing its complete irrelevance, its anaesthetic effect, its contradiction of the creative impulse." By characterizing this impulse as intimately connected with dreams, the subconscious, and the unconscious (or, to use his own language, its indentification with the "principle of life, of creation, of liberation"), Read proposes romanticism and surrealism as essentially identical, aesthetically as well as psychologically, socially, and politically. In sum, romanticism is art: all art worthy of the name is romanticism. If one can detect a basic antipathy to the views of Babbitt and the other neohumanist critics, as well as to those of Praz, and can be irritated by Read's ignoring of the claims of the literary historians and quasi-historical critics, one must also recognize that none of these is essentially pertinent to his thoroughly positive intent—to center art, morality, even salvation and apocalypse in the imaginative and creative impulse that, for him, is undissociable from romanticism.

The Marxism inherent in parts of Read's approach is seen much more clearly in Christopher Caudwell's relentless, often awkward and repetitious, *Illusion and Reality*, also published first in 1936. Romantic poetry for him can be viewed adequately only in terms of the "bourgeois dream"—"the dream of the one man alone producing the phenomena of the world," whether Faust, Hamlet, Robinson Crusoe, Satan, or Prufrock. That dream, however, is finally illusion, and Caudwell's analysis of each major romantic poet's relationship to ideological revolution leads him to see them tragically doomed as a group by virtue of the very circumstances and individual impetus that gave rise to the revolution in the first place. With each fresh demand the romantic poet makes for "individualism, free competition, absence of social relations, and more equality" comes the birth of what Caudwell calls "greater organization, more complex social relations, higher degrees of trustification and combination, more inequality." The failure of the bourgeois poets of the romantic period, then, is summed up in the fact that "the misery of the world, including their own special misery, will not let them rest, and yet the temper of the time forces them to support the class which causes it."

F. L. Lucas also considers romanticism as fundamentally an ideology, but he establishes it as psychologically rather than economically based. His position (1938) is diametrically opposed to that of Read and related in some ways to the moral, humanistic objections of Babbitt and to the emphasis on erotic sensibility espoused by Praz. For Lucas, the romantic is always a dreamer, both spawner and prey of the "crocodiles of the unconscious." As such, intoxication, loss of control, and finally Goethe's *das Kranke* are the inevitable results. But like Praz, Lucas has his disclaimer, for "one may be better for wine as well as the worse for it. The century since the romantic revival [presumably 1798 or thereabouts] produced work of creative worth in greater abundance than any before it." But it also produced the decadence of the end of the century as well as the "romanticism gone rotten" of modern fascism.

A refreshingly new note is also heard in the 1930's, with the rise of the New Critics. Often eschewing political, sociological, moral, and ideological considerations, critics like Cleanth Brooks submitted the poetry of the romantics to a hard scrutiny denied it by most earlier commentators. Their central concern was the nature of metaphor, wit, and irony, and with distinct echoes of Hulme's call for a new dry, hard verse, Brooks in *Modern Poetry and the Tradition* (1939) charges the romantics (with the exception of Blake) with distrust of the intellect, lack of irony and wit, flaccid and nonstructural metaphor, a persistent belief that poetry inhered in certain materials, and a fundamental absence of dramatic quality. The most flagrant offender was Shelley. Thus, Brooks concludes, in any new history of English literature, one that must have "emphasis on a more vital conception of the nature of poetry," the romantics must be seen as standing aside, perpetuating many of the errors of the eighteenth century and compounding them with lapses of their own.

Such a view, shared rather widely in the 1930's and 1940's, helped to turn many readers of poetry back to their texts with a new seriousness and critical eye; but it also spurred sharp reactions against its monism, its severely narrow view of "tradition" and the nature of poetry. Among these reactions Richard Harter Fogle's "Romantic Bards and Metaphysical Reviewers" (1945) provides a kind of epitome. The earlier attacks by Babbitt,

Lovejoy, Praz, Caudwell, and Lucas notwithstanding, Fogle correctly saw the New Critical attack as peculiarly influential and of fundamental importance, because of the basic seriousness of the critics themselves "and their undoubted regard for the estate of poetry." After summarizing the general New Critical position toward the romantics—by quoting liberally from Hulme, T. S. Eliot, I. A. Richards, John Crowe Ransom, Allen Tate, and Brooks—Fogle goes on to demonstrate the dangers inherent in the narrowness of their approach; and by his own analysis of romantic imagery, he vigorously defends the organic unity and fundamental excellence of romantic poetry.

The Second World War, however, brought forth more than the flowering of the New Critical controversy. The conflict of ideologies and the worldwide bloodshed helped to trigger a return to considerations earlier voiced by Read, Caudwell, Lucas, and others. In one of the most spirited and polemical of the discussions of romanticism as an ideology, Alex Comfort in *Art and Social Responsibility* (1946) sees the difference between classic and romantic as follows: "The classic sees man as master, the romantic sees him as victim of his environment." The romantic is dedicated to the preservation of humanness—"mind, purpose, consciousness, will, personality"—in the face of imminent death and all other barbaric efforts to destroy or enchain it. Man's responsibilities are thus to his fellow men as individuals, not to a society or any group; and the romantic artist takes it upon himself to provide a voice for all those in this hostile universe who have no voice. At once a personal confession, an anguished recoil from the horror of war and indiscriminate exercise of power, and the advancement of an ideological program, Comfort's essay speaks less to literature than to the way men think and believe; and in an age of war in Viet Nam, an occupation of Czechoslovakia, and continuing warfare in the Middle East, his essay seems to have established a view of romantic ideology pertinent to our time as well as his own.

Despite such concerns, though, which press upon us often to the exclusion of others, A. O. Lovejoy's challenge of twenty-five years earlier was not to go unanswered, even in the late 1940's. Rejecting the totally nominalistic view taken by Lovejoy, René Wellek confirmed in 1949 his earlier defense of period terms in literary history and then proceeded to establish the particular validity of the concept of romanticism as properly descriptive of "a unified European romantic movement." After an historical account of the evolution of the terms "romantic" and "romanticism," Wellek examines "the characteristics of the actual literature which called itself or was called 'romantic'" and finds "the same conceptions of poetry and of the workings and nature of poetic imagination, the same conception of nature and its relation to man, and basically the same poetic style, with a use of imagery, symbolism, and myth that is clearly distinct from that of eighteenth-century neoclassicism." Characteristically, all romantic literature for Wellek exhibits "imagination for the view of poetry, nature for the view of the world, and symbol and myth for poetic style." Viewing literary history not merely in terms of shifts of sensibility (as in Praz) nor in terms of a poetic-stylistic "tradition" such as that posited by Brooks, but rather as the study of "the sequence of periods, the rise, dominance, and disintegration of conventions and norms," Wellek supports the respectability and viability of romanticism as a term as well as a genuine literary phenomenon through a painstaking and detailed analysis of its basic norms.

Although several previous scholars had dealt with the religious aspects of romanticism—most notably in this collection Babbitt, Grierson, and Hulme—no one before Hoxie N. Fairchild, in his series of volumes entitled *Religious Trends in English Poetry*, examined this important subject with thoroughness. Guided by the conviction that romanticism (or at least its "spirit" and its expression in art) was an "attempt to achieve, to retain, or to justify that emotional experience which is produced by an imaginative interfusion of real and ideal, natural and supernatural, finite and infinite, man and God," Fairchild in the third volume of *Religious Trends* (1949) carefully dissociates romantic religion from Christianity while at the same time confessing his own preference for the latter. Romanticism is thus seen as a vain longing and struggle to believe in a creed based on faith in man's "natural goodness, his spiritual and intellectual energies, his power to see into the life of things, his kinship with divinity"—or again, as Fairchild had defined it in his earlier *Romantic Quest*, published in 1931, an "endeavor, in the face of growing factual obstacles, to achieve, to retain, or to justify" an "illusioned view of the universe" produced by the interfusion noted above. Although romantic religion gave us "the best qualities of romantic poetry," it was also responsible, Fairchild believes, for its major deficiencies and its inevitable reduction to a "cult" of self-worship. This is a notable attack, generated out of solid Anglican orthodoxy, quite contrary to Grierson's view of the relationship between Christianity and romanticism, and is at least vaguely related to Babbitt's and Hulme's earlier assaults.

In the same year there appeared another essay that may be taken as partly an answer to Brooks's and other New Critical attacks on the imaginative structure of romantic poetry as well as considerable support for the position taken earlier by Fogle on romantic imagery. W. K. Wimsatt, in his "The Structure of Romantic Nature Imagery" (1949), shares the view of Praz and others that romanticism is a "shift in sensibility," but he interprets that shift quite differently, pointing out the distinction between metaphysical and romantic metaphor and the consequent difference in quality of wit. He finds romantic nature poetry achieving "iconicity by a more direct sensory imitation of something headlong and impassioned, less ordered, nearer perhaps to the subrational"—and thus perhaps closer to symbolist and postsymbolist poetry than is the metaphysical tradition espoused by the New Critics as the normative forerunner of modern poetry. The essay in one sense turns the New Criticism of romanticism back upon itself in a more pointed way than the more extensive and broad "defense" advanced by Fogle earlier.

The literary-historical debate, however, was still not over—whether one thinks of it in terms of Grierson's vague historicism, the Prazian shift of sensibility in certain ages, the new history of Brooks, or the assiduous efforts in defense of periodization by Wellek. In two separate essays ten years apart (1951 and 1961) Morse Peckham undertook the unenviable task of trying to reconcile the positions taken earlier by Lovejoy and Wellek—with particular reference to the former's 1941 essay, "The Meaning of Romanticism for the Historian of Ideas," and his influential *The Great Chain of Being* (1936). Wellek's three criteria of organicism, imagination, and symbolism Peckham absorbs into what he calls "dynamic organicism": he concludes that romanticism is characterized by opposition to "thinking in terms of static mechanism and the redirection of the mind to thinking in terms of dynamic organicism. Its values are change, imperfection, growth, diversity, the creative imagination, the unconscious." To explain the seeming aberration of Byron from these norms, Peckham posits the idea of "negative romanticism," a stage wherein man has grown beyond static mechanism but has not yet arrived at "a reintegration of his thought and art in terms of dynamic organicism" (i.e., a "positive romanticism" incorporating not only Wellek's criteria but the same Lovejovian principles—organicism, dynamism, and diversitarianism—that led to his nominalistic view). Such positive romanticism Peckham sees, finally, as leading directly to modern art, which he characterizes as "the triumph of romanticism," an escape not *from* reality but rather *into* it. If Peckham's approach tends to lead us further toward an identification of modern culture with romanticism than many are willing to go, its firm reiteration of the fundamental coherence of romanticism provides a salutary balance to the several narrower, if often more insistent, studies of only certain "dominant aspects" of the movement.

Albert Gérard's "On the Logic of Romanticism" (1957) comes to a somewhat similar conclusion but by a more general route. He seeks to characterize the whole or "the vital core" of romanticism, to identify its own internal logic and cohesiveness by analyzing "the experiences which the romantics thought crucial and from which all their intellectual activity arose." Gérard finds a number of these experiences to have central common features. The poetic experience for the romantics is both emotional and cognitive, including both sensory and intellectual elements, and is "rich in moral and metaphysical ramifications." From this base Gérard analyzes the romantics' conception of unity, nature, epistemology, the symbol, egotism, poetic form, and moral significance. Unlike Peckham, Comfort, Read, and others, Gérard believes that "the romantic doctrine is obviously out-of-date in numerous ways," but that its "permanent merits" are substantial —in that it was "loyal to itself" (i.e., to its own principle of development), that "it was distinguished by a remarkable unity" and, perhaps most important, that it established a distinct and "special mode of statement, an original language almost."

Strikingly different from Gérard's approach and more sharply focused than Peckham upon the relationship between romanticism and "culture" is Raymond Williams's chapter on "The Romantic Artist" in this *Culture and Society 1780–1950* (1958). After establishing that "a main root of the idea of culture" is the "radical change . . . in ideas of art, of the artist, and of their place in society," Williams identifies and analyzes five such changes in the late eighteenth and early nineteenth centuries, the interrelationships of which tend to define romanticism in a way quite different from other approaches in this collection. These changes are (1) in the relationship between the writer and his readers; (2) in the habitual attitude toward the "public"; (3) in the relationship between "general production" and the production of art; (4) in the general attitude toward the "superior reality" of art as "the seat of imaginative truth"; and (5) in the idea of the artist himself as "autonomous genius." Neither an attack nor a defense, Williams's essay points out clearly the "high courage and actual utility" of the romantic claims for the imagination, but also the basic weakness inherent in what for him was an over-simplification. Deep insights and great works of art resulted from the inevitable conflict between the artist and the society of the early nineteenth century; but "in the continuous pressure of living, the free play of genius found it increasingly difficult to consort with the free play of the market, and the difficulty was not solved, but cushioned, by an idealization."

The artist's concern for his self—whether in relation to society or simply in relation to his art—is approached from another point of view by Geoffrey Hartman in his essay on "Anti–Self-Consciousness" (1962). One of the most distinguishing characteristics of the romantics, he finds, is their exploration of "the dangerous passage-ways of adolescence," of the transition from unself-consciousness to self-consciousness to a kind of "anti–self-consciousness" (or imagination). Their poetry is a record of their quest to find a way "not to escape from or limit knowledge but to convert it into an energy finer than intellectual"—or, to put it another way, to effect the reintegration of the self that is divided by the natural processes of growth and increased self-awareness. Romanticism, then, to Hartman is not merely an idiosyncratic surrogate for religion, but rather the redeemer of religion—in that it represents a time when art properly "frees itself from its subordination to religion or religiously inspired myth, and continues or even replaces them."

In substantial agreement with Hartman that romanticism is not primarily a profound change in belief (and thus differing sharply with those writers who see romanticism basically as a kind of ideology), Northrop Frye in 1963 proposed that it is "the effect of a profound change . . . in the spatial projection of reality," in the cosmic framework (or mythological account of it) that underlies belief. If earlier views presupposed or espoused the idea of a superior world "outside," the natural metaphorical direction of the romantics' world "is inside and downward, into the profounder depths of consciousness"; and that outside world is seen merely "as a mirror reflecting and making visible what is within." Romantic poetry, then, according to Frye, de-emphasizes "sense" and concentrates on (as well as originates from) "the constructive power of the mind, where reality is brought into being by experience." This inwardness of creative power is not only inherently revolutionary, it also represents that sense of unity with a creative power greater than the poet's own that leads to the mythopoeic nature of romantic poetry.

Unlike Frye's archetypal approach, yet clearly related to his characterization of the revolutionary element in romanticism is Meyer Abrams's "English Romanticism: The Spirit of the Age" (1963). In this essay, faintly reminiscent of Grierson's point, he deals with the ways in which the substance and form of romantic poetry were affected by its historical age of violent and inclusive change, particularly the French Revolution. Emerging from this analysis are a number of elements the romantics (particularly Blake, Wordsworth, Southey, and Coleridge) had in common: (1) they were "all centrally political and social poets"; (2) their "politics of vision" were more often than not proclaimed via the persona of the inspired prophet–priest; (3) they tried to incorporate the great events of their age into suitably great poetic forms, fusing "history, politics, philosophy, and religion into one grand design." This early coherence Abrams sees as giving way to a pervasive mood of revolutionary disillusionment or despair that characterizes the greatest of the romantics' poems—poems that "continue to exhibit, in a transformed but recognizable fashion, the scope, the poetic voice, the design, the ideas, and the imagery developed" earlier. Even in the apolitical poems of romanticism's maturity Abrams identifies the "need to reconstitute the grounds of hope" with the pervasive "shattered trust in premature political revolution." Although studies have been made of the political ideas of the romantics, Abrams's essay is the first substantial treatment of the relationship between the political revolutions, hopes, and defeats of the age and the unity of response—in substance and form—by the romantics to that age.

Equally substantial and important in its establishment of the epistemological base of romanticism is Earl R. Wasserman's "The English Romantics: The Grounds of Knowledge" (1963). Although he chooses to "sack" the term "romanticism" for the purposes of his essay, defining his subject instead as "Wordsworth, Coleridge, Keats, and Shelley," Wasserman establishes clear relationships among the four poets by analyzing their responses to two central questions: "How do subject and object meet in a meaningful relationship? By what means do we have a significant awareness of the world?" Although their answers, perhaps inevitably, reaffirm their essential individuality (if not uniqueness), they, unlike their predecessors, "all share the necessity to resolve the question." As a result, Wasserman believes, the role each poet assigns his raw materials, "how he will confront them, and how he will mold them into a poem," provides an important common base upon which romantic poetry characteristically rests. Without denying that poetry, romantic or otherwise, is made up of "features" (in the sense that Brooks, for example, understands the romantic view of poetry), Wasserman insists that it is "made *by* purposes." In this light his analysis of a basic consistency amid apparent wide disagreement speaks to a fundamental unity of concern that constitutes a common ground often ignored, or only paid lip service to, in various of the points of view taken toward romanticism.

III

Final assessment of the value, collective and individual, of the essays here gathered, as well as of those cited in the notes and bibliographies, poses significant and possibly insoluble problems. Although it would seem logical to advance here, however tentatively, a definition (or at least sense) of romanticism, or to disentangle evaluatively the woof of critical comment woven by critics from Pater to the present, yet another definition would serve little. To proceed in another manner is more to the point of this collection.

In Act II, Scene iii, of Shelley's *Prometheus Unbound*, Panthea describes her first reactions to the realm of Demogorgon as follows:

> ... The mighty portal,
> Like a volcano's meteor-breathing chasm,
> Whence the oracular vapor is hurled up
> Which lonely men drink wandering in their youth,
> And call truth, virtue, love, genius, or joy,
> That maddening wine of life, whose dregs they drain
> To deep intoxication and uplift,
> Like Maenads who cry loud, Evoe! Evoe!
> The voice which is contagion to the world.

The passage is a remarkable collocation of ideas and images that may be seen to reflect the peculiar density and complexity—the mystery—of romanticism; but, leaving aside my earlier Faulknerian reference it may also be seen as prophetically foreshadowing the myriad shapes and forms that critics, scholars, and commentators have given romanticism.

To define is to limit; an *ism* is "oracular vapor" condensed or, as Shelley himself put it, "a consideration of thoughts not in their integral unity, but as the algebraical representations which conduct to certain general results." Too often we tend to ignore or even forget that all the major romantics resisted the human tendency to manufacture isms, to cramp the idea in a slogan, to make the intangible tangible. "Energy is eternal delight," said Blake; isms (Blake used the word "Reason" here) are the "bound or outward circumference of energy." The idea implicit in the image of oracular vapor above, as well as Blake's point, is echoed in Shelley's *Defence of Poetry*, where poetry is defined as "at once the center and circumference of knowledge . . . at the same time the root and blossom. . . ." A hundred years later Yeats appropriated the same idea:

> . . . great rooted blossomer,
> Are you the leaf, the blossom or the bole!
> O body, swayed to music, O brightening glance,
> How can we know the dancer from the dance?

Obviously the answer is that we cannot distinguish "the dancer
from the dance"—but we persist in trying. Coleridge in *The
Statesman's Manual* puts the matter somewhat differently, reminding us that romantic poetry is symbolic, that "It always partakes
of the reality which it renders intelligible; and while it enunciates
the whole, abides itself as a living part in that unity of which it
is the representative." If we do not see this, now applying Coleridge's words in a way he did not intend, romantic literature and
romanticism "is either to be buried in the dead letter, or its
name and honors usurped by a counterfeit product of the mechanical understanding. . . ." That is, in Wordsworth's terms,
"We murder to dissect"; for dissection is definition, not creation—
a destruction of the artist's world-created-anew in an apparently
misguided attempt to find its center. "Philosophy," Keats said,
"will clip an Angel's wings,"

> Conquer all mysteries by rule and line,
> Empty the haunted air, and gnomed mine—
> Unweave the rainbow. . . .

The "ism" leads us to know but not to see; yields a photograph,
not a Renoir.

Yet the romantics themselves all recognized (with a clarity
we tend to begrudge them) the worldly dilemma inherent in
trying to fuse the center and the circumference, the essence and
the identity, in indissoluble unity. As Byron writes in *Childe
Harold*,

> Could I embody and unbosom now
> That which is most within me,—could I wreak
> My thoughts upon expression, and thus throw
> Soul, heart, mind, passions, feelings, strong or weak,
> All that I would have sought, and all I seek,
> Bear, know, feel, and yet breathe—into *one* word,
> And that one word were Lightning, I would speak.

I *would* speak. Coleridge, in "Kubla Khan," used the same
tense:

Could I revive within me
Her symphony and song,—

.   .   .

I would build that dome in air.

And Shelley, in the "Epipsychidion":

The wingèd words on which my soul would pierce
Into the height of Love's rare Universe,
Are chains of lead around its flight of fire—
I pant, I sink, I tremble, I expire!

For man is not a god, however much of a poet–prophet he may
be. Still, romantic art does represent that Keatsian "tip-toe"
moment, that "still point of the turning world" at which the
fusion takes place, at which Coleridge's "symbolic" poetry
achieves its fulness, at which, Keats said, "Life's self is nourish'd
by its proper pith"—and there is neither murder nor dissection.
Such synthesis or fusion is of course religious as well as aesthetic
(to Blake, we recall, Christ was the greatest artist, and to Eliot
"to apprehend/The point of intersection of the timeless/With
time, is an occupation for the saint")—but it is a religion that
transcends sectarianism and resists definition.

Though the critic is almost inevitably pushed by his particular
task to examine the circumference *or* the center, the critic who
endures will acknowledge the necessity of fusing them or may
indeed see them as fused. His own personal formulation, he will
recall, is neither art nor symbol but an abstraction from art and
symbol, at very best twice removed from the oracular vapor and
constructed from blocks and forms created by another. Blake said
that he who sees the "ratio" only (that is, the parts only) "sees
himself only." Although one should be reluctant to accuse the
critics of romantic poetry or of romanticism of seeing themselves
only, there is point to this remark. To return to the passage from
Prometheus Unbound, we can see there many "ratios," many critical
selves in embryo: the image of oracular vapor, isolated from the
others, will yield its own peculiarly limited view of Shelley's
poetry, or of romantic poetry in general, or of romanticism; the
fact that youthful "lonely men" wander and drink this vapor
suggests a curiously hybrid Shelleyan-Byronic romanticism;
the "truth, virtue, love, genius, or joy" suggests another, the

"maddening wine" that intoxicates one to Maenad-like madness, another; and so on.

This is not to say, of course, that the critics' ratios are by definition without value. In a sense this collection is dedicated to the principle that they have enduring value for us all. But just as Shelley's images in this passage do not operate, or even convey meaning, apart from each other and from the total context of *Prometheus Unbound*, so no formulation of romanticism can be seen rightly apart from the rest. Although the oracular vapor is vapor indeed, it is also given shape and form and meaning by men; and whereas the Maenads in the throes of Bacchanalian frenzy are "mad," the image is only an image or analogy, not a statement of fact or an assertion of belief or an "ism." The men who "uplift" the "voice which is contagion to the world" are only mad in the eyes of a world that knows itself to be sane—a "knowledge" that is the supreme self-complacency.

The romantic poet himself, however, is often guilty of or subject to the same sort of limiting as that ascribable to the critic-definer. Wordsworth's Nature, Coleridge's "joy" or "honeydew," Blake's "energy," Byron's "fancy," Keats's "mystery" or "intensity," as well Shelley's "vapor," can exist for the reader only insofar as they are made palpable—conceivable as well as perceivable. They must, as in the passage from *Prometheus Unbound*, be "called" something, given the shape, form, and substance that constitutes communicability. Blake asks:

> Can Wisdom be put in a silver rod?
> Or Love in a golden bowl?

The answer, of course, is no; yet the poet must "put" them into some *thing*, must give to airy nothingness a habitation and a name. If the Grecian urn is to be a "friend to man," it must speak to him. Words are not vain, merely necessary. The difference between this sort of "limiting" and that of the critic is the difference between creation and what was called earlier "condensation"—though at least one critic has characterized certain modern criticism as poetry. As Coleridge wrote,

> I may not hope from outward forms to win
> The passion and the life, whose fountains are within.

Through his creative imagination, those fountains erupted (like Shelley's volcano) into a poem, "Dejection: An Ode." The critic as critic is not concerned with fountains but with outward forms.

Thus even without murder in his heart the critic dissects, and perhaps we would have it no other way. For as romanticism becomes more and more a term for a large coherence of thought and practice in the literature of the late eighteenth and early nineteenth centuries (perhaps of "modern" literature as well), we must rely on the critic to provide us with appropriate angles of vision from which to view it. Dissection, after all, can yield truth and isolate error. However much we may wish to temper the views of a Goethe, Babbitt, Lucas, Praz, or Brooks, we must be grateful for their provocation, for they have all in their own ways, directly or indirectly, contributed rather remarkably to the making of something like a consensus. As was noted in the first edition, in the apparent chaos of conflicting ideas and opinions about romanticism, a fairly clear progression is already discernible. There is no reason to alter that opinion now. The epistemological, perceptual, and conceptual bases of romanticism seem sure, as the choice of essays hopefully shows. We shall continue to argue not about them (though even here semantic differences continue to obscure commonality of view), but rather about their manifold ramifications in the artifacts, psychology, sociology, politics, religion, culture, and lives of the age. The center is what we have begun to get at, and most of the works that have helped us get at it—some represented more fully than others, some remaining more vital than others, some central even if apparently superseded—are contained or referred to in these pages.

On Classical
and Romantic

Walter Pater

The words, *classical* and *romantic*, although, like many other critical
expressions, sometimes abused by those who have understood them too
vaguely or too absolutely, yet define two real tendencies in the history
of art and literature. Used in an exaggerated sense, to express a greater
opposition between those tendencies than really exists, they have at
times tended to divide people of taste into opposite camps. But in
that *House Beautiful*, which the creative minds of all generations—the
artists and those who have treated life in the spirit of art—are always
building together, for the refreshment of the human spirit, these
oppositions cease; and the *Interpreter* of the *House Beautiful*, the true
æsthetic critic, uses these divisions, only so far as they enable him to
enter into the peculiarities of the objects with which he has to do.
The term *classical*, fixed, as it is, to a well-defined literature, and a
well-defined group in art, is clear, indeed; but then it has often been
used in a hard, and merely scholastic sense, by the praisers of what is
old and accustomed, at the expense of what is new, by critics who
would never have discovered for themselves the charm of any work,
whether new or old, who value what is old, in art or literature, for its

ON CLASSICAL AND ROMANTIC: From *Appreciations* by Walter Pater (New York: The
Macmillan Company, 1889), pp. 241–61.

19

accessories, and chiefly for the conventional authority that has gathered about it—people who would never really have been made glad by any Venus fresh-risen from the sea, and who praise the Venus of old Greece and Rome, only because they fancy her grown now into something staid and tame.

And as the term, *classical*, has been used in a too absolute, and therefore in a misleading sense, so the term, *romantic*, has been used much too vaguely, in various accidental senses. The sense in which Scott is called a romantic writer is chiefly this; that, in opposition to the literary tradition of the last century, he loved strange adventure, and sought it in the Middle Age. Much later, in a Yorkshire village, the spirit of romanticism bore a more really characteristic fruit in the work of a young girl, Emily Brontë, the romance of *Wuthering Heights;* the figures of Hareton Earnshaw, of Catherine Linton, and of Heath-cliffe—tearing open Catherine's grave, removing one side of her coffin, that he may really lie beside her in death—figures so passionate, yet woven on a background of delicately beautiful, moorland scenery, being typical examples of that spirit. . . . The romantic spirit is, in reality, an everpresent, an enduring principle, in the artistic tempera-ment; and the qualities of thought and style which that, and other similar uses of the word *romantic* really indicate, are indeed but symp-toms of a very continuous and widely working influence.

Though the words *classical* and *romantic*, then, have acquired an almost technical meaning, in application to certain developments of German and French taste, yet this is but one variation of an old opposition, which may be traced from the very beginning of the forma-tion of European art and literature. From the first formation of any-thing like a standard of taste in these things, the restless curiosity of their more eager lovers necessarily made itself felt, in the craving for new motives, new subjects of interest, new modifications of style. Hence, the opposition between the classicists and the romanticists—between the adherents, in the culture of beauty, of the principles of liberty, and authority, respectively—of strength, and order or what the Greeks called κοσμιότης.

Sainte-Beuve, in the third volume of the *Causeries du Lundi*, has discussed the question, *What is meant by a classic?* It was a question he was well fitted to answer, having himself lived through many phases of taste, and having been in earlier life an enthusiastic member of the romantic school: he was also a great master of that sort of "philosophy of literature," which delights in tracing traditions in it, and the way in which various phases of thought and sentiment maintain themselves, through successive modifications, from epoch to epoch. His aim, then, is to give the word *classic* a wider and, as he says, a more generous sense than it commonly bears, to make it expressly *grandiose et flottant;* and, in doing this, he develops, in a masterly manner, those qualities of measure, purity, temperance, of which it is the especial function of classical art and literature, whatever meaning, narrower or wider, we attach to the term, to take care.

The charm, therefore, of what is classical, in art or literature, is that of the well-known tale, to which we can, nevertheless, listen over and over again, because it is told so well. To the absolute beauty of its artistic form, is added the accidental, tranquil, charm of familiarity. There are times, indeed, at which these charms fail to work on our spirits at all, because they fail to excite us. "*Romanticism,*" says Stendhal, "is the art of presenting to people the literary works which, in the actual state of their habits and beliefs, are capable of giving them the greatest possible pleasure; *Classicism,* on the contrary, of presenting them with that which gave the greatest possible pleasure to their grandfathers." But then, beneath all changes of habits and beliefs, our love of that mere abstract proportion—of music—which what is classical in literature possesses, still maintains itself in the best of us, and what pleased our grandparents may at least tranquillise us. The "classic" comes to us out of the cool and quiet of other times, as the measure of what a long experience has shown will at least never displease us. And in the classical literature of Greece and Rome, as in the classics of the last century, the essentially classical element is that quality of order in beauty, which they possess, indeed, in a pre-eminent degree, and which impresses some minds to the exclusion of everything else in them.

It is the addition of strangeness to beauty, that constitutes the romantic character in art; and the desire of beauty being a fixed element in every artistic organisation, it is the addition of curiosity to this desire of beauty, that constitutes the romantic temper. Curiosity and the desire of beauty, have each their place in art, as in all true criticism. When one's curiosity is deficient, when one is not eager enough for new impressions, and new pleasures, one is liable to value mere academical proprieties too highly, to be satisfied with worn-out or conventional types, with the insipid ornament of Racine, or the prettiness of that later Greek sculpture, which passed so long for true Hellenic work; to miss those places where the handiwork of nature, or of the artist, has been most cunning; to find the most stimulating products of art a mere irritation. And when one's curiosity is in excess, when it overbalances the desire of beauty, then one is liable to value in works of art what is inartistic in them; to be satisfied with what is exaggerated in art, with productions like some of those of the romantic school in Germany; not to distinguish, jealously enough, between what is admirably done, and what is done not quite so well, in the writings, for instance, of Jean Paul. And if I had to give instances of these defects, then I should say, that Pope, in common with the age of literature to which he belonged, had too little curiosity, so that there is always a certain insipidity in the effect of his work, exquisite as it is; and, coming down to our own time, that Balzac had an excess of curiosity—curiosity not duly tempered with the desire of beauty.

But, however falsely those two tendencies may be opposed by critics, or exaggerated by artists themselves, they are tendencies really at work at all times in art, moulding it, with the balance sometimes a little on one side, sometimes a little on the other, generating, respectively, as the balance inclines on this side or that, two principles, two traditions, in art, and in literature so far as it partakes of the spirit of art. If there is a great overbalance of curiosity, then, we have the grotesque in art: if the union of strangeness and beauty, under very difficult and complex conditions, be a successful one, if the union be entire, then the resultant beauty is very exquisite, very attractive. With a passionate care for beauty, the romantic spirit refuses to have it, unless the condition of strangeness be first fulfilled. Its desire is for a beauty born of unlikely elements, by a profound alchemy, by a difficult initiation, by the charm which wrings it even out of terrible things; and a trace of distortion, of the grotesque, may perhaps linger, as an additional element of expression, about its ultimate grace. Its eager, excited spirit will have strength, the grotesque, first of all—the trees shrieking as you tear off the leaves; for Jean Valjean, the long years of convict life; for Redgauntlet, the quicksands of Solway Moss; then, incorporate with this strangeness, and intensified by restraint, as much sweetness, as much beauty, as is compatible with that. *Énergique, frais, et dispos*—these, according to Sainte-Beuve, are the characteristics of a genuine classic—*les ouvrages anciens ne sont pas classiques parce qu'ils sont vieux, mais parce qu'ils sont énergiques, frais, et dispos.* Energy, freshness, intelligent and masterly

disposition:—these are characteristics of Victor Hugo when his alchemy is complete, in certain figures, like Marius and Cosette, in certain
scenes, like that in the opening of *Les Travailleurs de la Mer*, where
Déruchette writes the name of *Gilliatt* in the snow, on Christmas
morning; but always there is a certain note of strangeness discernible
there, as well.

The essential elements, then, of the romantic spirit are curiosity
and the love of beauty; and it is only as an illustration of these qualities,
that it seeks the Middle Age, beause, in the overcharged atmosphere
of the Middle Age, there are unworked sources of romantic effect, of a
strange beauty, to be won, by strong imagination, out of things unlikely
or remote.

> [Pater here points out that although "many English readers," influenced
> by Madame de Staël's *De L'Allemagne* and Heine's *Romantische Schule*,
> still consider romanticism and Germany to be inseparably connected,
> neither Germany nor England "is nearly so representative of the romantic
> temper as France"—particularly in the writings of Murger, Gautier,
> Hugo, Rousseau, and Chateaubriand. The major characteristics of this
> literature Pater sees as curiosity, "a deep thirst for intellectual excite-
> ment," grotesqueness, strength of passion, "a feverishness, an incompre-
> hensible straining and excitement . . . to be *énergique, frais, et dispos*,"
> strangeness and distortion, intensity and the exceptional, pity or pathos,
> antinomianism, novelty, and the "desire for beauty and sweetness."]

Romanticism, then, although it has its epochs, is in its essential
characteristics rather a spirit which shows itself at all times, in various
degrees, in individual workmen and their work, and the amount of
which criticism has to estimate in them taken one by one, than the
peculiarity of a time or a school. Depending on the varying proportion
of curiosity and the desire of beauty, natural tendencies of the artistic
spirit at all times, it must always be partly a matter of individual temperament. The eighteenth century in England has been regarded as
almost exclusively a classical period; yet William Blake, a type of so
much which breaks through what are conventionally thought the
influences of that century, is still a noticeable phenomenon in it, and
the reaction in favor of naturalism in poetry begins in that century,
early. There are, thus, the born romanticists and the born classicists.
There are the born classicists who start with *form*, to whose minds the
comeliness of the old, immemorial, well-recognised types in art and
literature, have revealed themselves impressively; who will entertain

no matter which will not go easily and flexibly into them; whose work
aspires only to be a variation upon, or study from, the older masters.
"'Tis art's decline, my son!" they are always saying, to the progressive
element in their own generation; to those who care for that which in
fifty years' time every one will be caring for. On the other hand, there
are the born romanticists, who start with an original, untried *matter*,
still in fusion; who conceive this vividly, and hold by it as the essence
of their work; who, by the very vividness and heat of their conception,
purge away, sooner or later, all that is not organically appropriate to it,
till the whole effect adjusts itself in clear, orderly, proportionate form;
which form, after a very little time, becomes classical in its turn.

The romantic or classical character of a picture, a poem, a literary
work, depends, then, on the balance of certain qualities in it; and in
this sense, a very real distinction may be drawn between good classical
and good romantic work. But all critical terms are relative; and there
is at least a valuable suggestion in that theory of Stendhal's, that all
good art was romantic in its day. In the beauties of Homer and Phie-
dias, quiet as they now seem, there must have been, for those who
confronted them for the first time, excitement and surprise, the sudden,
unforeseen satisfaction of the desire of beauty. Yet the *Odyssey*, with
its marvellous adventure, is more romantic than the *Iliad*, which nevertheless contains, among many other romantic episodes, that of the
immortal horses of Achilles, who weep at the death of Patroclus.
Æschylus is more romantic than Sophocles, whose *Philoctetes*, were it
written now, might figure, for the strangeness of its motive and the
perfectness of its execution, as typically romantic; while, of Euripides,
it may be said, that his method in writing his plays is to sacrifice readily
almost everything else, so that he may attain the fulness of a single
romantic effect. These two tendencies, indeed, might be applied as a
measure or standard, all through Greek and Roman art and poetry,
with very illuminating results; and for an analyst of the romantic
principle in art, no exercise would be more profitable, than to walk
through the collection of classical antiquities at the Louvre, or the
British Museum, or to examine some representative collection of Greek
coins, and note how the element of curiosity, of the love of strangeness,
insinuates itself into classical design, and record the effects of the romantic spirit there, the traces of struggle, of the grotesque even, though
overbalanced here by sweetness; as in the sculpture of Chartres and

Rheims, the real sweetness of mind in the sculptor is often overbalanced by the grotesque, by the rudeness of his strength.

Classicism, then, means for Stendhal, for that younger enthusiastic band of French writers whose unconscious method he formulated into principles, the reign of what is pedantic, conventional, and narrowly academical in art; for him, all good art is romantic.* To Sainte-Beuve, who understands the term in a more liberal sense, it is the characteristic of certain epochs, of certain spirits in every epoch, not given to the exercise of original imagination, but rather to the working out of refinement of manner on some authorised matter; and who bring to their perfection, in this way, the elements of sanity, of order and beauty in manner. In general criticism, again, it means the spirit of Greece and Rome, of some phases in literature and art that may seem of equal authority with Greece and Rome, the age of Louis the Fourteenth, the age of Johnson; though this is at best an uncritical use of the term, because in Greek and Roman work there are typical examples of the romantic spirit. But explain the terms as we may, in application to particular epochs, there are these two elements always recognisable; united in perfect art—in Sophocles, in Dante, in the highest work of Goethe, though not always absolutely balanced there; and these two elements may be not inappropriately termed the classical and romantic tendencies.

BIBLIOGRAPHICAL NOTE: Other late-nineteenth-century works dealing with romanticism include Leslie Stephen, *History of English Thought in the Eighteenth Century*, 2 vols. (London and New York, 1876); F. H. Hedge, "Classic and Romantic," *Atlantic Monthly*, LVII (1886), 309–16; W. D. MacClintock, "The Romantic and Classical in English Literature," *The Chautauquan*, XIV (1891), 187–91; W. L. Phelps, *The Beginnings of the English Romantic Movement* (Boston, 1893); E. Dowden, *The French Revolution and English Literature* (New York and London, 1897); C. H. Herford, *The Age of Wordsworth* (London, 1897); and H. A. Beers, *A History of English Romanticism in the Eighteenth Century* (New York, 1898).

* See his *Racine and Shakespeare* (1823).

The Present Outlook

Irving Babbitt

It has been my endeavor [in the preceding chapters of *Rousseau and Romanticism*] to show that classic and romantic art, though both at their best highly imaginative, differ in the quality of the imagination. I pointed out in my first chapter that in his recoil from the intellectual romanticism of the Renaissance and the medieval romanticism of actual adventure the neo-classicist came to rest his literary faith on "reason" (by which he meant either ordinary good sense or abstract reasoning), and then opposed this reason or judgment to imagination. This supposed opposition between reason and imagination was accepted by the romantic rebels against neo-classicism and has been an endless source of confusion to the present day. Though both neo-classicists and romanticists achieved much admirable work, work which is likely to have a permanent appeal, it is surely no small matter that they both failed on the whole to deal adequately with the imagination and its rôle whether in literature or life. Thus Dryden attributes the immortality of the *Æneid* to its being "a well-weighed judicious poem. Whereas poems which are produced by the vigor of imagination only

THE PRESENT OUTLOOK: From *Rousseau and Romanticism* (Boston: Houghton Mifflin Co., 1919), pp. 353–93. © 1919 by Irving Babbitt. © 1947 by Esther Babbitt Howe. Reprinted by permission of Meridian Books and Edward S. Babbitt.

have a gloss upon them at the first which time wears off, the works of judgment are like the diamond; the more they are polished, the more lustre they receive." Read on and you will find that Dryden thus stresses judgment by way of protest against the Cavalier Marini and the imaginative unrestraint that he and other intellectual romanticists display. Dryden thus obscures the fact that what gives the immortalizing touch to the *Æneid* is not mere judgment but imagination—a certain quality of imagination. Even the reader who is to enter properly into the spirit of Virgil needs more than judgment—he needs to possess in some measure the same quality of imagination. The romantic answer to the neo-classic distrust of the imagination was the apotheosis of the imagination, but without sufficient discrimination as to its quality, and this led only too often to an anarchy of the imagination—an anarchy associated, as we have seen, in the case of the Rousseauist, with emotion rather than with thought or action.

The modern world has thus tended to oscillate between extremes in its attitude towards the imagination, so that we still have to turn to ancient Greece for the best examples of works in which the imagination is at once disciplined and supreme. Aristotle, I pointed out, is doing little more than give an account of this Greek practice when he says that the poet ranks higher than the historian because he achieves a more general truth, but that he can achieve this more general truth only by being a master of illusion. Art in which the illusion is not disciplined to the higher reality counts at best on the recreative side of life. "Imagination," says Poe, "feeling herself for once unshackled, roamed at will among the ever-changing wonders of a shadowy and unstable land." To take seriously the creations of this type of imagination is to be on the way towards madness. Every madhouse, indeed, has inmates who are very imaginative in the fashion Poe here describes. We must not confuse the concentric or ethical with the eccentric imagination if we are to define rightly the terms "classic" and "romantic" or indeed to attain to sound criticism at all. My whole aim [in *Rousseau and Romanticism*] has been to show that a main stream of emotional sophistry that takes its rise in the eighteenth century and flows down through the nineteenth involves just such a confusion.

The general distinction between the two types of imagination would seem sufficiently clear. To apply the distinction concretely is, it must be admitted, a task infinitely difficult and delicate, a task that calls for the utmost degree of the *esprit de finesse*. In any particular case there enters

an element of vital novelty. The relation of this vital novelty to the
ethical or permanent element in life is something that cannot be determined by any process of abstract reasoning or by any rule of thumb;
it is a matter of immediate perception. The art of the critic is thus
hedged about with peculiar difficulties. It does not follow that Aristotle
himself because he has laid down sound principles in his *Poetics* would
always have been right in applying them. Our evidence on this point
is as a matter of fact somewhat scanty.

Having thus admitted the difficulty of the undertaking we may ourselves attempt a few concrete illustrations of how sound critical standards tended to suffer in connection with the romantic movement.
Leaving aside for the moment certain larger aspects of the ethical
imagination that I am going to discuss presently, let us confine ourselves
to poetry. Inasmuch as the ethical imagination does not in itself give
poetry but wisdom, various cases may evidently arise: a man may be
wise without being poetical; he may be poetical without being wise;
he may be both wise and poetical.

We may take as an example of the person who was wise without
being poetical Dr. Johnson. Though most persons would grant that
Dr. Johnson was not poetical, it is well to remember that this generalization has only the approximate truth that a literary generalization
can have. The lines on Levet have been inserted and rightly in anthologies. If not on the whole poetical, Johnson was, as Boswell says,
eminently fitted to be a "majestic teacher of moral and religious wisdom." Few men have had a firmer grasp on the moral law or been freer
from the various forms of sophistry that tend to obscure it. Unlike
Socrates, however, of whom he reminds us at times by his ethical
realism, Johnson rests his insight not on a positive but on a traditional
basis. To say that Johnson was truly religious is only another way of
saying that he was truly humble, and one of the reasons for his humility
was his perception of the ease with which illusion in man passes over
into delusion, and even into madness. His chapter on the "Dangerous
Prevalence of Imagination" in *Rasselas* not only gives the key to that
work but to much else in his writings. What he opposes to this dangerous
prevalence of imagination is not a different type of imagination but
the usual neo-classical reason or judgment or "sober probability."
His defence of widom against the gathering naturalistic sophistries of
his time is therefore somewhat lacking in imaginative prestige. He
seemed to be opposing innovation on purely formalistic and traditional

grounds in an age which was more and more resolutely untraditional and which was determined above all to emancipate the imagination from its strait-jacket of formalism. Keats would not have hesitated to rank Johnson among those who "blasphemed the bright Lyrist to his face."

Keats himself may serve as a type of the new imaginative spontaneity and of the new fullness and freshness of sensuous perception. If Johnson is wise without being poetical, Keats is poetical without being wise, and here again we need to remember that distinctions of this kind are only approximately true. Keats has written lines that have high seriousness. He has written other lines which without being wise seem to lay claim to wisdom—notably the lines in which, following Shaftesbury and other æsthetes, he identifies truth and beauty; an identification that was disproved for practical purposes at least as far back as the Trojan War. Helen was beautiful, but was neither good nor true. In general, however, Keats's poetry is not sophistical. It is simply delightfully recreative. There are signs that Keats himself would not have been content in the long run with a purely recreative rôle—to "be the idle singer of an idle day." Whether he would ever have achieved genuine ethical purpose is a question. In working out a wise view of life he did not, like Dante, have the support of a great and generally accepted tradition. It is not certain again that he would ever have developed the critical keenness that enabled a Sophocles to work out a wise view of life in a less traditional age than that of Dante. The evidence is rather that Keats would have succumbed, to his own poetical detriment, to some of the forms of sham wisdom current in his day, especially the new humanitarian evangel.*

• • •

If Keats is highly imaginative and poetic without on the whole rising to high seriousness or sinking to sophistry, Shelley, on the other hand, illustrates in his imaginative activity the confusion of values that was so fostered by romanticism. Here again I do not wish to be too absolute. Shelley has passages especially in his *Adonais* that are on a high level. Yet nothing is more certain than that the quality of his imagination is on the whole not ethical but Arcadian or pastoral. In

---

* Babbitt refers here to Keats's "dismal failure" to "rewrite *Hyperion* from a humanitarian point of view."

the name of his Arcadia conceived as the "ideal" he refuses to face the facts of life. I have already spoken of the flimsiness of his *Prometheus Unbound* as a solution of the problem of evil. What is found in this play is the exact opposite of imaginative concentration on the human law. The imagination wanders irresponsibly in a region quite outside of normal human experience. We are hindered from enjoying the gorgeous iridescences of Shelley's cloudland by Shelley's own evident conviction that it is not a cloudland, an "intense inane," but a true empyrean of the spirit. And our irritation at Shelley's own confusion is further increased by the long train of his indiscreet admirers. Thus Professor C. H. Herford writes in the *Cambridge History of English Literature* that what Shelley has done in the *Prometheus Unbound,* is to give "magnificent expression to the faith of Plato and of Christ"! Such a statement in such a place is a veritable danger signal, an indication of some grave spiritual bewilderment in the present age. To show the inanity of these attempts to make a wise man of Shelley it is enough to compare him not with Plato and Christ, but with the poet whom he set out at once to continue and contradict—with Æschylus. The *Prometheus Bound* has the informing ethical imagination that the *Prometheus Unbound* lacks, and so in its total structure belongs to an entirely different order of art. Shelley, indeed, has admirable details. The romanticism of nympholeptic longing may almost be said to culminate, at least in England, in the passage [beginning] "My soul is an enchanted boat." There is no reason why in recreative moods one should not imagine one's soul an enchanted boat and float away in a musical rapture with the ideal dream companion towards Arcady. But to suppose that revery of this kind has anything to do with the faith of Plato and of Christ is to fall from illusion into dangerous delusion.

> [Babitt goes on here to consider Goethe as a poet who exemplifies "progress from emotional sophistry to ethical insight" in contrast to Shelley's lack of such progress.]

The examples I have chosen should suffice to show how my distinction between two main types of imagination—the ethical type that gives high seriousness to creative writing and the Arcadian or dalliant type that does not raise it above the recreative level—works out in practice. Some such distinction is necessary if we are to understand the imagination in its relation to the human law. But in order to grasp the present situation firmly we need also to consider the imagination in its relation to the natural law. I have just said that most men have escaped from the imaginative anarchy of the emotional romanticist through science. Now the man of science at his best is like the humanist at his best, at once highly imaginative and highly critical. By this coöperation of imagination and intellect they are both enabled to concentrate effectively on the facts, though on facts of a very different order. The imagination reaches out and perceives likenesses and analogies whereas the power in man that separates and discriminates and traces causes and effects tests in turn these likenesses and analogies as to their reality: for we can scarcely repeat too often that though the imagination gives unity it does not give reality. If we were all Aristotles or even Goethes we might concentrate imaginatively on both laws, and so be both scientific and humanistic: but as a matter of fact the ordinary man's capacity for concentration is limited. After a spell of concentration on either law he aspires to what Aristotle calls "relief from tension." Now the very conditions of modern life require an almost tyrannical concentration on the natural law. The problems that have been engaging more and more the attention of the Occident since the rise of the great Baconian movement have been the problems of power and speed and utility. The enormous mass of machinery that has been accumulated in the pursuit of these ends requires the closest attention and concentration if it is to be worked efficiently. At the same time the man of the West is not willing to admit that he is growing in power alone, he likes to think that he is growing also in wisdom. Only by keeping this situation in mind can we hope to understand how emotional romanticism has been able to develop into a vast system of sham spirituality. I have said that the Rousseauist wants unity without reality. If we are to move towards reality, the imagination must be controlled by the power of discrimination and the Rousseauist has repudiated this power as "false and secondary," But a unity that lacks reality can scarcely be accounted wise. The Baconian, however, accepts this unity gladly. He has spent so much energy in working according to the natural law that he has no energy left for work according to the human law. By turning to the Rousseauist he can get the "relief from tension" that he needs and at the same time enjoy the illusion of receiving a vast spiritual illumination. Neither Rousseauist nor Baconian carry into the realm of the human law the keen analysis that is necessary to distinguish between genuine insight and some mere phantasmagoria of the emotions.

I am speaking especially, of course, of the interplay of Rousseauistic and Baconian elements that appear in certain recent philosophies like that of Bergson. According to Bergson one becomes spiritual by throwing overboard both thought and action, and this is a very convenient notion of spirituality for those who wish to devote both thought and action to utilitarian and material ends. It is hard to see in Bergson's intuition of the creative flux and perception of real duration anything more than the latest form of Rousseau's transcendental idling. To work with something approaching frenzy according to the natural law and to be idle according to the human law must be accounted a rather one-sided view of life. The price the man of today has paid for his increase in power is, it should seem, an appalling superficiality in dealing with the law of his own nature. What brings together Baconian and Rousseauist in spite of their surface differences is that they are both intent on the element of novelty. But if wonder is associated with the Many, wisdom is associated with the One. Wisdom and wonder are moving not in the same but in opposite directions. The nineteenth century may very well prove to have been the most wonderful and the least wise of centuries. The men of this period—and I am speaking of course of the main drift—were so busy being wonderful that they had no time, apparently, to be wise. Yet their extreme absorption in wonder and the manifoldness of things can scarcely be commended unless it can be shown that happiness also results from all this revelling in the element of change.* The Rousseauist is not quite consistent on this point. At times he bids us boldly set our hearts on the transitory. "*Aimez*," says Vigny, "*ce que jamais on ne verra deux fois.*" But the Rousseauist strikes perhaps a deeper chord when looking forth on a world of flux he utters the anguished exclamation of Leconte de Lisle: "*Qu'est-ce que tout cela qui n'est pas éternel?*" Even as one swallow, says Aristotle, does not make a spring, so no short time is enough to determine whether a man deserves to be called happy. The weakness of the romantic pursuit of novelty and wonder and in general of the philosophy of the beautiful moment—whether the erotic moment or the moment of cosmic revery—is that it does not reckon sufficiently with the something deep down in the human breast that craves the

---

* Babbitt may have in mind here Theodore Watts-Dunton's characterization of romanticism as "the renascence of wonder" in his *Poetry and the Renascence of Wonder* (New York, 1916).

abiding. To pin one's hope of happiness to the fact that "the world is so full of a number of things" is an appropriate sentiment for a *Child's Garden of Verse*. For the adult to maintain an exclusive Bergsonian interest in "the perpetual gushing forth of novelties" would seem to betray an inability to mature. The effect on a mature observer of an age so entirely turned from the One to the Many as that in which we are living must be that of a prodigious peripheral richness joined to a great central void.

• • •

I have no quarrel, it is scarcely necessary to add, either with the man of science or the romanticist when they keep in their proper place. As soon however as they try, whether separately or in unison, to set up some substitute for humanism or religion, they should be at once attacked, the man of science for not being sufficiently positive and critical, the romanticist for not being rightly imaginative.

This brings us back to the problem of the ethical imagination—the imagination that has accepted the veto power. . . . This problem is indeed in a peculiar sense the problem of civilization itself. A curious circumstance should be noted here: a civilization that rests on dogma and outer authority cannot afford to face the whole truth about the imagination and its rôle. A civilization in which dogma and outer authority have been undermined by the critical spirit, not only can but must do this very thing if it is to continue at all. Man, a being ever changing and living in a world of change, is, as I said at the outset, cut off from immediate access to anything abiding and therefore worthy to be called real, and condemned to live in an element of fiction or illusion. Yet civilization must rest on the recognition of something abiding. It follows that the truths on the survival of which civilization depends cannot be conveyed to man directly but only through imaginative symbols. It seems hard, however, for man to analyze critically this disability under which he labors, and, facing courageously the results of his analysis, to submit his imagination to the necessary control. He consents to limit his expansive desires only when the truths that are symbolically true are presented to him as literally true. The salutary check upon his imagination is thus won at the expense of the critical spirit. The pure gold of faith needs, it should seem, if it is to gain currency, to be alloyed with credulity. But the civilization that results from humanistic or religious control tends to produce the critical spirit. Sooner or later some Voltaire utters his fatal message:

Les prêtres ne sont pas ce qu'un vain peuple pense;
Notre crédulité fait toute leur science.

The emancipation from credulous belief leads to an anarchic individualism that tends in turn to destroy civilization.

• • •

... What I have myself been opposing to naturalistic excess, such as appears in the new realism,* is insight; but insight is in itself only a word, and unless it can be shown to have its own working and its own fruits, entirely different from those of work according to the natural law, the positivist at all events will have none of it.

The positivist will not only insist upon fruits, but will rate these fruits themselves according to their bearing upon his main purpose. Life, says Bergson, can have no purpose in the human sense of the word. The positivist will reply to Bergson and to the Rousseauistic drifter in general, in the words of Aristotle, that the end is the chief thing of all and that the end of ends is happiness. To the Baconian who wants work and purpose but according to the natural law alone, the complete positivist will reply that happiness cannot be shown to result from this one-sided working; that in itself it affords no escape from the misery of moral solitude, that we move towards true communion and so towards peace and happiness only by work according to the human law. Now the more individualistic we are, I have been saying, the more we must depend for the apprehension of this law on the imagination, the imagination, let me hasten to add, supplemented by the intellect. It is not enough to put the brakes on the natural man—and that is what work according to the human law means—we must do it intelligently. Right knowing must here as elsewhere precede right doing. Even a Buddha admitted that at one period in his life he had not been intelligent in his self-discipline. I need only to amplify here what I have said in a previous chapter about the proper use of the "false secondary power" by those who wish to be either religious or humanistic in a positive fashion. They will employ their analytical faculties, not in building up some abstract system, but in discriminating between

* Which, says Babbitt, holds "that the only thing real in the view of life that has prevailed of late [i.e., the "scientific" view] has been its working according to the natural law and the fruits of this working."

the actual data of experience with a view to happiness, just as the man of science at his best employs the same faculties in discriminating between the data of experience with a view to power and utility.

I have pointed out another important use of the analytical intellect in its relation to the imagination. Since the imagination by itself gives unity but does not give reality, it is possible to discover whether a unification of life has reality only by subjecting it to the keenest analysis. Otherwise what we take to be wisdom may turn out to be only an empty dream. To take as wise something that is unreal is to fall into sophistry. For a man like Rousseau whose imagination was in its ultimate quality not ethical at all but overwhelmingly idyllic to set up as an inspired teacher was to become an arch-sophist. Whether or not he was sincere in his sophistry is a question which the emotionalist is very fond of discussing, but which the sensible person will dismiss as somewhat secondary. Sophistry of all kinds always has a powerful ally in man's moral indolence. It is so pleasant to let one's self go and at the same time deem one's self on the way to wisdom. We need to keep in mind the special quality of Rousseau's sophistry if we wish to understand a very extraordinary circumstance during the past century. During this period men were moving steadily towards the naturalistic level, where the law of cunning and the law of force prevail, and at the same time had the illusion—or at least multitudes had the illusion—that they were moving towards peace and brotherhood. The explanation is found in the endless tricks played upon the uncritical and still more upon the half-critical by the Arcadian imagination.

· · ·

Rousseau would have us get rid of analysis in favor of the "heart." No small part of my endeavor in this work and elsewhere* has been to show the different meanings that may attach to the term "heart" (and the closely allied terms "soul" and "intuition")—meanings that are a world apart, when tested by their fruits. Heart may refer to outer perception and the emotional self or to inner perception and the ethical self. The heart of Pascal is not the heart of Rousseau. With this distinction once obliterated the way is open for the Rousseauistic corruption

---

* See, e.g., Babbitt's early *Literature and the American College* (1908), *New Laokoon* (1910), and the later *Democracy and Leadership* (1924).

of such words as "virtue" and "conscience," and this is to fling wide the door to every manner of confusion. The whole vocabulary that is properly applicable only to the super-sensuous realm is then transferred to the region of the sub-rational. The impulsive self proceeds to cover its nakedness with all these fair phrases as it would with a garment. A recent student of wartime psychology asks: "Is it that the natural man in us has been masquerading as the spiritual man by hiding himself under splendid words—courage, patriotism, justice—and now he rises up and glares at us with blood-red eyes?" That is precisely what has been happening.

But after all, the heart in any sense of the word is controlled by the imagination, so that a still more fundamental dichotomy, perhaps the most fundamental of all, is that of the imagination itself. We have seen how often the Arcadian dreaming of the emotional naturalist has been labeled the "ideal." Our views of this type of imagination will therefore determine our views of much that now passes current as idealism. Now the term "idealist" may have a sound meaning: it may designate the man who is realistic according to the human law. But to be an idealist in Shelley's sense or that of innumerable other Rousseauists is to fall into sheer unreality. This type of idealist shrinks from the sharp discriminations of the critic: they are like the descent of a douche of ice-water upon his hot illusions. But it is pleasanter, after all, to be awakened by a douche of ice-water than by an explosion of dynamite under the bed; and that has been the frequent fate of the romantic idealist. It is scarcely safe to neglect any important aspect of reality in favor of one's private dream, even if this dream be dubbed the ideal. The aspect of reality that one is seeking to exclude finally comes crashing through the walls of the ivory tower and abolishes the dream and at times the dreamer.

The transformation of the Arcadian dreamer into the Utopist is a veritable menace to civilization. The ends that the Utopist proposes are often in themselves desirable and the evils that he denounces are real. But when we come to scrutinize critically his means, what we find is not a firm grip on the ascertained facts of human nature but what Bagehot calls the feeble idealities of the romantic imagination. Moreover various Utopists may come together as to what they wish to destroy, which is likely to include the whole existing social order; but what they wish to erect on the ruins of this order will be found to be not only in dreamland, but in different dreamlands. For with the elimination of the veto power from personality—the only power that can pull men back to some common centre—the ideal will amount to little more than the projection of this or that man's temperament upon the void. In a purely temperamental world an affirmative reply may be given to the question of Euryalus in Virgil: "Is each man's God but his own fell desire?" ("*An sua cuique deus fit dira cupido?*")

The task of the Socratic critic at the present time is, then, seen to consist largely in stripping idealistic disguises from egoism, in exposing what I have called sham spirituality. If the word "spirituality" means anything, it must imply, it should seem, some degree of escape from the ordinary self, an escape that calls in turn for effort according to the human law. Even when he is not an open and avowed advocate of a "wise passiveness," the Rousseauistic idealist is only too manifestly not making any such effort—it would interfere with his passion for self-expression which is even more deeply rooted in him than his passion for saving society. He inclines like Rousseau to look upon every constraint whether from within or from without as incompatible with liberty. A right definition of liberty is almost as important as a right definition of imagination and derives from it very directly. Where in our anarchical age will such a definition be found, a definition that is at once modern and in accord with the psychological facts? "A man has only to declare himself free," says Goethe, "and he will at once feel himself dependent. If he ventures to declare himself dependent, he will feel himself free." In other words he is not free to do whatever he pleases unless he wishes to enjoy the freedom of the lunatic, but only to adjust himself to the reality of either the natural or the human law. A progressive adjustment to the human law gives ethical efficiency, and this is the proper corrective of material efficiency, and not love alone as the sentimentalist is so fond of preaching. Love is another word that cries aloud for Socratic treatment.

A liberty that means only emancipation from outer control will result, I have tried to show, in the most dangerous form of anarchy—anarchy of the imagination. On the degree of our perception of this fact will hinge the soundness of our use of another general term—"democracy." We should beware above all of surrendering our imaginations to this word until it has been hedged about on every side with discriminations that have behind them all the experience of the past with this form of government. Only in this way may the democrat know whether he is aiming at anything real or merely dreaming of the golden age.

Here as elsewhere there are pitfalls manifold for the uncritical enthusiast. A democracy that produces in sufficient numbers sound individualists who look up imaginatively to standards set above their ordinary selves, may well deserve enthusiasm. A democracy, on the other hand, that is not rightly imaginative, but is impelled by vague emotional intoxications, may mean all kinds of lovely things in dreamland, but in the real world it will prove an especially unpleasant way of returning to barbarism. It is a bad sign that Rousseau, who is more than any other one person the father of radical democracy, is also the first of the great anti-intellectualists.

> [There follows here a long section in which Babbitt discusses the relationship between humanism and religion, the necessity of grounding humanism in humility, and the "dehumanizing influences" of Rousseauistic romanticism in the modern world. He concludes the section as follows:]

The most disreputable aspect of human nature, I have said, is its proneness to look for scapegoats; and my chief objection to the movement I have been studying is that more perhaps than any other in history it has encouraged the evasion of moral responsibility and the setting up of scapegoats.* But as an offset to this disreputable aspect of man, one may note a creditable trait: he is very sensitive to the force of a right example. If the leaders of a community look up to a sound model and work humanistically with reference to it, all the evidence goes to show that they will be looked up to and imitated in turn by enough of the rank and file to keep that community from lapsing into barbarism. Societies always decay from the top. It is therefore not enough, as the humanitarian would have us believe, that our leaders should act vigorously on the outer world and at the same time be filled with the spirit of "service." Purely expansive leaders of this kind we have seen who have the word "humanity" always on their lips and are at the same time ceasing to be human. "That wherein the superior man cannot be equalled," say Confucius, "is simply this—his work which other men cannot see." It is this inner work and the habits that result from it that above all humanize a man and make him exemplary to the multitude. To perform this work he needs to look to a centre and a model.

---

* In the Introduction to *Rousseau and Romanticism* Babbitt describes his "main objection to the movement" as its failure "to produce complete positivists."

We are brought back here to the final gap that opens between classicist and romanticist. To look to a centre according to the romanticist is at the best to display "reason," at the worst to be smug and philistine. To look to a true centre is, on the contrary, according to the classicist, to grasp the abiding human element through all the change in which it is implicated, and this calls for the highest use of the imagination. The abiding human element exists, even though it cannot be exhausted by dogmas and creeds, is not subject to rules and refuses to be locked up in formulae. A knowledge of it results from experience— experience vivified by the imagination. To do justice to writing which has this note of centrality we ourselves need to be in some measure experienced and imaginative. Writing that is romantic, writing in which the imagination is not disciplined to a true centre is best enjoyed while we are young. The person who is as much taken by Shelley at forty as he was at twenty has, one may surmise, failed to grow up.* Shelley himself wrote to John Gisborne (October 22, 1821): "As to real flesh and blood, you know that I do not deal in those articles; you might as well go to a ginshop for a leg of mutton as expect anything human or earthly from me." The mature man is likely to be dissatisfied with poetry so unsubstantial as this even as an intoxicant and still more when it is offered to him as the "ideal." The very mark of genuinely classical work, on the other hand, is that it yields its full meaning only to the mature. Young and old are, as Cardinal Newman says, affected very differently by the words of some classic author, such as Homer or Horace.

> Passages, which to a boy are but rhetorical commonplaces, neither better nor worse than a hundred others which any clever writer might supply . . . at length come home to him, when long years have passed, and he has had experience of life, and pierce him, as if he had never before known them, with their sad earnestness and vivid exactness. Then he comes to understand how it is that lines, the birth of some chance morning or evening at an Ionian festival or among the Sabine hills, have lasted generation after generation for thousands of years, with a power over the mind and a charm which the current literature of his own day, with all its obvious advantages, is utterly unable to rival.

In the poets whom Newman praises the imagination is, as it were,

---

* Cf. T. S. Eliot's similar comments on Shelley in *The Use of Poetry and the Use of Criticism* (London, 1933), pp. 89 ff. It should also be noted that Eliot was one of Babbitt's students at Harvard.

centripetal. The neo-classic proneness to oppose good sense to imagination, and the romantic proneness to oppose imagination to good sense,
have at least this justification, that in many persons, perhaps in most
persons, the two actually conflict, but surely the point to emphasize
is that they may come together, that good sense may be imaginative
and imagination sensible. If imagination is not sensible, as is plainly
the case in Victor Hugo, for example, we may suspect a lack of the
universal and ethical quality. All men, even great poets, are more or
less immersed in their personal conceit and in the zones of illusion
peculiar to their age. But there is the question of degree. The poets to
whom the world has finally accorded its suffrage have not been mega-
lomaniacs; they have not threatened like Hugo to out-bellow the
thunder or pull comets around by the tail. Bossuet's saying that "good
sense is the master of human life" does not contradict but complete
Pascal's saying that "the imagination disposes of everything," provided
only due stress be laid on the word "human." It would not be easy to
live a more imaginative life than Hugo, but his imagination was so
unrestrained that we may ask whether he lived a very human life,
whether he was not rather, in Tennyson's phrase, a "weird Titan." Man
realizes that immensity of this being of which Joubert speaks only in
so far as he ceases to be the thrall of his own ego. This human breadth
he achieves not by throwing off but by taking on limitations, and
what he limits is above all his imagination. The reason why he should
strive for a life that is thus increasingly full and complete is simply, as
Joubert suggests, that it is more delectable, that it is found practically
to make for happiness.

BIBLIOGRAPHICAL NOTE: For a survey of the neohumanist controversy, in which
Babbitt is a central figure, see *The English Romantic Poets: A Review of Re-
search*, ed. T. M. Raysor (New York, 1956), pp. 28–30, and R. H. Fogle,
"The Romantic Movement," in *Contemporary Literary Scholarship*, ed. L.
Leary (New York, 1958), pp. 109–12. An important earlier neohumanist
attack on romanticism is Paul Elmer More's "The Drift of Romanticism,"
Shelburne Essays, 8th ser. (Boston, 1913). Refutations of the neohumanist
position may be found in C. H. Herford, "Romanticism in the Modern
World," *Essays and Studies*, VIII (1922), 109–34; Hugh I'A. Fausset, *The
Proving of Psyche* (London, 1929); and J. W. Beach, *A Romantic View of
Poetry* (Minneapolis, 1944). The influence of the New Humanist critics
may be seen in the essays by T. E. Hulme, F. L. Lucas, and H. N. Fairchild
in this collection.

Classical and Romantic: A Point of View

H. J. C. Grierson

"Classical" and "romantic," not meaning simply Greek and Roman art and literature on the one hand, mediæval on the other, but used, as they have been since the so-called romantic revival, to indicate certain qualities which distinguish, not only periods of art and literature, but individual pictures and poems of the same epoch, it may be of today—these are terms no attempts to define which ever seem entirely convincing to oneself or others. . . . It may prove on careful scrutiny that the words are not the best which could be used, that "romantic" at any rate is either too definite or too indefinite to indicate all I shall propose to bring under it, and yet we may agree that some words were needed to indicate what is a recurrent—or if that beg the question as to the future—has been a recurring sequence of tendencies in the actual history of thought and art and literature. My effort is in this essay—and I would stress the word, and ask you to remember that if I speak dogmatically it is to save time, and that my whole thesis is exploratory—my endeavour is to see the history of Western European literature in a perspective which seems to me valuable and has not, so far as I know, been attempted in so broad a fashion.

CLASSICAL AND ROMANTIC: A POINT OF VIEW: From CLASSICAL AND ROMANTIC by H. J. C. Grierson, reprinted by permission of Chatto & Windus Ltd. (The Leslie Stephen Lecture, 1923).

[Grierson next surveys various definitions of the terms "romantic" and "classical," rejecting medievalism (and particularly medieval Christianity) as the sole or main base of romanticism and "definiteness and perfection of form" as the sole or main base of classicism.]

Nor am I entirely at one with Brunetière when . . . he affirms that a classical period can come but once in a nation's literature, at the moment when its language attains perfection and before the inevitable process of decay has set in. Brunetière was too much dominated by the organic conceptions of his century. After a certain stage of development has been reached, a language may change without necessarily improving or decaying. . . . Allowing all this, I would still maintain that Brunetière does describe the main conditions under which a classical literature has at different times appeared, and what are its chief qualities. It is the product of a nation and a generation which has consciously achieved a definite advance, moral, political, intellectual; and is filled with the belief that its view of life is more natural, human, universal and wise than that from which it has escaped. It has effected a synthesis which enables it to look round on life with a sense of its wholeness, its unity in variety; and the work of the artist is to give expression to that consciousness, hence the solidity of his work and hence too its definiteness, and in the hands of great artists its beauty. Literature at such a period is not personal—at least in quite the same sense or to the same degree as it is, say, in Rousseau or Byron or Carlyle or Ibsen, because there is, as it were, a common consciousness throbbing in the mind and heart of each individual representative of the age, or of the circle for which he writes, for one must admit, and this is significant, that a classical literature has generally been the product of a relatively small society—Athens, Rome, Paris, London. The work of the classical artist is to give individual expression, the beauty of form, to a body of common sentiments and thoughts which he shares with his audience, thoughts and views which have for his generation the validity of universal truths. His preoccupation with form is not, as with those whom Bacon describes, due to disregard of weight of matter and worth of subject, but to the fact that the matter is given to him by his age, has for him the weight and worth it possesses for his audience; and so we find critics stressing opposite things in classical literature. Matthew Arnold, trying to wean his countrymen from the luxuries of romance, dwells on "the all-importance of the subject matter, the necessity of accurate construction, the subordinate character of expression," whereas Brunetière, in the same spirit, declares that substance is nothing, *"C'est la forme qui est tout."* And they mean much the same thing.

A classical age, again, is an age of reason—good sense—not of rationalism which is reason dogmatising beyond the limits that its premises, the experience on which it rests, will sanction—but there is nothing of which such an age is so acutely conscious as that it has escaped from the weight of tradition into the free life of intelligence. But the individual is still controlled by the social consciousness which checks eccentricity, compels a regard for the mean, and so literature and art approximate at any rate to that balance of qualities which Brunetière describes: "A classic is a classic because in his work all the faculties find their legitimate function—without imagination overstepping reason, without logic impeding the flight of imagination, without sentiment encroaching on the rights of good sense, without good sense killing the warmth of sentiment, without the matter allowing itself to be despoiled of the persuasive authority it should borrow from the charm of form, and without the form ever usurping an interest which should belong only to the matter."

I have not time now to justify this by an examination of the classical literature of a period, but must just point to three such epochs—the age of Pericles, when the defeat of the Persians had given Athens confidence, prestige, and hegemony, while at the same time she was absorbing and making her own the philosophical culture of Ionia, the rhetoric of the West. Its great product was the Attic drama; and that Aeschylus and Sophocles reflected in different ways the best convictions of their age is at any rate suggested by Aristophanes' indignation with the disintegrating spirit of Euripides. In Rome the classic age, I would suggest, extends through the later republic and reign of Augustus, from Cicero and Lucretius to Virgil and Horace—writers conscious of having mastered and made their own the literary inheritance of Greece, but who are using these forms to express a spirit that is not Greek but Roman, inspired by the greatness and mission of Imperial Rome. The third such age was the age of Louis XIV in France, and that which was inaugurated by Dryden in this country, running closely parallel to one another and yet interestingly divergent, the idea of authority, for example, having for the French of the classical period a universal validity that it had not for Englishmen, to whom constitutional liberty and religious toleration were rather the achievements which gave them a right to look back on the past with a complacent sense of their own advance; with this difference also that our classical writers were conscious that there had been giants in the age which preceded their own. No French critic—Malherbe, Boileau, or Bouhours—ever spoke of Ronsard and his generation with the respect which Dryden, sweeping Rymer aside, taught his age and successors to feel for Shakespeare and Jonson and Milton.

•   •   •

Achievement, then, I suggest, is the note of a living, healthy, classical literature and art. It reflects the spirit of a self-confident society seeking in art and literature the expression of its ideals and convictions, and requiring of art the same attention to form, to correctness, which it seeks in manners and all the gestures of life. A weakness, indeed, of classical art is that its work may be controlled by a spirit of etiquette rather than the requirements of essentially artistic form. The enforcement of the Unities by the French Academy, the proscription of words which have been "sullied by passing through the mouth of the vulgar," are examples of what I mean. But the great defect of a classical period and art is that it cannot endure. It represents, a synthesis, a balance; and a synthesis effected by the human mind involves exclusions, sacrifices, which will sooner or later be realised; all balances in human affairs are precarious. A classical literature perishes in different ways. It gradually dries up. The forms which have established themselves are reproduced mechanically; convictions become conventions. Greek literature lived on in a remarkable way after the great age was over, and threw out some charming shoots, Middle-Comedy and the pastorals of Theocritus. In the later epics of Apollonius it threw out a romantic shoot, for love is a perennially romantic motive; and Apollonius was to inspire Virgil—but that was not an immediately important development. No new and profound spirit quickened Greek poetry. The old forms became conventional and academic.

Again the classical synthesis may disintegrate, the fine balance of intellect and feeling, of form and matter, may give way to exaggeration of one or other. So Brunetière describes *"la déformation de l'idéal classique"* in French literature of the eighteenth century. Feeling was overstressed, at the expense of good sense, by the sentimentalists, *"C'est ici, dans les romans de Prévost que la sensibilité se déborde."* Reason became dogmatic, ignoring the incompleteness of its premises, the experience on which it built, in the work of the Encyclopædists. And, as regards form, the purification of the vocabulary became an impoverishment, Voltaire condemning the extravagances of Corneille (as Dryden had in a mood of spleen criticised Shakespeare), Condorcet condemning Pascal's use of familiar and proverbial phrases.

But something may happen as this process of desiccation or disintegration goes on. Disintegration may become violent disruption, because a fresh sap is beginning to rise in the veins of the human spirit, a wave of fresh thought and emotion is pouring over the nation or the world of which this or that nation is a conscious part. The minds of men become aware of what has been left out in the synthesis, the balance of which a classical art is the reflection. The *spiritual,* or it may be the *secular,* side of man's nature has been repressed or ignored. A new vision dawns on the imagination. In some of its manifestations the new movement, and the literature which expresses it, will be sentimental and fanciful, a literature of *Sturm und Drang;* to some minds it will come, at some period at any rate, as almost entirely an artistic movement, a rejection of old forms, a delight in new experiments in vocabulary and metres; but for its greatest minds it is a spiritual and philosophical movement also. At all times *"Le romantisme"* has been *"tout traversé de frissons métaphysiques."* But this spiritual quickening reacts on the form of literature, hence the qualities which distinguish the literature of such a movement from classical literature. It lacks the confident clarity, the balanced humanism, the well-proportioned form, the finished correctness of the literature of a period which knows its own mind. But it is shot through and through with new and strange beauties of thought and vision, of phrase and rhythm. Language grows richer, for words become symbols, not labels, full of colour and suggestion as well as clear, definable meaning; and the rhythms of verse and prose grow more varied and subtle to express subtler if vaguer currents of thought and feeling.

That is the character of a romantic movement, and I think we can point to three such movements in the history of Western European literature. The first is felt to some extent, but mainly as a disintegrating force, in the tragedies of Euripides, more certainly, distinctly, positively, I think, in the dialogues of Plato. I feel disposed, despite the diffidence with which I must speak before an audience in Cambridge, to claim Plato as the first great romantic; and if I feel like Socrates encountering a mighty wave, let me take shelter for a moment under the undeniable fact that it is to Plato the greatest romantics have always turned to find philosophical expression for their mood—Spenser, Wordsworth, Shelley, the German romantic philosophers Schelling and Fichte. Nor does it invalidate my contention to urge that if ever there was a classical prose it is the perfect prose of Plato, for it would not be the first time in which a romantic movement was generated in the very heart of a classical literature. To take a much lesser instance, Addison's classical essays on the ballad of "Chevy Chase"—and he criticises from a classical point of view, finds in the ballads qualities of classical master-pieces—awakened a geni which was to quicken the dormant spirit of romance. It was Plato who, despite his condemnation of the poets, effected that interrelation of philosophy and poetry which has char-acterised every great romantic movement. Is there anything that gives more of the romantic thrill than the myths of the Cave, of Er, of the chariot of the soul in the *Phaedrus*? Plato was the first great romantic because his thought, his romantic conception of an ideal world behind the visible, his "city laid up in heaven," his daring deduction of all being and knowledge from the Idea of Good, was the ferment which disintegrated the ancient view of life, of man and his relation to the divine; and working through the Stoics and the neo-Platonics, helped to beget the great romantic movement which we know as the Christian religion, for the next great romantic after Plato is St. Paul.

Wilamowitz-Moellendorf's description of St. Paul's irruption into Greek religious thought and Greek prose seems to me a complete, at least an essential, description of what I mean by a romantic movement, its spirit, and the reaction of that spirit on the form, the vehicle—an effect at once disintegrating and revivifying. I wish I could quote it in full, but I must content myself with a few sentences:

> At last, at last someone speaks in Greek from a fresh, inner experience of life; that is Paul's faith; he is sure of the hope within him, and his ardent love embraces humanity—a fresh life of the soul bubbles up wherever he sets his foot. . . . For him all literature is a plaything, he has no artistic vein, but all the higher must we estimate the artistic effects which he all the same achieves. . . . In the Hellenic world of conventional form, smooth beauty, this absence of form in a style which is yet quite adequate to the thoughts and feelings expressed, has a quick-ening force. What stylistic effect could heighten the intimate charm of the Epistle to the Philippians? . . . The whole of Greek classicist litera-ture stands hereby condemned that the imitation of the classics was productive of new classics only in Latin—in Cicero, Horace, Virgil. The Greek language, when it came straight from the heart, had to be devoid of art, as it is in Paul, in Epictetus, in Plotinus. "*Dann ist auch das vorbei*" [the ellipses are Grierson's].

There is much in these words relevant to my theme. Let me for the moment insist only on this that they describe exactly, allowing for such reduction of the scale as individually you may wish to make, the spirit in which William Blake turned away from the technique of art, in painting and poetry, when his "message" came upon him, in which Wordsworth called upon poetry to cast away "the bracelets and snuff-boxes and adulterous trinkets" of poetic diction and return to her legitimate home in the heart of men and the language which is uttered by men under the actual pressure of passion, or at least of passion recollected in tranquillity; for "poetry is the image of man and nature, the breath and finer spirit of all knowledge, the impassioned expression which is in the countenance of all science."

The effect of Christianity, this new romantic ferment, on the subsequent history of literature* is, of course, beyond my scope but I would just remind you of this. The new spirit would not adjust itself, despite the efforts of Prudentius and others, to the traditional classical forms. The Christian temper found adequate poetic expression in the Greek and Latin hymns of the Eastern and Western Churches; and, ever since, the hymn has been the special vehicle of Christian sentiment, accompanying every spiritual revival. Remember the great hymns in which the troubled spirit of Germany found utterance in the seventeenth century, the hymns which accompanied the Wesleyan and Evangelical movements, and every subsequent revival. I am not concerned for the moment with the quality of the hymns. Such a mood as we have described, the romantic mood, tends to rhapsody, and a hymn is rather a rhapsody of love or penitence or praise or doctrinal confession than, like a lyric proper, the full expression of an, perhaps complex, individual mood. Religious lyrics, like those of Donne, Herbert, Crashaw, and Vaughan, are not hymns.

The *third* great romantic movement, for I wish to keep the *second* in reserve for a moment, is that from which I started, the flame which Rousseau kindled and which spread to Germany and England. . . . It has its spiritual, its religious aspect in the poetry of Blake and Wordsworth, perhaps of Shelley, in the philosophy of Schelling and Fichte and Schleiermacher, in the revival of mediæval Catholic feeling. . . . It has the antinomian aspect, the note of rebellion, of expansion, of surrender to impulse and passion on which Mr. Paul Elmer More [*The Drift of Romanticism*] and Professor Babbitt [*Rousseau and Romanticism*] have dwelt, in some phases of the work of Blake and Shelley, and in what Goethe calls the "dreadful negativity" of Byron. It has its

---

* A fuller study of the relationship between medieval Christianity and the development of the romantic tradition is Christopher Dawson's "The Origins of the Romantic Tradition," in *Medieval Essays* (New York, 1954). For a quite different view of the relationship between the rise of Christianity and romanticism, see H. N. Fairchild's essay below.

purely artistic aspect, as in Keats's delight in new beauties of language and harmony, though as you are aware he was not quite content with this. Its themes are as numerous as its spirit is manifold—the worship of nature, the revival of mediævalism, dreams of a golden age, a new Hellenism.

But instead of dwelling on this, I wish, if you will bear with me a very little longer, because it is essential to my argument, to turn back to my starting point and ask what was the significance of the mediæval element in the romantic revival, or rather to ask what was the *differentia* of mediæval romance? Am I justified in claiming the romantic literature of the twelfth and thirteenth centuries as the *second* of the movements, as romantic not in virtue of its themes Germanic, Celtic, Oriental, but because of its spirit of revolt, of emancipation? Heine's view, as I said, was inadequate as a description of the romantic revival, apart from the German school which gave so much trouble to Schiller and Goethe and evoked the brief and final statement of the latter: *"Classisch is das Gesunde, Romantisch das Kranke."* The romantic cult of mediæval Catholicism was, after all, only a phase of the spiritual element in the revolt, its reaction from the temper of the *Aufklärung,* the bondage of the *secular,* which led others to the worship of Humanity and Liberty and Nature. But Heine is equally or more misleading in his description of mediæval romance, of the spirit of mediæval poetry. Are *Launcelot and Guinivere, Tristram and Iseult, Aucassin and Nicolette* really passion-flowers which have sprung from the blood of Christ? "In Paradise what have I to win?" cries Aucassin,

> therein I seek not to enter but only to have Nicolette, my sweet lady that I love so well. For into Paradise go none but such folk as I shall tell thee now. Thither go these same old priests, and halt old men and marred, who all day and night cower continually before the altars and in the crypts; and such folk as wear old arrices and clouted frocks, and naked folk and shoeless, and covered with sores, perishing of hunger and of thirst, and of cold, and of little ease. These be they that go into Paradise, with them have I naught to make. But into Hell would I fain go; for into Hell fare the goodly clerks, and goodly knights that fall in tourneys and great wars, and stout men at arms, and all men noble. With these am I lief to go. And thither pass the sweet ladies and courteous that have two lovers, or three, and their lords also thereto. Thither goes the gold, and the silver, and the cloth of vair, and cloth of gris, and harpers, and poets, and the princes of this world. With these I would gladly go, let me but have with me Nicolette my sweetest lady.

That is a strange flower to blossom from the blood of the cross, or from the pure worship of the Virgin. Heine, indeed, recognises that there are romances, or elements in romance, which are not Christian but pagan: "in them still rules the whole pre-Christian mode of thought and feeling, the raw power not yet softened into knighthood; there they stand like stone figures, the stubborn champions of the North, and the soft light and moral atmosphere of Christianity has not yet penetrated their iron mail." This is true enough, but it is not the whole truth or the most important one. That is this—that the spirit of chivalry as it took shape in the love-lyrics of the Provençals and the Arthurian and other romances was itself a spirit of revolt, the revolt of the secular spirit of man against the long preoccupation with theological and ascetic ideals. The important thing is not that the ideals of romance may be traceable to pagan sources, Teutonic, Celtic, and classical; the important thing is the new value, the new treatment they received. In romantic poetry the spirit of man found an outlet for feelings that Christianity condemned and strove to repress, for ideals which the Church might and did strive to annex and to modify, but which are essentially anti-Christian, the ideal of personal prowess and honour, the ideal of passionate love and devoted service, not of God, but of a woman. Romance was not, of course, heretical, it was not concerned with dogma—though one must not forget the connection of the troubadours with the Albigensians, the part they took in ridiculing clerical teaching about Hell and Purgatory (of which there is perhaps an echo in *Aucassin and Nicolette*)—but the spirit of romance, the glorification of personal honour and passionate love, was not in truth compatible with Christian ethics. The Church had no place in its scheme of life for secular literature. When Boccaccio and Chaucer are afflicted with a fit of remorse their first thought is to burn *all* their secular writings.

. . .

But, and this is the other side of the picture, the centuries of romance, the twelfth and thirteenth, were just those in which the Church built up for herself a complete, well-articulated body of reasoned dogma in the work of the schoolmen, of Thomas Aquinas; presented mankind with, not only the claims of authority, and an appeal to the heart and imagination, as a romantic, lyrical impulse and ferment, but with a reasoned, comprehensive conception of life. The Church, as Signor Papini says, "represented throughout the Middle Ages the classical spirit." But for that spirit to create a classical literature there was needed a more living medium than Latin, and none of the vernaculars was quite ready. But one was nearly so. Dante is the classical poet of Catholic Christianity because he, controlling and transmuting the romantic spirit which he inherited from his Provençal progenitors, carried so much of it as might be purified or transmuted into the poetic expression of the reasoned and comprehensive, Catholic view of life; and transcending the limits of the lyric, even the great *canzone*, created one of the larger, more comprehensive forms in which the classical spirit delights, his great dramatic epic, the *Divina Commedia*, Nowhere is the difference between the classical and the romantic spirit seen more clearly than in Dante's treatment of love. Aucassin would go to Hell to live with Nicolette. Dante meets two lovers, Paolo and Francesca, who have thus gone to Hell, drawn thither by love, and he has no illusions about their happiness: "While the one spirit thus spake the other so wept that I fainted with pity: '*E caddi, come corpo morto cade.*'" He knows where all the romantic lovers, the saints of Love's Calendar, are. They are in Hell—Dido, Cleopatra, Helen, Achilles, Paris, Tristan—more than a thousand others: "*Che la ragion sommettono al talento.*" But the crucial test is Beatrice. Another classical poet before Dante had treated love as a motive in a poem intended to be a comprehensive pictue of human virtue and life. "Dido," says an historian of Latin literature, "blocks the advance of fate. . . . Aeneas's alliance with Dido was wrong. His interests were the interests of Rome. . . . Desertion of Dido becomes a duty: it cannot be judged—or at least understood—by standards of chivalry" [Grierson's ellipses]. In like manner, one might add, Titus is called on to part from Bérénice in Racine's beautiful play. But Virgil's chivalry, his poetic feeling, the romantic in Virgil, defeated his purpose. The world has declared for Dido against Aeneas and Rome. It was not so that Dante dealt with Beatrice. Instead of rejecting her and human love he sublimates them. She remains her whom he had loved in youth, but no word approaching earthly love ever falls from his lips or hers. She is always theology, divine wisdom whose inspiration is love, but love that is the fulfillment of the Law. For the romantic, Love; for the classic, Law—but in the end these are one.

One cannot speak, therefore, of a classical age at the end of the thirteenth century, producing an abundant classical literature, as in the Periclean age in Athens or the age of Louis XIV; but there was a classical mood, a classical spirit, a classical synthesis, of which Dante's poem is the great expression. He speaks for Italy primarily, but for all Western Christendom also; and this is significant because if a classical age came again it could not, even Brunetière sees this, be confined to one people. It would have to be at least European and American.

But to sum up, what I have tried to bring out is this:

1. That the word "classical"—like the word "heroic" applied to "heroic poetry"—has its full meaning only historically. Classical literature is the literature of such a society as I have tried to describe, a generation conscious of achievement, advance, the attainment of a reasonable and comprehensive view of life and the attainment in language and artistic forms of a fitting medium for the expression of its mind. It is thus quite a distinct thing from a literature which simply imitates the ancients, what one might call a "classicist" literature, following Wilamowitz, who calls the later Greek epic and other poetry *"die griechische Literatur des Klassizismus."* The essential difference is this, that such a literature looks back. The poet is consciously and deliberately endeavouring to revive old modes and old moods—Virgil in as far as he merely imitates Homer, Goethe in *Iphigenie* (though this is not the whole truth), Arnold, Swinburne in *Atalanta* and *Erechtheus,* Landor. These are genuine products of the romantic quest for new refinements. The *differentia* of the true classic, Sophocles, Virgil in all that is greatest in his poem, Racine, Johnson,* is that he stands firmly on his own age, is consciously and proudly the mouthpiece of his own age of reason and enlightenment. Racine's dramas are more truly classical than Goethe's or Arnold's just because they express so entirely the spirit of the Frenchman of that age; and because their form is no mere imitation of the antique but a living form, the product of a conflict between the need of a living stage tradition for action, story, suspense, and the demand of cultured circles—represented by the Academy—for the beauty and regularity of ancient drama. Corneille and Racine completed a movement which began with Hardy when he realized that the classic plays of Garnier and the *Pléiade* could not live on the stage.

2. When the word is not used in this historical sense it is applied in a merely relative and rather vague way to literature that seems to the critic to have the qualities of the great writers of such a period; "classical" art is that in which good sense, a comprehensive view of life, a balance of reason and feeling, of matter and form predominate. "Poetry in Goethe's view," says Hume-Brown, "should deal with worthy subjects and should be inspired by reason as well as by imagination. To achieve the highest effects it must be restrained by law; there must

* In later editions Grierson substituted Addison for Johnson.

be precision of detail and harmony of all the parts and a latent logic even in its wildest flights." We in this country are familiar with that ideal from the criticism of Matthew Arnold—the all-importance of the subject, the necessity for construction, etc.—all very admirable, but not things to be obtained by any poet merely through sitting down in a cool hour to take thought; for a poet is the child of his age, and not every age is sure of itself, is convinced as to what are worthy subjects or what is a reasonable view of life. A classical age believes it knows, is convinced of the reasonableness and naturalness of many things, feels that it has achieved an equilibrium between faith and reason, sense and feeling, matter and form. Time invariably proves that the balance was imperfect and precarious. But if we are to call the poetry of Goethe and Arnold "classical" it should, I think, not be because they cultivated Greek forms but because, by virtue of worth of substance and beauty of form, their work has in it the promise of endurance, *some* of the elements which every classical synthesis must include. And here perhaps we descry a possible reconciliation of classical and romantic. Some works that are the genuine product of such a period of ferment as I have described may, in virtue of some elements in them, some essential solidity and beauty, outline the movement that begot them, while others that once sparkled as brightly remain like withered, if richly coloured, weeds, left by a tide that came in like a spring-flood but has receded now out of sight and out of hearing.

With the epithet "romantic" we must proceed even more tentatively though perhaps less relatively. The romantic mood is always with us. We are all romantics at times, even if it be only "When sleep comes to close each difficult day," or when we are in love; and so there will at all times be more or less romantic poets and artists. But a romantic *movement* is a definite and justifiable phenomenon in the history of thought and literature and art. Classical and romantic—these are the systole and diastole of the human heart in history. They represent on the one hand our need of order, of synthesis, of a comprehensive yet definite, therefore *exclusive* as well as inclusive, ordering of thought and feeling and action; and on the other hand the inevitable finiteness of every human synthesis, the inevitable discovery that, in Carlyle's metaphor, our clothes no longer fit us, that the classical has become the conventional, that our spiritual aspirations are being starved, or that our secular impulses are "cribb'd, cabin'd, and confined"; and the heart and imagination bursts its cerements and reaches out, it may be with Faust, after the joys of this world:

> Had I as many souls as there be stars,
> I'd give them all for Mephistophelis;

it may be with Rousseau and Wordsworth and Shelley after a "return to nature," a freer, juster, kinder world:

> When love is an unerring light
> And joy its own security;

it may be after "a past that never was a present," "the glory that was Greece," for

> Greece and her foundations are
> Built below the tide of war,
> Based on the crystalline sea
> Of thought and its eternity;

or it may be the ages of faith, the Gothic Rose:

> The Middle Ages sleep in alabaster.
> A delicate fine sleep. They never knew
> The irreparable Hell of that disaster,
> That broke with hammers Heaven's fragile blue.
>
> .   .   .
>
> All gone, it was too beautiful to die:
> It was too beautiful to live; the world
> Ne'er rotted it with her slow-creeping hells:
> Men shall not see the vision crowned and pearled,
> When Jerusalem blossomed in the noon-tide bells.

But it is not the subject matter which in itself, at any time, makes poetry romantic. It is not the fairies and magicians of Celtic literature, the heroisms of Germanic tradition, the marvels of Oriental tales which make romantic the poems of the Middle Ages, it is the use which was made of them. To their original authors and audiences, Celtic, Germanic, and Eastern, we do not know how these stories appealed. Marvellous, doubtless, but perhaps in the main quite credible. It is the conscious contrast with reason that makes romance in the full sense. It is not because it reflects the life and serious thought of the age that mediæval romance is interesting, but because it does not, but represents men's dreams. This is, I think, the very essence of the word "romantic" as we apply it to the literature of these great periods and

great poets—this conscious contrast of what the heart and the imagination envisage and beckon us to follow, and reason, not the scientific
reason which has thought out the matter and attained conviction, but
reason in the sense of what the society in which a man lives deems reasonable. Paul is a romantic Christian because he realizes, as possibly few
of his fellow-apostles did, the tremendous venture on which he has
embarked; he knows that Christ crucified is "unto the Jews a stumbling-
block, and unto the Greeks foolishness." The romantic quality of the
mediæval Christian hymns resides in nothing so much as in the definite,
matter-of-fact way in which dogmas are affirmed in sonorous language
and the tremendous, reason-transcending character of the content of
these dogmas. To an earlier people the symbols of the Grail—the lance,
the plate, the sword, the wounded Fisher-King—had, if I may believe
Miss Weston, a definite enough character in a fertilising ritual. For the
romantic poets of the Middle Ages they were consciously mysterious,
inexplicable things which they wove into their expression of ideals
transcending all rational limits, ideals secular and sacred, ideals of
honour and love, of humility and asceticism. And in like manner at
the romantic revival there is a conscious transcendence of reason in
Wordsworth's

> sense sublime
> Of something far more deeply interfused
> Whose dwelling is the light of setting suns,
> And the round ocean and the living air,
> And the blue sky, and in the mind of man;

the romantic poet who reviews mediæval chivalry or Catholicism knows
that he is dreaming, though the dream may have for him elements of
perennial value. If Shelley, despite the ardour and music of his poetry,
yet seems sometimes hardly a romantic in the sense that Wordsworth
and Coleridge and Keats and Morris are, it is not, as Crabbe, because he
is a realist but for the very opposite reason because he has *no* grasp of
reality, no clear definable consciousness of the contrast between what
is and what he dreams of and desires, or, as far as he has it, can express
it only in musical lament. The great romantic knows that he lives by
faith and not by reason.

BIBLIOGRAPHICAL NOTE: For other essays that juxtapose in different ways
    classic and romantic as "a recurring sequence of tendencies" rather than
    distinct periods of literary history, see Lascelles Abercrombie, *Romanticism*
    (London, 1926), and the selections by Walter Pater, Mario Praz, Herbert
    Read, F. L. Lucas, and Alex Comfort in this collection.

Romanticism and Classicism

T. E. Hulme

I want to maintain that after a hundred years of romanticism, we are in for a classical revival, and that the particular weapon of this new classical spirit, when it works in verse, will be fancy. And in this I imply the superiority of fancy—not superior generally or absolutely, for that would be obvious nonsense, but superior in the sense that we use the word "good" in empirical ethics—good for something, superior for something. I shall have to prove then two things, first that a classical revival is coming, and, secondly, for its particular purposes, fancy will be superior to imagination.

So banal have the terms Imagination and Fancy become that we imagine they must have always been in the language. Their history as two differing terms in the vocabulary of criticism is comparatively short. Originally, of course, they both mean the same thing; they first began to be differentiated by the German writers on æsthetics in the eighteenth century.

I know that in using the words "classic" and "romantic" I am doing a dangerous thing. They represent five or six different kinds of anti-

ROMANTICISM AND CLASSICISM: FROM *Speculations* by T. E. Hulme (New York: Harcourt, Brace & World, Inc., 1936), pp. 113–40. Reprinted by permission of Harcourt, Brace & World, Inc.

theses, and while I may be using them in one sense you may be interpreting them in another. . . .

. . .

The best way of gliding into a proper definition of my terms would be to start with a set of people who are prepared to fight about it—for in them you will have no vagueness. (Other people take the infamous attitude of the person with catholic tastes who says he likes both.)

About a year ago, a man whose name I think was Fauchois gave a lecture at the Odéon on Racine, in the course of which he made some disparaging remarks about his dullness, lack of invention and the rest of it. This caused an immediate riot: fights took place all over the house; several people were arrested and imprisoned, and the rest of the series of lectures took place with hundreds of gendarmes and detectives scattered all over the place. These people interrupted because the classical ideal is a living thing to them and Racine is the great classic. That is what I call a real vital interest in literature. They regard romanticism as an awful disease from which France had just recovered.

The thing is complicated in their case by the fact that it was romanticism that made the revolution. They hate the revolution, so they hate romanticism.

I make no apology for dragging in politics here; romanticism both in England and France is associated with certain political views, and it is in taking a concrete example of the working out of a principle in action that you can get its best definition.

What was the positive principle behind all the other principles of '89? I am talking here of the revolution in as far as it was an idea; I leave out material causes—they only produce the forces. The barriers which could easily have resisted or guided these forces had been previously rotted away by ideas. This always seems to be the case in successful changes; the privileged class is beaten only when it has lost faith in itself, when it has itself been penetrated with the ideas which are working against it.

It was not the rights of man—that was a good solid practical warcry. The thing which created enthusiasm, which made the revolution practically a new religion, was something more positive than that. People of all classes, people who stood to lose by it, were in a positive ferment about the idea of liberty. There must have been some idea which enabled them to think that something positive could come out

of so essentially negative a thing. There was, and here I get my definition of romanticism. They had been taught by Rousseau that man was
by nature good, that it was only bad laws and customs that had suppressed him. Remove all these and the infinite possibilities of man would
have a chance. This is what made them think that something positive
could come out of disorder, this is what created the religious enthusiasm. Here is the root of all romanticism: that man, the individual, is an
infinite reservoir of possibilities; and if you can so rearrange society by
the destruction of oppressive order then these possibilities will have a
chance and you will get Progress.

One can define the classical quite clearly as the exact opposite to
this. Man is an extraordinarily fixed and limited animal whose nature
is absolutely constant. It is only by tradition and organisation that
anything decent can be got out of him.

This view was a little shaken at the time of Darwin. You remember
his particular hypothesis, that new species came into existence by the
cumulative effect of small variations—this seems to admit the possibility of future progress. But at the present day the contrary hypothesis
makes headway in the shape of De Vries's mutation theory, that each
new species comes into existence, not gradually by the accumulation
of small steps, but suddenly in a jump, a kind of sport, and that once in
existence it remains absolutely fixed. This enables me to keep the
classical view with an appearance of scientific backing.

Put shortly, these are the two views, then. One, that man is intrinsically good, spoilt by circumstance; and the other that he is intrinsically limited, but disciplined by order and tradition to something fairly
decent. To the one party man's nature is like a well, to the other like
a bucket. The view which regards man as a well, a reservoir full of
possibilities, I call the romantic; the one which regards him as a very
finite and fixed creature, I call the classical.

One may note here that the Church has always taken the classical
view since the defeat of the Pelagian heresy and the adoption of the
same classical dogma of original sin.

It would be a mistake to identify the classical view with that of
materialism. On the contrary it is absolutely identical with the normal
religious attitude. I should put it in this way: That part of the fixed
nature of man is the belief in the Deity. This should be as fixed and true
for every man as belief in the existence of matter and in the objective

world. It is parallel to appetite, the instinct of sex, and all the other
fixed qualities. Now at certain times, by the use of either force or
rhetoric, these instincts have been suppressed—in Florence under
Savonarola, in Geneva under Calvin, and [in England] under the
Roundheads. The inevitable result of such a process is that the repressed
instinct bursts out in some abnormal directon. So with religion. By the
perverted rhetoric of rationalism, your natural instincts are suppressed
and you are converted into an agnostic. Just as in the case of the other
instincts, Nature has her revenge. The instincts that find their right and
proper outlet in religion must come out in some other way. You don't
believe in a God, so you begin to believe that man is a god. You don't
believe in Heaven, so you begin to believe in a heaven on earth. In
other words, you get romanticism. The concepts that are right and
proper in their own sphere are spread over, and so mess up, falsify,
and blur the clear outlines of human experience. It is like pouring a
pot of treacle over the dinner table. Romanticism, then, and this is
the best definition I can give of it, is spilt religion.*

I must now shirk the difficulty of saying exactly what I mean by
romantic and classical in verse. I can only say that it means the result
of these two attitudes toward the cosmos, toward man, in so far as it
gets reflected in verse. The romantic, because he thinks man infinite,
must always be talking about the infinite; and as there is always the
bitter contrast between what you think you ought to be able to do and
what man actually can, it always tends, in its later stages at any rate,
to be gloomy. I really can't go any further than to say it is the reflection of these two temperaments, and point out examples of the different
spirits. On the one hand I would take such diverse people as Horace,
most of the Elizabethans and the writers of the Augustan age, and on
the other side Lamartine, Hugo, parts of Keats, Coleridge, Byron,
Shelley, and Swinburne.

I know quite well that when people think of classical and romantic
in verse, the contrast at once comes into their mind between, say,
Racine and Shakespeare. I don't mean this; the dividing line that I
intend is here misplaced a little from the true middle. That Racine is on
the extreme classical side I agree, but if you call Shakespeare romantic,
you are using a different definition to the one I give. You are thinking
of the difference between classic and romantic as being merely one
between restraint and exuberance. I should say with Nietzsche that

---

* Cf. Babbitt's idea of romanticism's "sham spirituality," p. 31 above, and H. N.
Fairchild's assessment of romantic religion as "a tissue of heresies" p. 209 below.

there are two kinds of classicism, the static and the dynamic. Shakespeare is the classic of motion.

What I mean by classical in verse, then, is this. That even in the most imaginative flights there is always a holding back, a reservation. The classical poet never forgets this finiteness, this limit of man. He remembers always that he is mixed up with earth. He may jump, but he always returns back; he never flies away into the circumambient gas.

You might say if you wished that the whole of the romantic attitude seems to crystallise in verse round metaphors of flight. Hugo is always flying, flying over abysses, flying up into the eternal gases. The word "infinite" in every other line.

In the classical attitude you never seem to swing right along to the infinite nothing. If you say an extravagant thing which does exceed the limits inside which you know man to be fastened, yet there is always conveyed in some way at the end an impression of yourself standing outside it, and not quite believing it, or consciously putting it forward as a flourish. You never go blindly into an atmosphere more than the truth, an atmosphere too rarefied for man to breathe for long. You are always faithful to the conception of a limit. It is a question of pitch; in romantic verse you move at a certain pitch of rhetoric which you know, man being what he is, to be a little high-falutin. The kind of thing you get in Hugo or Swinburne. In the coming classical reaction that will feel just wrong. For an example of the opposite thing, a verse written in the proper classical spirit, I can take the song from *Cymbeline* beginning with "Fear no more the heat of the sun." I am just using this as a parable. I don't quite mean what I say here. Take the last two lines:

> Golden lads and girls all must,
> Like chimney sweepers come to dust.

Now, no romantic would have ever written that. Indeed, so ingrained is romanticism, so objectionable is this to it, that people have asserted that these were not part of the original song.

Apart from the pun, the thing that I think quite classical is the word "lad." Your modern romantic could never write that. He would have to write golden youth, and take up the thing at least a couple of notes in pitch.

I want now to give the reasons which make me think that we are nearing the end of the romantic movement.

The first lies in the nature of any convention or tradition in art. A

particular convention or attitude in art has a strict analogy to the phenomena of organic life. It grows old and decays. It has a definite period
of life and must die. All the possible tunes get played on it and then it
is exhausted; moreover its best period is its youngest. . . . Each field of
artistic activity is exhausted by the first great artist who gathers a full
harvest from it. This period of exhaustion seems to me to have been
reached in romanticism. We shall not get any new efflorescence of
verse until we get a new technique, a new convention, to turn ourselves
loose in.

Objection might be taken to this. It might be said that a century
as an organic unity doesn't exist, that I am being deluded by a wrong
metaphor, that I am treating a collection of literary people as if they
were an organism or state department. Whatever we may be in other
things, an objector might urge, in literature in as far as we are anything at all—in as far as we are worth considering—we are individuals,
we are persons, and as distinct persons we cannot be subordinated to
any general treatment. At any period at any time, an individual poet
may be a classic or a romantic just as he feels like it. You at any particular moment may think that you can stand outside a movement. You
may think that as an individual you observe both the classic and the
romantic spirit and decide from a purely detached point of view that
one is superior to the other.

The answer to this is that no one, in a matter of judgment of
beauty, can take a detached standpoint in this way. Just as physically
you are not born that abstract entity, man, but the child of particular
parents, so you are in matters of literary judgment. Your opinion is
almost entirely of the literary history that came just before you, and
you are governed by that whatever you may think.

•   •   •

When I say that I dislike the romantics, I dissociate two things:
the part of them in which they resemble all the great poets, and the
part in which they differ and which gives them their character as
romantics. It is this minor element which constitutes the particular
note of a century, and which, while it excites contemporaries, annoys
the next generation. It was precisely that quality in Pope which pleased
his friends, which we detest. Now, anyone just before the romantics
who felt that, could have predicted that a change was coming. It seems
to me that we stand just in the same position now. I think that there

is an increasing proportion of people who simply can't stand Swinburne.

When I say that there will be another classical revival I don't necessarily anticipate a return to Pope. I say merely that now is the time for such a revival. Given people of the necessary capacity, it may be a vital thing; without them we may get a formalism something like Pope. When it does come we may not even recognise it as classical. Although it will be classical it will be different because it has passed through a romantic period. To take a parallel example: I remember being very surprised, after seeing the post-impressionists, to find in Maurice Denis's account of the matter that they consider themselves classical in the sense that they were trying to impose the same order on the mere flux of new material provided by the impressionist movement, that existed in the more limited materials of the painting before.

There is something now to be cleared away before I get on with my argument, which is that while romanticism is dead in reality, yet the critical attitude appropriate to it still continues to exist. To make this a little clearer: For every kind of verse, there is a corresponding receptive attitude. In a romantic period we demand from verse certain qualities. In a classical period we demand others. At the present time I should say that this receptive attitude has outlasted the thing from which it was formed. But while the romantic tradition has run dry, yet the critical attitude of mind, which demands romantic qualities from verse, still survives. So that if good classical verse were to be written to-morrow very few people would be able to stand it.

I object even to the best of the romantics. I object still more to the receptive attitude. I object to the sloppiness which doesn't consider that a poem is a poem unless it is moaning or whining about something or other. I always think in this connection of the last line of a poem of John Webster's which ends with a request I cordially endorse: "End your moan and come away." The thing has got so bad now that a poem which is all dry and hard, a properly classical poem, would not be considered poetry at all. How many people now can lay their hands on their hearts and say they like either Horace or Pope? They feel a kind of chill when they read them.

The dry hardness which you get in the classics is absolutely repugnant to them. Poetry that isn't damp isn't poetry at all. They cannot see that accurate description is a legitimate object of verse. Verse to them always means a bringing in of some of the emotions that are grouped round the word "infinite."

The essence of poetry to most people is that it must lead them to a beyond of some kind. Verse strictly confined to the earthly and the definite (Keats is full of it) might seem to them to be excellent writing, excellent craftsmanship, but not poetry. So much has romanticism debauched us, that, without some form of vagueness, we deny the highest.

In the classic it is always the light of ordinary day, never the light that never was on land or sea. It is always perfectly human and never exaggerated: man is always man and never a god.

But the awful result of romanticism is that, accustomed to this strange light, you can never live without it. Its effect on you is that of a drug.

There is a general tendency to think that verse means little else than the expression of unsatisfied emotion. People say: "But how can you have verse without sentiment?" You see what it is: the prospect alarms them. A classical revival to them would mean the prospect of an arid desert and the death of poetry as they understand it, and could only come to fill the gap caused by that death. Exactly why this dry classical spirit should have a positive and legitimate necessity to express itself in poetry is utterly inconceivable to them. What this positive need is, I shall show later. It follows from the fact that there is another quality, not the emotion produced, which is at the root of excellence in verse.

> [Hulme next argues that this "reluctance to understand classical verse" is due to "a bad metaphysic of art," one "unable to admit the existence of beauty without the infinite being in some way or another dragged in."]

It is essential to prove that beauty may be in small, dry things.

The great aim is accurate, precise, and definite description. The first thing is to recognise how extraordinarily difficult this is. It is no mere matter of carefulness; you have to use language, and language is by its very nature a communal thing; that is, it expresses never the exact thing but a compromise—that which is common to you, me, and everybody. But each man sees a little differently, and to get out clearly and exactly what he does see, he must have a terrific struggle with language, whether it be with words or the technique of other arts.

Language has its own special nature, its own conventions and communal ideas. It is only by a concentrated effort of the mind that you can hold it fixed to your own purpose. I always think that the fundamental process at the back of all the arts might be represented by the following metaphor. You know what I call architect's curves—flat pieces of wood with all different kinds of curvature. By a suitable selection from these you can draw approximately any curve you like. The artist I take to be the man who simply can't bear the idea of that "approximately." He will get the exact curve of what he sees whether it be an object or an idea in the mind. I shall here have to change my metaphor a little to get the process in his mind. Suppose that instead of your curved pieces of wood you have a springy piece of steel of the same types of curvature as the wood. Now the state of tension or concentration of mind, if he is doing anything really good in this struggle against the ingrained habit of the technique, may be represented by a man employing all his fingers to bend the steel out of its own curve and into the exact curve which you want. Something different to what it would assume naturally.

There are then two things to distinguish, first the particular faculty of mind to see things as they really are, and apart from the conventional ways in which you have been trained to see them. This is itself rare enough in all consciousness. Second, the concentrated state of mind, the grip over oneself which is necessary in the actual expression of what one sees. To prevent one falling into the conventional curves of ingrained technique, to hold on through infinite detail and trouble to the exact curve you want. Wherever you get this sincerity, you get the fundamental quality of good art without dragging in infinite or serious.

I can now get at that positive fundamental quality of verse which constitutes excellence, which has nothing to do with infinity, with mystery or with emotions.

This is the point I aim at, then, in my argument. I prophesy that a period of dry, hard, classical verse is coming. I have met the preliminary objection founded on the bad romantic æsthetic that in such verse, from which the infinite is excluded, you cannot have the essence of poetry at all.

After attempting to sketch out what this positive quality is, I can get on to the end of my paper in this way: That where you get this quality exhibited in the realm of the emotions you get imagination, and that where you get this quality exhibited in the contemplation of finite things you get fancy.

. . . Poetry . . . is not a counter language, but a visual concrete one.* It is a compromise for a language of intuition which would hand over sensations bodily. It always endeavours to arrest you, and to make you continuously see a physical thing, to prevent you gliding through an abstract process. It chooses fresh epithets and fresh metaphors, not so much because they are new, and we are tired of the old, but because the old cease to convey a physical thing and become abstract counters. A poet says a ship "coursed the seas" to get a physical image, instead of the counter word "sailed." Visual meanings can only be transferred by the new bowl of metaphor; prose is an old pot that lets them leak out. Images in verse are not mere decoration, but the very essence of an intuitive language. Verse is a pedestrian taking you over the ground, prose—a train which delivers you at a destination. . . . [Verse] is the avoidance of conventional language in order to get the exact curve of the thing.

I have still to show that in the verse which to is come, fancy will be the necessary weapon of the classical school. . . . Fancy is not mere decoration added on to plain speech. Plain speech is essentially in-accurate. It is only by new metaphors, that is, by fancy, that it can be made precise.

When the analogy has not enough connection with the thing described to be quite parallel with it, where it overlays the thing it described and there is a certain excess, there you have the play of fancy—that I grant is inferior to imagination.

But where the analogy is every bit of it necessary for accurate descrip-tion . . . and your only objection to this kind of fancy is that it is not serious in the effect it produces, then I think the objection to be entirely invalid. If it is sincere in the accurate sense, when the whole of the analogy is necessary to get out the exact curve of the feeling or thing you want to express—there you seem to me to have the highest verse, even though the subject be trivial and the emotions of the infinite far away. . . .

A romantic movement must have an end of the very nature of the thing. It may be deplored, but it can't be helped—wonder must cease to be wonder.**

* Hulme defines prose as the embodiment of things " in signs or counters which are moved about according to rules, without being visualised at all in the process."

** Hulme, as Babbitt before him, is probably referring to Watts-Dunton's descrip-tion of romanticism as "the renascence of wonder."

I guard myself here from all the consequences of the analogy, but it expresses at any rate the inevitableness of the process. A literature of wonder must have an end as inevitably as a strange land loses its strangeness when one lives in it. Think of the lost ecstasy of the Elizabethans: "Oh my America, my new found land," think of what it meant to them and of what it means to us. Wonder can only be the attitude of a man passing from one stage to another, it can never be a permanently fixed thing.

BIBLIOGRAPHICAL NOTE: The origins of Hulme's basic position may be found in the general neohumanist view of romanticism, which is most explicit in Babbitt's essay above and in P. E. More's *The Drift of Romanticism*. Hulme's position in turn is similar to T. S. Eliot's in, e.g., *The Sacred Wood* (London, 1920); "Andrew Marvell," *Selected Essays 1917–1932* (New York, 1932); "Shelley and Keats," *The Use of Poetry and the Use of Criticism* (New York, 1933). Their influence may be seen particularly in the selection by Cleanth Brooks below, and in John Crowe Ransom's *The World's Body* (New York, 1938), and Allen Tate's *Reactionary Essays* (New York, 1936) and *Reason in Madness* (New York, 1941). For specific attacks on Hulme's view see R. H. Fogle's essay below, and the conclusion of Northrop Frye's essay below. On the other hand, see Frank Kermode's chapter on Hulme in his *Romantic Image* (New York, 1957), in which Hulme is seen as affiliated with "that organicist, anti-positivist stream of ideas that stems from the romantic movement"; also Murray Krieger's chapter, "T. E. Hulme: Classicism and the Imagination," in his *The New Apologists for Poetry* (Minneapolis, 1956).

On the Discrimination
of Romanticisms

Arthur O. Lovejoy

[Lovejoy begins by surveying the various, confusing, and even contradictory accounts of the origins and definitions of romanticism.]

All this is a mere hint, a suggestion by means of random samples,
of the richness of the collection which might be brought together. . . .
The result is a ‚confusion of terms, and of ideas, beside which that of a
hundred years ago—mind-shaking though it was to the honest inquirers
[Dupuis and Cotonet]*—seems pure lucidity. The word "romantic"
has come to mean so many things that, by itself, it means nothing.
It has ceased to perform the function of a verbal sign. When a man is
asked . . . to discuss romanticism, it is impossible to know what ideas
or tendencies he is to talk about, when they are supposed to have

On the Discrimination of Romanticisms: From *PMLA*, XXXIX (1924), 229–253.
Reprinted by permission of the Modern Language Association of America.

* In 1824 Alfred de Musset published his *Lettres de Dupuis et Cotonet*, a *reductio ad
absurdum* of efforts to define romanticism. For a convenient list of twenty-eight definitions of romanticism, "selected from many hundreds" as he puts it, see Ernest Bernbaum's *Guide through the Romantic Movement* (New York, 1949), p. 301. Other interesting
compilations of definitions, Continental as well as English, appear in *The Portable
Romantic Reader*, ed. Howard E. Hugo (New York, 1957), pp. 51–73, and Anthony
Thorlby, *The Romantic Movement* (London, 1966), pp. 14–18.

flourished, or in whom they are supposed to be chiefly exemplified. Perhaps there are some who think the rich ambiguity of the word not regrettable. In 1824, as Victor Hugo then testified, there were those who preferred to leave "*à ce mot de romantique un certain vague fantastique et indéfinissable qui en redouble l'horreur*"; and it may be that the taste is not extinct. But for one of the philosopher's trade, at least, the situation is embarrassing and exasperating; for philosophers, in spite of a popular belief to the contrary, are persons who suffer from a morbid solicitude to know precisely what they are talking about.

Least of all does it seem possible, while the present uncertainty concerning the nature and *locus* of romanticism prevails, to take sides in the controversy which still goes on so briskly with respect to its merits, the character of its general influence upon art and life. To do so would be too much like consenting to sit on a jury to try a criminal not yet identified, for a series of apparently incompatible crimes, before a bench of learned judges engaged in accusing one another of being accessories to whatever mischief has been done. . . .*

What, then, can be done to clear up, or to diminish, this confusion of terminology and of thought which has for a century been the scandal of literary history and criticism, and is still, as it would not be difficult to show, copiously productive of historical errors and of dangerously undiscriminating diagnoses of the moral and æsthetic maladies of our age? . . . There are . . . two possible historical inquiries which, if carried out more thoroughly and carefully than has yet been done, would, I think, do much to rectify the present muddle, and would at the same time promote a clearer understanding of the general movement of ideas, the logical and psychological relations between the chief episodes and transitions, in modern thought and taste.

One of these measures would be somewhat analogous to the procedure of contemporary psychopathologists in the treatment of certain types of disorder. It has been found that some mental disturbances can be cured or alleviated by making the patient explicitly aware of the genesis of his troublesome "complex," i.e., by enabling him to reconstruct those processes of association of ideas through which it was formed. The result of such analysis is sometimes a disassociation of a

---

* Lovejoy refers here to Pierre Lasserre, *Le romantisme français* (Paris, 1919), Ernest Seillière, *Le mal romantique* (Paris, 1908), Irving Babbitt, and Paul Elmer More, all of whom agree "that something called romanticism is the chief cause of the spiritual evils from which the nineteenth century and our own have suffered," but none of whom quite agree as to what those evils are and how they may be remedied.

very benign sort. Similarly in the present case, I think, it would be useful to trace the associative processes through which the word "romantic" has attained its present amazing diversity, and consequent uncertainty, of connotation and denotation; in other words, to carry out an adequate semasiological study of the term. For one of the few things certain about romanticism is that the name of it offers one of the most complicated, fascinating, and instructive of all problems in semantics. It is, in short, a part of the task of the historian of ideas, when he applies himself to the study of the thing or things called romanticism, to render it, if possible, psychologically intelligible how such manifold and discrepant phenomena have all come to receive one name. Such an analysis would, I am convinced, show us a large mass of purely verbal confusions operative as actual factors in the movement of thought in the past century and a quarter; and it would, by making these confusions explicit, make it easier to avoid them.

But this inquiry would in practice, for the most part, be inseparable from a second, which is the remedy that I wish, on this occasion, especially to recommend. The first step in this second mode of treatment of the disorder is that we should learn to use the word "romanticism" in the plural. This, of course, is already the practice of the more cautious and observant literary historians, in so far as they recognize that the "romanticism" of one country may have little in common with that of another,* and at all events ought to be defined in distinctive terms. But the discrimination of the romanticisms which I have in mind is not solely or chiefly a division upon lines of nationality or language. What is needed is that any study of the subject should begin with a recognition of a *prima facie* plurality of romanticisms, of possibly quite distinct thought-complexes, a number of which may appear in one country. There is no hope of clear thinking on the part of the student of modern literature, if—as, alas! has been repeatedly done by eminent writers—he vaguely hypostatizes the term, and starts with the presumption that "romanticism" is the heaven-appointed designation of some single real entity, or type of entities, to be found in nature. He must set out from the simple and obvious fact that there are various historic episodes or movements to which different historians of our own or other periods have, for one reason or another, given the name.

* It is precisely to this point, as well as to the whole idea of a plurality of romanticisms, that René Wellek addresses himself in the essay reprinted in this collection.

There is a movement which began in Germany in the seventeen-nineties—the only one which has an indisputable title to be called romanticism, since it invented the term for its own use. There is another movement which began pretty definitely in England in the seventeen-forties. There is a movement which began in France in 1801. There is another movement which began in France in the second decade of the century, is linked with the German movement, and took over the German name. There is the rich and incongruous collection of ideas to be found in Rousseau. There are numerous other things called romanticism by various writers whom I cited at the outset. The fact that the same name has been given by different scholars to all of these episodes is no evidence, and scarcely even establishes a presumption, that they are identical in essentials. There may be some least common denominator of them all; but if so, it has never yet been clearly exhibited, and its presence is not to be assumed *a priori*. In any case, each of these so-called romanticisms was a highly complex and usually an exceedingly unstable intellectual compound; each, in other words, was made up of various unit-ideas linked together, for the most part, not by any indissoluble bonds of logical necessity, but by alogical associative processes, greatly facilitated and partly caused, in the case of the romanticisms which grew up after the appellation "romantic" was invented, by the congenital and acquired ambiguities of the word. And when certain of these romanticisms have in truth significant elements in common, they are not necessarily the same elements in any two cases. Romanticism A may have one characteristic presupposition or impulse, X, which it shares with romanticism B, another characteristic, Y, which it shares with romanticism C, to which X is wholly foreign. In the case, moreover, of those movements or schools to which the label was applied in their own time, the contents under the label sometimes changed radically and rapidly. At the end of a decade or two you had the same men and the same party appellation, but profoundly different ideas. As everyone knows, this is precisely what happened in the case of what is called French romanticism. . . . In most of its practically significant sympathies and affiliations of a literary, ethical, political, and religious sort, the French "romanticism" of the eighteen-thirties was the antithesis of that of the beginning of the century.

But the essential of the second remedy is that each of these romanticisms—after they are first thus roughly discriminated with respect to their representatives or their dates—should be resolved, by a more

thorough and discerning analysis than is yet customary, into its elements—into the several ideas and æsthetic susceptibilities of which it
is composed. Only after these fundamental thought-factors in it are
clearly discriminated and fairly exhaustively enumerated, shall we be
in a position to judge of the degree of its affinity with other complexes
to which the same name has been applied, to see precisely what tacit
preconceptions or controlling motives or explicit contentions were
common to any two or more of them, and wherein they manifested
distinct and divergent tendencies.

Of the needfulness of such analytic comparison and discrimination
of the romanticisms let me attempt three illustrations.

1. In an interesting lecture before the British Academy a few years
since, Mr. [Edmund] Gosse described Joseph Warton's youthful poem,
"The Enthusiast," written in 1740, as the first clear manifestation of

> the great romantic movement, such as it has enlarged and dwindled
> down to our day. . . . Here for the first time we find unwaveringly
> emphasized and repeated what was entirely new in literature, the essence
> of romantic hysteria. "The Enthusiast" is the earliest expression of
> complete revolt against the classical attitude which had been sovereign
> in all European literature for nearly a century. So completely is this
> expressed by Joseph Warton that it is extremely difficult to realize that
> he could not have come under the fascination of Rousseau. . . who was
> not to write anything characteristic until ten years later [Lovejoy's
> ellipses].[1]

Let us, then, compare the ideas distinctive of this poem with the conception of *romantische Poesie* formulated by Friedrich Schlegel and his
fellow-romanticists in Germany after 1796. The two have plainly
certain common elements. Both are forms of revolt against the neoclassical aesthetics; both are partly inspired by an ardent admiration
for Shakespeare; both proclaim the creative artist's independence of
"rules." It might at first appear, therefore, that these two romanticisms,
in spite of natural differences of phraseology, are identical in essence—
are separate outcroppings of the same vein of metal, precious or base,
according to your taste.

But a more careful scrutiny shows a contrast between them not less
important—indeed, as it seems to me, more important—than their

[1] "Two Pioneers of Romanticism," *Proceedings of the British Academy* (1915), pp.
146–48.

resemblance. The general theme of Joseph Warton's poem (of which, it will be remembered, the sub-title is "The Lover of Nature") is one which had been a commonplace for two centuries: the superiority of "nature" to "art."

. . .

. . . This, if I may be permitted the expression, was old stuff. The principal thing that was original and significant in the poem was that Warton boldly applied the doctrine of the superiority of "nature" over conscious art to the theory of poetry:

> What are the lays of artful Addison,
> Coldly correct, to Shakespeare's warblings wild?

That Nature herself was wild, untamed, was notorious, almost tautological; and it was Shakespeare's supposed "wildness," his nonconformity to the conventional rules, the spontaneous freedom of his imagination and his expression, that proved him Nature's true pupil.

Now this æsthetic inference had not, during the neo-classical period, ordinarily been drawn from the current assumption of the superiority of nature to art. The principle of "following nature" had in æsthetics usually been taken in another, or more than one other, of the several dozen senses of the sacred word.[2] Yet in other provinces of thought an analogous inference had long since and repeatedly been suggested. From the first the fashion of conceiving of "nature" (in the sense in which it was antithetic to "art") as norm had made for antinomianism, in some degree or other—for a depreciation of restraint, for the ideal of "letting yourself go." . . .

Aside from a certain heightening of the emotional tone, then, the chief novelty of Warton's poem lay in its suggesting the application of these ideas to a field from which they had been curiously and inconsistently excluded, in its introduction of antinomianism, of a rather mild sort, into the conception of poetic excellence. But this extension was obviously implicit from the outset in the logic of that protean "naturalism" which had been the most characteristic and potent force in modern thought since the late Renaissance; it was bound to be made by somebody sooner or later. Nor was Warton's the first æsthetic ap-

---

[2] This is not rhetorical exaggeration; at least sixty different senses or applications of the notion of "nature" as norm can be clearly distinguished. [See, e.g., Lovejoy's "'Nature' as Aesthetic Norm," *MLN*, XLII (1927), 444–50.]

plication of the principle; it had already been applied to an art in the theory and practice of which eighteenth-century Englishmen were keenly interested—the art of landscape design. The first great revolt against the neo-classical æsthetics was not in literature at all, but in gardening;* the second, I think, was in architectural taste; and all three were inspired by the same ideas. Since, the "artful Addison" had observed, "artificial works receive a greater advantage from their resemblance of such as are natural," and since Nature is distinguished by her "rough, careless strokes," the layer-out of gardens should aim at "an artificial rudeness much more charming than that neatness and elegancy usually met with." This horticultural romanticism had been preached likewise by Sir William Temple, Pope, Horace Walpole, Batty Langley, and others, and ostensibly exemplified in the work of Kent, Brown, and Bridgeman. Warton in the poem in question describes Kent as at least doing his best to imitate in his gardens the wildness of Nature:

> He, by rules unfettered, boldly scorns
> Formality and method; round and square
> Disdaining, plans irregularly great.

It was no far cry from this to the rejection of the rules in the drama, to a revulsion against the strait-laced regularity and symmetry of the heroic couplet, to a general turning from convention, formality, method, artifice, in all the arts.

There had, however, from the first been a curious duality of meaning in the antithesis of "nature" and "art"—one of the most pregnant of the long succession of confusions of ideas which make up much of the history of human thought. While the "natural" was, on the one hand, conceived as the wild and spontaneous and "irregular," it was also conceived as the simple, the naïve, the unsophisticated. No two words were more fixedly associated in the mind of the sixteenth, seventeenth and early eighteenth centuries than "Nature" and "simple." Consequently the idea of preferring nature to custom and to art usually carried with it the suggestion of a program of simplification, of reform by elimination; in other words, it implied primitivism. The "natural" was a thing you reached by going back and by leaving out. And this

---

* For an interesting account of the origins of romanticism in treatises on gardening, see Raymond Immerwahr's "The First Romantic Æsthetic," *MLQ*, XXI (1959), 3–26.

association of ideas—already obvious in Montaigne, in Pope, and scores of other extollers of "Nature"—is still conspicuous in Warton's poem. It was the "bards of old" who were "fair Nature's friends." The poet envies

> The first of men, ere yet confined
> In smoky cities.

He yearns to dwell in some

> Isles of innocence from mortal view
> Deeply retired beneath a plantane's shade,
> Where Happiness and Quiet sit enthroned,
> With simple Indian swains.

For one term of the comparison, then, I limit myself, for brevity's sake, to this poem to which Mr. Gosse has assigned so important a place in literary history. . . . For the present purpose it suffices to take "The Enthusiast" as typical, in one especially important way, of a great deal of the so-called romanticism before the seventeen-nineties— a romanticism, namely, which, whatever further characteristics it may have had, was based upon naturalism (in the sense of the word which I have indicated) and was associated with primitivism of some mode or degree.

2. For in this fundamental point this earlier "romanticism" differed essentially from that of the German æsthetic theorists and poets who chose the term "romantic poetry" as the most suitable designation for their own literary ideals and program. The latter "romanticism" is in its very essence a denial of the older naturalistic presuppositions, which Warton's poem had manifested in a special and somewhat novel way. The German movement received its immediate and decisive impetus from Schiller's essay *On Naïve and Sentimental Poetry;* and what it derived from that confused work was the conviction that "harmony with nature," in any sense which implied an opposition to "culture," to "art," to reflection and self-conscious effort, was neither possible nor desirable for the modern man or the modern artist.[3] The *Frühromantiker* learned from Schiller the idea of an art which should look back no more to the primitive than to the classical—the notions of which,

[3] Cf. the writer's "Schiller and the Genesis of Romanticism," *MLN*, XXXV (1920), 1–9, 136–46.

incidentally, Schiller had curiously fused—for its models and ideals; which should be the appropriate expression, not of a *natürliche* but of a *künstliche Bildung*; which, so far from desiring simplification, so far from aiming at the sort of harmony in art and life which is to be attained by the method of leaving out, should seek first fullness of content, should have for its program the adequate expression of the entire range of human experience and the entire reach of the human imagination. For man, the artificial, Friedrich Schlegel observed, *is* "natural." "*Die Abstraktion ist ein künstlicher Zustand. Dies ist kein Grund gegen sie, denn es ist dem Menschen gewiss natürlich, sich dann und wann auch in künstliche Zustände zu versetzen.*" And again: "*Eine nur im Gegensatz der Kunst und Bildung natürliche Denkart soll es gar nicht geben.*" To be unsophisticated, to revert to the mental state of "simple Indian swains," was the least of the ambitions of a German romantic—though, since the unsophisticated is one type of human character, his art was not, at least in theory, indifferent even to that. The Shakespeare whom he admired was no gifted child of nature addicted to "warblings wild." Shakespeare, said A. W. Schlegel, is not "*ein blindes wildlaufendes Genie*"; he had "a system in his artistic practise and an astonishingly profound and deeply meditated one." The same critic seems to be consciously attacking either Joseph Warton's or Gray's famous lines about Shakespeare when he writes: "Those poets whom it is customary to represent as carefree nurslings of nature, without art and without schooling, if they produce works of genuine excellence, give evidence of exceptional cultivation (*Kultur*) of their mental powers, of practised art, of ripely pondered and just designs." The greatness of Shakespeare, in the eyes of *these* romantics, lay in his *Universalität*, his sophisticated insight into human nature and the many-sidedness of his portrayal of character; it was this, as Friedrich Schlegel said, that made him "*wie der Mittelpunkt der romantischen Kunst.*" It may be added that another trait of the romanticism found by Mr. Gosse in Joseph Warton, namely, the feeling that didactic poetry is not poetic, was also repudiated by early German romanticism: "How," asked F. Schlegel again, "can it be said that ethics (*die Moral*) belongs merely to philosophy, when the greatest part of poetry relates to the art of living and to the knowledge of human nature?"

The difference, then, I suggest, is more significant, more pregnant, than the likeness between these two romanticisms. Between the assertion of the superiority of "nature" over conscious "art" and that of the superiority of conscious art over mere "nature"; between a way of thinking of which primitivism is of the essence and one of which the idea of perpetual self-transcendence is of the essence; between a fundamental preference for simplicity—even though a "wild" simplicity—and a fundamental preference for diversity and complexity; between the sort of ingenuous naiveté characteristic of "The Enthusiast" and the sophisticated subtlety of the conception of romantic irony: between these the antithesis is one of the most radical that modern thought and taste have to show. I don't deny anyone's right to call both these things romanticism, if he likes; but I cannot but obseve that the fashion of giving both the same name has led to a good deal of unconscious falsification of the history of ideas. The elements of the one romanticism tend to be read into the other; the nature and profundity of the oppositions between them tend to be overlooked; and the relative importance of the different changes of preconceptions in modern thought, and of susceptibilities in modern taste, tends to be wrongly estimated. I shall not attempt to cite here what seem to me examples of such historical errors; but the sum of them is, I think, far from negligible.

Between the "romanticism" which is but a special and belated manifestation of the naturalism that dates from the Renaissance, and the "romanticism" which began at the end of the eighteenth century in Germany (as well as that which appeared a little later in France) there is another difference not less significant. This is due to the identification of the meaning of "romantic" in the later movement with "Christian"—and mainly with the medieval implications of the latter term. This was not the central idea in the original notion of "romantic poetry" as conceived by Friedrich Schlegel. Primarily, as I have elsewhere tried to show,[4] the adjective meant for him and the entire school *"das eigentümlich Moderne"* in contrast with *"das eigentümlich Antike."* But it early occurred to him that the historic cause of the supposed radical differentiation of modern from classical art could lie only in the influence of Christianity. . . .

"Romantic" art thus came to mean—for one thing—an art inspired by or expressive of some idea or some ethical temper supposed to be essential in Christianity. *"Ursprung und Charakter der ganzen neuern Poesie lässt sich so leicht aus dem Christentume ableiten, dass man die romantische eben so gut die chistliche nennen könnte,"* said Richter in 1804, repeating

---

[4] "The Meaning of 'Romantic' in Early German Romanticism," *MLN,* XXXI (1916), 385–96; XXXII (1916–17), 65–77.

what had by that time become a commonplace. But the nature of the essentially Christian, and therefore essentially romantic, spirit was variously conceived. Upon one characteristic of it there was, indeed, rather general agreement among the German romanticists: the habit of mind introduced by Christianity was distinguished by a certain insatiability; it aimed at infinite objectives and was incapable of lasting satisfacton with any goods actually reached. It became a favorite platitude to say that the Greeks and Romans set themselves limited ends to attain, were able to attain them, and were thus capable of self-satisfaction and finality; and that modern or "romantic" art differed from this most fundamentally, by reason of its Christian origin, in being, as Schiller had said, a *Kunst des Unendlichen. "Absolute Abstraktion, Vernichtung des Jetzigen, Apotheose der Zukunft, dieser eigentlich bessern Welt!; dies ist der Kern der Geheisse des Christentums,"* declared Novalis. In its application to artistic practice this "apotheosis of the future" meant the ideal of endless progress, of *"eine progressive Universalpoesie"* in the words of Fr. Schlegel's familiar definition; it implied the demand that art shall always go on bringing new provinces of life within its domain and achieving ever fresh and original effects. But anything which was, or was supposed to be, especially characteristic of the Christian *Weltanschauung* tended to become a part of the current connotation of "romantic," and also a part of the actual ideals of the school. Preoccupation with supersensible realities and a feeling of the illusoriness of ordinary existence was thus often held to be a distinctive trait of romantic art, on the ground that Christanity is an otherworldly religion: *"in der christlichen Ansicht,"* said A. W. Schlegel, *"die Anschauung des Unendlichen hat das Endliche vernichtet; das Leben ist zur Schattenwelt und zur Nacht geworden."* Another recognized characteristic of Christianity, and therefore of the "romantic," was ethical dualism, a conviction that there are in man's constitution two natures ceaselessly at war. The Greek ideal, in the elder Schlegel's words, was *"volkommene Eintracht und Ebenmass aller Kräfte, natürliche Harmonie. Die Neueren hingegen sind zum Bewusstsein der inneren Entzweiung gekommen, welche ein solches Ideal unmöglich macht."* Directly related to this, it was perceived, was the "inwardness" of Christianity, its preoccupation with "the heart" as distinguished from the outward act, its tendency to introspection; and hence, as Mme. de Staël and others observed, "modern" or "romantic" art has discovered, and has for its peculiar province, the inexhaustible realm of the inner life of man. . . .

It is one of the many paradoxes of the history of the word, and of the controversies centering about it, that several eminent literary historians and critics of our time have conceived the moral essence of romanticism as consisting in a kind of "this-worldliness" and a negation of what one of them has termed "the Christian and classical dualism." Its most deplorable and dangerous error, in the judgment of these critics, is its deficient realization of the "civil war in the cave" of man's soul, its belief in the "natural goodness" of man. They thus define "romanticism" in terms precisely opposite to those in which it was often defined by the writers who first called their own ideals romantic; and this fashion, I can't but think, has done a good deal to obscure the palpable and important historical fact that the one romanticism which has thus (as I have said) an unequivocal title to the name was—among other and often incongruous things—a rediscovery and revival, for better or worse, of what these critics, at least, regard as characteristically Christian modes of thought and feeling—of a mystical and otherworldly type of religion and a sense of the inner moral struggle as the distinctive fact in human experience—such as had been for a century alien to the dominant tendencies in "polite" literature. The new movement was, almost from the first, a revolt against what was conceived to be paganism in religion and ethics as definitely as against classicism in art. The earliest important formulation of its implications for religious philosophy was Schleiermacher's famous *Reden* (1799) addressed "to the cultivated contemners of religion," a work profoundly—sometimes, indeed, morbidly—dualistic in its ethical temper. Christianity, declares Schleiermacher, is *"durch und durch polemisch"*; it knows no truce in the warfare of the spiritual with the natural man, it finds no end in the task of inner self-discipline. And the *Reden*, it must be remembered, were (in the words of a German literary historian) "greeted by the votaries of romanticism as a gospel."

Now it is not untrue to describe the ethical tendency of the "romanticism" which had its roots in naturalism—that is, in the assumption of the sole excellence of what in man is native, primitive, "wild," attainable without other struggle than that required for emancipation from social conventions and artificialities—as anti-dualistic and essentially non-moral. This aspect of it can be seen even in the poem of the "blameless Warton," when he describes the life of the state of nature for which he yearns. But as a consequence of the prevalent neglect to discriminate the romanticisms, the very movement which was the begin-

ning of a deliberate and vigorous insurrection against the naturalistic
assumptions that had been potent, and usually dominant, in modern
thought for more than three centuries, is actually treated as if it were
a continuation of that tendency. Thesis and antithesis have, partly
through accidents of language, and partly through a lack of careful
observation on the part of historians of literature, been called by the
same name, and consequently have frequently been assumed to be the
same thing. An ideal of ceaseless striving towards goals too vast or too
exacting ever to be wholly attained has been confused with a nostalgia
for the untroubled, because unaspiring, indolent, and unselfconscious,
life of the man of nature. Thus one of the widest and deepest-reaching
lines of cleavage in modern thought has been more or less effectually
concealed by a word.

3. This cleavage between naturalistic and anti-naturalistic "romanticism" crosses national lines; and it manifestly cuts, so to say, directly
through the person of one great writer commonly classed among the
initiators of the romantic movement in France. The author of the *Essai
sur les révolutions* and of the earlier-written parts of *Atala* may perhaps
properly be called a romantic; the author of the later-written parts of
the latter work and of the *Génie du Christianisme* may perhaps properly
be called a romantic; but it is obvious that the word has, in most
important respects, not merely different but antithetic senses in these
two applications of it to the same person. Chateaubriand before 1799
represented in some sort the culmination of the naturalistic and primitivistic romanticism of which Mr. Gosse sees the beginning in Joseph
Warton; he had not only felt intensely but had even gratified the
yearning to live "with simple Indian swains." That the Chateaubriand
of 1801 represents just as clearly a revolt against this entire tendency
is sufficiently evident from the repudiation of primitivism in the first
preface to *Atala*:

> *Je ne suis point, comme M. Rousseau, un enthousiaste des sauvages; ... je ne
> crois point que la* pure nature *soit la plus belle chose du monde. Je l'ai toujours
> trouvée fort laide partout où j'ai eu occasion de la voir.* ... *Avec ce mot de nature
> on a tout perdu* [Lovejoy's ellipses].

Thus the magic word upon which the whole scheme of ideas of the
earlier writing had depended is now plainly characterized as the
fruitful source of error and confusion that it was. And in his views
about the drama the Chateaubriand of 1801 was opposed *both* to the

movement represented by "The Enthusiast" and to the German Romanticism of his own time. Shakespeare was (though mainly, as we have seen, for differing reasons) the idol of both; but Chateaubriand in his *Essai sur la littérature anglaise* writes of Shakespeare in the vein, and partly in the words, of Voltaire and Pope. In point of natural genius, he grants, the English dramatist was without a peer in his own age, and perhaps in any age: "*je ne sais si jamais homme a jeté des regards plus profounds sur la nature humaine.*" But Shakespeare knew almost nothing of the requirements of the drama as an art:

> *Il faut se persuader d'abord qu' écrire est un art; que cet art a nécessairement ses genres, et que chaque genre a ses régles. Et qu'on ne dise pas que les genres et les régles sont arbitraires; ils sont nés de la nature même; l'art a seulement séparé ce que la nature a confondu. . . . On peut dire que Racine, dans toute l'excellence de son art, est plus naturel que Shakespeare* [Lovejoy's ellipsis].

Chateaubriand here, to be sure, still finds the standard of art in "nature"; but it is "nature" in the sense of the neo-classical critics, a sense in which it is not opposed, but equivalent, to an art that rigorously conforms to fixed rules. And the "great literary paradox of the partisans of Shakespeare," he observes, is that their arguments imply that "there are *no* rules of the drama," which is equivalent to asserting "that an art is not an art." Voltaire rightly felt that "by banishing all rules and returning to *pure nature* nothing was easier than to equal the *chefs-d'oeuvre* of the English stage"; and he was well advised in recanting his earlier too enthusiastic utterances about Shakespeare, since he saw that "*en relevant les beautés des barbares, il avait séduit des hommes qui, comme lui, ne sauraient séparer l'alliage de l'or.*" Chateaubriand regrets that "the *Cato* of Addison is no longer played" and that consequently "*on ne se délasse au théâtre anglais des monstruosités de Shakespeare que par les horreurs d'Otway.*" "*Comment,*" he exclaims, "*ne pas gémir de voir une nation éclairée, et qui compte parmi ses critiques les Pope et les Addison, de la voir s'extasier sur le portrait de l'apothicaire dans* Roméo et Juliette. *C'est le burlesque le plus hideux et le plus dégoûtant.*" The entire passage might almost have been written with Warton's poem in mind, so completely and methodically does this later "romanticist" controvert the æsthetic principles and deride the enthusiasms of the English "romanticist" of 1740. It is worth noting, also, that Chateaubriand at this time thinks almost as ill of Gothic architecture as of Shakespeare and of *la pure nature. . . .*

We have, then, observed and compared—very far from exhaustively, of course, yet in some of their most fundamental and determinative ideas—three "romanticisms." In the first and second we have found certain common elements, but still more significant oppostions; in the second and third we have found certain other common elements, but likewise significant oppositions. But between the first and third the common elements are very scanty; such as there are, it could, I think, be shown, are not the same as those subsisting between either the first and second or the second and third; and in their ethical preconceptions and implications and the crucial articles of their literary creeds, the opposition between them is almost absolute.

All three of these historic episodes, it is true, are far more complex than I have time to show. I am attempting only to illustrate the nature of a certain procedure in the study of what is called romanticism, to suggest its importance, and to present one or two specific results of the use of it. A complete analysis would qualify, without invalidating, these results, in several ways. It would (for one thing) bring out certain important connections between the revolt against the neo-classical æsthetics (common to two of the episodes mentioned) and other aspects of eighteenth-century thought. It would, again, exhibit fully certain *internal* oppositions in at least two of the romanticisms considered. For example, in German romanticism between 1797 and 1800 there grew up, and mainly from a single root, *both* an "apotheosis of the future" and a tendency to retrospection—a retrospection directed, not, indeed, towards classical antiquity or towards the primitive, but towards the mediæval. A belief in progress and a spirit of reaction were, paradoxically, twin offspring of the same idea, and were nurtured for a time in the same minds. But it is just these internal incongruities which make it most of all evident, as it seems to me, that any attempt at a *general* appraisal even of a single chronologically determinate romanticism— still more, of "romanticism" as a whole—is a fatuity. When a romanticism has been analyzed into the distinct "strains" or ideas which compose it, the true philosophic affinities and the eventual practical influence in life and art of these several strains will usually be found to be exceedingly diverse and often conflicting. It will, no doubt, remain abstractly possible to raise the question whether the preponderant effect, moral or æsthetic, of one or another large movement which has been called by the name was good or bad. But that ambitious inquiry cannot even be legitimately begun until a prior task of analysis and detailed comparison—of the sort that I have attempted here to indicate—has been accomplished. And when this has been done, I doubt whether the larger question will seem to have much importance or meaning. . . .

BIBLIOGRAPHICAL NOTE: René Wellek responded to Lovejoy's challenge in a two-part essay, "The Concept of 'Romanticism' in Literary History," *Comparative Literature*, I (1949), 1–23, 147–72, a major portion of which appears in this collection. Referring to Lovejoy's "Discrimination of Romanticisms" but also to his later "The Meaning of Romanticism for the Historian of Ideas" (*Journal of the History of Ideas*, II [1941], 237–78) and *The Great Chain of Being* (Cambridge, 1936), Morse Peckham tries to "reconcile Wellek and Lovejoy" in his essay, "Toward a Theory of Romanticism." Wellek's response to Peckham may be found in his "Romanticism Re-examined," in *Romanticism Reconsidered*, ed. Northrop Frye (New York and London, 1963).

Romantic Sensibility

Mario Praz

The epithet "romantic" and the antithetical terms "classic" and "romantic" are approximate labels which have long been in use. The philosopher solemnly refuses to allow them, exorcising them with unerring logic, but they creep quietly in again and are always obtruding themselves, elusive, tiresome, indispensable; the grammarian attempts to give them their proper status, their rank and fixed definition, but in spite of all his laborious efforts he discovers that he has been treating shadows as though they were solid substance.

Like an infinite number of other words in current usage, these approximate terms have a value and answer a useful purpose, provided that they are treated at their proper value—that is, as approximate terms—and that what they cannot give—exact and cogent definition of thought—is not demanded of them. They are serviceable make-shifts, and their fictitious character can be easily proved, but if the proof of their relatively arbitrary nature should cause us to dispense with their services, I do not see that literary history would benefit by it.

The case is similar to that of literary "genres." Let them be abolished:

ROMANTIC SENSIBILITY: From *The Romantic Agony* by Mario Praz (Oxford University Press, 1933), reprinted by permission of Oxford University Press. This English translation, by Angus Davidson, is of the original 1931 Italian edition.

soon they will crop up again in the shape of more elaborate distinctions and categories, more in accordance with the spirit of the particular moment, but no less approximate. . . . The mistake is to wish to graft æsthetic problems on the ideas which are intended only to be practical and informative, but there is nothing to prevent the same use being made of these ideas as Ampère made of the imaginary swimmer in the electric current.

•   •   •

Literary criticism assumes the existence of a history of culture—the culture of a particular *milieu* or of a particular individual. If the merging of the work of art into the general history of culture results in losing sight of the individual artist, it is impossible, on the other hand, to think of the latter without recurring to the former. Tendencies, themes, and mannerisms current in a writer's own day provide an indispensable aid to the interpretation of his work. True, for the purpose of æsthetic appreciation, this work forms a unique world shut up in itself, rounded off and perfected, an *individuum ineffabile*; but this philosophical truism would leave the critic no other alternative but a mystical, admiring silence.

But there is more to it than that. If it is true that the life of a work of art is in direct ratio to its being, so to speak, eternally contemporary, or able to reflect, with a universal application, the sentiments of periods in history which are in themselves diverse and remote, it is yet true that, in separating the work of art from its own particular cultural substratum, it is easy to fall into arbitrary, fantastic interpretations which alter the nature of the·work even to the extent of making it unrecognisable. . . . Now the use of formulas such as "romantic," "baroque," etc., serves to give some guidance to the interpretation of a work of art, or, in other words, to define the limits within which the activity of the critic is to be confined and beyond which lie mere arbitrary and anachronistic judgments. The sole object of these formulas is to keep in mind the character of the period in which the work was produced, in such a way as to avoid the danger of a combination of words, sounds, colours, or forms becoming surreptitiously invested with ideas which are aroused in the mind of the interpreter, but which certainly did not exist in the mind of the artist. Similar results may arise out of very different artistic intentions. Thus in a seventeenth-century writer like Alessandro Adimari one finds a love-sonnet on a beautiful lady recently buried, but one must be careful not to see in it a manifestation of romantic necrophily; when, elsewhere, he goes into ecstasies over a "wounded beauty," one must refrain from imagining in such a composition a morbid exquisiteness of feeling such as is found in Baudelaire's *Une Martyre;* but keeping in mind the partiality of the baroque period for every form of wit, one must attribute the choice of these unattractive subjects mainly to the desire of provoking astonishment through the conceit which can be elicited from them.

So also, when one reads in Alcman: "O maidens of honey voice so loud and clear, my limbs can carry me no more. Would, O would God I were but a ceryl, such as flies fearless of heart with the halcyons over the bloom of the wave, the Spring's own bird that is purple as the sea!" one must not try to discern in him signs already of an aspiration similar to that which made Shelley invoke the wild spirit of the West Wind. . . because such aspirations are the property of the romantics, and Alcman is not a romantic. Actually Alcman's artistic intention is shown by the passage from Antigonus Carystius which accompanies the quotation of the above lines: "He says that old age has made him feeble, and unable to join the choruses in their evolutions or the maidens in the dance." Alcman evokes the "ceryl" as an example of those qualities which he no longer possesses—freedom of movement and spring-like youthful ardour. The image sticks closely to the situation (the halcyons corresponding to the maidens with whom the poet will never dance again), and there is no room for the vague *Stimmung*, the thirst for the infinite, which animates the lines of the romantics. But there is nothing to prevent a modern critic who confines himself to its external values and separates it from the confines of time and mentality from distorting the fragment of Alcman to a romantic significance. . . .

•   •   •

Approximate terms such as "baroque," "romantic," "decadent," etc., have their origins in definite revolutions of sensibility, and it serves no purpose to detach them from their historical foundations and apply them generously to artists of varied types, according to the more or less extravagant whims of the critics. It happens only too often that the unsuccessful artist which lurks repressed in the soul of the critic seeks an outlet in the composition of a critical novel, or in projecting on to some author or other a light which is quite alien to him, which alters his appearance and brings it up to date, greatly to the detriment of the correct interpretation. For such purposes are these approximate terms used capriciously by critics, just as a clever cook uses sauces and seasonings to disguise the food. So Petrarch is found to be baroque, Tasso a romantic, Marino to resemble D'Annunzio, *"miraturque novas frondes et non sua poma."* These terms, however, are intended merely to indicate where the accent falls, and have no meaning outside the circumference of certain historical periods. The same idea may assume quite a different significance in Petrarch, where it is used for the first time, and in Marino, who imitates it from Petrarch; for Marino invests it with a feeling of baroque which is alien to Petrarch, and also draws the reader's special attention to it. In Petrarch the idea is incidental, in Marino deliberate and essential. Hence the highly problematical value of any research into the forerunners of seventeenth-century literature, of romanticism, and, indeed, of futurism—a form of research which is as elegantly literary as it is generally arbitrary and inconclusive, since these empirical formulas cannot be applied to every period and every place. It is, I believe, to the neglect of this criterion that one may ascribe the discredit into which certain of these terms have fallen, particularly the antithetical terms "classic" and "romantic."

These two terms, introduced, as is well known, by Goethe and Schiller, have ended by being adopted as the criteria of interpretation for all periods and all literatures; in the case of literature, as well as in that of the plastic arts and music, people frequently speak of classic and romantic in the same way as, in politics, they speak, universally, of conservative and liberal, with an extension of meaning which is, quite obviously, arbitrary.

[Praz here summarizes and quotes extensively from Grierson's essay reprinted in this collection.]

Extended in this way the terms "classic" and "romantic" come finally to denote, respectively, "equilibrium" and "interruption of equilibrium," and come very near to Goethe's definition, *"Classisch ist das Gesunde, Romantisch das Kranke"*; on the one hand, there is the serene state of mind of the man who does not notice his own health precisely because he is healthy; on the other, the state of ferment and struggle of the invalid who fights to overcome his own fever, or in other words to achieve a new equilibrium. Such an extension of the terms ends by being of an apparent rather than of a real use, since, generalised in this way, they are bound finally to become identified, the one with the passionate, practical element in the artistic process, the other with the theoretical and synthetic element, in which matter is converted into form (Croce): so they lose all value as historical categories and merely indicate the process which goes on universally in every artist. This is evident, for instance, in the following passage from Paul Valery:

> Tout classicisme suppose un romantisme antérieur. *Tous les avantages que l'on attribue, toutes les objections que l'on fait à un art "classique" sont relatifs à cet axiome.* L'essence du classicisme est de venir après. L'ordre *suppose un certain désordre qu'il vient réduire. La* composition, *qui est artifice, succède à quelque chaos primitif d'intuitions et de dévelopements naturels. La* pureté *est le résultat d'opérations infinies sur le langage, et le soin de la forme n'est autre chose que la réorganisation méditée des moyens d'expression. Le classique implique donc des actes volontaires et réfléchis qui modifient une production "naturelle" conformément à une conception* claire et rationnelle *de l'homme et de l'art*[1]

However, if one wishes to protect the useful function of the word "romantic" as an approximate term, one must first of all distinguish this function from that of its so-called opposite "classic," which has become nothing more than a secondary abstract reflection of the term "romantic": then, returning to the original use of the word, one must accept it as the definition of a peculiar kind of sensibility at a fixed historical period. The indiscriminate use of the word can only cause misunderstanding and confusion, as it does when Grierson speaks of the "romantic thrill" one feels when reading the myths of the Cave, of Er, and of the Chariot of the Soul in the *Phaedrus*, and of the "romantic conception" of Plato "of an ideal world behind the visible"; here the epithet "romantic" is surreptitiously transferred from the modern reader's impression to the Platonic conception itself, and Plato is shown as a romantic because the reader is pleased to interpret his legends in a romantic way.

> [Praz here attacks what he calls "the most curious example of arbitrary generalisation to which the 'classic–romantic' antithesis has given rise— Fritz Strich's *Deutsche Klassik und Romantik, oder Vollendung und Unendlichkeit, ein Vergleich* (Munich, 1922). Strich's attempt to coordinate "approximate terms in an organic system" Praz believes "is no less desperate than an attempt to build a house on quicksands."]

Strich's book is a *reductio ad absurdum* of the "classic–romantic" antithesis. Nevertheless I think that Croce's conclusion—that "romantic" and "classic" are moments of the human spirit, existing in every individual man, identifiable with matter and form, i.e., abstract moments of a process which is in reality indivisible—I think that this

---

[1] "Situation de Baudelaire," *Revue de France*, V (Sept.–Oct. 1924), 224.

conclusion does justice only to the secondary meaning of these formulas, taking off from their value as useful approximate terms and indications of definite historical characteristics. Or, to be more exact, from the value of one of them—the term "romantic," since the other—"classic"— is a derivative and has meaning only in the sense of *playing at being classical*, that is, as the definition of the programme of a school opposed to the romantic school, which, in its turn, inasmuch as it is a school, or conscious, organised manifestation, stands in relation to romantic sensibility as the chastened to the spontaneous. Classicism, then, is a phenomenon by no means alien to the romantic spirit; on the contrary, inasmuch as it seeks to revive manners and ideas belonging to the past, inasmuch as it strives longingly towards a fantastic pagan world, rather than sharing in the state of serene equilibrium proper to so-called classical works of art (which are serene without knowing it), it shares in the same spiritual travail which is usually defined as characteristically and *par excellence* "romantic." It is not the content which decides whether a work should be labelled "romantic" or not, but the spirit, and, in this sense, a Hölderlin or a Keats, worshipping, as they do, a vanished world, is no less romantic than a Coleridge or a Shelley. In other words, there is such a thing as a "romantic movement," and classicism is only an aspect of it. There is no opposite pole to "romantic," merely because "romantic" indicates a certain state of sensibility which, simply, is different from any other, and not comparable either by coördination or by contrast.

How can one describe the new state of sensibility which came into full flower towards the end of the eighteenth century? What does "romantic" mean? The evolution of this word has been traced by Logan Pearsall Smith,[2] to whose lucid exposition I owe a great deal of what follows.

The word "romantic" appears for the first time in the English language about the middle of the seventeenth century, meaning "like the old romances," and shows how there began to be felt, about this time, a real need to give names to certain characteristics of the chivalrous and pastoral romances. These characteristics, thrown into relief by contrast with the growing rationalistic spirit which was soon to

---

[2] "Four Romantic Words," in *Words and Idioms: Studies in the English Language* (London, 1925). On the word "romantic" see also the letters of J. Butt in *The Times Literary Supplement* for August 3rd, 1933, of W. Lee Ustick in the same periodical for December 21st, 1933, and of C. T. Onions in the issue for January 1st, 1934. [See also René Wellek's essay below.]

triumph in Pope and Dr. Johnson, lay in the falsity, the unreality, the fantastic and irrational nature of events and sentiments described in these romances. Like the terms "gothic" and "baroque," therefore, "romantic" started in a bad sense. The shade of meaning indicated by "romantic," at this stage of its development, is clearly evinced by the other words with which it was usually coupled, words such as "chimerical," "ridiculous," "unnatural," "bombast." One reads of childish and romantic poems," of "romantic absurdities and incredible fictions," and so on. Nature's truth is contrasted with the falsity of the romances. Everything that seemed to have been produced by a disorderly imagination came to be called "romantic." The contrast is well presented in a couplet of Pope's:

> . . . that not in Fancy's maze he wandered long,
> But stooped to Truth, and moraliz'd his song.

But a new current in taste can be discerned right from the beginning of the eighteenth century: there is a growing tendency to recognise the importance of imagination in works of art. "Romantic," though continuing to mean something slightly absurd, takes on the flavour of *attractive*, suited to please the imagination. "The subject and scene of this tragedy, so *romantic* and uncommon, are highly pleasing to the imagination," wrote J. Warton in 1757. Side by side with the depreciatory use of the word in relation to the events and sentiments of the old romances, "romantic" came to be used also to describe scenes and landscapes similar to those described in them, and, this time, without any note of scorn. As early as the middle of the seventeenth century examples are found of similar usage, especially in the case of old castles (as early as 1666 Pepys wrote of Windsor Castle, "the most *romantique* castle that is in the world"), of mountains, forests, pastoral plains, desolate and solitary places. The two meanings are both to be found in Dr. Johnson, who, while on the one hand he speaks of "romantic and superfluous," "ridiculous and romantic," "romantic absurdities and incredible fictions," on the other hand writes, without a hint of scorn, "When night overshadows a romantic scene, all is stillness, silence and quiet," etc. In this second sense, the adjective has gradually ceased to retain its connexion with the literary *genre* (the romances) from which it was originally derived, and has come to express more and more the growing love for wild and melancholy aspects of nature. It is so closely connected with certain qualities of landscape that French translators of English books of the period, when the word "romantic" is used, often render it with *pittoresque:* which shows that the French were not yet aware of the new state of sensibility suggested by the word "romantic." It was not until 1776 that Letourneur, translator of Shakespeare, and the Marquis de Girardin, author of a book on landscape, deliberately use the word *romantique*, noting the reasons in favour of the adoption of this *mot anglais*. It is possible to see from their notes how these French writers had finally grasped the exact shade of meaning. "Romantic," they say, means more than *romanesque* (chimerical, fabulous)[3] or

[3] In his essay on "Romantisch und Romanesk," in *Britannia, Max Förster zum sechzigsten Geburtstage* (Leipzig, 1929), M. Deutschbein has tried to make use of the two terms in order to distinguish between external romanticism, to be associated with fancy, and inner romanticism, the product of imagination. *Romanesk* should be employed to designate certain tendencies to the strange, the exotic, the grotesque, which have made their appearance many times throughout history (e.g., in the Greek romances), whereas *romantisch* ought to be used for genuine romanticism, whose essence according to Deutschbein, lies in a deep understanding of the harmony of the universe. ... Such a distinction, he remarks, had been foreshadowed by Brande in *A Dictionary of Science*, 1842. ... However, Deutschbein goes on to say, nowadays "romantic" stands in English for both *romantisch* and *romanesk*. Deutschbein's distinction is, after all, of little utility, for every work of art worth the name is *romantisch* in the sense he gives to this word. ... This idea of the meaning of romanticism seems to be shared by Lascelles Abercrombie (*Romanticism*, London, 1926), who opposes to it the term "realism". ... One of the most important characteristics of romanticism consists for this critic in a kind of retreat from the external world to an "inner" world. Realism "loves to go out into the world, and live confidently and busily in the stirring multitude of external things" (cf. Deutschbein's *romanesk*!). Romanticism is at least a withdrawal from these outer things into inner experience. Roughly and approximately it is a transition from "perception" to "conception." Therefore, also for Abercrombie, the term "romanticism" becomes identical with the inner urge of every artistic inspiration.

According to I. Babbitt (*Rousseau and Romanticism*) "the so-called realism does not represent any fundamental change of direction as compared with the earlier romanticism. ... What binds together realism and romanticism is their common repudiation of decorum as something external and artificial. ... At the bottom of much so-called realism ... is a special type of satire, a satire that is the product of violent emotional disillusion." It is obvious that by "realism" Babbitt means something quite different from Abercrombie's use of the same word. For Babbitt romanticism is a return to a hypothetical spontaneity of nature conceived as essentially good, an emancipation of (mainly sexual) impulses, a cult of emotional intensity by getting rid of the rules of discipline and decorum devised by man in the course of civilisation, a substitution for ethical effort of a mere lazy floating on the stream of mood and temperament; therefore a manner of living in the stirring multitude of phenomena, of going out into the world ... so that in a way romanticism according to Babbitt's idea (which seems convincing enough) corresponds to Abercrombie's realism. The romantic tendency is to push every emotion to an extreme, regardless of decorum, so that Babbitt inclines to see also in erotic exasperation a corollary of this general principle ... [*the ellipses in this second paragraph are Praz's*].

pittoresque (used to describe a scene which strikes the eye and arouses admiration); "romantic" describes not only the scene but the particular emotion aroused in the person who contemplates it. Rousseau probably came by the word from his friend Girardin, and conferred upon it full French citizenship in the well-known *Rêverie du promeneur solitaire*. In *romantique* Rousseau found the appropriate word to define that elusive and indistinct thing which hitherto he had vaguely expressed by *je ne sais quoi: "Enfin, ce spectacle a je ne sais quoi de magique, de surnaturel, qui ravit l'esprit et les sens"* (*Nouvelle Héloïse*). In this sense, "romantic" assumes a subjective character, like "interesting," "charming," "exciting," which describe not so much the property of the objects as our reactions to them, the effects which they arouse in an impressionable onlooker. Besides, as L. P. Smith observes, Nature described as "romantic" is seen through a veil of associations and feelings extracted from poetry and literature in general.

The term *pittoresque*, which arose at the same time, expresses a similar phenomenon. The subjective element, implicit in "romantic," rendered this word particularly suitable to describe the new kind of literature in which suggestion and aspiration had so large a part. It is true that in England, where the word "romanticism" only came to be used later, the antithesis between "romantic" and "classic," German in its origin, was at first expressed by the contrasting of "magical and evocative poetry" with rhetorical and didactic poetry as exemplified by Pope. *Magie der Einbildungskraft* (Magic of the Imagination) is the title of the well-known essay in which Jean Paul defines the essence of romantic sensibility. How does it come about—asks Jean Paul—that everything which exists only in aspiration (*Sehnsucht*) and in remembrance, everything which is remote, dead, unknown, possesses this magic transfiguring charm? Because—the answer is—everything, when inwardly represented, loses its precise outline, since the imagination possesses the magic virtue of making things infinite. And Novalis: *"Alles wird in der Entfernung Poesie: ferne Berge, ferne Menschen, ferne Begebenheiten. Alles wird romantisch."*

The word "romantic" thus comes to be associated with another group of ideas, such as "magic," "suggestive," "nostalgic," and above all with words expressing states of mind which cannot be described, such as the German *"Sehnsucht"* and the English "wistful." It is curious to note that these two words have no equivalent in the Romance languages—a clear sign of the Nordic, Anglo-Germanic origin of the sentiments they express. Such ideas have this in common, that they furnish only a vague indication, leaving it to the imagination to make the final evocation. A Freudian would say that these ideas appeal to the unconscious in us.* It is the appeal of Yeats's *Land of Heart's Desire.*

The essence of romanticism consequently comes to consist in that which cannot be described. The word and the form, says Schlegel in *Lucinde,* are only accessories. The essential is the thought and the poetic image, and these are rendered possible only in a passive state. The romantic exalts the artist who does not give a material form to his dreams—the poet ecstatic in front of a forever blank page, the musician who listens to the prodigious concerts of his soul without attempting to translate them into notes. It is romantic to consider concrete expression as a decadence, a contamination. How many times has the magic of the ineffable been celebrated, from Keats, with his "Heard melodies are sweet, but those unheard / Are sweeter," to Maeterlinck, with his theory that silence is more musical than any sound!

But these are extreme cases, in which the romantic tends to merge in the mystical. The normal is that of suggestive expression, which evokes much more than it states. Whenever we encounter such a method, we do not hesitate to define the artist who makes use of it as "romantic." But the legitimate use of this term depends upon the deliberate method of the artist, not upon the mere interpretation of the reader. In these lines of Dante:

> Quale ne' plenilunii sereni
> Trivia ride tra le ninfe eterne
> Che dipingon lo ciel per tutti i seni

the modern reader is inclined to detect one of the most obvious cases of evocative magic, in virtue of their purity of sound, of the play of diæreses, of the use of certain words in themselves suggestive—*plenilunii, eterne*—and of others which bring legends to the mind—*Trivia, ninfe.* Are we to say, therefore, that Dante, in these lines, is a romantic? Is it not, rather, a romantic education, which has by now become traditional, that causes the modern reader to interpret these lines in this way? If each century had left us a list of what, in its own opinion, were the greatest beauties in Dante, we should be able to trace an interesting

* See Albert Gérard's essay below for a fuller discussion of romantic *"Sehnsucht"* and F. L. Lucas's essay, also below, for an analysis of romanticism and the unconscious.

history of taste, but would it be possible to base on these anthologies a reconstruction of Dante's inspiration? One line of Petrarch—"*Fior, frondi, erbe, ombre, antri, onde, aure soavi*"—used to send the writers of the sixteenth century into ecstasies. "This is the loftiest, the most sonorous, and the fullest line to be found in modern or ancient writers," wrote Sebastiano Fausto da Longiano. But who among us at the present day would be capable of seeing in this line all that the writers of the sixteenth century saw?

A knowledge of the tastes and preferences which belong to each period is a *sine qua non* of the interpretation of a work of art, and literary history cannot afford to dispense with approximate terms such as those we have been discussing, terms which do not claim to be more than symbols of specific tendencies of sensibility. They are intended to be empirical categories, and to condemn them as futile abstractions is as great an error as to exalt them into realities of universal import.

•   •   •

The aim of the greater part of this book [*The Romantic Agony*] is a study of romantic literature (of which the Decadent movement of the end of the last century is only a development) under one of its most characteristic aspects, that of erotic sensibility. It is, therefore, a study of certain states of mind and peculiarities of behaviour, which are given a definite direction by various types and themes that recur as insistently as myths engendered in the ferment of the blood.

Looked at from this point of view, the literature of the nineteenth century appears as a unique, clearly distinct whole, which the various formulas such as "romanticism," "realism," "decadence," etc., tend to disrupt. In no other literary period, I think, has sex been so obviously the mainspring of works of imagination: but it is more profitable to study the historical development of such a tendency than to repeat from hearsay, and as though incidentally, the vague accusations of sensuality and perversity with which critics of that period are generally content to label the darker portions of the picture. . . . It is much easier to label as monsters certain writers who were tormented by obsessions, than to discern the universal human background which is visible behind their paroxysms. The sexual idiosyncrasies which will be discussed in the following pages offer, so to speak, a distorted image of characteristics common to all mankind. The remark made by Edmond Jaloux about Lafourcade's study of Swinburne is apposite: "*Pourquoi alors ne pas s'expliquer franchement sur le sadisme et ne pas vouloir accepter qu'il soit un des ferments les plus naturels de l'âme humaine? On ne l'en débusquera que plus facilement si on le connaît bien."*

To any one who may protest, therefore, that the intimate examination of an artist's life is irreverent, or worse, we may answer with Sainte-Beuve: *"Quand on fait une étude sur un homme considérable, il faut oser tout voir, tout regarder, et au moins tout indiquer."* We must not pay so much attention to momentary exclamations of satisfied curiosity—such as *"Habemus confitentem," "nous touchons ici à la clef"*—as to the more general aim of casting some light upon the most profound instincts of humanity —an aim in which a study like the present may perhaps, in the end, succeed.

It must, however, be stated without further delay that a study such as the present one differs from a medico-scientific treatise in that the recurrence of certain morbid themes in a particular period of literature is not invariably treated as an indication of a psychopathic state in the writers discussed. The genetic link is in this case provided by taste and fashion; literary sources are discussed, and not—is it necessary to mention?—resemblances due to physiological causes, so that, side by side with writers of genuinely specialised sensibility are to be found others who give a mere superficial echo of certain themes. Again, this study has not even a remote connexion with the sociological study or the study of collective psychology, in which case it would have had to include documentations from police and assize reports, scientific or pseudo-scientific works, and anonymous or popular literary productions.

The Marquis de Sade, in whom Sainte-Beuve saw "one of the greatest inspirers of the moderns," will be frequently mentioned in the following pages. But an immediate word of warning is needed, no longer (as would have been necessary a few years ago) against the time-honoured condemnation of the author of *Justine,* but against the reaction in his favour which a few years ago became fashionable in certain literary circles in France.

The conclusions of the present study will prove, even to those who are least well-informed, that Sade's work is a monument—not indeed, as Guillaume Apollinaire was pleased to declare, *"de la pensée humaine"*— but at least of something. But that the light which his work throws upon the less mentionable impulses of the man-animal should suffice immediately to classify the author as an original thinker, or, without further ado, as a man of genius, is a conclusion only to be pardoned if the ignorance and momentary infatuation of its formulator are taken

into account. .... Let us give Sade his due, as having been the first
to expose, in all its crudity, the mechanism of *homo sensualis*, let us even
assign him a place of honour as a psycho-pathologist and admit his
influence on a whole century of literature; but courage (to give a
nobler name to what most people would call shamelessness) does not
suffice to give originality to a thought, nor does the hurried jotting
down of all the cruel fantasies which obsess the mind suffice to give a
work mastery of style. It is true that the surrealists, who have now made
themselves the champions of Sade's greatness, hold a curious theory on
the subject of "automatic writing," as being the only kind of writing to
reveal the whole man, without hypocrisy or changes of mind;* but this
theory of untrammelled self-expression is precisely an extreme application of that very romanticism which, being so open to Sade's influence,
is on that account the least fitted to judge him dispassionately. The most
elementary qualities of a writer—let us not say, of a writer of genius—
are lacking in Sade. Though more worthy of the title of polygrapher
and pornographer than a writer such as Aretino, his whole merit lies
in having left documents illustrative of the mythological, infantile
phase of psycho-pathology: he gives, in the form of a fantastic tale, the
first systematized account of sexual perversions.

Was Sade a "*surromantique*"? No, but he was certainly a sinister force
in the romantic movement, a familiar spirit whispering in the ear of the
"*mauvais maîtres*" and the "*poètes maudits*"; actually he did nothing more
than give a name to an impulse which exists in every man, an impulse
mysterious as the very forces of life and death with which it is inextri-
cably connected.

Isolating, as it does, one particular aspect, fundamental though it
may be, of romantic literature—that is, the education of sensibility,
and more especially of erotic sensibility—this study must be considered as a monograph, not as a synthesis, and the point of view of its
author might be compared to that of some one who, in Poe's well-
known story, examined merely the crack which runs zig-zag across
the front of the House of Usher, without troubling about its general
architecture.

> [Praz here defends his book against the attack on its method and conclu-
> sions by Benedetto Croce in *La Critica*, XXIX (March 20, 1931). Croce's
> main point is that romanticism cannot be seen merely as the formation

* For a discussion of the relationship between romanticism and surrealism, see
Herbert Read's essay below.

of a particular kind of new sensibility that is displayed in the "various tendencies and fantasies" Praz "so amply expounds." It is, rather, a much more complex thing, rich "not only in theoretical values" but also in "moral values, and even in maladies and crises which are less shameful than those" Praz examines. Croce's own literary-historian approach, Praz believes, can account "only very indirectly for particular tendencies of sensibility." At most such an approach limits "the screen on which the visions are projected, but they do not say why exactly those visions, and not others, appear.]

If, therefore, the history of ideas and ideals during the nineteenth century constitutes a necessary frame for the picture I have painted, it is a part which completes, rather than conditions, the whole; there was no obligation for me to examine it afresh, nor to deal with phenomena of other kinds, which in any case have been fully discussed by others.

Why was it that, towards the end of the eighteenth century, people came to consider landscape with different eyes? why did they look for a *je ne sais quoi* which they had not looked for before? Why, at about the same time, did the "beauty of the horrid" become a source, no longer of conceits, as in the seventeenth century, but of sensations? To such questions adequate answers are not to be found in the history of the religious, philosophical, moral, and practical development of the period. In this field of ideas is to be found a confirmation of the axiom propounded by Wilde, as to Nature imitating Art (in *The Decay of Lying*). Education of sensibility came about through works of art; what it is therefore chiefly important to establish is the means by which the transmission of themes from one artist to another is effected. The mysterious bond between pleasure and suffering has certainly always existed; it is one of the *vulnera naturae* which is as old as man himself. But it became the common inheritance of romantic and decadent sensibility through a particular chain of literary influences.

BIBLIOGRAPHICAL NOTE: For a different interpretation of the romantic shift of sensibility see W. K. Wimsatt's essay below, and David Wright's introduction to *The Penguin Book of English Romantic Verse* (Baltimore, 1968). See also Northrop Frye's "Towards Defining an Age of Sensibility," *ELH*, XXIII (1956), 144–52. For discussions of T. S. Eliot's idea of the "dissociation of sensibility" which he regards as precipitating both neoclassicism and romanticism, see R. H. Fogle's essay below, and Frank Kermode's chapter, "'Dissociation of Sensibility': Modern Symbolist Readings of Literary History," in his *Romantic Image* (New York, 1957). On the use of "romantic" as an approximate term only, see Ian Jack, *English Literature: 1815–1832* (Oxford, 1963), pp. 408–21.

Surrealism and the Romantic Principle

Herbert Read

No critic of experience will return to a discussion of the terms "romanticism" and "classicism" with anything but extreme reluctance; no subject has provoked so much weary logomachy since the Scholastics argued themselves out on the question of nominalism. I only take up the discussion again (eating my own words in the process) because I think that surrealism has settled it. So long as romanticism and classicism were considered as alternative attitudes, rival camps, professions of *faith*, an interminable struggle was in prospect, with the critics as profiteers. But what in effect surrealism claims to do is to resolve the conflict—not, as I formerly hoped, by establishing a synthesis which I was prepared to call "reason" or "humanism"[1]—but by liquidating

SURREALISM AND THE ROMANTIC PRINCIPLE: From Introduction to *Surrealism* by André Breton and others (London: Faber & Faber Ltd., 1936). Reprinted by permission of Faber and Faber Ltd.

[1] My use of the word "reason" in my . . . *Reason and Romanticism*, 1926, has led to some misunderstanding. . . . If we think of reason as an intellectual censor external to the instinctual life of man, wielding a blue (*blue-de-roi*) pencil against our romantic impulses, then we fall into the classical error. That was never my conception of reason. Reason, I said, "should rather connote the widest evidence of the senses, and of all processes and instincts developed in the long history of man. It is the sum total of awareness, ordained and ordered to some specific end or object of attention." I see no necessity now to vary that statement. Super-realism is also super-rationalism.

classicism, by showing its complete irrelevance, its *anæsthetic* effect, its contradiction of the creative impulse. Classicism, let it be stated without further preface, represents for us now, and has always represented, the forces of oppression.* Classicism is the intellectual counterpart of political tyranny. It was so in the ancient world and in the mediæval empires; it was renewed to express the dictatorships of the Renaissance and has ever since been the official creed of capitalism. Wherever the blood of martyrs stains the ground, there you will find a doric column or perhaps a statue of Minerva.

Academic critics have not been unaware of this alignment, but have united, of course, to give living colours to the corpse they have embalmed. I have often praised Sir Herbert Grierson's clean handling of this problem; like Brunetière, whose main line of demarcation he follows, he is not altogether unsympathetic toward romanticism, but there is a question of values involved which must be challenged.

[Here Read quotes two passages from Grierson's *Classical and Romantic* (pp. 42 and 52–53 above).]

The particular danger of this argument is due to its false dialecticism. A certain type of society is regarded as a "synthesis," a natural order or balance of forces, a state of equilibrium; and any deviation from that standard is regarded as abnormal, degenerate, or revolutionary. Actually such types of society merely represent the dominance of one particular class—the economic dominance and therefore the cultural dominance of that class. For the stability of such a society a certain uniformity of ideas and modes of expression is a fundamental necessity; and the less novelty these ideas and modes of expression show the better. This explains the constant return to the norms of classical art; for these norms (in architecture we call them the "orders") are the typical patterns of order, proportion, symmetry, equilibrium, harmony, and of all static and inorganic qualities. They are intellectual concepts which control or repress the vital instincts on which growth and therefore change depend, and in no sense represent a freely determined preference, but merely an imposed ideal.

* On this point Read's essay should be compared with Alex Comfort's below. Read's subsequent identification of romanticism as anti-capitalistic should be seen in the context of Marxian essays such as Christopher Caudwell's below and Alick West's "Romantic Criticism" and "Marx and Romanticism" in his book *Crisis and Criticism* (London, 1937).

98

The fallacy we are discussing is logical in its origin. It is a sophism by means of which two terms are conceived as dialectical opposites whereas actually they represent types of action and reaction. This is a very important distinction, and its neglect is the cause of much confusion. In dialectics the thesis and the antithesis are both objective facts, and the necessity for a resolution or synthesis is due to the real existence of a contradiction. But "classic" and "romantic" do not represent such a contradiction. They correspond rather to the husk and the seed, the shell and the kernel. There is a principle of life, of creation, of liberation, and that is the romantic spirit; there is a principle of order, of control, and of repression, and that is the classical spirit. Naturally there is some purpose in the latter principle—the instincts are curbed in the interest of some particular ideal or set of values; but on analysis it always resolves into the defence of some particular structure of society, the perpetuation of the rule of some particular class. To identify romanticism with revolt as Grierson does is true enough as an historical generalisation; but it merely distorts the values involved if such revolt is conceived in purely literary or academic terms. It would be much nearer the truth to identify romanticism with the artist and classicism with society; classicism being the political concept of art to which the artist is expected to conform.

It may be as well to forestall at once the criticism that on this showing the artist is merely the individualist in conflict with society. To a certain extent, as I have shown elsewhere,[2] this is true; the mental personality of the artist is originally determined by a failure in social adaptation. But his whole effort is directed towards a reconciliation with society, and what he offers to society is not a bagful of his own tricks, his idiosyncrasies, but rather some knowledge of the secrets to which he has had access, the secrets of the self which are buried in every man alike, but which only the sensibility of the artist can reveal to us in all their actuality. This "self" is not the personal possession we imagine it to be; it is largely made up of elements from the unconscious, and the more we learn about the unconscious, the more collective it appears to be—in fact, "a body of common sentiments and thoughts . . . universal truths" such as Grierson assumes to be the exclusive concern of the classical artist. But whereas the universal truths of

[2] *Art and Society* (London, 1936), Ch. 6.

classicism may be merely the temporal prejudices of an epoch, the universal truths of romanticism are coeval with the evolving consciousness of mankind.

It is in this sense, then, that surrealism is a reaffirmation of the romantic principle; and though poets and painters in all ages have clung to a belief in the inspirational and even the obsessional nature of their gifts, repudiating in deeds if not in words the rigid bonds of classical theory, it is only now, with the aid of modern dialectics and modern psychology, in the name of Marx and Freud, that they have found themselves in a position to put their beliefs and practices on a scientific basis, thereby initiating a continuous and deliberate creative activity whose only laws are the laws of its own dynamics.

Before passing on to a more precise examination of the romantic principle as actually manifested in English art and literature, there is one further interpretation of the classic-romantic antithesis which is worth referring to, especially as it finds its justification in modern psychology—I mean the theory that the two terms correspond to the general distinction between "extravert" and "introvert" types of personality. The comparison is valid enough if it has reference to the personalities involved; what is questionable is the very existence of such a type as an extravert *artist*. To the degree in which he becomes extravert the artist, we would say, ceases to be, in any essential sense of the word, an artist. Now admittedly there is much in the process of producing a work of art which involves, or may involve, an objective attitude towards the materials the artist is using; only the purely automatic text or drawing is purely subjective, and though the surrealist insists on the significance of such automatic expression, he is far from asserting that all art must of necessity be produced under such conditions. What he does assert, however, is the absolute impossibility of producing a work of art by the conscious exercise of talents. The notion that a work of art can be created by observing a set of rules is only to be compared with the notion that a human being can be produced in a test-tube.

"Verbal and graphic automatism," Breton has said, "only represents a *limit* towards which the poet or artist should tend." The opposed limit is represented by all those "arts of poetry," those academic discourses on painting, in which various ages have sought to codify for all time the laws of art. Between these limits we find the whole range of æsthetic expression, but it is towards the limit of automatism, and

away from the limit of rational control, that we find the most enduring
vitality, the words which live when the poet is dead, when even his
name is forgotten—

> A rose-red city half as old as time

—a single line surviving from the complete works of a poet and surviving precisely by virtue of its irrationality.

It is very difficult to determine the factors which lead to the survival
of any particular work of art. There is a considerable element of
chance, even under modern conditions of publishing and propaganda.
We know that contemporary judgment is very uncertain, very arbitrary; every age has its Ossians and there may still be Donnes to be
redeemed from a neglected past. We ascribe this fickleness of public
estimation to changes in sensibility, but sensibility itself does not change,
only the control of it. The sensibility which appreciated the poems of
Donne at the time of their first appearance was lively and direct; it
needed the colossal irrelevance of a Johnsonian intellect and the general
diffusion of a rational spirit to throw them into obscurity. The sensibility
which we have now recovered and by virtue of which we once more
appreciate the poetry of Donne is the identical sensibility for which his
poems were written; and it is no gust of fashion which has re-established
his fame, but a revival of poetic sensibility itself—the same revival
which has once more placed Shakespeare at the utmost pinnacle of
fame, which has given Blake his due eminence and has secured immediate recognition for Hopkins and Eliot.* No doubt we are age-bound
like the rest and our standards are relative to our circumstances; but it
is difficult to imagine, in any form of society congenial to our elementary
demands of economic security and intellectual liberty, any return to
the standards which tended to exalt a Dryden or a Pope above Shakespeare, and which misled so genuine a poet as Milton into the barren
wastes of his later works.

Some recognition of the truth which I am affirming—the identity
of art and romanticism—has been given by the philosophers of art;
not by all philosophers, but particularly by those who have shown the
greatest appreciation of art, or who have been like Plato, great artists
themselves.

* For a somewhat different view of this "recovered sensibility," see Cleanth Brooks's
Modern Poetry and the Tradition and the selection from it reprinted in this collection.

[Read here quotes Plato's description of the poet in *Ion*.]

It is pointless to observe that because of their irrational character Plato excluded poets from his ideal republic. Within the logic of his rational philosophy, this was inevitable; just as later it was inevitable that Hegel, for quite similar reasons, should come to the conclusion that "the fair days of Greek art, as also the golden time of the later middle ages, are over." Both philosophers held the view that a reflective, idealistic, and ratiocinative culture was not merely desirable, but actually represented a higher stage in human evolution. They were both right in considering that the sensuous phenomena of art—the completely irrational basis of the imaginative faculty—are inconsistent with such a reflective culture. But what we now assert with the strongest conviction is our disbelief in either the inevitability or desirability of such a culture. The whole evidence of history, as well as of modern psychology, causes us to reject without hesitation such a fool's paradise of idealism. For good or for evil the instinctive and impulsive components of our being are irreducible and irreplaceable, and we ignore them or repress them at our peril. Not merely the neuroses of individuals result from such repression, but there is more and more reason to believe that the mass hysteria manifested, for example, in such a nation as Germany, is the collective aspect of general repressions. The only absolutely pacifist races (if any such still exist) are those which live in a golden age of hedonism such as, apparently, the Minoan civilisation enjoyed for many centuries. Unfortunately we do not know enough about the Minoan civilisation to relate its freedom from war to, for example, its freedom from morality; but we are beginning to know sufficient about our own civilisation to be sure that war has no simple explanation in economic forces, but is most probably not unrelated to the frustration of certain primitive impulses during childhood, a frustration which is prolonged and reinforced by adult codes of morality. War is, in theory as in fact, the correlative of religion. Above all, the Christian religion in its Pauline rigour has induced the bloodiest epoch in the world's history. Piety and asceticism are inevitably accompanied by masochism and sadism, and the more Christianity has been deprived of a ritualistic and occult indulgence of the senses, rationalising itself in the form of moral precepts and social conventions, the deeper the world has plunged into compensatory orgies of hatred and bloodshed.

[Read then develops the idea of the horror, idiocy, and agony of war, and the incredible docility of man even in the face of its imminence.]

The only individuals who protest against injustices—or who make their protest vocal—are in effect the poets and artists of each age, who to the extent that they rely on their imaginative capacities and powers, despise and reject the acquisitive materialism of men of action.*

I am not leaving it open for anyone to suggest that in this respect—in its adoption of a revolutionary political attitude, its protest against injustice and inhumanity—surrealism merely represents a sentimental movement of the heart. Surrealism is anti-rational, but it is equally anti-emotional. If you wish to reduce surrealism to its foundations you will find the only basic elements on which any useful structure can be built—the basic elements of natural science and psychology. We build on that materialistic basis. But we build. We create. And we have our method of building, our craft of logic, our dialectic.

The philosophical justification of surrealism is to be found, if anywhere in the past, in Hegel. But it is a Hegel deprived for the most part of those elements which he would have considered of the greatest importance. Just as Marx, for his purposes, turned Hegel upside down, "sloughed off" the mystical form of Hegel's dialectic, so the surrealist, for his purposes, subjects the philosopher to the same indignity. If I am asked why, in this matter, we should return to Hegel rather than start our philosophy of art afresh, there are various answers to give— answers similar to those which have to be given in the field of political philosophy. One is that Hegel represents a convenient *crux* in philosophy: all previous philosophies seem to meet in him, to be sorted and smelted and reduced to the purest and least contradictory elements of human thought. Hegel is the great scavenger of philosophical systems; he cleans them up and leaves a tidy piece of ground on which we can build. More than that, he provides a scaffolding within which we can build—the scaffold of his dialectic.

This dreaded word "dialectic"—a word which the English-speaking public finds difficult to digest and which even our so-called socialists, with a few exceptions, would willingly forget—this word is actually the

---

* Alex Comfort makes this same point in his essay. For a more historical analysis of the origins of romantic social concern, see Edward A. Whitney's "Humanitarianism and Romanticism," *Huntington Library Quarterly*, II (1939), 159–78.

name of a very simple and very necessary process of thought. If we consider the natural world, we soon become aware that its most striking characteristic is not permanency, solidity, or stability, but *continuous change* or development. Physicists now affirm that not merely the organic world, not merely this earth we live on, but the whole universe is undergoing a process of continuous change. Dialectics is nothing more than a logical explanation of how such a change takes place. It does not suffice to say that "it grows," or "it decays," "it runs down," "it expands"; these phrases are vague abstractions. The change must take place in a definite way. Between one phase and another of that development there must intervene an active principle, and Hegel suggested that this principle was actually one of opposition and interaction. That is to say, to produce any new situation (i.e., any departure from an existing condition of equilibrium) there must previously exist two elements so opposed to each other and yet so related to each other that a solution or resolution is demanded; such a solution being in effect a new phase of development (temporary state of equilibrium) which preserves some of the elements of the interacting phases, eliminates others, but is qualitatively different from the previously existing state of opposition.

Such is the dialectical logic elaborated by Hegel for idealistic purposes and brilliantly adapted by Marx for materialistic purposes. . . . Surrealism is an application of the same logical method to the realm of art. By the dialectical method we can explain the development of art in the past and justify a revolutionary art at the present time.

In dialectical terms we claim that there is a continual state of opposition and interaction between the world of objective fact—the sensational and social world of active and economic existence—and the world of subjective fantasy. This opposition creates a state of disquietude, a lack of spiritual equilibrium, which it is the business of the artist to resolve. He resolves the contradiction by creating a synthesis, a work of art which combines elements from both these worlds, eliminates others, but which for the moment gives us a qualitatively new experience—an experience on which we can dwell with equanimity. Superficial critics may pretend to be unable to distinguish such a qualitatively new state from an ordinary compromise, and it is to be feared that in practice most dialectical solutions are of this kind. But a true synthesis is never a reversion; it is always a progression.

This is the central core of the surrealist claim, and any attempt to discredit or criticise surrealism must present an adequate philosophical alternative; just as any criticism of dialectical materialism as embodied in the socialism of Marx must present an adequate philosophical alternative. At present any alternatives worthy of our consideration are lacking.

•   •   •

Surrealism demands nothing less than . . . a revaluation of all æsthetic values. It has no respect for any academic tradition, least of all for the classical-capitalist tradition of the last four hundred years. It believes that as a general rule even men of genius during this period —and it has no difficulty in conceding genius where it is due—have been hampered and repressed by the conventions of their education and by their social environment. For poets like Dryden and Pope, for painters like Michelangelo, and Poussin, and for many lesser artists, we can only have an angry and in no sense patronising pity. The spectacle of the immense genius of Michelangelo, for example, caught in the toils of the rational ideas of the Grand Manner, is a titanic tragedy. On the other hand the exaltation of conforming mediocrities in every age into a position of authority is a melancholy farce. It is true that only a small proportion of them survive the inevitable ridicule of posterity, but there still remain on every self-styled Parnassus stuffed corpses that should be thrown on the dunghill.

That such a revaluation would be in effect merely a rehabilitation of romanticism is true enough, if the definition of romanticism I have already given is borne in mind. . . .

> [Read here discusses at length "the tasks awaiting us" to effect this revolution, under the following heads: "A fuller acknowledgement of the supreme poetic quality of our ballads and anonymous literature"; "Driving home the inescapable significance of Shakespeare"; "The exact relations between metaphysics and poetry"; "Lifting the moral ban"; "A reconsideration of all literature described as 'mad or nonsensical.'" This is followed by a section on dreams and the parallel between "dream-formation," as described by Freud, and poem-formation, in which, among other things, Read argues that "the whole irrationality of art, and the surrealist defense of irrationality, is explained by the Freudian theory of regression. An unconscious impulse creates the poem no less than the dream; it provides, that is to say, the mental energy required for its formation. That impulse seeks in the poem, no less and no otherwise than in the dream, its desired satisfaction. The latent ideas or thoughts are turned into visual images, are dramatised and illustrated, are finally liberated in the hallucinatory reality of the poem."]

The surrealist is opposed to current morality because he considers that it is rotten. We can have no respect for a code of ethics that tolerates extremes of poverty and riches; that wastes or deliberately destroys the products of the earth amidst a starving or undernourished people; that preaches a gospel of universal peace and wages aggressive war with all the appendages of horror and destruction which its evil genius can invent; that so distorts the sexual impulse that thousands of unsatisfied men and women go mad, millions waste their lives in unhappiness or poison their minds with hypocrisy. For such a morality (and these are merely its most general features) the surrealist has nothing but hatred and scorn.

His own code of morality is based on liberty and love. He sees no reason why the frailties of the human race should be erected into a doctrine of original sin, but he realises that most men are born imperfect and are made less perfect still by their circumstances. Such evils and imperfections cannot wholly be eradicated in any conceivable span of human development. But it is our belief that the whole system of organised control and repression which is the social aspect of present-day morality is psychologically misconceived and positively harmful. We believe, that is to say, in the fullest possible liberation of the impulses and are convinced that what law and oppression have failed to achieve will in due time be brought about by love and fraternity.

The surrealist is not a sentimental humanitarian; the super-realism of his art has its counterpart in the realism of his science. He is a psychologist of the strictest type, and if he uses words like "love" and "fraternity," it is because his analysis of the sexual and affective and of the economic life of man has given him the right to use such words cleanly, without the least surplus of sentimentality.

To close this essay without a personal note of explanation would be discreet, perhaps, but unnecessarily indefinite. . . . My main affiliations have always been romantic, in the sense in which I have interpreted romanticism in this essay. I have always had an instinctive preference for those poets and painters who have exceeded the limits of convention, which are the limits of moral experience; and in the history of criticism my interest quickens from the moment that romanticism begins to acquire a rational and scientific basis in psychology and philosophy: the line of development from Vico to Freud. . . .

In so far as such an attitude involves a political alignment and is thereby a clerk's *trahison*, such treason is committed in full awareness of the consequences. In normal circumstances the *detachment* of the artist from a party and therefore a partial point of view is a condition of his *attachment* to an integral view of life. But the conditions of the present time [1936] are not normal. It is the presumption of modern dictatorships to challenge in a most direct manner the artist's creative freedom. Whether done in the cause of "socialist realism" or "racial purity" or nationalism, the menace is the same—not merely repression and economic servitude such as the artist has suffered in all ages, but the actual extermination of the artist as such. Not since the Iconoclastic Controversy has the artist been forced into the position usually occupied by religious martyrs and political enemies. To the degree that the artist is directly attacked as an artist, he must actively defend himself; and to defend himself he must ally himself with whatever political forces seem to him to promise the requisite intellectual liberty. That choice may be a difficult one, for even communism, the creed of liberty and fraternity, has made the exigencies of a transitional epoch the excuse for an unnecessary and stupid form of æsthetic intolerance. Nevertheless, in a world of competing tyrannies, the artist can have only one allegiance: to that dictatorship which claims to end all forms of tyranny and promises, however, indefinitely, the complete liberation of man: the dictatorship of the proletariat.

The contradictions of the personality are resolved in the work of art: that is one of the first principles of surrealism.* One might even go so far as to say that the personality without contradictions is incapable of creating a work of art. It is incapable of entering into dialectical activity—of moving from the state of equilibrium which is the state of mental passivity. Art is more than description or "reportage"; it is an act of renewal. It renews vision, it renews language; but most essentially it renews life itself by enlarging the sensibility, by making men more conscious of the terror and the beauty, the *wonder* of the possible forms of being.

•   •   •

BIBLIOGRAPHICAL NOTE: For other essays that interpret romanticism in terms of the psychology of the "creative impulse" see those by F. L. Lucas and Mario Praz in this collection, and also Lucas's *Literature and Psychology* (London, 1951); P. L. Thorslev, "The Romantic Mind Is Its Own Place," *Comparative Literature*, XV (1963), 250–68; George Boas, "The Romantic

* In the original version of this essay, Read wrote "romanticism" here in place of "surrealism."

Self: An Historical Sketch," *Studies in Romanticism*, IV (1964), 1–16; and the section of "General Essays on Romanticism and Apocalypse" (by S. Schimanski and Henry Treece, Herbert Read, Alex Comfort, the Rev. E. F. F. Hill, and Walford Morgan) in *A New Romantic Anthology*, ed. Schimanski and Treece (London, 1949). For other studies dealing specifically with the relationship between surrealism and romanticism see Herbert S. Gershman, "Surrealism: Myth and Reality," in *Myth and Reality*, ed. Bernice Slote (Lincoln, Neb., 1963), pp. 51–57; and Anna Balakian, *Literary Origins of Surrealism* (New York, 1966) and *The Symbolist Movement* (New York, 1967).

The Bourgeois Illusion
and English Romantic Poetry

Christopher Caudwell

England has . . . been notable for the volume and variety of its contribution to modern poetry. The fact that England for three centuries led the world in the development of capitalism and that, during the same period, it led the world in the development of poetry, are not unrelated coincidences but part of the same movement of history.

> The bourgeoisie, historically, has played a most revolutionary part.
> The bourgeoisie, wherever it has got the upper hand, has put an end to all feudal, patriarchal, idyllic relations. It has pitilessly torn asunder the motley feudal ties that bound man to his "natural superiors," and has left no other nexus between man and man than naked self-interest, than callous "cash payment."
> The bourgeoisie cannot exist without constantly revolutionising the means of production, and thereby the relations of production, and with them the whole relations of society. Conservation of the old modes of production in unaltered form was, on the contrary, the first condition of existence for all earlier industrial classes. Constant revolutionising of production, uninterrupted disturbance of all social conditions, everlasting uncertainty and agitation distinguish the bourgeois epoch from all earlier ones. All fixed, fast-frozen relations, with their train of ancient and venerable prejudices and opinions, are swept away, all new-formed

THE BOURGEOIS ILLUSION AND ENGLISH ROMANTIC POETRY: From *Illusion and Reality*. Reprinted by permission of International Publishers Co., Inc., and Lawrence and Wishart Ltd. Copyright © 1947. Originally published in 1936.

ones become antiquated before they can ossify. All that is solid melts into air, all that is holy is profaned, and man is at last compelled to face with sober senses his real conditions of life and his relations with his kind [*The Communist Manifesto*].

Capitalist poetry reflects these conditions. It is the outcome of these conditions.

• • •

It is an art which constantly revolutionises its own conventions, just as bourgeois economy constantly revolutionises its own means of production. This constant revolution, this constant sweeping-away of "ancient and venerable prejudices and opinions," this "everlasting uncertainty and agitation," distinguishes bourgeois art from all previous art. Any bourgeois artist who even for a generation rests upon the conventions of his time becomes "academic" and his art lifeless. This same movement is characteristic of English poetry.

• • •

. . . Early poetry is essentially collective emotion, and is born in the group festival. It is not collective emotion of an unconditioned, instinctive kind, such as might be roused in a herd by a foe; it is the collective emotion of a response conditioned by the needs of economic association.

Now bourgeois culture is the culture of a class to whom freedom—man's realisation of all his instinctive powers—is secured by "individualism." It might therefore seem that bourgeois civilisation should be anti-poetic, because poetry is collective and the bourgeois is an individualist.

But this is to take the bourgeois *at his own valuation*. Certainly we must first of all do this, whether to understand him as capitalist or as poet. The bourgeois sees himself as an heroic figure fighting a lone fight for freedom—as the individualist battling against all the social relations which fetter the natural man, who is born free and is for some strange reason everywhere in chains. And in fact his individualism does lead to a continual technical advance and therefore to an increasing freedom. His fight against feudal social relations permits a great release of the productive forces of society. His individualism expresses the particular way in which the bourgeois economy continually revolutionises the base on which it stands, until the base becomes too much for the superstructure, and bourgeois economy explodes into its opposite.

And, in the same way, the bourgeois poet sees himself as an individualist striving to realise what is most *essentially* himself by an expansive outward movement of the energy of his heart, by a release of internal forces which outward forms are crippling. This is the bourgeois dream, the dream of the one man alone producing the phenomena of the world. He is Faust, Hamlet, Robinson Crusoe, Satan, and Prufrock.

This "individualism" of the bourgeois, which is born of the need to dissolve the restrictions of feudal society, causes a tremendous and ceaseless technical advance in production. In the same way it causes in poetry a tremendous and ceaseless advance in technique.

But both capitalist and poet become darker figures—first tragic, then pitiful, and finally vicious. The capitalist finds his very individualism, his very freedom, producing all the blind coercion of war, anarchy, slump, and revolution. The machine in its productiveness finally threatens even him. The market in its blindness becomes a terrifying force of nature. . . . The bourgeois poet treads a similar circle. He finds the loneliness which is the condition of his freedom unendurable and coercive. He finds more and more of his experience of the earth and the universe unfriendly and a restraint on his freedom. He ejects everything social from his soul, and finds that it deflates, leaving him petty, empty and insecure.

. . .

The bourgeois is a man who believes in an inborn spontaneity which secures man's free will. He does not see that man is only free in so far as he is conscious of the motive of his actions—as opposed to involuntary actions of a reflex character, like a tic, or imposed actions of a coercive character, like a shove in the back. To be conscious of the motive is to be conscious of the cause, that is of the necessity. But the bourgeois protests against this, because determinism seems to him the antithesis of free will.

To be conscious of one's motives is to will freely—to be conscious of the necessity of one's actions. Not to be conscious is to act instinctively like an animal, or blindly like a man propelled by a push from behind his back. This consciousness is not secured by introspection but by a struggle with reality which lays bare its laws, and secures to man the means of consciously using them.

. . .

Thus the root of the bourgeois illusion regarding freedom and the function of society in relation to the instincts, is seen to spring from the essential contradiction of bourgeois economy—private (i.e., individual) property in social means of production. The bourgeois ceases to be bourgeois as soon as he becomes conscious of the determinism of his social relations, for consciousness is not mere contemplation, it is the product of an active process. It is generated by his experiments in controlling social relations, just as his consciousness of Nature's determinism is generated by his experiments in controlling her. But before men can control their social relations, they must have the power to do so—that is, the power to control the means of production on which social relations rest. But how can they do this when these means are in the power of a privileged class?

The condition of freedom for the bourgeois class in a feudal society is the nonexistence of feudal rule. The condition of the freedom of the workers in a capitalist society is the nonexistence of capitalist rule. This is also the condition of freedom for a completely free society—that is, a classless society. Only in such a society can all men actively develop their consciousness of social determinism by controlling their associated destinies. The bourgeois can never accept this definition of freedom for all until he has ceased to be a bourgeois and comprehended the historical movement as a whole.

The nature of this contradiction in the bourgeois notion of freedom only becomes apparent in so far as bourgeois society decays, and the freedom of the bourgeois class becomes increasingly antagonistic to the freedom of society as a whole. The freedom of society as a whole consists in its economic products. These represent the freedom man has won in his struggle with Nature. In proportion as these expand, not only does the bourgeois feel himself free, thanks to the conditions of bourgeois economy, but the rest of society, which shares these products, is not proposed to challenge these conditions in a revolutionary way. It also—passively—accepts them. All this seems therefore a confirmation of the bourgeois theory of freedom. In these particular circumstances the bourgeois theory of freedom is true. It is an illusion, a phantastic illusion, which at this stage *realises* itself in practice. Man *is* gaining freedom by denying the relations of society, for these were feudal relations, already made obsolete by the development of bourgeois economy in their pores.

• • •

At this point, therefore, the contradictory nature of the bourgeois definition of freedom discloses itself because the advance of society has objectively negated it. This, therefore, gives way to a definition of freedom as a consciousness of determinism, and the condition of man's freedom is now seen to be the consciousness and the control of the determining causes of social relations—the productive forces. But this is a revolutionary demand—a demand for socialism and proletarian power, and it is opposed by the bourgeois as the negation of freedom— as indeed it is for him, as a bourgeois. He attempts to speak here in the name of all society, but the revolutionary movement of the bulk of society itself denies him this right.

Thus the bourgeois illusion regarding freedom, which counterposes freedom and individualism to determinism and society, overlooks the fact that society is the instrument whereby man, the unfree individual, in association realises his freedom and that the conditions of such association are the conditions of freedom. This illusion is itself the product of a particular class society, and a reflection of the special privilege on which bourgeois rule rests, and which rends society in two as long as it persists.

.   .   .

All bourgeois poetry is an expression of the movement of the bourgeois illusion, according as the contradiction rooted in bourgeois economy emerges in the course of the development of capitalism. Men are not blindly moulded by economy; economy is the result of their actions, and its movement reflects the nature of men. Poetry is then an expression of the real essence of associated men and derives its truth from this.

The bourgeois illusion is then seen to be a phantasy and bears the same relation to truth as the phantasy of primitive mythology. In the collective festival, where poetry is born, the phantastic world of poetry anticipates the harvest and, by so doing, makes possible the real harvest. But the illusion of this collective phantasy is not a mere drab copy of the harvest yet to be: it is a reflection of the emotional complex involved in the fact that man must stand in a certain relation to others and to the harvest, that his instincts must be adapted in a certain way to Nature and other men, to make the harvest possible. The collective poetry of the festival, although it is a confused perception of the real harvest-to-be, is an accurate picture of the instinctive adaptations involved in associated man's relation to the harvest process. It is a real picture of man's heart.

In the same way bourgeois poetry reflects, in all its variety and complexity, the instinctive adaptations of men to each other and Nature necessary in those social relations which will produce freedom—for freedom, as we saw, is merely man's phantastic and poetic expression for the economic product of society which secures his self-realisation. We include of course in this economic product not merely the commercial or saleable product of society, but the cultural and emotional products, including men's consciousnesses themselves. Hence this bourgeois illusion regarding freedom, of which bourgeois poetry is the expression, has a reality in so far as it produces, by its existence, freedom—I do not mean in any formal sense, I mean that just as primitive poetry is justified by the material harvest it produces, which is the means of the primitive's freedom, so bourgeois poetry is justified by the material product of the society which generates it in its movement. But it is a freedom not of all society but of the bourgeois class which appropriates the major part of society's products.

For freedom is not a state, it is a specific struggle with Nature. Freedom is always relative, relative to the success of the struggle. The consciousness of the nature of freedom is not the simple contemplation of a metaphysical problem, but the very act of living and behaving like a man in a certain state of society. Each stage of consciousness is definitely won; it is only maintained as a living thing by social movement—the movement we call labour. The working-out of the bourgeois illusion concerning freedom, first as a triumphant truth (the growth and increasing prosperity of capitalism), next as a gradually revealed lie (the decline and final crisis of capitalism), and finally as its passage into its opposite, freedom as the life-won consciousness of social necessity (the proletarian revolution), is a colossal movement of men, materials, emotions, and ideas, it is a whole history of toiling, learning, suffering, and hoping men. Because of the scale, energy, and material complexity of the movement, bourgeois poetry is the glittering, subtle, complex, many-sided thing it is. The bourgeois illusion which is also the condition of freedom for the bourgeoisie is realised in their own poetry, because bourgeois poets, like the rest of the bourgeoisie, realise it in their lives, in all its triumphant emotion, its tragedy, its power of analysis, and its spiritual disgust. And the consciousness of social necessity which is the condition of freedom for the people as a whole in classless, communist society, will be realised in communist poetry because it can only be realised in its essence, not as a metaphysical formula, but by living as men in a developing communist society, which includes living as poets and readers of poetry.

> [Caudwell next devotes a chapter to "The Period of Primitive Accumulation"—of capital and wage-labourers—a period encompassed by English literature from the Renaissance through the eighteenth century, the poetry of the latter being described as expressing "the spirit of the petty manufacturing bourgeoisie, beneath the wings of the big land-owning capitalists, giving birth to industrial capitalism."]

The bourgeois illusion now passes to another stage, that of the Industrial Revolution, the "explosive" stage of capitalism. Now the growth of capitalism transforms all idyllic patriarchal relations—including that of the poet to the class whose aspirations he voices—into "callous" cash-nexus.

Of course this does not make the poet regard himself as a shopkeeper and his poems as cheeses. To suppose this is to overlook the compensatory and dynamic nature of the connection between illusion and reality. In fact it has the opposite effect. It has the effect of making the poet increasingly regard himself as a man removed from society, as an individualist realising only the instincts of his heart and not responsible to society's demands—whether expressed in the duties of a citizen, a fearer of God, or a faithful servant of Mammon. At the same time his poems come increasingly to seem worthy ends-in-themselves.

This is the final explosive movement of the bourgeois contradiction. The bourgeois illusion has already swayed from antithesis to antithesis, but as a result of this final movement it can only pass, like a whirling piece of metal thrown off by an exploding flywheel, out of the orbit of the bourgeois categories of thought altogether.

As a result of the compromise of the eighteenth century, beneath the network of safeguards and protections which was characteristic of the era of manufacture, bourgeois economy developed to the stage where by the use of the machine, the steam-engine, and the power-loom it acquired an enormous power of self-expansion. At the same time the "factory" broke away from the farm of which it was the handicraft adjunct and challenged it as a mightier and opposed force.

On the one hand organised labour inside the factory progressively increased, on the other hand the individual anarchy of the external market also increased. On the one hand there was an increasingly public form of production, on the other hand an increasingly private form of appropriation. At the one pole was an increasingly landless and toolless proletariat, at the other an increasingly wealthy bourgeoisie. This self-contradiction in capitalist economy provided the terrific momentum of the Industrial Revolution.

The bourgeoisie, who had found its own revolutionary-puritan ideals of liberty "extreme," and returned to the compromise of mercantilist good taste that seemed eternal reason, now again found its heart had been right, and reason wrong.

This revealed itself first of all as a cleavage between the former landed aristocracy and the industrial bourgeoisie, expressing the rise of the factory to predominance over the farm. The landed aristocracy, and the restrictions it demanded for its growth, was now confronted by industrial capital and its demands. Capital had found an inexhaustible self-expansive power in machinery and outside sources of raw material. So far from any of the earlier forms being of value to it, they were so many restraints. The cost of labour power could safely be left to fall to its real value, for the machine by its competition creates the proletariat it requires to serve it. The real value of labour power in turn depends on the real value of wheat, which is less in the colonies and America than in England because there it embodies less socially necessary labour. The Corn Laws, which safeguard the agricultural capitalist, therefore hamper the industrialist. Their interests—reconciled during the period of wage-labour shortage—are now opposed. All the forms and restraints that oppose this free expansion of the industrial bourgeoisie must be shattered. To accomplish this shattering, the bourgeoisie called to its standard all other classes, precisely as in the time of the Puritan Revolution. It claimed to speak for the people as against the oppressors. It demanded reform and the repeal of the Corn Laws. It attacked the Church, either as Puritan (Methodist) or as open sceptic. It attacked all laws as restrictive of equality. It advanced the conception of the naturally good man, born free but everywhere in chains. Such revolts against existing systems of laws, canons, forms, and traditions always appear as a revolt of the heart against reason, a revolt of feeling and the sentiments against sterile formalism and the tyranny of the past. Marlowe, Shelley, Lawrence, and Dali have a certain parallelism here; each expresses this revolt in a manner appropriate to the period.

We cannot understand this final movement of poetry unless we understand that at every step the bourgeois is revolutionary in that he is revolutionising his own basis. But he revolutionises it only to make it consistently more bourgeois. In the same way each important bourgeois poet is revolutionary, but he expresses the very movement which brings more violently into the open the contradiction against which his revolutionary poetry is a protest. They are "mirror revolutionaries." They attempt to reach an object in a mirror, only to move farther away from the real object. And what can that object be but the common object of man as producer and as poet—freedom? The poignancy of their tragedy and pessimism derives its bite from this perpetual recession of the desired object as they advance to grasp it. "La Belle Dame Sans Merci" has them all in thrall. They wake up on the cold hillside.

Blake, Byron, Keats, Wordsworth, and Shelley express this ideological revolution, each in their different ways, as a romantic revolution.

Byron is an aristocrat—but he is one who is conscious of the break-up of his class as a force, and the necessity to go over to the bourgeoisie. Hence his mixture of cynicism and romanticism.

These deserters are in moments of revolution always useful and always dangerous allies. Too often their desertion of their class and their attachment to another, is not so much a "comprehension of the historical movement as a whole" as a revolt against the cramping circumstances imposed on them by their own class's dissolution, and in a mood of egoistic anarchy they seize upon the aspirations of the other class as a weapon in their private battle. They are always individualistic, romantic figures with a strong element of the *poseur*. They will the destruction of their own class but not the rise of the other, and this rise, when it becomes evident and demands that they change their merely destructive enmity to the dying class to a constructive loyalty to the new, may, in act if not in word, throw them back into the arms of the enemy. They become counter-revolutionaries. Danton and Trotsky are examples of this type. Byron's death at Missolonghi occurred before any such complete development, but it is significant that he was prepared to fight for liberty in Greece rather than England. In him the revolt of the heart against the reason appears as the revolt of the hero against circumstances, against morals, against all "pettiness" and convention. This Byronism is very symptomatic, and it is also symptomatic that in Byron it goes with a complete selfishness and carelessness for the sensibilities of others. Milton's Satan has taken on a new guise, one far less noble, petulant even.

Byron is most successful as a mocker—as a Don Juan. On the one hand to be cynical, to mock at the farce of human existence, on the other hand to be sentimental, and complain of the way in which the existing society has tortured one's magnificent capabilities—that is the essence of Byronism. It represents the demoralisation in the ranks of the aristocracy as much as a rebellion against the aristocracy. These men are therefore always full of death-thoughts: the death-thoughts of Fascism fighting in the last ditch, the death-thoughts of Jacobites; the glorification of a heroic death justifying a more dubious life. The same secret death-wishes are shown by these aristocrats if they turn revolutionary, performing deeds of outstanding individual heroism— sometimes unnecessary, sometimes useful, but always romantic and single-handed. They cannot rise beyond the conception of the desperate hero of revolution.

Shelley, however, expresses a far more genuinely dynamic force. He speaks for the bourgeoisie who, at this stage of history, feel themselves the dynamic force of society and therefore voice demands not merely for themselves but for the whole of suffering humanity. It seems to them that if only *they* could realise themselves, that is, bring into being the conditions necessary for their own freedom, this would of itself ensure the freedom of all. Shelley believes that he speaks for all men, for all sufferers, calls them all to a brighter future. The bourgeois trammelled by the restrains of the era of mercantilism is Prometheus, bringer of fire, fit symbol of the machine-wielding capitalist. Free him and the world is free. A Godwinist, Shelley believed that man is naturally good— institutions debase him. Shelley is the most revolutionary of the bourgeois poets of this era because *Prometheus Unbound* is not an excursion into the past, but a revolutionary programme for the present. It tallies with Shelley's own intimate participation in the bourgeois-democratic revolutionary movement of his day.

Although Shelley is an atheist, he is not a materialist. He is an idealist. His vocabulary is, for the first time, consciously idealist—that is, full of words like "brightness," "truth," "beauty," "soul," "æther," "wings," "fainting," "panting," which stir a whole world of indistinct emotions. Such complexes, because of the numerous emotional associations, appear to make the word indicate one distinct concrete entity, although in fact no such entity exists, but each word denotes a variety of different concepts.*

This idealism is a reflection of the revolutionary bourgeois belief that, once the existing social relations that hamper a human being are shattered, the "natural man will be realised"—his feelings, his emotions, his aspirations, will all be immediately bodied forth as material realities. Shelley does not see that these shattered social relations can only give place to the social relations of the class strong enough to shatter them and that in any case these feelings, aspirations, and emotions are the product of the social relations in which he exists and that to realise them a social act is necessary, which in turn has its effect upon a man's feelings, aspirations, and emotions.

The bourgeois illusion is, in the sphere of poetry, a revolt. In Wordsworth the revolt takes the form of a return to the natural man, just as it does in Shelley. Wordsworth, like Shelley profoundly influenced by French Rousseauism, seeks freedom, beauty—all that is not now in man because of his social relations—in "Nature." The French Revolution now intervenes. The bourgeois demand for freedom has now a regressive tinge. It no longer looks forward to freedom by revolt but by return to the natural man.

Wordsworth's "Nature" is of course a Nature freed of wild beasts and danger by æons of human work, a Nature in which the poet, enjoying a confortable income, lives on the product of industrialism even while he enjoys the natural scene "unspoilt" by industrialism. The very division of industrial capitalism from agricultural capitalism has now separated the country from the town. The division of labour involved in industrialism has made it possible for sufficient surplus produce to exist to maintain a poet in austere idleness in Cumberland. But to see the relation between the two, to see that the culture, gift of language, and leisure which distinguish a Nature poet from a dumb sub-human are the product of economic activity—to see this would be to pierce the bourgeois illusion and expose the artificiality of "Nature" poetry. Such poetry can only arise at a time when man by industrialism has mastered Nature—but not himself.

---

* In her studies in the language of English poetry Josephine Miles cites only "bright" and "soul" as occurring with significant frequency in Shelley's poetry. In connection with this, as well as with Caudwell's comment on Keats's vocabulary, see Miss Miles's *Renaissance, Eighteenth-Century, and Modern Language in English Poetry* (Berkeley and Los Angeles, 1960). See also *The Primary Language of Poetry in the 1740's and 1840's* (Berkeley and Los Angeles, 1950).

Wordsworth therefore is a pessimist. Unlike Shelley, he revolts regressively—but still in a bourgeois way—by demanding freedom from social relations, the specific social relations of industrialism, while still retaining the products, the freedom, which these relations alone make possible.

With this goes a theory that "natural," i.e., *conversational* language is better, and therefore more poetic than "artificial," i.e., *literary* language. He does not see that both are equally artificial—i.e., directed to a social end—and equally natural, i.e., products of man's struggle with Nature. They merely represent different spheres and stages of that struggle and are good or bad not in themselves, but in relation to this struggle. Under the spell of this theory some of Wordsworth's worst poetry is written.

Wordsworth's form of the bourgeois illusion has some kinship with Milton's. Both exalt the natural man, one in the form of Puritan "Spirit," the other in the more sophisticated form of pantheistic "Nature." One appeals to the primal Adam as proof of man's natural innocence, the other to the primal child. In the one case original sin, in the other social relations, account for the fall from grace. Both therefore are at their best when consciously noble and elevated. Milton, reacting against primitive accumulation and its deification of naïve princely desire and will, does not, however—as Wordsworth does—glorify the wild element in man, the natural primitive. Hence he is saved from a technical theory that conduces to "sinking" in poetry.

Keats is the first great poet to feel the strain of the poet's position in this stage of the bourgeois illusion, as producer for the free market. Wordsworth has a small income; Shelley, although always in want, belongs to a rich family and his want is due simply to carelessness, generosity, and the impracticability which is often the reaction of certain temperaments to a wealthy home. But Keats comes of a small bourgeois family and is always pestered by money problems. The sale of his poems is an important consideration to him.

For Keats therefore freedom does not lie, like Wordsworth, in a return to Nature; his returns to Nature were always accompanied by the uncomfortable worry, where was the money coming from? It could not lie, as with Shelley, in a release from the social relations of this world, for mere formal liberty would still leave the individual with the problem of earning a living. Keats's greater knowledge of bourgeois reality therefore led him to a position which was to set the keynote for future bourgeois poetry: "revolution" as a flight *from* reality. Keats is the banner bearer of the romantic revival. The poet now escapes upon the "rapid wings of poesy"* to a world of romance, beauty, and sensuous life separate from the poor, harsh, real world of everyday life, which it sweetens and by its own loveliness silently condemns.

This world is the shadowy enchanted world built by Lamia for her lover or by the Moon for Endymion. It is the golden-gated upper world of Hyperion, the word-painted lands of the nightingale, of the Grecian urn, of Baiae's isle. This other world is defiantly counterposed to the real world.

> "Beauty is truth, truth beauty"—that is all
> Ye know on earth, and all ye need to know.

And always it is threatened by stern reality in the shape of sages, rival powers, or the drab forces of everyday. Isabella's world of love is shattered by the two money-grubbing brothers. Even the wild loveliness of *The Eve of St. Agnes* is a mere interlude between storm and storm, a coloured dream snatched from the heart of cold and darkness—the last stanzas proclaim the triumph of decay. "La Belle Dame Sans Merci" gives her knight only a brief delight before he wakes. The flowering basil sprouts from the rotting head of Isabella's lover, and is watered with her tears.

> The fancy cannot cheat so well
> As she is famed to do, deceiving elf! . . .
> Was it a vision or a walking dream?
> Fled is that music—do I wake or sleep?

Like Cortez, Keats gazes entranced at the New World of poetry, Chapman's realms of gold, summoned into being to redress the balance of the old, but however much voyaged in, it is still only a world of fancy.

A new vocabulary emerges with Keats, the dominating vocabulary of future poetry. Not Wordsworth's—because the appeal is not to the unspoilt simplicity of the country. Not Shelley's—because the appeal is not to the "ideas" that float on the surface of real material life and can be skimmed off like froth. The country is a part of the real material world, and the froth of these metaphysical worlds is too unsubstantial and therefore is always a reminder of the real world which generated

---

* Keats actually wrote, of course, "viewless wings of poesy."

it. A world must be constructed which is more real precisely because it is more unreal and has sufficient inner stiffness to confront the real world with the self-confidence of a successful conjuring trick.

Instead of taking, like Wordsworth and Shelley, what is regarded as the most natural, spiritual, or beautiful part of the real world, a new world is built up out of words, as by a mosaic artist, and these words therefore must have solidity and reality. The Keatsian vocabulary is full of words with a hard material texture, like tesserae, but it is an "artificial" texture—all crimson, scented, archaic, stiff, jewelled, and anti-contemporary. It is as vivid as missal painting. Increasingly this world is set in the world of feudalism, but it is not a feudal world. It is a bourgeois world—the world of the Gothic cathedrals and all the growing life and vigour of the bourgeois class under late feudalism. Here too poetic revolution has a strong regressive character, just as it had with Wordsworth, but had not with the most genuinely revolutionary poet, Shelley.

The bourgeois, with each fresh demand he makes for individualism, free competition, absence of social relations, and more equality, only brings to birth greater organisation, more complex social relations, higher degrees of trustification and combination, more inequality. Yet each of these contradictory movements revolutionises his basis and creates new productive forces. In the same way the bourgeois revolution, expressed in the poetry of Shelley, Wordsworth, and Keats, although it is contradictory in its movement, yet brings into being vast new technical resources for poetry and revolutionises the whole apparatus of the art.

The basic movement is in many ways parallel to the movement of primitive accumulation which gave rise to Elizabethan poetry. Hence there was at this era among poets a revival of interest in Shakespeare and the Elizabethans. The insurgent outburst of the genetic individuality which is expressed in Elizabethan poetry had a collective guise, because it was focussed on that collective figure, the prince. In romantic poetry it has a more artificial air as an expression of the sentiments and the emotions of the individual figure, the "independent" bourgeois. Poetry has separated itself from the story, the heart from the intellect, the individual from society; all is more artificial, differentiated, and complex.

The poet now begins to show the marks of commodity-production. We shall analyse this still further when, as in a later date, it sets the whole key for poetry. At present the most important sign is Keats's statement, that he could write for ever, burning his poems afterward. The poem has become already an end in itself.

But it is more important to note the air of tragedy that from now on looms over all bourgeois poetry that is worth the adjective "great." Poetry has become pessimistic and self-lacerating. Byron, Keats, and Shelley die young. And though it is usual to regret that they died with their best works unwritten, the examples of Wordsworth, Swinburne, and Tennyson make fairly clear that this is not the case, that the personal tragedy of their deaths, which in the case of Shelley and Byron at least seemed sought, prevented the tragedy of the bourgeois illusion working itself out impersonally in their poetry. For the contradiction which secures the movement of capitalism was now unfolding so rapidly that it exposed itself in the lifetime of a poet and always in the same way. The ardent hopes, the aspirations, the faiths of the poet's youth melted or else were repeated in the face of a changed reality with a stiffness and sterility that betrayed the lack of conviction and made them a mocking caricature of their youthful sincerity. True, all men grow old and lose their youthful hopes—but not in this way. A middle-aged Sophocles can speak with searching maturity of the tragedy of his life, and at eighty he writes a drama that reflects the open-eyed serenity of wisdom's child grown aged. But mature bourgeois poets are not capable of tragedy or resignation, only of a dull repetition of the faiths of youth— or silence. The movement of history betrays the contradiction for what it is, and yet forces the bourgeois to cling to it. From that moment the lie has entered his soul, and by shutting his eyes to the consciousness of necessity, he has delivered his soul to slavery.

In the French Revolution the bourgeoisie, in the name of liberty, equality, and fraternity, revolted against obsolete social relations. They claimed, like Shelley, to speak in the name of all mankind; but then arose, at first indistinctly, later with continually increasing clarity, the claim of the proletariat also demanding liberty, equality, and fraternity. But to grant these to the proletariat means the abolition of the very conditions which secure the existence of the bourgeois class and the exploitation of the proletariat. Therefore the movement for freedom, which at first speaks largely in the voice of mankind, is always halted at a state where the bourgeoisie must betray its ideal structure expressed in poetry, forget that it claimed to speak for humanity, and crush the class whose like demands are irreconcilable with its own existence. Once robbed of its mass support, the revolting bourgeoisie can always be beaten back a stage by the forces of reaction. True, these forces have learned "a sharp lesson" and do not proceed too far against the bourgeoisie who have shown their power. Both ally themselves against the proletariat. Ensues an equilibrium when the bourgeoisie have betrayed their talk of freedom, and compromised their ideal structure, only themselves to have lost part of the ideal fruit of their struggle to the more reactionary forces—feudal forces, if the struggle is against feudalism, landowning and big financial forces, if the struggle is between agricultural and industrial capitalism.

Such a movement was that from Robespierre to the Directory and the anti-Jacobin movement which as a result of the French Revolution swept Europe everywhere. The whole of the nineteenth century is a record of the same betrayal, which in the life of the poets expresses itself as a betrayal of youthful idealism. 1830, 1848 and, finally, 1871 are the dates which make all bourgeois poets now tread the path of Wordsworth, whose revolutionary fire, as the result of the proletarian content of the final stage of the French Revolution, was suddenly chilled and gave place to common sense, respectability, and piety.*

It was Keats who wrote:

> "None can usurp this height," the shade returned,
> "Save those to whom the misery of the world
> Is misery and will not let them rest."

The doom of bourgeois poets in this epoch is precisely that the misery of the world, including their own special misery, will not let them rest, and yet the temper of the time forces them to support the class which causes it. The proletarian revolution has not yet advanced to a stage where "some bourgeois ideologists, comprehending the historical movement as a whole," can ally themselves with it and really speak for suffering humanity and for a class which is the majority now and the whole world of men tomorrow. They speak only for a class that is creating the world of tomorrow willy-nilly, and at each step draws back and betrays its instinctive aspirations because of its conscious knowledge that this world of tomorrow it is creating, *cannot include itself.*

BIBLIOGRAPHICAL NOTE: Other essays that deal similarly with the relationship between romanticism and political and socio-economic forces are those by

---

* For a very different view of "the revolutionary climate" of the English romantic movement see M. H. Abrams's essay below.

Herbert Read and Alex Comfort in this collection, and Alick West, *Crisis and Criticism* (London, 1937); Edwin B. Burgum, "Romanticism," *Kenyon Review*, III (1941), 479–90; the "General Essays on Romanticism and Apocalypse" in *A New Romantic Anthology*, ed. S. Schimanski and H. Treece (London, 1949), pp. 17–58. For an important attack on Caudwell's views (as well as those of other Marxist writers on "culture") see Raymond Williams's chapter on "Marxism and Culture" in his *Culture and Society 1780–1950* (New York, 1958). Williams's own view of romanticism may be seen in the selection from this book, "The Romantic Artist," below.

La Princesse Lointaine:
or the Nature of Romanticism

F. L. Lucas

[Basing his position largely on Freudian concepts of the unconscious Lucas states that "romanticism remains . . . essentially a problem, not of politics or economics, but of psychology." After reviewing and rejecting earlier definitions of romanticism, he examines numerous quotations from assumed romantic works, and then answers the question: "What are the qualities that recur? Remoteness, the sad delight of desolation, silence and the supernatural, winter and dreariness; vampirine love and stolen trysts, the flowering of passion and the death of beauty; Radcliffe horrors and sadistic cruelty, disillusion, death, and madness; the Holy Grail and battles on the Border; the love of the impossible." In similar fashion he finds the "salient features" of classicism as "Grace, self-knowledge, self-control; the sense of form, the easy wearing of the chains of art hidden under flowers, as with some sculptured group that fills with life and litheness its straitened prison in the triangle of a pediment; idealism steadied by an unfaltering sense of reality; lamp and midnight-oil, rather than wine-cup."]

We may seem drifting back to the old antithesis: "classicism—romanticism, reason—emotion." But the human mind is more complex than that. What are the psychological differences behind these spontaneous associations of the two words?

LA PRINCESSE LOINTAINE: OR THE NATURE OF ROMANTICISM: From *The Decline and Fall of the Romantic Ideal* (1936), by permission of the Cambridge University Press.

Civilised man is pulled this way and that by conflicting forces within him, which it is the whole difficult art of life to reconcile. First, there are the instinctive impulses of the human animal: second, there are the influences of other human beings, beginning with his parents, which build up in him certain ideals of behaviour, a certain conscience about misbehaviour, till these too become second nature. A man not only likes or dislikes certain things; he likes or dislikes himself for liking or disliking them. Third, his intelligence presents him a shadow-show of what he calls "reality." Meredith has symbolized these three as blood (or the dragon, or the worm), spirit, and brain. Freud has more clearly pictured the unhappy lot of the "ego" torn three ways between the "id," the "super-ego," and the "reality-principle." It is no longer a case of "the world, the flesh, and the devil"; but of the world, the flesh, and the ideal.

Now the lives men live and the art they make depends, I think, enormously on how strict and oppressive, or relaxed and easygoing, are their sense of reality and their sense of the ideal, their consciousness and their conscience. Different periods vary widely in this—and, within periods, different individuals. It is as if some men loved (like D. H. Lawrence), and some even loathed (like Lord Chesterfield), the preconscious and instinctive side of personality. In each of us lies this dark lake from which our conscious, reasoning selves have gradually emerged; strange emanations dance by night, or at solitary moments, on its surface; still stranger shapes appear to inhabit its hidden depths. Some of us love to dream on the banks of this mysterious mere; some try to fish or dive in it; others labour to brick it over and blot it out beneath a laboratory, or business-premises, or a dancing-floor.

In art these differences are specially important because there seems a good deal in common between all artistic creation and dreaming. . . . So considered, the differences between classicism, romanticism, and realism* turn out, I think, to be differences mainly of degree; depending on the strictness with which, if we may call them so, the reality-principle and the super-ego control and censor such emanations from the unconscious mind. The realist writer tends to sacrifice everything to his sense of reality. The classic, while ruthless towards some forms of unreality in the name of "good sense," elaborately cultivates others in

* Lascelles Abercrombie's book-length essay, *Romanticism* (London, 1926), is devoted largely to the opposition between romanticism and realism. See also Mario Praz's comment on Abercrombie's interpretation of this opposition, p. 89n. above.

the name of "good taste"; his impulses and fantasies are much more dominated by a social ideal, formed under the pressure of a finely civilised class.*

•   •   •

The romantic is in fact, like Joseph, a "dreamer." He may indeed, like a nightmare, be vividly realistic at moments. At moments he may be ruled, like the classic, by a social ideal of conduct—partly social, at least, in its heroism and generosity, though in other ways rebelliously anti-social. But, essentially, he believes with Blake in letting his impulses and ideas run free—"Damn braces, bless relaxes"—"Exuberance is beauty."

> The Land of Dreams is better far
> Above the light of morning-star.

Alcohol, I gather, does not so much stimulate the brain as relax its higher controls. Romanticism is likewise an intoxication; though there are varying degrees of it, just as there are day-dreams, night-dreams, nightmares, drink-dreams, and drug-dreams. If I had to hazard an Aristotelian definition of romanticism, it might run—"romantic literature is a dream-picture of life; providing sustenance and fulfilment for impulses cramped by society or reality." Whereas the world of classicism, on the contrary, is wide awake and strictly sober. . . .

Similarly in England, at the very gateway of the revival, Horace

---

* In his later *Literature and Psychology* (London, 1951) Lucas elaborates on this three-way distinction as follows: "in literature realism corresponds to a dominance of the 'reality-principle'; classicism, very roughly, to a dominance of the 'super-ego'; romanticism, also very roughly, to a dominance of impulses from the 'id.'

"In other words, it is misleadingly incomplete to picture a duel between classicism and romanticism. This literary conflict is not really a duel; it is part of a three-cornered conflict between classicism, romanticism, and realism.

"On the whole, then, our primitive impulses lead us towards romanticism; our sense of reality towards realism; our social sense towards classicism,—the art of men who honour a code and a tradition. Naturally there are many other contributory causes that vary with time and place. But a fundamental part seems played by these three fundamental factors of the human mind; and the basis of all romanticism becomes clearest if approached from the side, not of literary or social history, but of psychology.

"Sometimes romantics have called in realism as an ally against the unreal conventions of classicism; sometimes classicists have appealed to realism against the fantastic dreams of romanticism. For the danger that lies in wait for the classical muse is of becoming a blue-stocking and a governess; the danger that besets her romantic sister is of becoming a drunken libertine" (p. 100).

Walpole's *Castle of Otranto* is built out of a dream and written half in
one. "Visions, you know," writes its wise and charming author, whose
memory, for some reason, critics treat so disdainfully, "have always
been my pasture; and so far from growing old enough to quarrel with
their emptiness, I almost think there is no wisdom comparable to that
of exchanging what is called the realities of life for dreams. Old castles,
old pictures, old histories, and the babble of old people, make one live
back into centuries that cannot disappoint one. The dead have exhausted their power of deceiving—one can trust Catherine of Medicis now."
Macpherson's *Ossian* is a monotonous dream of shadows. "Dream not,
Coleridge," cries Lamb, "of having tasted all the grandeur and wildness of fancy till you have gone mad." "You never dream," says Coleridge in his turn reproachfully to Hazlitt. And again: "I should much
wish, like the Indian Vishnu, to float about along an infinite ocean,
cradled in the flower of the lotus, and wake once in a million years for
a few minutes just to know that I was going to sleep a million years
more." Even as a boy, seized in the street by a gentleman for picking
his pocket, he turned out to have been merely waving his hands in a
day-dream that he was Leander swimming the Hellespont to Hero's
tower. In later years his dreams became less pleasant; the creator of
"Kubla Khan" fled through much of his life like the figure in his
Ancient Mariner who hears the stalking footsteps of a fiend behind.
"Dreams with me are no Shadows, but the very Substances and foot-
thick Calamities of my Life." And after him in the long pageant of
romantic dreamers follows de Quincey with his opium; Beddoes the
"Dream-Pedlar"; Keats, "a dreaming thing, A fever of thyself,"
whose "La Belle Dame" arose from a dream of Dante's Francesca, and
whose *Endymion* de Quincey found, with some justice, vaguer "than
the reveries of an oyster"; Shelley beating his wings high above the
clouds; Byron, whose "Dream" is among his still living poems, and
who slept with pistol under pillow to ward off the too real phantoms of
the night; Clare turning back to refuge in madness from "the living sea
of waking dreams"; Tennyson hypnotising himself into strange trances
by the repetition of his own name; Browning with his visionary visit to
Childe Roland's tower; Poe with his stud of speckled nightmares. . . .
Here too paces Rossetti,

> Master of the murmuring courts
> Where the shapes of sleep convene—

till sleeplessness and chloral mastered him; his sister Christina,

> Dreaming through the twilight
> That does not rise nor set;

Morris following to the World's End, like his own Pharamond, the beauty seen and loved in dream; Francis Thompson, dallying with his opium amid labouring London, like the idle poppy amid the wheat— "My fruit is dreams, as theirs is bread"; the languid O'Shaughnessy, the languider Dowson; de la Mare "crazed with the spell of far Arabia," Yeats in his Celtic twilight; and so to the *surréalistes*, whose principle it is to write not merely of dreams, or after dreaming, but in one.*

Not only did the romantics prefer to create their art in this atmosphere of dream. Even the critical power of appreciating art seemed to Stendhal something only to be acquired by a habit *"de rêverie un peu mélancolique."* Even history, not altogether to its advantage, became in romantic hands a dream likewise. *"L'Histoire de France de Michelet,"* says Heine, . . . *"est ce recueil de rêves, c'est tout le moyen âge rêveur qui vous regarde de ses yeux profonds, douloureux, avec son sourire de spectre, et l'on est presque effrayé par la criante vérité de la couleur et des formes. En fait, pour la peinture de cette époque somnambule, il fallait précisément un historien somnambule comme Michelet."* Less romantic critics will be more critical of this romanticised history; but the passage well brings out the persistent connection between the Middle Ages, romanticism, and dream. Even autobiography proved too real a form for romantics to write correctly. Even their own past lives danced in a coloured mist before their eyes. . . .

• • •

Romanticism, in a word, was the sleeping beauty dreaming of the fairy prince; unfortunately the fairy prince is apt to lose his way; and the sleeping beauty may then console herself with other spirits that come, like the Arabian kind, out of bottles, but end all too unromantically in *"delirium tremens."*

The eighteenth century had always had at its ear two voices, like the warning dæmon of Socrates; one whispering "That is not intelligent," the other, "That is not done." Romanticism seems to me, essentially, an attempt to drown these two voices and liberate the unconscious life from their tyrannical repressions. Like the accompany-

---

* On this point see Herbert Read's essay on surrealism and romanticism above.

ing French Revolution, it is the insurrection of a submerged population; but, this time, a population of the mind. *"Fancy,"* remarked
Rymer, the orthodox neoclassic, *"Fancy* leaps and frisks and away she's
gone, whilst *Reason* rattles the chains and follows after." Now at last
those chains were broken; the Bastille of those twin oppressors, Probability and Propriety, was stormed and obliterated. In this sense,
indeed, *"Le Romantisme, c'est la Révolution."*[1]

The views of writers themselves on the actual business of composition
help to confirm this, by differing significantly, according as they are
more classical or romantic. The romantic, depending more on processes
outside his conscious control, believes, like Plato, in "inspiration"
or *"furor poeticus,"* a divine drunkenness. Whereas Davenant, at the
dawn of neoclassicism, already sniffs at this idea. It is, for him, a relic
of the primitive days when poets, being also priests, were of course
charlatans, who found it politic to pretend to be possessed. . . .

At all events, whereas the diverse theories of romanticism quoted
earlier seemed one-sided—each like a single photograph of a building
taken from a different aspect—it now becomes possible, I think, to
assemble them as part of a more intelligible whole.

Thus romanticism is not, in Goethe's phrase, "disease." It is intoxicated dreaming. But it is easy to see, and we shall see, that such auto-
intoxication can often become the reverse of healthy.

Again, romanticism is not simply a revolt of emotion against reason, though it often is; nor yet of imagination against reason—a
"renascence of wonder"; it can be both of these, or either. As there
are two tyrants to rebel against—the sense of reality and the sense of
society, the rebellion may be highly imaginative yet not very passionate, like much of Coleridge; or passionate yet not highly imaginative,
like much of Byron; or both, like *Adonais.*

That rules like the Unities should be among the first things to be
flung aside by romanticism, follows naturally. For it is hard to dream
in a stiff shirt-front; and exhilarated revellers dislike being asked to toe
chalk lines on the floor. Far better Herrick's "wild civility." . . . And

---

[1] Jung, with his idea of the collective unconscious, would possibly put it that the
sensitive minds of poets and artists now became aware that an essential part of human
nature was being starved. But this seems only a rather mystical way of saying that
healthy instincts first reasserted themselves in certain more imaginative personalities;
because these artists were more sensitive, they felt more distinctly where their shoes
pinched.

so romanticism, in order that it may be free to dream, becomes a literary Protestantism, liberalism, or rule of *laissez-faire*. Again, the Middle Ages were its obvious spiritual home. For they were mystical, mysterious, and remote; and they had been finally killed at the Renaissance by this hated classicism, which the romantics now proposed to kill in its turn. But the mediæval is no essential part of the romantic.

Finally, romanticism is only partly opposed to realism; its true enemy is the hackneyed and humdrum present, whether squalid or academic—a very different thing. Snatches of realism remain very welcome to romantic sensationalists, especially as an escape from the starched dignities of classicism; just as a courtier of the old régime used, he said, on returning from the pomps of Versailles, to stand and stare at a dog gnawing a bone in the street—here at last was something "real."

Thus romantic diction shows fondness not only for the romantically remote, in place or time, but also for the realistic. While Coleridge, Keats, and Morris revived words long hoary and moss-grown, Wordsworth, on the contrary, copied the actual speech of "huts where poor men lie" and Hugo boasted that he had stuck a red cap of liberty on the dictionary of the Academy.

Further, from its relaxation of the censorship over the unconscious or the preconscious, follow naturally certain other features of romantic literature.

We have become familiar with the enormous part played by symbolism in all dreaming. It plays an enormous part also in enriching the imagery of this "literature of dream." Dryden with his classicism had already found Shakespeare's style "pestered" with figurative expressions. Aristotle and Longinus would certainly have shuddered at his extravagances. But with the romantic revival, after the hackneyed metaphors and similes of neoclassicism, appeared a new wealth of images, often as grotesque and fantastic as a dream. . . .

Again the romantic writers use language in a dreamier way; with vague overtones and associations that shall echo through a mind whose attention is not riveted but half relaxed. . . . In the romantic hands that thus "writ in water," other words besides Keats's "forlorn" grow "like a bell"; indeed a romantic sentence is often a whole carillon of such bells, an Easter chime that calls the ghosts of forgotten meanings to rise again.

> The fairy fancies range
> And, lightly stirr'd,
> Ring little bells of change
> From word to word.

We are far here from the days

> When *Phoebus* touch'd the Poet's trembling Ear
> With one supreme Commandment: "Be thou clear."

How blind by contrast the eighteenth century could be to the dream associations of words is well seen in an astonishing passage by the Abbé de Pons (1714), vindicating his right to judge Homer without even knowing Greek: "*Chaque nation a ses signes fixes pour représenter tous les objets que son intelligence embrasse. Qu'on ne dise donc plus que les beautés qu'on a senties en lisant Homère ne peuvent être parfaitement rendues en francais. Ce qu'on a senti ou pensé, on peut l'exprimer avec une élégance* égale *dans toutes les langues.*" To this good Abbé words are merely like algebraic symbols; his mind concentrates on the barest literal meaning; to let it wander away to half-conscious associations would be reprehensible wool-gathering. He did not guess that such wool might be the Golden Fleece of poetry. These neoclassics were not emotionally over-cold, but mentally over-alert; not unfeeling, but unsleeping.

So with metre. The essential difference between romantic verse, in England and France, and the immaculate heroics and Alexandrines of the classics is that rhythm has now become once more an intoxicant. "*Enivrez-vous!*" Pope or Gray, Racine or Boileau can speak perfectly; they can declaim magnificently; but they do not sing. Their verse is exquisite coffee in lordly porcelain; it "cheers but not inebriates"; it is not the wine of Dionysus. It hardly performs at all the essential task of more dancing rhythms—the task of hypnotising the reader into a dreamy trance, where his sense of reality is drugged and, at the same time, his suggestibility heightened. The music of Handel, Gluck, and Mozart (such a complete refutation of the supposed passionlessness of the eighteenth century) failed to infect the sister-art of poetry. In literature, for a century and a half Apollo had harped with a dignity sometimes splendid, often monotonous; now at last the wild flutings of Marsyas were once more to catch at the heart and go shuddering down the spine. . . .

To-day knights-errant are rust and dust, witches ashes, war a folly; but as the trees with Orpheus, so to such music we can still forget our most stiffly rooted convictions. It was not for nothing that in a realistic moment Shelley compared himself for unreality to a gin-palace. Intoxication is the essence of such poetry as this.

So with romantic settings and subject-matter. Always *"la princesse lointaine,"* the blue of distance. For remoteness is a feeling associated with dreams; and, again, remoteness makes it easier to dream—there is less danger of colliding with a brute fact. It may be remoteness in time. . . . Or it may be remoteness in space, as with Heine's fir-tree—the distance of far Arabia or Xanadu, of Tipperary or "the lands where the Jumblies live." . . . Or, again, it may be that other remoteness of undiscovered countries of the mind. "Who," says Fuller, "hath sailed about the world of his own heart, sounded each creek, surveyed each corner, but that there still remains much *terra incognita* in himself?"

The romantics found this *terra incognita* of the soul their happy hunting ground. And yet dreamers may not make the best explorers; the results, as we shall see, were not always very happy. . . .

Similarly in other fields where more conscious critical control is needed—in the construction of a plot, in the creation of a *prose* style—the romantic in his semi-trance is often inferior to the century before. Then, a gentleman regarded his readers as his guests. He considered it his duty to face the toil of hard writing in order to give them the pleasure of easy reading; unlike Mr. Joyce who has touchingly remarked "The demand that I make of my reader is that he should devote his whole life to reading my works." Of the more serious weaknesses which come from the romantic surrender to impulse it will be time to speak when we deal with its decadence.

· · ·

In these pages it has been suggested that the fundamental quality of romanticism is not mere anti-classicism nor mediævalism, nor "aspiration," nor "wonder," nor any of the other things its various formulas suggest; but rather a liberation of the less conscious levels of the mind. Health, both in life and in literature, lies between excess of self-consciousness and excess of impulsiveness, between too much self-control and too little. The romantic intoxication of the imagination suspends the over-rigid censorship exerted by our sense of what is fact and our sense of what is fitting. The first of these dominates the extreme realist; both inhibit the extreme classicist; the romantic escapes.

But it is not always into Paradise that he escapes. "Romanticism," said Goethe, "is a disease." If Keats be disease, then let us have more of

it. Nonetheless, Goethe has repeatedly proved right. Reality-principle
and super-ego are not devices of the Devil: they are necessities of all
civilised life. Again and again the romantic who drinks too deep, who
surrenders too much to the unconscious, who becomes too completely
a child once more, has fallen a victim to the neurotic maladies that beset
the childish adult who cannot cope with life but falls between two ages.
Then the "clouds of glory" have changed to the nightmares of ego-
maniac perversion; to the love of sensation even in torture; to the pursuit of strange fruit even in the Garden of Proserpine, whose beauty is
death.

The advantage of the Freudian viewpoint is that it links together
various characteristics of romanticism, some healthy and some morbid,
that hitherto seemed arbitrary and disconnected. Why, after all,
should the same movement have led from Sir Galahad to *Salome*, from
the Lady of the Lake to *La Charogne*, from chivalry to sadistic tortures,
from idealism to ordure? Freud, like all pioneers, may often have got
hold of the wrong end of the stick: it is hard to doubt that the sticks are
there. About our infancy, it seems, lies Caliban as well as Ariel; after
all, though it so horrified our grandparents, we accept the truth of that
for the human race as a whole. And so the romantic, I suggest, wandering in the woods of dream, has often wandered too far, and got lost like
the neurotic who takes refuge from reality among the phantoms that
haunt the mouldered lodges of his childish years. Those symptoms in
individuals have become familiar; they are strangely like those of
romantic decadence.

But one may be the better for wine as well as the worse for it. The
century since the romantic revival produced work of creative worth in
greater abundance than any before it. Its criticism, too, became far
more sensitive; but whereas eighteenth-century critics wrote often
admirable sense or, if not, at least lucid nonsense, romantic critics like
Coleridge and Hugo and Carlyle and Ruskin and Swinburne, with all
their brilliance, have tended to lapse into a transcendental nonsense
far more tiresome to the reader. These star-gazers fall so easily into
wells; and it is seldom Truth that they find at the bottom*. . . .

---

* In a note to a reprinting of *The Decline and Fall of the Romantic Ideal* (Cambridge,
1963), Lucas makes a further interesting comment on romanticism in the twentieth
century as well as on the relationship among romanticism, classicism, and realism:
"Nearly thirty years have passed since this book was written under the shadow of
coming war. The War came; and provided a grimmer example than ever of the destruc-

tiveness of a romanticism gone rotten. For Hitler, though he might pride himself on ruthless realism, remained, still more, a perverted romantic, who hated reason, boasted of marching to his goal like a somnambulist, and intoxicated both himself and his countrymen with megalomaniac dreams. And so, though far smaller than that other romantic, Napoleon, he proved even costlier. On the other hand I should like to make it clear from the outset that this book is *not* an indiscriminate attack on all romanticism. Both life and literature have, I believe, reached their best with those that kept a steady, yet flexible, balance between romanticism, realism, and classicism, all three. For it seems perilous to become either *too* imaginative, or *too* cynical, or *too* dominated even by good sense and great traditions. I have here tried to discuss both the triumphs and the dangers of romanticism; the triumphs remain; but the dangers also. 'Lilies that fester smell far worse than weeds.'"

Two other works that deal with the supposed relationship between romanticism and twentieth-century totalitarianism are Jacques Barzun, *Classic, Romantic, and Modern* (Garden City, N.Y., 1961)—a revision of his earlier *Romanticism and the Modern Ego* (Boston, 1943)—and Paul Roubiczek, *The Misinterpretation of Man* (London, 1949).

BIBLIOGRAPHICAL NOTE: For other psychological interpretations of romanticism see the essays by Mario Praz and Herbert Read in this collection. See also Lucas's *Literature and Psychology* (London, 1951) and the several works on romanticism and surrealism listed in the bibliographical note above, p. 107.

Romantic Poetry and the Tradition

Cleanth Brooks

[In his first chapter, "Metaphor and the Tradition," Brooks sets out to show the links between romantic and neoclassic principles, particularly in regard to metaphor. He charges both Wordsworth and Coleridge with opposing materials for poetry "which are technical, sharply realistic, definite in their details," with holding that "the play of the intellect is inimical to deep emotion," with believing that "certain words and objects are intrinsically poetic," and with condemning "the ingenious and exact figure."]

We think of the romantic revolt as being radically opposed to the whole neoclassic conception of poetry. But, in fact, the line of reasoning used by Wordsworth and Coleridge can be traced back into eighteenth-century criticism. Dr. Johnson, we may be sure, differed widely with the romantic critics in his judgment of particular figures. But the principles which he used to attack the figures which he does not like are precisely those which they themselves used. . . . Johnson, no less than his romantic successors, is anxious to preserve a certain sublimity which he feels is injured by too much show of ingenuity or the use of undignified and prosaic diction.

ROMANTIC POETRY AND THE TRADITION: From *Modern Poetry and the Tradition* (Chapel Hill, N.C.: University of North Carolina Press, 1939). Reprinted by permission of The University of North Carolina Press.

We can trace this process of reasoning still further back into the neoclassic period. At the beginning of the century, Addison, for example, thoroughly corroborates Johnson and Wordsworth. . . . However jejune Addison's critical summary [in the *Spectator* papers entitled "The Pleasures of the Imagination"] may seem to be, one observes that he has anticipated the two main points which his successors were to insist upon: (1) the assumption that some things are intrinsically poetic and (2) that the intellectual faculty is somehow opposed to the emotional (the poetic).

•   •   •

[Also] Wordsworth and Coleridge go too far in implying that only playfulness is served by the methods and materials which they assign to fancy.* There are complex attitudes in which there is an interplay— even a swift interplay—of intellect and emotion; and these romantic critics neglect the possibility that levity itself may sometimes be used to *intensify* seriousness.

One may sum up by saying that the methods and materials which Wordsworth and Coleridge confined to the fancy may sometimes be employed to attain heights of *imaginative* power. This is evidently the meaning of Eliot's comment that "the difference between imagination and fancy, in view of this poetry of wit [the poetry of Donne and his followers], is a narrow one." (I interpret Richards' remark that "Donne most often builds, in the mode of Fancy, with imaginative units formed in 'meaning's press and screw,'" as indicating that he is in substantial agreement with Eliot here.)

If the eighteenth- and nineteenth-century principles for testing the goodness of metaphor are too narrow, what is to be the test? When is a figure justified? One must not hope for a neat formulation which can be applied a priori. Indeed, it is just this a priori application of the conventional tests of simplicity and decoration which does most damage at the present time. Each figure must be dealt with separately and individually. But some of the values and functions of the radical comparison may be suggested. . . .

•   •   •

With the modern poet, the value of the figure must in all cases be referred to its function in the context in which it occurs, with the recognition that the range of possible functions is wide; the figure may have a negative function as well as a positive—may serve irony as well as

---

* Cf. T. E. Hulme's conception of fancy in his essay above.

ennoblement. Our only test for the validity of any figure must be an appeal to the whole context in which it occurs: Does it contribute to the total effect, or not?

Most clearly of all, the metaphysical poets reveal the essentially functional character of all metaphor. We cannot remove the comparisons from their poems. The comparison *is* the poem in a structural sense.

And now one may consider the fundamental fallacy which underlies the romantic and neoclassical account of the functions of figurative language. In that account, metaphor is merely subsidiary. For "to illustrate" is to illustrate something, and the illustration of a proposition implies that the proposition could be made without recourse to the illustration. Obviously, the phrase "to decorate" assumes for the decoration merely a subsidiary function.*

> [Brooks next discusses the "tradition" of wit and irony** as it developed in Elizabethan and Jacobean poetry, as well as the relationship between the development of science in the middle of the seventeenth century and the structure of poetry. He summarizes this relationship as follows:]

We have abundant evidence of the esteem in which such poets as Cowley, D'Avenant, and Dryden held Thomas Hobbes, and as Ransom has admirably put it: "What Bacon with his disparagement of poetry had begun, in the cause of science and protestantism, Hobbes completed. . . . The name [of Hobbes] stood for common sense and naturalism, and the monopoly of the scientific spirit over the mind." The weakening of metaphor, the development of a specifically "poetic" subject matter and diction, the emphasis on simplicity and clarity, the simplification of the poet's attitude, the segregation of the witty and the ironical from the serious, the stricter separation of the various genres—all these items testify to the monopoly of the scientific spirit. This process of clarification involved the *exclusion* of certain elements from poetry—the prosaic, the unrefined, and the obscure. The imagi-

---

* For contrary views of the nature of romantic metaphor see the essays by R. H. Fogle, René Wellek, W. K. Wimsatt, and Albert Gérard in this collection, and Frank Kermode's *Romantic Image* (London, 1957).

** For a very different view of the "tradition," of which both romanticism and modern criticism (including T. E. Hulme and T. S. Eliot) are seen to be a part, see again Kermode's *Romantic Image*. See also Robert Langbaum's "Romanticism as a Modern Tradition" in his *The Poetry of Experience* (New York, 1957).

nation was weakened from a "magic and synthetic" power to Hobbes's conception of it as the file-clerk of the memory. It was obviously the antirationalistic magic that Hobbes was anxious to eliminate.

This change in taste constitutes the first great critical revolution that has occurred in the history of modern English poetry. The second major critical revolution, the romantic revolt, had as its ostensible objective, the liberation of the imagination. Unfortunately it failed to be revolutionary enough. As we have seen, the romantic poets, in attacking the neoclassic conception of the poetic, tended to offer new poetic objects rather than to discard altogether the conception of a special poetic material. Even Coleridge himself, with all his critical acumen, did not completely free himself from the didactic conception. The didactic function, clad in iridescent colors as a revelation of the Divine, remained to confuse his critical theory.

The importance of the third critical revolution lies in the fact that it attempts a complete liberation of the imagination. The successful use of prosaic or unpleasant materials and the union of the intellectual with the emotional are symptoms of imaginative power—not, as Mr. F. L. Lucas would interpret them, symptoms of the death of poetry. Moreover, the important resemblance between the modern poet and the poets of the sixteenth and seventeenth centuries lies not in the borrowing of a few "metaphysical" adjectives or images, or the cultivation of a few clever "conceits." That is why the "metaphysical" quality of the best of the moderns is not the result of a revival, or the aping of a period style. The fundamental resemblance is in the attitude which the poets of both periods take toward their materials and in the method which both, at their best, employ.

• • •

In our revised interpretation of the history of English literature, the romantic movement obviously is to be classed as an antiscientific revulsion.* It retreated, as we know, from the rationalistic, the ordered, and the classified. But it did not have the capacity to undo the damage done by Hobbes. In a sense it understood that the issue was science, but its reaction was confused. Hence we have on one hand Wordsworth's drivel about the botanist who would peek and botanize on his mother's grave, and on the other, Shelley's attempt to found a poetry

* With this statement compare A. N. Whitehead's "The Romantic Reaction" in his *Science and the Modern World* (New York, 1925).

of wonder and of humanitarianism on the latest findings of science. Moreover, as a reaction to neoclassicism, the movement was too much centered in the personal and the lyrical, and it has a cult of simplicity of its own. It substituted romantic subjectivism for neoclassic objectivism instead of fusing the two as they were fused in a great dramatic period such as the Elizabethan. Wordsworth has a little of the dramatic as does Shelley, and where we find an overt attempt at the dramatic, it is the personal self-dramatization of Byron—the self-conscious actor, not the objectifying dramatist. Keats, oddly enough, comes closest to giving us dramatic poems—in the great odes; and Keats himself had recognized before his death the need for a stiffening and toughening of his poetry. If, as Eliot has pointed out, wit is a quality that is lacking in the romantic poets, one can point out a concomitant lack of the dramatic. And, as we have seen, the second statement is but a restatement of the first.

But, one may inquire, how does the re-emergence of a metaphysical poetry in our time fit into the scheme? I cannot but feel that it is more than mere coincidence that it should occur today when the course of science has come full circle from the age of Hobbes to the age of Einstein, and when the scientists themselves have come to point out that their science is, in one sense at least, a fiction—a construct. This perception, by removing the curse of *fiction* from poetry, allows the poet to develop *his* kind of *fiction* in accord with its own principles, unconfused by those of another.

To put the matter in slightly different terms: The concept of progress developed concomitantly with the advance of science and dominated men's imaginations in proportion as the scientific method won its successes. Thus, the doctrine of progress dominated the nineteenth century. It has not been until the twentieth century that the concept of progress has been seriously challenged. With the weakening of that concept, men are becoming ready once more to accept a poetry which will give a view of the human situation as total as that given by tragedy. To admit the advance of science (as all must) and yet to deny that the results of scientific advancement are automatically beneficial, is to take a more critical view of the nature of scientific description, and therefore, perhaps, open the way to a clearer, more just view of the nature of poetic description.

The principles of poetic organization, developed to their logical conclusion, we have argued, carry the poem over into drama, with the characteristics of tragedy—concreteness, dramatic ambiguity, irony, resolution through struggle—as perhaps their highest expression. Probably our best proof that the principles *are* essentially dramatic is the fact that one finds that the easiest introduction of a modern reader to the metaphysical poets today is made on the analogy of drama, and specifically, on the analogy of Shakespeare's drama. To conceive of the poem as a little drama may be the only way in which the overliteral-minded reader can proceed at all. Our sense of a poem as a dramatic context, in general, is slight; it has hardly been nourished by the poetry of the last two hundred years.

[Brooks here begins his last chapter, "Notes for a Revised History of English Poetry," by demonstrating the "tradition of wit" (as opposed to Spenserian allegory) in the early seventeenth century as the basis for his revision of "standard" literary history.]

At its best the literature of the early eighteenth century shows the structure of early seventeenth-century poetry, but constricted and narrowed in scope. . . . Indeed, the relative failure of neoclassic poetry has long been put down to the neoclassic poets' preoccupation with satire.

This romantic criticism of neoclassic poetry deserves a little further commentary. Satire is not in itself inimical to the poetic impulse, though most formal satires, one may grant, fail to achieve the qualities of the greatest poetry. Perhaps one may best consider the matter in this way. We have already argued that particular scenes, words, or situations are not in themselves poetic or unpoetic; and by saying this, we may have seemed to remove altogether the possibility of setting up a distinction between satire and the other forms of poetry. Certainly we shall have removed the basis on which satire has been distinguished from the other forms in the past.* But one may still make the distinction on the basis of the poet's attitude.

It is possible to isolate, on the one hand, an attitude of almost pure approval or sympathy, and, on the other, one of almost complete disapproval (the negative or satiric). The extremes, of course, are never

---

* For an essay that defines lyric and satire "as incompatible modes" and then constructs a definition of romanticism on the basis of "that set of mind (or literary mode) of which the lyric is the characteristic expression," see Calvin S. Brown, "Toward a Definition of Romanticism," in *Varieties of Literary Experience*, ed. Stanley Burnshaw (New York, 1962).

realized in absolute purity; but we can point to a simple and affectionate love poem as tending to mark one limit, and to a simple and direct satire as marking the other. Now it is apparent that an attitude of almost any complexity will involve a mixture of these basic attitudes, whether it be in love poetry, or religious poetry, or tragedy. If this is true, the highest type of satire will hardly be recognized as such. It will merge imperceptibly into some form like tragedy, for example. Seen in these terms, the Elizabethan period, no less than the eighteenth century, turns out to be a period in which the satiric element was very great though we shall have to look for examples to such works as *Hamlet, Timon of Athens,* and *Lear* rather than to the formal satires of Hall and Marston.

The prime mistake of the neoclassic period, then, was not that it gave vent to the satiric impulse but rather that it segregated it from other impulses, leaving its tragedy too noble and too easily didactic; or, on the other hand, when it attempted to stir the heartstrings, too sentimental. Neoclassic love poetry is too exclusively love poetry; neoclassic satire, too narrowly satiric.

The apparent exceptions test and corroborate the rule. The "Portrait of Atticus," we have said, is better than most of the portraits of *The Dunciad* because there Pope's judgment is most mixed and his attitude least simple. And to turn back to Dryden for a moment, Dryden's greatest sustained poem, in some respects, is his *Hind and the Panther;* for his earlier allegiance to the Anglican Church and a continuing sympathy with, and understanding of, its position, make his satire complex and rich.

In general, the terms used commonly in the textbooks to describe neoclassic poetry need a thorough overhauling. The poetry of the Age of Reason is not, as we have seen, "intellectual." Its "perfection of form" is valid æsthetically only in so far as we subscribe to the limitations of form which the poets of the period accepted. If we mean by *form* the arrangement of the various elements of the poem in order to further the poet's total intention, then Keats's "Ode to Autumn" has perfection of form quite as much as does Pope's *Rape of the Lock;* and so, for that matter, does Donne's "Nocturnal on St. Lucy's Day." So also with terms like "propriety," "correctness," and "finish."

We have spoken thus far primarily of poets like Pope, Swift, and Gray. The so-called preromantic poets require some further attention. . . . It is perfectly valid to consider them as "preromantics," and the textbooks have doubtless been right in emphasizing the romantic qualities to be found in them. But the textbooks have insisted rather too much on the metaphor of these poets "struggling to burst the fetters of neo-classicism." There is, in fact, a great deal of continuity in the poetry of the century.

The preromantic poets, hardly less than Pope, are descriptive and didactic. There is little change in the structure of their poetry, though the descriptive and didactic matter is changed: rural landscapes for London ballrooms; didactic accounts of wool-raising, hunting, cane-growing, for the didactic *Moral Essays.*

 • • •

A realization of the basic continuity of eighteenth-century poetry will explain many matters which most historians of English literature tend to obscure: for instance, why Collins and Gray, two poets who make consistent use of the romantic materials—Gothic, Celtic, and Norse stories, and the scenery of country graveyards, for example—are justly regarded as two of the most "classic" of the English poets; or why a poet like Young could be a satirist in the manner of Pope and at the same time a member of the Graveyard School.

What it is important to see is that the changes introduced by the forerunners of romanticism did little to reinvigorate metaphor or to make verse more flexible and varied ("rough"). The preromantics do tend, as the century advanced, toward more "wildness" (though they stop far short of the wildness of a Sandburg or a Whitman). They become bolder in their emphasis on the emotions, avowing themselves frankly to be enthusiasts. Most of all, they go to an extreme in insisting on the intrinsic poetic quality of certain classes of objects. But these tendencies lead them still farther away from the structure of Elizabethan poetry.

With many of the preromantics, it is almost sufficient merely to point to the new poetic objects—owls, ivy, ruined towers, and yew trees. Indeed, some of their poems may be considered as little more than display cases filled with collections of such objects tied loosely together with appropriate interjections. . . . Perhaps never before or since have poetic terms become clichés so rapidly; and this is a measure of the weight of the dependence placed upon them in securing the poetic effect.

In such poetry there is the very minimum of metaphor. We can describe the process by which the metaphor was sloughed off as follows: The neoclassic poets had tended to use poetic materials in order to decorate or dignify the subject in question. The preromantic poets (with a change, of course, in the kind of objects considered poetic) were often content merely to point to the objects themselves.

... Ironically, for those who insist on "nature," it was not the romantic plowman who restored liberty to the imagination, but the cockney Blake. Blake represents, as Burns does not, the return to the daring of Elizabethan metaphor, to the use of serious irony, to a bold willingness to risk obscurity, and even to something very close to metaphysical wit.

Blake's metaphor is vigorous. In "London," a sigh is made to "run in tears down palace walls"; "the youthful harlot's curse" blasts "the new-born infant's ear";* in "The Mental Traveler" shrieks can be caught "in cups of gold"; in "The Scoffers" the grains of sand, blown back into the scoffers' eyes, became, in turn, "gems" shining in the light of truth, and then sands along the Red Sea shore over which the Chosen People are to pass. The metaphor is made to define and carry the idea; it represents a fusion of image and idea, and is thus a successful attempt to break through the deadening influence of Hobbes. In its kind it stands almost alone in its period.

One further comment on Blake's wit. Consider the following lines from "London":

> How the chimney-sweeper's cry
> Every blackening church appalls.

The blackening of the church walls by the soot becomes a sign of the church's sin in failing to protest against the un-Christian exploitation of children as chimney sweepers, the soot of the sweeps' trade besmirching the churches themselves. But Blake goes further and states it as if the cry of the child had the effect of a curse, and there is a suggestion that the church is blackened at the cry as well as appalled. Moreover, by the word *appalled*, Blake suggests that the cry throws a pall over the church; the church is dead. The poets of the early seventeenth century would have had no trouble in recognizing this as a witty comparison, brilliantly and successfully executed. Blake is a metaphysical poet. But the elements which make him such a poet appeared rarely in the poetry of his period and never elsewhere in a form so extreme. He remains an isolated and exceptional figure.

With the flowering of the romantic tendencies early in the nineteenth century there were signs of more radical changes. There was a

---

* The correct readings of two of these lines are: "Runs in blood down Palace walls" and "the new-born Infant's tear."

reconsideration of poetic diction and an attempt to found it on a broader base and to incorporate the unpoetic. Metaphor became somewhat
more vigorous and daring. The metaphysical poets were read and
elicited some praise even though no poems were modeled upon them.
Coleridge, as we have seen, even provided a new charter for the imagination. But the belief that poetry inhered in certain materials persisted.
Most of all, the poets distrusted the intellect.

The key to the problem lies in the new cult of simplicity. As we have
said in an earlier chapter, the neoclassic poets, too, had desired to be
simple. But they had wished to be simple in order to be logically clear.
They had even wished to be "natural," but their naturalness consisted
in an approximation to the inevitable and, since this was the eighteenth
century, the *logical* order of the world.

Romantic simplicity, on the other hand, was something quite
different from logical clarity. The emphasis had shifted from the logical
perspicuity of the poetry to the emotional lucidity of the poet. The
romantic poet distrusted the intellect as inimical to emotion and
destructive of spontaneity.

Wordsworth will illustrate. His distrust of the intellect and the subtleties of wit rarely allows him to make use of indirection in his poetry.
It is no accident, therefore, that many of his best poems are long. His
finest effects—as in *Michael*—are usually the result of the use of a
cumulative process rather than the use of a few, carefully selected
dramatic symbols.

We have already quoted Yeats's account of Wordsworth's characteristic limitation as an artist—that he lacks dramatic quality, and
because he lacks this, is often flat and heavy. "This," Yeats goes on to
say, "increases his popularity with the better kind of journalists and
politicians who have written books." Quite so. For a Wordsworth who
was consciously dramatic, a Wordsworth behind the mask, might
puzzle such readers—might have puzzled himself.

One of the most striking evidences of the inaccuracy of the traditional account of English poetry is seen in the ease with which Shelley
and Keats are paired. I do not mean to say that critics have not always
been aware of differences of method and effect between the two poets;
I have in mind differences of poetic caliber. The traditional historian
hardly sees Shelley as a very unsatisfactory poet greatly inferior to
Keats. A more considered view must surely hold him so.

Shelley is not merely guilty of poor craftsmanship—slovenly riming,
loosely decorative and sometimes too gaudy metaphor. Consideration

of the two poets on the basis of tone and attitude will reveal more important differences. Keats is rarely sentimental, Shelley frequently so. Keats is too much the artist to risk Shelley's sometimes embarrassing declarations—"I die, I faint, I fail," or "I fall upon the thorns of life! I bleed!" Keats, even in his apprentice stage, attempts to give his lyricism a restraining form; he maintains his objectivity as in "To Autumn"; he attempts a qualifying self-irony as in the "Ode to a Nightingale."

There is surely no attempt to turn Keats into a Donne, or, for that matter, into a Shakespeare or Milton, if one observes that his most mature poetry can be brought under the general principles of symbolist-metaphysical poetry. And if Shelley, measured by these principles, comes off rather badly, the issue may be more important than some readers will at first be willing to allow. For the charges of sentimentality, lack of proportion, confusion of abstract generalization with symbol, and confusion of propaganda with imaginative insight are not charges to be dismissed lightly.

Does it add any clarification to say with one of the popular histories of English poetry that Keats "worships beauty for beauty's sake, with none of the secondary moral intentions of . . . Shelley"? [Brooks's ellipses] Cannot the essential distinction between them be stated somewhat as follows: Shelley tends to make a point, to state a dogma, decking it with the beautiful and the ethereal. When his poetry fails, it fails through oversimplification or cloying floweriness. Keats, on the other hand, explores a particular experience—not as a favorite generalization to be beautified—but as an object to be explored in its full ramifications. Even the abstract statement, "Beauty is Truth, Truth Beauty—that is all / Ye know on earth," cannot be removed from the poem without violence. It is defined and given meaning only in terms of the context, and is taken legitimately only as a statement elicited by the preceding lines of the poem, and as one element in the whole experience. It is not intended to be a generalization which can march out of the poem and take its place alongside the scientific and practical generalizations of the workaday world.

Both Keats and Coleridge, indeed, are separated from their contemporaries by a reluctance to force didacticism. They respect the complexity of experience too much to violate it by oversimplification; the concrete, too much to indulge in easy abstractions. They think through their images. Instead of the formula employed by Shelley in his "Ode to a Skylark"—lush imagery followed by the abstract

> Our sweetest songs are those that tell
> of saddest thought . . .

Keats gives us the "Ode to a Nightingale." Instead of Wordsworth's rather flat generalization,

> The eye—it cannot choose but see;
> We cannot bid the ear be still;
> Our bodies feel, where'er they be,
> Against or with our will.
>
> Nor less I deem that there are Powers
> Which of themselves our minds impress;
> That we can feed this mind of ours
> In a wise passiveness. . . .

Coleridge, finding adequate symbols for the theme, gives us the *Rime of the Ancient Mariner*, and the mariner achieves in his experience a dramatic contact with those Powers. But what a difference between the *experience* which Wordsworth's lines abstract and summarize and that which Coleridge's symbolist poem transmits. The comparison is unfair to Wordsworth because it measures one of his inferior poems against Coleridge's best poem; but it may throw light on Wordsworth's typical method and may indicate why Coleridge's great poem so far exceeds the triviality of its apparent subject.

• • •

This sketch of a new history of English poetry since the Renaissance may well be regarded as an impertinence. Some of the judgments are trite; other, heretical. Moreover, its brevity allows no room for saving qualifications or convincing illustrations. It is frankly a sketch, but it may serve to suggest the general theory of the history of English poetry implied by the practice of the modern poets.

At the worst, at least this much may be said in its defense: the orthodox histories of English poetry do not offer a valid alternative. They will have to be rewritten—if not as expansion of the sketch just given, at least with more consistency than they now possess, and with emphasis on a more vital conception of the nature of poetry than that which now underlies them.

BIBLIOGRAPHICAL NOTE: With Brooks's position on romanticism should be compared T. E. Hulme's essay above, and T. S. Eliot's *The Sacred Wood* (London, 1920) and "Shelley and Keats" in his *The Use of Poetry and the Use of Criticism* (London, 1933); John Crowe Ransom's *The World's Body* (New York, 1938); Allen Tate's *Reactionary Essays* (New York, 1936) and *Reason in Madness* (New York, 1941). Defenses of the romantics, particularly Shelley, against the New Critics' attacks may be found in R. H. Fogle's essay below, and in Lorna Reynolds, "In Defense of Romanticism," *Dublin Magazine*, XXI (Oct.–Dec. 1946), 24–34; and F. A. Pottle, "The Case of Shelley," *PMLA*, LXVII (1952), 589–608. For a broader view of the "tradition" see B. Ifor Evans, *Tradition and Romanticism* (London, 1940).

Romantic Bards and Metaphysical Reviewers

Richard H. Fogle

The reputations of all the English romantic poets, and of Shelley in particular, have been vigorously attacked by an influential coterie of modern critics: the "New" Critics, as John Crowe Ransom has called them. They are too powerful to be ignored. They command respect because of their seriousness and their undoubted regard for the estate of poetry. They have, I think, succeeded in damaging Shelley seriously in the minds even of intelligent readers. The time seems ripe, therefore, for a detailed defense against their charges, lest the case be thought to have gone by default. Since their attack has been in the main centered upon romantic and especially Shelleyan imagery, I am accordingly devoting this article to an examination of this particular aspect of the controversy. In order to do so, however, it will be necessary first to give some account of the nature and development of the imaginal doctrine of the New Critics, so as to make clear the issues at stake. For the present purpose the men chiefly to be considered are T. S. Eliot, John Crowe Ransom, Allen Tate, F. R. Leavis, and Cleanth Brooks, with I. A. Richards indirectly figuring in the movement insofar as he furnishes the bases of its theory.

Romantic Bards and Metaphysical Reviewers: From *ELH*, XII, No. 3 (1945), 221–50. Reprinted by permission of The Johns Hopkins Press.

The attitude of the New Critics toward the romantics and toward Shelley is foreshadowed in T. E. Hulme's tentative but highly significant "Romanticism and Classicism,"* an opening gun against the English poets of the early nineteenth century. . . . In this account there are several points of special significance. First to be noticed is the sweeping contemptuousness of Hulme's attitude toward romanticism. He formulates an extremely narrow and rigid definition, epigrammatic and denunciatory to the detriment of candor. Although at the outset he warns the reader that he is using the terms "romanticism" and "classicism" in a limited and special sense, he permits them throughout his essay to assume a general significance. He confesses that there are other things in the poetry of the romantics besides the qualities which he condemns, but the general effect of his remarks is implicitly damaging to the men themselves.

Of interest, too, is his assertion that the justification of poetry lies in its accurate delineation of things and experiences, which it is able to do because it speaks a visual, concrete language, almost a substitute for the intuition of the things and experiences themselves. There is the germ here of a theory of poetry as knowledge, which as formulated by Hulme one need not be very far gone in idealism to protest against. In the first place, he assumes that all sensory images are visual: an assumption obviously false. Second, and more important, such a view as this deprives poetry of its significance and individuality. If poetry is a substitute for consciousness itself, by which we intuit things and experiences, what reason is there for reading it? It can in that case only do poorly what we ourselves can do supremely well. A word is not, after all, equivalent to a thing.

The implications of this theory of imagery are that poetry ought to occupy itself with objects, and that the nature of these objects does not really matter, at any rate qualitatively. Practically, they should be small, with definite limits, so as to present the minimum of difficulty to perception. Hulme predicts that the new poetry will be "cheerful, dry, and sophisticated," in keeping with the finite quality of its subject matter.

It is noticeable that Hulme's distaste for romanticism is in some measure due to what he regards as its monism. The classicist will be dualistic; he will not seek to impose a factitious unity upon the natural

* Hulme's essay appears in this collection.

world. In the brilliant series of detached aphorisms collected under the name of "Cinders" he declares that there is no comprehensive scheme of the cosmos, that all is flux, and that "only in the fact of consciousness is there a unity of the world." Elsewhere he divides the world into two parts: "cinders," and "the part built up." Taken together with his explicit utterances upon imagery, these pronouncements suggest, I believe, an artistic preoccupation with the single image and a relative indifference to the unity of the whole, in keeping with his general *Weltanschauung*.

Hulme expresses for the first time in English an attitude and a set of beliefs about romanticism, poetry, and imagery which become part and parcel of the work of his successors. His ideas recur in a greater or less degree in the criticism of all of them. His attitude toward the romantics, for example, his love of definiteness and concreteness in imagery, and his desire for "a period of dry, hard, classical verse," are all apparent in the essays of T. S. Eliot.

Hulme's attitude is faithfully reproduced in Eliot's superbly supercilious judgment upon romanticism:

> . . . the only cure for romanticism is to analyse it. What is permanent and good in romanticism is curiosity . . . a curiosity which recognises that any life, if accurately and profoundly penetrated, is interesting and always strange. Romanticism is a short cut to the strangeness without the reality, and it leads its disciples only back upon themselves. . . . there may be a good deal to be said for romanticism in life, there is no place for it in letters.[1]

In Eliot is the same narrowness of definition, the same epigrammatic brilliance, the same over-awing certainty that one finds in Hulme. So confident is the tone, so nervous and closepacked the expression, that one is inclined to take this statement for more than it is. Actually it is a definition in a vacuum, without referents; what, where, and how extensive is the romanticism of which Eliot is thinking?

Eliot's liking for hard precision and concreteness in imagery is evident in his doctrine of "the objective correlative," and in such a comparison as he makes between Morris's "The Nymph's Song to Hylas" and Marvell's "The Nymph and the Fawn": "the effect of Morris's charming poem depends upon the mistiness of the feeling and

---

[1] *The Sacred Wood* (London, 1920), pp. 31–32. [The ellipses are Fogle's.]

the vagueness of its object; the effect of Marvell's upon its bright, hard precision. . . . A curious result of the comparison of Morris's poem with Marvell's is that the former, though it appears to be more serious, is found to be the slighter. . ."[2] [Fogle's ellipses].

Akin to Hulme's demand for poetry which shall be "cheerful, dry, and sophisticated" is Eliot's defense of wit, a quality without which he deems poetry incomplete. "It involves, probably, a recognition, implicit in the expression of every experience, of other kinds of experience which are possible, which we find as clearly in the greatest as in poets like Marvell." Wit furnishes an "internal equilibrium" not to be found in the poets after the seventeenth century; particularly not to be found in the great romantics.*

Eliot's greatest contribution to the New Criticism, "the unified sensibility," is, however, a complete departure from the ideas of Hulme. In his important essay on "The Metaphysical Poets" Eliot suggested a view of literary history and a criterion for poetry which were later extended and systematized by others. The metaphysical poets of the seventeenth century, along with many of the late Elizabethan and Jacobean dramatists, possessed a unity of sensibility, "a mechanism of sensibility which could devour any kind of experience." Through the influence of two powerful poets, Milton and Dryden, this unity was lost. The metaphysicals, however, were in the direct current of English poetry, not those who followed. Judged by this standard of sensibility, the eighteenth and nineteenth centuries were found wanting. Thought and feeling were separated. "The poets revolted against the ratiocinative, the descriptive; they thought and felt by fits, unbalanced; they reflected." To a poet like Donne, however, "A thought . . . was an experience; it modified his sensibility."

At this point Eliot proposes a definition of the proper psychology for the poet which we find reflected again and again in later critics:

> When a poet's mind is properly equipped for its work, it is constantly amalgamating disparate experience; the ordinary man's experience is chaotic, irregular, fragmentary. The latter falls in love, or reads Spinoza, and these two experiences have nothing to do with each other, or with the noise of the typewriter or the smell of cooking; in the mind of the poet these experiences are always forming new wholes.

[2] *Homage to John Dryden* (London, 1927), p. 26 [all references to Eliot in Fogle's discussion of the metaphysical poets are to this work, pp. 26–46.]

* For an account of the "tradition of wit" see Cleanth Brooks's essay above.

Closely allied to this statement is his shrewd remark on Johnson's condemnation of the metaphysical poets for "yoking the most hetero-geneous ideas by violence together."

> The force of this impeachment [says Eliot] lies in the failure of the con-junction, the fact that often the ideas are yoked but not united. . . . But a degree of heterogeneity of material compelled into unity is omnipresent in poetry.

Akin to this remark, with its emphasis upon heterogeneity, is his observation about the probable nature of the poetry of the future. This poetry, in his opinion, will be difficult and complex:

> Our civilisation comprehends great variety and complexity, and this variety and complexity, playing upon a refined sensibility, must become more and more comprehensive, more allusive, more indirect, in order to force, to dislocate if necessary, language into his meaning.

It is to be assumed, on the strength of these quotations, that good poetic imagery is likely to be heterogeneous in material, comprehen-sive, and difficult, but unified by the amalgamating power of the poet's mind.

• • •

Mr. Eliot's apologia for the metaphysical poets performed a valuable service to readers of poetry in helping to return to favor a group which had suffered long and undeserved neglect. Unfortunately, in so doing he suggests a whole æsthetic and theory of literary history, dangerously narrow and intolerant in its implications if taken literally. The breadth of outlook which he advocates for poetry he rigidly excludes from his criticism. And his stimulating but tentative pronouncements harden into dogma as the New Criticism proceeds.

The doctrine of poetry and of imagery which in Eliot appears as "unified sensibility" or "heterogeneity of material compelled into unity by the operation of the poet's mind" is more elaborately formu-lated by I. A. Richards, upon whose work most of the New Critics draw heavily. Professor Richards divides poetry into "Synthetic" and "Exclu-sive," a classification roughly correspondent to the "unified" and "divided" sensibility of Eliot. In Synthetic Poetry there is an "equili-brium of opposed impulses, which we suspect to be the groundplan of the most valuable æsthetic responses." The distinction between Exclu-sive and Synthetic Poetry is as follows:

A poem of the first group is built out of sets of impulses which run parallel, which have the same direction. In a poem of the second group the most obvious feature is the extraordinary heterogeneity of the distinguishable impulses. But they are more than heterogeneous, they are opposed. They are such that in ordinary, nonpoetic, nonimaginative experience, one or other set would be suppressed to give as it might appear freer development to the others.[3]

From this distinction Richards evolves his theory of Irony. To him Exclusive Poetry is sentimental poetry, incomplete in its view of life and open to attack by irony. Synthetic Poetry, being itself ironic, is invulnerable:

> Irony in this sense consists in the bringing in of the opposite; the complementary impulses; that is why poetry which is exposed to it is not of the highest order, and why irony itself is so constantly a characteristic of poetry which is.

This principle of irony is apotheosized under the name of Synæsthesis as the ultimate æsthetic experience, as Beauty itself, in *Foundations of Æsthetics*. Synæsthesis is an equilibrium and harmony of various impulses, bringing into play all the faculties. By this equilibrium and harmony "we are enabled to appreciate relationships in a way which would not be possible under normal circumstances. Through no other experience can the full richness and complexity of our environment be realized."[4]

Richards then elaborates a conception of poetry and of poetic imagery closely parallel to the more tentative and fragmentary notions of Eliot. Although he is not primarily interested in assaying by means of it the value of specific poets, his examples are so chosen as to be implicitly damaging to the romantics, especially to Shelley. His views support the conception of English literary history proposed by Eliot.

Richards's Irony is frankly derivative from Coleridge's theory of the Imagination,[5] in which opposite or discordant qualities are reconciled, a more than usual state of emotion is conjoined with more than usual order, and judgment and self-possession are combined with

[3] *Principles of Literary Criticism* (New York, 1924), p. 250.

[4] C. K. Ogden, I. A. Richards, and James Wood, *The Foundations of Æsthetics* (London, 1925), p. 91.

[5] See Richards, *Coleridge on Imagination* (London, 1934).

enthusiasm and feeling. There is, however, a significant difference of emphasis. Coleridge would reconcile opposites in an organic synthesis of emotion and order, judgment and feeling. In Richards the synthesizing elements are slighted, the discordant and opposing materials emphasized. It is the opposition and heterogeneity itself upon which his attention is focussed, and aside from a vague hint of "poetic and imaginative experience" the balancing and harmonizing is left to take care of itself. The reader is left with the notion that the important thing in poetic imagery is not the synthesizing into unity, but the discordance and heterogeneity of the materials to be synthesized. Eliot, I think, has put his finger on the vital point in commenting upon Johnson's criticism of the metaphysical poets. "Heterogeneous ideas" are often yoked without being united.

The concept of Irony, or heterogeneity, or "unified sensibility" is the basic tenet of the New Criticism. Obviously it calls for complexity and heterogeneity of elements in poetic imagery. Richards's theory of the infinite flexibility and variety of words according to their context and situation has had a like effect. Richards also, like Hulme and Eliot, prefers verse to be urbane, social, and easy in tone: a preference which has had its influence upon later critics. I believe that I do not distort his intention by saying that this urbanity of tone is with him a standard of judgment, and that it is very close to what Eliot means by "wit." It is closely linked with the theory of irony, in which harmony and calm result from an equilibrium of opposed elements. It implies a certain dandyism and imperturbability, a refusal to be disturbed by inconvenient and excessive emotions. Like Eliot, Professor Richards finds this quality absent in the romantics.

In the criticism of John Crowe Ransom and Allen Tate one finds the same general view of literary history as Eliot's; the same love of complexity and heterogeneity in imagery as in Eliot and Richards; the same demand for dry urbanity of tone.* One finds in them also, however, a preoccupation with form unexampled even in Eliot, an exclusive and intransigent æstheticism. Poetry to them is an absolute substance, related to the affairs of the world only at several removes. It "finds its true usefulness in its perfect inutility." It is "the art of apprehending and concentrating our experience in the mysterious limitations

---

* Fogle's discussion here is based on, and his quotations are from, John Crowe Ransom, *The World's Body* (New York, 1938); and Allen Tate, *Reactionary Essays* (New York, 1936), and *Reason in Madness* (New York, 1941).

of form." The objective reality of poetry is in its formal qualities, which
it is therefore the chief business of the critic to examine. Poetry, however, gives us the only complete knowledge of the world, "that unique
and formed intelligence of the world of which man alone is capable."

To Ransom and Tate romantic poetry is imperfect poetry because
it attempts to communicate ideas, because it employs mass language,
the only effective means of communication, and because it is "associa-
tionist," vaguely musical, cloudy, and "pretty." The best poetry, and
the best imagery, is complex and ironic, "metaphysical." In the words
of Tate, "The poet attains to a mastery over experience by facing its
utmost implications. There is the clash of powerful opposites." Ransom
speak approvingly of the deliberate obscurity of Tate's poem, "Death of
Little Boys"; to him complexity is an absolute value. A poem is "nothing short of a desperate ontological or metaphysical manoeuvre."
"The kind of poetry which interests us," he declares, speaking as it
were for the New Critics *en masse*, "is not the act of a child . . . but the
act of a fallen mind, since ours too are fallen." In other words, such a
poetry must be ironic; world-weary, yet mocking at its own weariness.
The antithesis of this is romanticism. "The poetry I am disparaging is
. . . the poetry written by romantics, in a common sense of that term."
Romantic poetry is also to be condemned because it is "Platonic." It
is "allegory, a discourse in things, but on the understanding that they
are translatable at every point into ideas."

Applied specifically to the problem of poetic imagery, the theories
of Ransom and Tate correspond approximately with the ideas of
Hulme and Eliot, and in a lesser degree with those of I.A. Richards.
They take over the attitude toward the romantics, the doctrine of
"unified sensibility" or "irony," with its corollary of heterogeneity of
poetic materials, almost unaltered. Their view of poetry as knowledge
is very close to Hulme's "poetry of things," and Eliot's "objective correlative," and is open to the same objections. Ransom, in commenting
upon Aristotle, declares, like Hulme, that the accurate description of
things is enough for poetry; that the end of art is an infinite degree of
particularity. He sees the difficulty, but deals with it in a fashion entirely
inadequate. The realism of technique thus to be employed is not "pho-
tographic," but "psychological." The value and the distinction of the
artistic process lie in the pains lavished by the artist upon technique.
But this technique, by Ransom's account of it, is an isolated entity
related neither to subject or object. He tells us nothing either of the
consciousness of the artist by which the thing is perceived, or in what

manner words are able to express the essential qualities of things. Tate is more cautious, less willing to commit himself. He goes no further than the statement that poetry is *complete* knowledge, knowledge of whole objects, unlike the limited knowledge offered us by the positivist sciences. Beyond this essentially negative pronouncement he offers little.

The basic flaw in the criticism of Ransom and Tate, in their approach specifically to Shelley, is its absolutism. They are well on their way toward transforming a set of interesting but essentially ungrounded and provisional insights, attitudes, and reactions into critical absolutes. They mistake their own speculations, often acute but always limited in validity, for truths of universal application. They establish categories, and these categories suddenly become independent, fixed, and permanent. They generalize with astounding haste. Like T. E. Hulme, they formulate a definition of romanticism, for example, which they at first intend to be limited to a single context; but end by applying it indiscriminately to vast tracts of poetry and legions of poets. Consequently they are at their worst, in spite of their unprecedented emphasis on close reading, when they are dealing with the individual phenomenon of a poem by a poet to whom they are theoretically and temperamentally opposed, and who had the misfortune of being born in the wrong period.

[Fogle here summarizes and answers some New Critical attacks upon Shelley's poetry, particularly Tate's in *Reason in Madness*; F. R. Leavis's in *Revaluation* (London, 1936); and Ransom's in *The World's Body*. He argues that these attacks are completely arbitrary, devised for poets whom the critics dislike, using methods which would never be used against such poets as Donne, Hopkins, or Eliot, whom they generally admire. He further argues that the methods of analysis used by such critics are based upon confusion of "poetry with representation, as if words were absolute, mirrorlike reflections of the visible world."]

In Cleanth Brooks's *Modern Poetry and the Tradition** the doctrines of the New Criticism are hardened and set in a fully developed and rounded system. Drawing heavily upon Eliot, Richards, Ransom, and Tate, Professor Brooks rationalizes and sets in order their views upon poetic imagery, æsthetics, and literary history in a single coherent structure. The true "tradition," as one might guess, is the tradition of metaphysical wit and complexity. Following Eliot and possibly

---

* Unless otherwise indicated, all quotations from Brooks here are from this work, a selection from which appears above.

Basil Willey* he traces its downfall to Hobbes and the scientific rationalism of the late seventeenth century, and hails its resurgence in the moderns of the twentieth.

Romanticism he finds unsatisfactory both in theory and in practice. The romantics attempted to break loose from the bonds of eighteenth century neoclassicism, but failed to go far enough. Instead of repudiating completely the eighteenth-century belief in the inherent beauty and poetic value of certain types of objects, they merely substituted other objects. By denying the importance of the intellect in poetry in favor of emotion and spontaneity they fell into the fallacy of dissociating the elements of poetic sensibility. The modern poet and theorist, on the other hand, resposes his confidence in the power of his imagination, which fuses and harmonizes disparate, incongruous, and apparently unattactive materials into unity. He does not make the error of distinguishing fancy from imagination, wit from high poetry.

In a separate essay Professor Brooks joins Ransom and Tate in condemning "the fallacy of communication." The poem itself is "the linguistic vehicle which conveys the thing most clearly and accurately"; therefore it is erroneous to attempt to abstract its ideas in order to understand it. The poet employs the methods characteristic of poetry: indirection, "the use of symbol rather than abstraction, suggestion rather explicit pronouncement, metaphor rather than direct statement."[6] In a later article Brooks declares that paradox is the very stuff of poetry.[7]

Since Brooks applies specifically to Shelley his strictures against romantic theory in general, it is appropriate to examine these a little more at length. He attributes to the romantics a doctrine of the inherent beauty of poetic objects which he has found in Addison, relating it to romanticism on the strength of a single ambiguous remark of Wordsworth: "Fancy depends upon the rapidity . . . with which she scatters her thoughts and images; trusting that their number, and the felicity with which they are linked together, will make amends for the want of individual value." It seems less than fair to saddle the romantics with the naïveté of Addison's pioneering essays in æsthetics, especially as Wordsworth devoted his famous 1800 Preface to the *Lyrical Ballads* to declaring that he meant something quite different.

The principal object . . . [says Wordsworth] proposed in these Poems

[6] "What Does Modern Poetry Communicate," *American Prefaces* (Autumn, 1940), pp. 25, 27.

[7] "The Language of Paradox," *The Language of Poetry* (Princeton, 1942).

* In *The Seventeenth Century Background* (London, 1924).

> was to choose incidents and situations from common life, and to relate
> or describe them throughout, as far as was possible, in a selection of
> language really used by men, and at the same time, to throw over them
> a certain colouring of imagination, whereby ordinary things should be
> presented to the mind in an unusual aspect.

The passage seems to me to suggest that Wordsworth is relying very little upon the inherent qualities of his material, and very much upon the powers of his imagination.

Professor Brooks is to some extent the victim of his own terminology; his use of the phrase, "poetic objects," misleads him. In support of his thesis he cites Coleridge's remark on a figure of Cowley's: "Surely, no unusual taste is requisite to see clearly, that this compulsory juxtaposition is not produced by the presentation of impressive or delightful forms to the inward vision. . . . " To Coleridge, however, these "impressive and delightful forms" are subjective, not objective. He does not fall into the error of confusing poetry with the objects and forms of nature.

Brooks's examples of the separation of emotion and intellect in romantic theory are equally unconvincing. He finds in Wordsworth "warrant for the view that the play of the intellect is inimical to deep emotion" only by adding his own "implied antithesis." He is somewhat hasty in using Wordsworth's definition of poetry as "a spontaneous overflow of emotion" for the same purpose, since Wordsworth continues, "and though this be true, Poems to which any value can be attached were never produced on any variety of subjects but by a man who, being possessed of more than usual organic sensibility, had also thought long and deeply." One would say that the relation between emotion and intellect here suggested was rather intimate.

The application of these statements to Shelley is as follows: Shelley, in the opinion of Professor Brooks, occupies much too high a place in the ranks of the English poets. . . . Shelley is condemned, first, for "loosely decorative" and "sometimes too gaudy" metaphor. Since Brooks offers no evidence of these poetical sins in Shelley, the assertion is somewhat difficult to cope with. The accusation of "loosely decorative metaphor" is clearly based, however, on the objection of the New Critics to "communication," and of "gaudiness" on the critic's dislike of the doctrine of the inherent beauty of poetic objects, which he attributes to romantic theory.

Now, of his refusal to permit poetry to "communicate," one may say that it is salutary insofar as it demands of the poet conscientious artistic effort, but that in theory it is too narrow, since direct statement may itself contribute to the sum-total of poetic effect, which is conceptual as well as emotional and sensuous; and that in practice it is positively baneful, since it encourages the poet to make a fetish of unintelligibility. James Russell Lowell in the *Fable for Critics* says of Emerson that he builds beautiful temples, but leaves no door to get into them. The New Criticism would leave no door for the reader to get into the poem. In *The World's Body*, for example, John Crowe Ransom praises Allen Tate for retiring into private imagery in the second stanza of "Death of Little Boys," after in the first stanza having hovered on the verge of hinting that there was something tragic about little boys dying. Faced with an exclusiveness so magnificent what can the reader do but retire in embarrassment, ashamed of his momentary desire to intrude upon it?

The New Critical doctrine of imagery which Professor Brooks is employing here maintains that imagery is functional and organic, that poetry works by means of images. The poet must not depart from the artistic working out of images into direct statement. Since the metaphor of the metaphysical poets is most functional and least detachable from their poems, they wrote the best type of poetry. The writers of romantic poetry, however, in the opinion of Brooks, were led astray by a fallacious belief that imagery was an extrinsic and external decoration, not an integral part of the poem in which it occurs. Romantic imagery, therefore, lacks the courage of its convictions. It is half-way, half-hearted, unlike metaphysical imagery.

As a matter of fact the great romantics held no such theory as Professor Brooks imputes to them. Keats required that "the rise, the progress, the setting of imagery should like the Sun come natural." Wordsworth declared that good imagery arises naturally from poetic feeling:

> if the Poet's subject be judiciously chosen, it will naturally, and upon fit occasion, lead him to passions, the language of which, if selected truly and judiciously, must necessarily be dignified and variegated, and alive with metaphors and figures.

In commenting upon Wordsworth's Preface Coleridge referred to the highest poetry as "the natural language of impassioned feeling." Finally Shelley regarded metaphor as the very essence of poetry. The language of poets, said he, is vitally metaphorical; that is, it marks the before unapprehended relations of things and perpetuates their apprehension, until the words which represent them become, through time, signs for portions or classes of thoughts instead of pictures of integral thoughts; and then if no new poets should arise to create afresh the associations which have thus been disorganized, language will be dead to all the nobler purposes of human intercourse.

While charging, incorrectly as I think, the romantics with a dualist theory of imagery, the New Critics themselves fall into difficulties. They give no account of imagery, making implicitly an absolute distinction between image and idea in poetry which leads back to the over-simplified "poetry of things" of T. E. Hulme, as well as to his dualism. They mingle in their criticism "imagery" in its psychological sense and "metaphor" as a logical process, failing to differentiate between them, so that they find themselves demanding simultaneously from poetry the clearest and most detailed representation and the most elaborate logic, the while insisting that poetry is not logical at all. The ultimate result of their doctrine is the anomaly of finding that poetry and imagery are synonymous, without being able to account for imagery itself. Thus Professor Brooks accuses Shelley of "loosely decorative metaphor" in the light of his own absolute distinction between "things" and "idea," "image" and "statement," whereas Shelley fuses the two in his definition of metaphors as "pictures of integral thoughts." Shelley's conception, I think, is the more truly organic.

The allegation that Shelley's metaphor is "too gaudy," since it is unsupported, can be answered simply by the statement that Shelley uses color and brightness in his poetry functionally, in relation to the total meaning he desires to convey. He does not splash his canvases indiscriminately with the hues of the rainbow. The "gaudiest" passage which I recall in Shelley is from the beginning of Act II in *Prometheus Unbound*:

> The point of one white star is quivering still
> Deep in the orange light of widening morn
> Beyond the purple mountains; through a chasm
> Of wind-divided mist the darker lake
> Reflects it; now it wanes; it gleams again
> As the waves fade, and as the burning threads
> Of woven cloud unravel in pale air;
> 'Tis lost! and through yon peaks of cloud-like snow

The roseate sunlight quivers; hear I not
The Aeolian music of her sea-green plumes
Winnowing the crimson dawn?

This lavish use of color is justifiable both naturalistically and symbolically. As representation it is faithful to the brilliance of a mountain-
dawn, while as symbol it presents in radiant hues the opening of the
day of deliverence for Prometheus and for mankind, contrasting the
vivid and joyous coloring of full daylight to the night of ignorance and
bondage which slowly fades away.

As to the distinction made by Professor Brooks between the "tone"
and "attitude" of Shelley and Keats, these terms are meaningless when
considered as independent and absolute. One may admit them as
elements in terms of which a poem may be described and distinguished
from other poems, so long as the presence of other elements is not
ignored; but apart from the poem which gives them being they have no
existence, and they can have no standing as criteria for qualitative
judgment. A poet has a "tone" and an "attitude" only in relation to his
poetic materials. Shelley is "sentimental" in the eyes of Brooks because
he sometimes makes direct, subjective statements, and Brooks is rigidly
committed to the view that poetry never states, that it is always dramatic, impersonal, and concrete. Therefore he complains of "Shelley's
sometimes embarrassing declarations." Taken from its context, "I die,
I faint, I fail," etc., is somewhat startling. But this statement must be
considered in relation to the poem in which it occurs. Brooks himself
has declared that the assertions made by the poet must be "a quality of
the whole poem," and that "the terms of the poem work and have their
meaning" only in the total context of the poem."[8] If one returns "I die, I
faint, I fail," to its context it proves to be perfectly in keeping with its
surroundings, and, to the hardy, not at all embarrassing. Shelley has
written in "The Indian Serenade," from which the line comes, a slight
but pleasant love-poem, integral and artistic in design, but admittedly
of no great consequence. The lover who speaks is uttering the conventional sentiments belonging to his situation. Professor Brooks elsewhere
attacks "The Indian Serenade" at length,[9] but his summary judgment

[8] "The Poem as Organism," *English Institute Annual* (New York, 1940), p. 37.
[9] *Understanding Poetry* (New York, 1938), pp. 320–23.

of Shelley is unsupported by any analysis of Shelley's really significant poetry.

For the most part Shelley receives even worse treatment than this from the New Critics. He is generally condemned without even a show of evidence. In a well-known and extremely influential essay, "Shelley and Keats," T. S. Eliot explains that he cannot stomach Shelley's verse, but he expends very little effort upon explaining why, devoting his attention instead to an honest but abortive attempt to expound the relation of belief to poetry. Mr. Eliot probably established some sort of record in criticism by writing an essay on Shelley and Keats with only casual reference to their verse.

One cannot quarrel with Mr. Eliot for having opinions. One ought not, perhaps, even to insist upon his grounding these opinions more firmly in critical, æsthetic, and psychological theory; we should not ask for everything. His criticism is the work of an original and sensitive mind, although it is also the work of a dilettante. But when his casual and tentative judgments are seized upon as dogma by over-hasty and zealous followers the need for protest is patent.

[Fogle's "protest" here extends to an attack on the doctrine of irony and unified sensibility, which he says "has become a Procrustean bed in which poetry is arbitrarily stretched or lopped off." Shelley he sees as "closer to carrying out their doctrines than the New Critics themselves, fusing and reconciling opposing and disparate elements, grappling "with the totality of his thought and experience" with a "really 'unified sensibility,' " using irony but not merely as a "conscious attitude," and employing a language not "loosely decorative" but "vitally metaphorical."]

By the doctrine of Irony the New Critics claim to have reunited emotion and intellect, which the eighteenth century and the romantics had divided. Actually they have drawn them farther apart than ever. They have banished emotion completely, although giving her lip-service, so that only intellect remains, mutilated by this forcible separation. Instead of liberating the imagination, they have done away with it. They have proposed materials for poetry, "opposing impulses," "conflicting attitudes," but have left these oppositions and conflicts to "reconcile" and "harmonize" themselves, without formulating any agency of mind to act upon them. Only I. A. Richards has suggested a hypothesis, and his account of the imaginative process is frankly mythical and incomplete. The theory of irony, which descends directly from Coleridge's account of imagination, is a distorted and withered version of its forebear. . . .

• • •

Conceiving of poetry in the last analysis as a disjunctive series of metaphors existing in a void, and committed to a simplistic naturalism which draws an absolute distinction between the thing and the idea, the New Critics are unfitted for dealing with a poetry like Shelley's, in which form and content, thought and emotion, thing and idea, are truly and imaginatively conjoined.

BIBLIOGRAPHICAL NOTE: For a survey of the New-Critical controversy over romanticism see *The English Romantic Poets: A Review of Research*, ed. T. M. Raysor (New York, 1956), pp. 31–34, and R. H. Fogle, "The Romantic Movement," in *Contemporary Literary Scholarship*, ed. L. Leary (New York, 1968), pp. 111–12, 115–16. See also the bibliographical note to the Brooks essay above, pp. 147–48.

The Ideology
of Romanticism

Alex Comfort

[The] . . . terms, "classic" and "romantic," stand for more than differences of style. The classic sees man as master, the romantic sees him as victim of his environment. That seems to me to be the real difference. I regard the periods of English literature as an alternation between these two concepts. It is as if the awareness of death, the factor which, at root, determines the degree to which we feel masters of our circumstances, ebbed and flowed, alternately emphasised and obscured as a factor in interpretative art. The classical periods are periods of economic and mental security, when the drive is towards action and where the majority of the people is in possession of a satisfactory interpretation of the universe and of themselves, religious or political (it can be either). They are periods during which the burden of realising and interpreting the most ghastly of all conflicts, between the man's and the artist's desperate desire for permanence, and factual death which he discovers, falls upon individual shoulders. These artists, standing in a period of general complacency, are the major poets—frequently psychopathic, since their insecurity is endogenous. The Victorian period

THE IDEOLOGY OF ROMANTICISM: From *Art and Social Responsibility*: *Lectures on the Ideology of Romanticism* (London: The Falcon Press, 1946).

165

was one such, and it produced its Arnolds and Mark Rutherfords who agonised as much quantitatively if not qualitatively within the structure of the times as did Rilke or Thompson, or Unamuno and Lorca in contemporary Europe.

The active periods with their extroverted public alternate with ages when the realisation of the Tragic Sense becomes general, spreads over continents, reaches men who are conscious only of being afraid. There are no major poets, because what they have to say, everybody already knows. The times need not revealers but concealers, a hierarchy of men who will hide the truth of death from humanity, or life becomes empty. I am convinced that a large part of cultural barbarism arises from this source. Perhaps this is the true failure of nerve. Major poetry is the vicarious function of the single artist—he takes the weight of tragic awareness to shield the rest of humanity from it. I rather doubt if ever in history there have been so many who realised the emotional fact of death. Megalopolitan civilisation is living under a death sentence. That has become a personal realisation over great areas of the world. We are at the turn of a major period of classicism (Victorian) which produced major romantic poets, and finally classical poets using the husk of romantic technique. Slack water was at about 1900, and suddenly the face of social disintegration and personal death began to be seen by more and more people. The private knowledge of the Dostoievskys and Unamunos of the past was becoming general. A numb silence fell on everyone, except Monro and his Georgians, who could not understand what was happening and shouted to fill the gap. There were few attempts to reinstate a classical, secure approach. The imagists wrote with increasing tragic awareness. The socialist poets attempted to deny the awareness and to turn to society, but in Spain the face of the unpleasant black figure was unveiled. The poets went out to fight, taking Marx with them, and came back with Unamuno and Lorca. It was then that the dialectical-historical approach became hollow. In some strange fashion the same knowledge, unconditioned by history, was growing up in innumerable childhoods—Dylan Thomas knew it early in life, long before the Spanish defeat. Art does not move always by sudden transition—Steiner's concept of the *Zeitgeist* is truer than it looks. The transition is a matter of relative numbers who reach a viewpoint together, independently. Artists reflect it now only because it is the general temper of the public.

The awareness of death, the quasi-priestly but secular attitude, are omnipresent for anyone who knows contemporary English art and letters. No artist of my generation is uninfluenced by them. I should make it clear that I do not wish to argue for them, only to state that they are here. The new climate is a thing into which we grew up. The ideas that lie behind it are . . . these.

1. That there is no correspondence between the physical essence of the universe and the psychological and so-called "spiritual" aspirations of man—that no human activity can be said to have "permanent" or "absolute" significance, and that ethics and æsthetics exist because we make them and assert them, not in conformity with Platonic absolutes but in the teeth of material reality. That the common enemy of man is Death, that the common tie of man is ultimate victimhood, and that anyone who, in attempting to escape the realisation of that victimhood in himself, increases its incidence upon others, is a traitor to humanity and an ally of Death.

2. That history, in so far as it is the history of power, is not to be regarded as a steady progress in any direction, whether moral or political, e.g., towards civilisation, goodness, socialism, but as an oscillation about a fixed point, a series of self-limiting ecological changes, an ebb and flow between certain fixed limits which have not within human record been exceeded. We see it as a fluctuating conflict between biological freedom and power. One cannot suggest on the recorded evidence that man is either "morally better" (however that be defined) or politically more capable of forming a society which does not involve the abuse of power. His achievement fluctuates sufficiently for one to be able to say that democracy is "better"—i.e., more humane or less exacting— than fascism, or that the Greece of 450 B.C. was preferable to the Rome of A.D. 50, but the statement that absolute qualitative change has taken place between 500 B.C. and A.D. 1943 is without meaning for us. Such comparisons are in themselves historically meaningless. We do not believe that irresponsible society now is any less of an evil than irresponsible society then, or society when Godwin saw it. Every society based upon power is, to us, vitiated by that fact, whoever the rulers may be, and where free communities have come into existence their freedom has to be constantly asserted, or they degenerate slowly or rapidly into the adoption of power. In other words, the recurrent tendency of society is to degenerate into barbarism. We accept this hypothesis for the same reason that we call the tendency to live between fifty and eighty years a human property—evidence tends to suggest that in

a majority of cases it is factually true. One does not detect the tendency
so freely in individuals as the Adlerians would lead us to believe—it
is not a question of individual lust-for-power, but a different property,
belonging to masses, and able to vitiate the most enlightened decisions.
It seems that in any society, acting as a society, once responsibility and
mutual aid are submerged, the constructive impulses tend to cancel out,
and the negative and destructive summate. This is as true of the Communist Party as it is of feudal Poland or the Roman Empire. It is as
though we were to have a boat full of blindfold rowers. They pull in
different directions, and no progress is made, but the weights of the
crew add up, and she sinks. There is a good deal of argument possible
whether education can in any degree remedy this tendency. One can
call it original sin if one wishes.* I do not care what name I give it—
for me as an artist it is real, the most real feature of society in all ages.
It is possible that, in reality, it is a feature of the collapse-phase only—
certainly its recognition is—yet all ages speak of deterioration as a
journey *down* hill. Social conduct is described as harder than its opposite. It is no new idea. But the state of irresponsibility once reached, the
viciousness of an organisation tends to be proportional to its size.
Democracy in a barbarian state is a priori impossible, because it
involves the refusal to admit that the majority is never right. Fascism
is the attempt to summate the destructive impulses and to use them as
a basis for a society. It teaches that the individual is unreal, and therefore death, the termination of the individual, is unreal also. If this
does not explain the genuine satisfaction which all authoritarian societies give to their adherents, then I have misunderstood society. But I
have no use for a Swedenborgian Hell by common consent. One
cannot propel the boat by the weight of its rowers.

Romanticism is our ideology. It is based upon a metaphysical theory.
The most serious difficulty in the discussion of romanticism and its
place in sociological and literary criticism is the progressive loss of
meaning which critical illiteracy has inflicted on the name itself.
Romanticism is not a stylistic term, and the criterion of its application
is not how the subject writes, but what he believes—otherwise we
might find it difficult to explain the clarity and definition with which
we can speak of romantic painting, romantic poetry, romantic sculp-

---

* Cf. T. E. Hulme's characterization of original sin as "sane classical dogma,"
the romantic view of man as "intrinsically good, spoilt by circumstance" (p. 57 above).

ture, and romantic music, with equal readiness and an exact correspondence in the quality described.* It has become fashionable to
deride any attempt to relate artistic criticism to cosmological theory,
except among those who confuse mystical speculation with metaphysics.
To attempt such a relation is one of the stigmata which characterizes
"loss of nerve" in the eyes of the neoclassicists. But without coherent
metaphysics art is no more a comprehensible activity than travel without a sense of direction. The nature of reality is the first concern not
only of poetry but of intelligent biology or political ethics, and the only
claim of romanticism to the status of an ideology, and a historically
valid ideology, lies in the coherence of its metaphysics, and its root in
observed fact.

The romantic believes that the particular qualities which make
up humanness—mind, purpose, consciousness, will, personality—are
unique in known phylogeny, and are so far at variance with the
physical conditions in which man exists that they are irrelevant to the
general structure of physical reality. Christian and pagan metaphysicians of opposing ideologies (including the Marxists, who believe in
historical inevitability) have contended either that Man was made in
God's image, in which case ethical obligation corresponded with the
nature of a Creator, or that the Universe was made in Man's image,
and that some of the values to which human individuals tend to aspire
(beauty, goodness, or order) were incorporated in the physical universe
itself. The distinguishing feature of the metaphysical theory which
underlies romanticism is that it rejects the inevitable victory or in-
herence of these ideals without rejecting the ideals themselves. They
exist only so long as Man himself exists and fights for them. The entire
romantic ethic and body of art rests upon this assumption of insecurity,
an insecurity which begins at the personal level of mortality, and
extends into all the intellectual fields where insecurity is least tolerable.
It is comical that such a view should be characterised as wish-fulfil-
ment. The romantic has only two basic certainties—the certainty of
irresoluble conflict which cannot be won but must be continued, and the
certainty that there exists between all human beings who are involved
in this conflict an indefeasible responsibility to one another. The romantic has two enemies, Death, and the obedient who, by conformity to

* For a contrary view see Josephine Miles, "Classic and Romantic," in *The
Primary Language of Poetry in the 1740's and 1840's* (Berkeley and Los Angeles, 1950),
and, of course Cleanth Brooks and other "New Critics."

power and irresponsibility, ally themselves with Death. There is no hint of mysticism in this—romanticism is the ideology of a whole human being looking at the whole universe.

Romanticism, the belief in the human conflict against the Universe and against power, seems to me to be the driving force of all art and of all science which deserves the name. In Western civilisation today, there are only two recognisable elements which can be said to differentiate it from total barbarism, our art and our medical science, and both are based upon this romantic ideology. The ethical content of romanticism has always been the same. The romantic bases his ethic upon his belief in the hostility or the neutrality of the Universe. He does not deny the existence of absolute standards, but he denies their existence apart from Man. The conceptions of artistic beauty or moral goodness did not exist before the emergence of consciousness, and they will return to oblivion with its extinction, but they are none the less good for their impermanence. And because of this one-sided battle which the romantic believes himself to be fighting, he recognises an absolute and imperative responsibility to his fellow men as individuals—both because he, unlike the Christian, is defending standards in which he believes but which are not by nature assured of triumph, which he feels will only exist so long as they are defended, and because his pessimistic interpretation of philosophy makes him feel towards his fellow men much as you might feel towards fellow survivors on a raft.

It is from this metaphysical idea of conflict, of principles which are maintained only by struggle, that romanticism draws the tremendous force of its social and philosophical criticism, and the equally tremendous emotional and intellectual appeal of its artistic statements. It is a force which alone among artistic forces seems to preserve perpetual virility and perpetual youth. . . .

The romantic recognizes a perpetual struggle upon two levels, the fight against Death which I have described, and the struggle against those men and institutions who ally themselves with Death against humanity, the struggle against barbarism. These are the two subjects of the Brueghel paintings, *The Triumph of Death* and *The Massacre of the Holy Innocents*. In the first, a gigantic host of skeletons is riding down mankind. In the second the Duke of Alva's soldiery are butchering Flemish peasants and their children. I regard these paintings as the highest level which the expression of the romantic ideology has ever reached—and Brueghel is not in any lecture catalogue of romantic painters. These are the enemies of humanity, and of the standards of beauty and of truth which exist only for and in humanity—Death and Death's ally, irresponsibility. The relevance of romanticism today lies in the fact that of all ideologies it alone declares this basic antagonism and moulds its course accordingly.

I suppose that I would summarise the social conclusions of contemporary romantics in some such form as this:

1. Man, considered individually, seems to be internally maladapted. He possesses a conscious sense of personality which, as far as one can reasonably guess, is not shared by other organisms, and which renders the emotional realisation of Death intolerable and incompatible with continued enjoyment of existence. He therefore attempts universally to deny either that Death is real or that his personality is really personal.

2. At the present time, one of the main human refuges in the past (the negation of Death) is apparently sealed by scientific research. I say apparently, because the important factor from the viewpoint of social psychology is not the actual evidence but the acceptance of Death as real and final by a high proportion of the populations which have so far evaded the realisation.[1] This acceptance, coming upon people whose humanity has been undermined by social organisation, is a root cause of the flight into barbarism.

3. Accordingly, the emphasis is laid more than ever before on the negation of individual personality and responsibility, since to admit that I am an individual I must also admit that I shall cease to exist. The negation takes the form of a growing belief in the conception of an immortal, invisible, and only wise society, which can exact responsibilities and demand allegiances. The concept is as old as human

---

[1] Singularly enough some critics again attempt to depict this view as a form of religious mysticism, largely because it uses the term "human nature" and discusses the relationship of man to the Universe. Except in so far as philosophical pessimism is a "religion," it is difficult to see in what way a romantic interpretation of history is any more "religious" than a Marxist or physiochemical interpretation. It certainly rejects every form of supernaturalism. As to Whitehead's conception of romanticism as a revolt against science [in Chapter 5 of *Science and the Modern World*, entitled "The Romantic Reaction"] the romantic conception of metaphysics and politics is constituted in the same way as any scientific hypothesis—by reference to the observed facts of history or of psychology. Its interpretation may be fallible, but its method is surely above reproach, even from the rationalists, whose notion of the economic reform of society has no historical evidence to support it. I would have placed the romantic awareness high in the list of causes of scientific progress.

thought, but its acceptance is becoming more and more a refuge from the reality of self. Society is not only a form of abrogating moral responsibility, it is a womb into which one can crawl back and become immortal because unborn.

4. But we have seen that it is a property of over-specialised groups that they submerge constructive impulses and summate destructive ones, so that the product of any group[2] action is by tendency destructive and irrational. The courses of action which the group mode of thought imposes upon the individual members are so grotesque and so wildly at variance with reason and with normal constructive activity that by reference to individual standards of human responsibility they are clinically insane. The consciousness of personal responsibility is the factor which differentiates human relationships from superficially similar animal societies: and contemporary irresponsibility has thrown it overboard.

The barbarian revolution occurs without external change at the point where mutual aid becomes detached from political organisation, civic delegation passes out of the control of the delegators, at the transition between a community of responsible individuals and a society of irresponsible citizens. At a definite point in the history of every civilisation, and shortly before its economic peak, there occurs a transfer of civic obligation, from the community based on mutual aid to the society based upon common irresponsibility. It may manifest itself as an industrial revolution, a megalopolitan development of the city, or as a change in national attitude from community to communal aggression. Every society has its Melian Dialogues, and thereafter the barbarian revolution has taken place, and the actions of that society are irresponsible, and of its members insane. . . . To call them insane, over the range of those actions, is not a figure of speech but a clinical fact. If insanity is a divorce between reality and perception which, by depriving a man of insight, renders him a peril to himself and others, then these men . . . are insane, over the whole section of their activity

---

[2] I do not say that all groups are bad, any more than I say that because all men have stomachs they are all dyspeptics. The tendency to degenerate into irresponsibility is inherent in every group, once its members cease to act as individuals, and transfer their responsibility from their fellow men to the group. Where I use the word "Society" in a derogatory sense, I mean a society in which this change for the worse has taken place.

which is involved with the madhouse group. What else does the tag concerning Salus Populi mean, save that society abrogates rational conduct? What else is the contemporary phrase Military Necessity but a prelude to some grotesque piece of bestiality which we are being asked to accept? We are living in a madhouse whenever society is allowed to become personalised and regarded as a super-individual. We are living in a madhouse now.

What will the artist, as an individual, have to say for himself when he looks at the results of this process in the present time? He will lay down, and I believe he is laying down, a set of cynical but reliable guides to conduct.

In a barbarian society, we are forced to live in an asylum, where we are both patients and explorers. Certain rules, arrived at empirically, will govern our conduct in terms of that analogy.

First, I recognise the seeds of madness in myself. I know that if ever, for any purpose, I allow myself to act as a member of such a group and to forfeit my responsibility to my fellows, from that moment I am a madman, and the degree of my insanity will be purely fortuitous.

Second, I must suspect all bodies, groups, teams, gangs, based on power, for where two or three are gathered together, there is the potentiality of lunacy in the midst of them, whether lunacy that kills Jews, lunacy that flogs Indians, lunacy that believes Lord George Gordon or the Ku Klux Klan, or lunacy that bombs Berlin. Yet I shall not hate or distrust any of my fellow patients singly. They are exactly as I am. I can see how dangerous they are, but I can be as dangerous to them if I allow myself to become involved. It will be said that I deny social responsibility. I do not—I believe that responsibility is boundless. We have boundless responsibility to every person we meet. The foreman owes it to his men not to persecute them—he owes it as a man, not because there is an abstract power vested in the T.U.C. which demands it. Barbarism is a flight from responsibility, an attempt to exercise it towards a nonexistent scarecrow rather than to real people. Each sincere citizen feels responsibility to society in the abstract, and none to the people he kills. The furious obedience of the Good Citizens is basically irresponsible. "The simple love of country and home and soil, a love that needs neither reasons nor justifications, is turned by the official apologists of the state into the demented cult of 'patriotism':

coercive group unanimity: blind support of the rulers of the state: maudlin national egoism: an imbecile willingness to commit collective atrocities for the sake of 'national glory.' "[3] We have no responsibility whatever to a barbarian society (we recognise no moral duties towards a gang of madmen); our responsibilities to each other I believe to be boundless.

Third, one must aim at concealment. When lunacy is a norm, cynicism is a duty. The chief task will be to remain unnoticed by these ranging gangs of fellow patients. Their main fury falls on anybody who, by remaining a person, reminds them of personality and Death. One lives in perpetual danger from the hatred or the equally destructive desire of the Good Citizens, and we shall need to humour, to cajole, to deceive, to appease, to compromise, to run at the right moments. When two of these squealing packs are murdering each other we shall be denounced by both as traitors for failing to join in. The most we can do is to attempt to snatch out of the mob one or two of the pathetic figures, urged on by scamps, who compose such mobs. They are our friends.

The positive expression of such ideas is not in the ballot box but in the individual restoration of responsible citizenship, the practice of recalcitrant mutual aid, not in political organisation but in the fostering of individual disobedience, individual thought, small responsible mutual-aid bodies which can survive the collapse and concentrate their efforts upon the practice of civilisation. It is the philosophy of direct action, of the deserter and the Maquis, the two most significant and human figures of every barbarian age.

In future, our responsibilities are to our fellow men, not to a society. The point at which responsibility becomes finally submerged is the point at which we no longer have common ground with society. Once the choice of barbarism has been made, the only remedy is in direct action. We now accept no responsibility to any group, only to individuals. This repudiation is not confined to "artists"—"artists" have made it because they happen to be human beings. They enjoy no rights that shoemakers, doctors, or housewives are not equally entitled to demand. The claim of society on bakers is just as much vitiated by irresponsibility as its claim on poets. There are no corporate allegiances. All our politics are atomised.

[3] Lewis Mumford, *The Culture of Cities* [New York, 1938], p. 273.

It is not that as artists we have deserted society. It has deserted or ejected us, and we live on in contact with it as tenants whom the landlord has not troubled to have thrown out. We have not seceded, but in clinging to personality we cling to something which everyone knows is the harbinger of Death. They hate us for reminding them of it. They burrow deeper into society to lose sight of the fact which towers over them. Rather than face it, they become insane. Fascism is a refuge from Death in death. And fascism epitomises the historical tendency of barbarian society.*

These are the necessary conclusions of an age in which a concept of society and of the universe—I mean the Victorian-liberal-bourgeois concept—has collapsed. To describe them as obscurantist or a "failure of nerve" contributes little to their discussion. They are the almost inevitable product of the time, and in practice they exercise everybody, even Marxist writers who repudiate them and find it hard to sympathise with "romantics" who express them. They are far more a fact of social history than a result of conscious thought.

Further, they represent the conscious or unconscious state of mind of an entire generation of writers, both those who profess individualism and those who reject it. They are manifestly not identical with the ideas behind "Art for Art's sake"—it would be far fairer to regard them as art for responsibility's sake. The generation which is influenced by such ideas is certainly making no special claims for itself, either of privilege or of insight. This set of ideas, this metaphysical and political attitude, is an ideology, and that ideology is correctly termed romanticism. . . . However, the romantic is certainly obliged to face the criticism that he denounces other people's doings when he cannot say what principles guide his own actions. I say emphatically that war is wrong, and do not know why I say it. The position is illogical, but I see no way out. I cannot give so many reasons for believing any one action to be wrong as I can give for believing a work of art to be bad. Yet as I am confident that æsthetics are real, and find myself obliged to act accordingly, so in the field of ethics I must act on some of the convictions that compose humanity. The only coherent ethic is that of responsible humanness. I believe, therefore, in reason against insanity, in respon-

* This is interestingly contrary to the view that romanticism is the forerunner of fascism. See Jacques Barzun's discussion of this in *Classic, Romantic, and Modern* (Garden City, N.Y., 1961) and Paul Roubiczek, *The Misinterpretation of Man* (London, 1949).

sibility against barbarism. A society of irresponsible, obedient citizens to my mind is as morally null as it is historically doomed. The ethic of romanticism is an ethic derived entirely from man, and for the artist and the scientist, concerned with humanity and nothing else, it is true and coherent. Apart from human beings, neither "goodness" nor "beauty" have any absolute significance. They are human things and the seeking of them is a human obligation. The romantic launches his protest and bases his conduct upon an ethic, an agathistic utilitarianism, which he finds in the alliance for mutual aid of all human beings against a universe which does not exist for their comfort nor share their aspirations. . . .

Romanticism postulates the alliance of all human beings against the hostility of the universe, and against power, which is the attempt to push off the burden of personal responsibility on to other shoulders. Both biologically and historically, it is a wholly realistic view. It comprises no conclusion which is reached by any process save the examination of human experience and observation, and the anger of the classicists against it is based entirely upon the romantic rejection both of the wholly illusory ideas of historical and inevitable progress and of the implicit metaphysical assumption that human ideals have some unexplained entity, in a psychophysical vacuum called "ultimate reality"—the ideals to which the most hardened dialectical materialist unconsciously appeals when he talks about "social justice."

Even more urgently romanticism rejects the form of social order in which human responsibilities are curtailed, to a point at which none of the conceptions which constitute justice or freedom retain any meaning save that which the stateholders confer on them, the condition of society in which we now live, and which is correctly termed barbarism. With the moral extinction of Christianity, romanticism remains the only ideology which has a coherent system of moral judgments on which it can rely, and because its morals and its sociology, its conception of human need and of human duty, coincide and have a common historic and scientific origin, it can confidently predict the self-destruction of every barbarian order.

•   •   •

I have described romanticism sympathetically, but not because I fail to see its fallacies. The classicist is running the perpetual risk of forfeiting his responsibility—the romantic of forfeiting his sanity. He is performing a continual tight-rope walk over a series of intellectual abysses, of self-pity, self-dramatisation, mysticism, conversion to Roman Catholicism, acquiescence in political reaction, or pathological despair. The danger of such a collapse is greatest when the romantic ideology is thrown up half-consciously by a semi-emotional sense of impending social disaster, just as revolutionary classicism is at its most irresponsible when it comes into violent conflict with historical and sociological fact. But we are no more entitled to denounce romanticism in terms of romantics who have lost their nerve than we are entitled to abolish coal gas because some persons use it as a means of suicide. Every idea and every ideology carries in itself the potential destruction of its adherents. The prediction that a social order is bound to destroy itself, while it is an unnerving conclusion, is no more a loss of nerve in itself than the conclusion upon scientific observation or common experience that a man is likely to die or a volcano to erupt. It is in the consciousness of common humanity and the retention of this wholly scientific conception of history that the validity of romanticism persists.

... The essential prerequisite on which all romantic theory is founded [is] the community of the artist with his fellow men: in other words, his humanity. He must cater for the need to stand aside by regarding all movements and societies neutrally, not in that he refuses to judge them *at all*, but that he judges on the same basis. He cannot afford to have in his bag divers weights—that is one of the traits of civic lunacy. The artist's isolation and humanity are no different from the isolation and humanity of other responsible people—isolation from barbarism, solidarity with other human beings. It is a tribute to English letters that in a period of almost unparalleled national insanity England should have produced Trevelyan's *Social History*. This is the history of the relationships and the experience from which there is no standing aside, the story of humanity in its incessant war with society. If the artist is to take the side of man, he is fulfilling both his duties of isolation and humanity.

I disagree with the idea that the artist is primarily the interpreter of the symptoms and processes of economic change—to follow Caudwell's conception* is to limit the number of levels on which art could or should exist. The unit with which the artist is concerned is first of all the individual human being. The romantic artist sees him exactly as the physician sees him—an individual who shares his organs and a high propor-

* See pp. 112–16.

tion of his psychological make-up with every individual who has existed within historical time, and with the artist himself. Like the physician, the artist is one of humanity, subject to every branch of human experience, from politics to death, but possessing by virtue of his talent the faculty which the physician acquires through training, or elucidating, interpreting, assisting. His sensibility corresponds to the physician's medical training—consciously or unconsciously he is aware of the individual's position and of the roots in anthropology, psychology, and evolution which make up humanness. He is neither a superman nor a privileged person, any more than the physician is. It is with this quality of humanness that the romantic is primarily concerned—it is the origin of the romantic sympathy, the concept of shared, responsible experience, and of man as the product and victim of environment, which makes romanticism and defines it. In addition to this prerequisite consciousness, there is the technical mastery, learned or acquired, which is needed to express it. One might almost continue the analogy and say that classicism bears some resemblance to operative surgery—there is the same emphasis on technical virtuosity and the same preoccupation with intervention rather than with organic process. To the artist as a human being, and to the physician in his practice, the sense of continuity of circumstance and difference of environment are perpetually present— the human being and the patient, for the purposes of art and medicine, are fundamental constants. There is no difference between Hagesichora and any other young girl dancing, between the Homeric warriors and any other soldier—you cannot tell whether the man under the theatre towels is a Nazi or an anarchist; that aspect of his existence concerns you very little—you are interested in him as a man. The neutrality of medicine has survived this war well. The neutrality of romantic art will also survive it, because it is based on the far larger community of man, which society tends to destroy, which one finds only in London's slums or America's prisons. It seems to me that it is this universality in art which Marxist classicism misses, just as in the political sphere it does not extend "working-class solidarity" into the responsible and anti-authoritarian conception of human solidarity. It is the extension of this evaluation of man into politics which makes up anarchism, and the common foundation of anarchism and romanticism* renders them inseparable in

---

* Herbert Read, to whom Comfort's book is dedicated, has written widely on romanticism and anarchism, as well as on the relationship between the two.

the evolution of art, just as medicine as a practice, if we are to oppose it to the technical veterinary surgery of such people as army psychologists, whose aim is something other than plain human welfare, is inseparable from a similar human neutrality.

The value of Marxist criticism has lain, however, in its perpetual emphasis on the environmental concern of the artist. Once fortified with this conception of humanity and his knowledge that he is a part of it, not an observer, the artist is under an obligation to concern himself with the entire environment of the times, both by interpreting it and by modifying it. Writers who are afraid to throw their weight into the cause of the humanity they recognise will find little in the tradition of romanticism to support their abstention. This criticism is valuable in itself, but at present it is pretty consistently directed against the wrong people. It is the concept of irresponsible society, whatever its social organisation, that is now, and always has been, the enemy of the romantic conception of man, and in a period of disintegration, with irresponsibility at a premium, the artist who reflects and interprets is accused of decadence, and the artist who advocates responsibility is accused of disruption. I cannot see an iota of difference between the attacks of sycophants and clowns who propagate a theory of cultural bolshevism (that Joyce and Proust were responsible for the fall of France, for instance) and those of the political actives who charge romantic individualism with losing its nerve. They are both imitating the man who smashes the barometer because it points to rain.

• • •

. . . One finds islands of community which have escaped the curse of personified societies scattered everywhere—the shelters during the air-raids, the Cossack villages, some primitive tribes, prisoners in Dachau or Huyton, the Russian collective farms. These are the largest communities in which anarchism is real and the standing aside preliminary to creation is not resented to the same degree as in the societies of clock-faces, whose sole virtue is their unanimity in error. This virtue is a virtue of death. They do not escape death by evading it in the renunciation of life. It is not for nothing that Brueghel's skeletons have all the same faces.

And artistic responsibility consists in taking all this upon our shoulders—in providing voices for all those who have not voices. The romantic ideology of art is the ideology of that responsibility, a responsibility born out of a sense of victimhood, of community in a hostile universe, and destined like Prometheus, its central creation, to be the perpetual advocate and defender of Man against barbarism, community against irresponsibility, life against homicidal and suicidal obedience.

BIBLIOGRAPHICAL NOTE: Other essays that deal with the relationship between romanticism and political and socio-economic forces are listed in the bibliographical note to Christopher Caudwell's essay above, pp. 123–24. For very different views of the place of romanticism in the history of culture, see particularly Raymond Williams's *Culture and Society 1780–1950* (New York, 1958) and Morse Peckham's *Beyond the Tragic Vision* (New York, 1962) and *Romanticism: The Culture of the Nineteenth Century* (New York, 1965).

The Concept of Romanticism in Literary History

René Wellek

I

The terms "romanticism" and "romantic" have been under attack for a long time. In a well-known paper, "On the Discrimination of Romanticisms," Arthur O. Lovejoy has argued impressively that "the word 'romantic' has come to mean so many things that, by itself, it means nothing. It has ceased to perform the function of a verbal sign." Lovejoy proposed to remedy this "scandal of literary history and criticism" by showing that "the 'romanticism' of one country may have little in common with that of another, that there is, in fact, a plurality of romanticisms, of possibly quite distinct thought-complexes." He grants that "there may be some common denominator to them all; but if so, it has never been clearly exhibited." Moreover, according to Lovejoy, "the romantic ideas were in large part heterogeneous, logically independent, and sometimes essentially antithetic to one another in their implications."

As far as I know, this challenge has never been taken up by those who still consider the terms useful and will continue to speak of a unified European romantic movement. While Lovejoy makes reserva-

THE CONCEPT OF ROMANTICISM IN LITERARY HISTORY: From *Comparative Literature*, I (1949), 1–23, 147–72, reprinted with permission of the author and of the Editor of *Comparative Literature*.

181

tions and some concessions to the older view, the impression seems widespread today, especially among American scholars, that his thesis has been established securely. I propose to show that there is no basis for this extreme nominalism, that the major romantic movements form a unity of theories, philosophies, and style, and that these, in turn, form a coherent group of ideas each of which implicates the other.

I have tried elsewhere to make a theoretical defense of the use and function of period terms.[1] I concluded that one must conceive of them, not as arbitrary linguistic labels nor as metaphysical entities, but as names for systems of norms which dominate literature at a specific time of the historical process. The term "norms" is a convenient term for conventions, themes, philosophies, styles, and the like, while the word "domination" means the prevalence of one set of norms compared with the prevalence of another set in the past. The term "domination" must not be conceived of statistically: it is entirely possible to envisage a situation in which older norms still prevailed numerically while the new conventions were created or used by writers of greatest artistic importance. It thus seems to me impossible to avoid the critical problem of evaluation in literary history. The literary theories, terms, and slogans of a time need not have prescriptive force for the modern literary historian. We are justified in speaking of "Renaissance" and "Baroque," though both of these terms were introduced centuries after the events to which they refer. Still, the history of literary criticism, its terms and slogans, affords important clues to the modern historian, since it shows the degree of self-consciousness of the artists themselves and may have profoundly influenced the practice of writing. But this is a question which has to be decided case by case, since there have been ages of low self-consciousness and ages in which theoretical awareness lagged far behind practice or even conflicted with it.

In the case of romanticism the question of the terminology, its spread and establishment, is especially complicated because it is contemporary or nearly contemporary with the phenomena described. The adoption of the terms points to an awareness of certain changes. But this awareness may have existed without these terms, or these terms may have been introduced before the actual changes took place, merely as a program, as the expression of a wish, an incitement to change. The situation differs in different countries; but this is, of course, in itself

[1] Cf. "Periods and Movements in Literary History," *English Institute Annual 1940* (New York, 1941), pp. 73–93, and *Theory of Literature*, with Austin Warren (New York, 1949), especially pp. 274ff.

no argument that the phenomena to which the terms refer showed substantial differences.

The semantic history of the term "romantic" has been very fully studied in its early stages in France, England, and Germany, and for the later stages in Germany.[2] But, unfortunately, little attention has been paid to it in other countries and, even where materials are abundant, it is still difficult to ascertain when, for the first time, a work of literature and which works of literature were designated as "romantic," when the contrast of "classical-romantic" was introduced, when a contemporary writer referred to himself first as a "romanticist," when the term "romanticism" was first adopted in a country, etc. Some attempt, however imperfect in detail, can be made to straighten out this history on an international scale and to answer some of these questions.

We are not concerned here with the early history of "romantic" which shows an expansion of its use from "romance-like," "extravagant," "absurd," etc., to "picturesque." If we limit ourselves to the history of the term as used in criticism and literary history, there is little difficulty about its main outlines. The term "romantic poetry" was used first of Ariosto and Tasso and the mediæval romances from which their themes and "machinery" were derived. It occurs in this sense in France in 1669, in England in 1674, and certainly Thomas Warton understood it to mean this when he wrote his introductory dissertation to his *History of English Poetry* (1774), "The Origin of Romantic Fiction in Europe." In Warton's writings and those of several of his contemporaries a contrast is implied between this "romantic" literature, both mediæval and Renaissance, and the whole tradition of literary art as it came down from classical antiquity. The composition and "machinery" of Ariosto, Tasso, and Spenser are defended against the charges of neoclassical criticism with arguments which derive from the Renaissance defenders of Ariosto (Patrizzi, Cinthio) and which had been repeated by such good neoclassicists as Jean Chapelain. An attempt is made to justify a special taste for such "romantic" fiction and its noncompliance with classical standards and rules, even though these

[2] Fernand Baldensperger, "'Romantique'—ses analogues et équivalents," *Harvard Studies and Notes in Philology and Literature*, XIV (1937), 13–105, is the fullest list. Unfortunately there is no interpretation and it goes only to 1810. . . . Logan P. Smith, *Four Words, Romantic, Originality, Creative, Genius* (Society for Pure English Tract no. 17, London, 1924), reprinted in *Words and Idioms* (Boston, 1925), is still the only piece on English developments and is for this purpose valuable; the comments on the further story in Germany are injudicious. [See also Mario Praz's discussion of the word "romantic" above, pp. 87–91.]

are not challenged for other genres. The dichotomy implied has obvious analogues in other contrasts common in the eighteenth century: between the ancients and moderns, between artificial and popular poetry, the "natural" poetry of Shakespeare unconfined by rules and French classical tragedy. A definite juxtaposition of "Gothic" and "classical" occurs in Hurd and Warton. Hurd speaks of Tasso as "trimming between the Gothic and the Classic," and of the *Faerie Queene* as a "Gothic, not a classical poem." Warton calls Dante's *Divine Comedy* a "wonderful compound of classical and romantic fancy." Here the two famous words meet, possibly for the first time, but Warton probably meant little more than that Dante used both classical mythology and chivalric *motifs*.

> [Wellek next traces the historical development of the concept of romanticism in Germany, France, and other European countries in the late eighteenth and early nineteenth centuries.]

We have left the English story, the most unusual development, for the conclusion. After Warton there had begun in England an extensive study of mediæval romances and of "romantic fiction." But there is no instance of a juxtaposition of "classical" and "romantic," nor any awareness that the new literature inaugurated by the *Lyrical Ballads* could be called romantic. Scott, in his edition of *Sir Tristram*, calls his text, "the first classical English romance." An essay by John Forster, "On the Application of the Epithet Romantic" [*Essays in a Series of Letters* (London, 1805)], is merely a commonplace discussion of the relation between imagination and judgment with no hint of a literary application except to chivalrous romances.

The distinction of classical–romantic occurs for the first time [in England] in Coleridge's lectures, given in 1811, and is there clearly derived from Schlegel, since the distinction is associated with that of organic and mechanical, painterly and sculpturesque, in close verbal adherence to Schlegel's phrasing.[3] But these lectures were not published at that time, and thus the distinction was popularized in England only

[3] Coleridge's *Shakespearean Criticism*, ed. Thomas M. Raysor (Cambridge, Mass., 1930), I, 196–98, II, 265; and *Miscellaneous Criticism*, ed. T. M. Raysor (Cambridge, Mass., 1936), pp. 7, 148. Coleridge himself says that he received a copy of Schlegel's *Lectures* on Dec. 12, 1811; see S. T. Coleridge's *Unpublished Letters*, ed. Earl L. Griggs (London, 1932), 11, 61–67. A MS. by Henry Crabb Robinson, written about 1803, "Kant's Analysis of Beauty," now in the Williams Library, London, contains the distinction of classical-romantic; see my *Immanuel Kant in England* (Princeton, 1931), p. 158.

through Madame de Staël, who made Schlegel and Sismondi known in England. *De L'Allemagne*, first published in London, appeared almost simultaneously in an English translation. Two reviews, by Sir James Mackintosh and William Taylor of Norwich, reproduce the distinction between classical and romantic, and Taylor mentions Schlegel and knows of Madame de Staël's indebtedness to him.[4] Schlegel was in the company of Madame de Staël in England in 1814. The French translation of the *Lectures* was very favorably reviewed in the *Quarterly Review*,[5] and in 1815 John Black, an Edinburgh journalist, published his English translation. This was also very well received. Some reviews reproduce Schlegel's distinction quite extensively: for instance, Hazlitt's in the *Edinburgh Review*.[6] Schlegel's distinctions and views on many aspects of Shakespeare were used and quoted by Hazlitt, by Nathan Drake in his *Shakespeare* (1817), by Scott in his *Essay on Drama* (1819), and in *Ollier's Literary Magazine* (1820), which contains a translation of Schlegel's old essay on *Romeo and Juliet*. The use to which Coleridge put Schlegel in his lectures given after the publication of the English translation, needs no repetition.

The usual impression that the classical–romantic distinction was little known in England seems not quite correct.[7] It is discussed in Thomas Campbell's *Essay on Poetry* (1819), though Campbell finds Schlegel's defense of Shakespeare's irregularities on "romantic principles" "too romantic for his conception." In Sir Edgerton Brydges's *Gnomica* and *Sylvan Wanderer*, there is striking praise of romantic mediæval poetry and its derivations in Tasso and Ariosto in contrast to the classical abstract poetry of the eighteenth century.[8] We find only a few practical uses of these terms at that time. Samuel Singer, in his introduction to Marlowe's *Hero and Leander*, says that "Musaeus is more classical, Hunt more romantic." He defends Marlowe's extravagancies which might excite the ridicule of French critics: "but here in England their reign is over and thanks to the Germans, with the Schlegels at their

---

[4] *Edinburgh Review*, XXII (Oct. 1813), 198–238; *Monthly Review*, LXXII (1813), 421–26, LXXIII (1814), 63–68, 352–65, especially 364.

[5] *Quarterly Review*, XX (Jan. 1814), 355–409. I do not know the author: he is not given in the list of contributors in the *Gentleman's Magazine*, 1844, or in W. Graham's *Tory Criticism in the Quarterly Review* (New York, 1921).

[6] Feb. 1816. Reprinted in *Complete Works*, ed. Howe, XVI, 57–99.

[7] Further examples in Herbert Weisinger, "English Treatment of the Classical–Romantic Problem," in *Modern Language Quarterly*, VII (1946), 477–88.

[8] Issues dated Apr. 20, 1819, and Oct. 23, 1818.

head, a truer philosophical method of judging is beginning to obtain among us."[9] De Quincey in 1835 attempted a more original elaboration of the dichotomy by stressing the role of Christianity and the difference in the attitudes toward death; but even these ideas are all derived from the Germans.[10]

But none of the English poets, we must stress, recognized himself as a romanticist or recognized the relevance of the debate to his own time and country.

> [Wellek points out here that despite their knowledge of Schlegel's *Lectures*, Coleridge, Hazlitt, and Byron, for example, do not show any conciousness of themselves as "romantics." "Actual application of the term 'romantic' to English literature of the early nineteenth century" comes much later, as do the English terms "a romantic," "a romanticist," and "romanticism"—and even then they occur in accounts of Continental literature. There are a few exceptions (see p. 16 of Wellek's article), but the great bulk of evidence shows that:]

The history of the term and its introduction cannot regulate the usage of the modern historian, since he would be forced to recognize milestones in his history which are not justified by the actual state of the literatures in question. The great changes happened independently of the introduction of these terms either before or after them and only rarely approximately at the same time.

On the other hand, the usual conclusion drawn from examinations of the history of the words, that they are used in contradictory senses, seems to me greatly exaggerated. One must grant that many German æstheticians juggle the terms in extravagant and personal ways, nor can one deny that the emphasis on different aspects of their meaning shifts from writer to writer and sometimes from nation to nation. But, on the whole, there was really no misunderstanding about the meaning of "romanticism" as a new designation for poetry, opposed to the poetry of neoclassicism, and drawing its inspiration and models from the Middle Ages and the Renaissance. The term is understood in this sense all over Europe, and everywhere we find references to August Wilhelm Schlegel or Madame de Staël and their particular formulas opposing "classical" and "romantic." . . .

---

[9] London, 1821, p. lvii.
[10] Cf. a full discussion in my "De Quincey's Status in the History of Ideas," *Philological Quarterly*, XXIII (1944), 248–72.

The mere use of the terms "romantic" and "romanticism" must not be overrated. English writers early had a clear consciousness that there was a movement which rejected the critical concepts and poetic practice of the eighteenth century, that it formed a unity, and had its parallels on the continent, especially in Germany. Without the term "romantic" we can trace, within a short period, the shift from the earlier conception of the history of English poetry as one of a uniform progress from Waller and Denham to Dryden and Pope, still accepted in Johnson's *Lives of the Poets*, to Southey's opposite view in 1807, that the "time which elapsed from the days of Dryden to those of Pope is the dark age of English poetry." The reformation began with Thomson and the Wartons. The real turning point was Percy's *Reliques*, "the great literary epocha of the present reign." Shortly afterward, in Leigh Hunt's *Feast of the Poets* (1814) we have the view established that Wordsworth is "capable of being at the head of a new and great age of poetry; and in point of fact, I do not deny that he is so already, as the greatest poet of the present." In Wordsworth's own postscript to the 1815 edition of the *Poems*, the role of Percy's *Reliques* is again emphasized: "The poetry of the age has been absolutely redeemed by it." In 1816, Lord Jeffrey acknowledged that the "wits of Queen Anne's time have been gradually brought down from the supremacy which they had enjoyed, without competition, for the best part of a century." He recognized that the "present revolution in literature" was due to the "French revolution—the genius of Burke—the impression of the new literature of Germany, evidently the original of our Lake School of poetry."[11] In Nathan Drake's book on *Shakespeare* (1817) the role of the revival of Elizabethan poetry is recognized. "Several of our bards," he says, "have in great degree reverted to the ancient school." In Hazlitt's *Lectures on the English Poets* (1818) a new age dominated by Wordsworth is described quite clearly, with its sources in the French revolution, in German literature, and its opposition to the mechanical conventions of the followers of Pope and the old French school of poetry. An article in *Blackwood's* sees the connection between the "great change in the poetical temper of the country" and the Elizabethan revival. "A nation must revert to the ancient spirit of its own. The living and creative spirit of literature is its nationality."[12] Scott uses Schlegel extensively and describes the general

[11] Review of Scott's edition of Swift, in *Edinburgh Review*, Sept. 1816; *Contributions to Edinburgh Review* (2nd ed., London, 1846), I, 158–60.
[12] *Blackwood's Magazine* (1818), IV, 264–66.

change as a "fresh turning up of the soil" due to the Germans and neces-
sitated by the "wearing out" of the French models.[13] Carlyle in his
introduction to selections from Ludwig Tieck draws the English-German
parallel quite explicitly:

> Neither can the change be said to have originated in Schiller and Goethe:
> for it is a change originating not in individuals, but in universal circum-
> stances, and belongs not to Germany, but to Europe. Among ourselves,
> for instance, within the last thirty years, who has not lifted his voice with
> double vigour in praise of Shakespeare and Nature, and vituperation of
> French taste and French philosophy? Who has not heard of the glories
> of old English literature, the wealth of Queen Elizabeth's age: the penury
> of Queen Anne's and the inquiry whether Pope was a poet? A similar
> temper is breaking out in France itself, hermetically sealed as that
> country seemed to be against all foreign influence; and doubts are
> beginning to be entertained, and even expressed, about Corneille and
> the Three Unities. It seems substantially the same thing which has
> occurred in Germany . . . only that the revolution, which is there
> proceeding, and in France commencing, appears in Germany to be
> completed.[14]

All of this is broadly true and applicable even today and has been
wrongly forgotten by modern sceptics.

Scott, in a retrospect, "Essay on Imitations of the Ancient Ballads"
(1830), also stressed the role of Percy and the Germans in the revival.

> As far back as 1788 a new species of literature began to be introduced
> into the country. Germany . . . was then for the first time heard of as
> the cradle of a style of poetry and literature much more analogous to
> that of Britain than either the French, Spanish, or Italian schools
> [Scott's ellipsis].

Scott tells of a lecture of Henry Mackenzie where the audience
learned that the "taste which dictated the German compositions was
of a kind as nearly allied to the English as their language." Scott learned
German from Dr. Willich, who later expounded Kant in English.
But, according to Scott, M. G. Lewis was the first who attempted to
introduce something like German taste into English composition.[15]

---

[13] In "Essay on Drama," contributed to *Encyclopedia Britannica*, Supplement, vol.
III, 1819; *Miscellaneous Prose Works* (Edinburgh, 1834), VI, 380.

[14] "German Romance," in *Miscellanies* (London, 1890), I, 246 [Carlyle's ellipsis].

[15] In new edition of *Minstrelsy of the Scottish Border* (1830), ed. T. Henderson (New
York, 1931), pp. 535–62, expecially pp. 549–50. On Willich, see my *Kant in England*
(Princeton, 1931), pp. 11–15.

Probably the most widely read of these pronouncements was T. B. Macaulay's account in his review of Moore's *Life of Byron*. There the period of 1750–80 is called the "most deplorable part of our literary history." The revival of Shakespeare, the ballads, Chatterton's forgeries, and Cowper are mentioned as the main agents of change. Byron and Scott are singled out as the great names. Most significantly, Macaulay realizes that

> Byron, though always sneering at Mr. Wordsworth, was yet, though, perhaps unconsciously, the interpreter between Mr. Wordsworth and the multitude . . . Lord Byron founded what may be called an exoteric Lake School—what Mr. Wordsworth had said like a recluse, Lord Byron said like a man of the world.[16]

Macaulay thus long before he knew a term for it, recognized the unity of the English romantic movement.

James Montgomery, in his *Lectures on General Literature* (1833), described the age since Cowper as the third era of modern literature. Southey, Wordsworth, and Coleridge are called the "three pioneers, if not the absolute founders, of the existing style of English literature."

The most boldly formulated definition of the new view is again in Southey, in the "Sketches of the Progress of English Poetry from Chaucer to Cowper" (1833). There the "age from Dryden to Pope" is called "the worst age of English poetry: the age of Pope was the pinchbeck age of poetry." "If Pope closed the door against poetry, Cowper opened it." The same view, though less sharply expressed, can be found with increasing frequency even in textbooks, such as Robert Chambers' *History of the English Language and Literature* (1836), in De Quincey's writings, and R. H. Horne's *New Spirit of the Age* (1844).

None of these publications uses the term "romantic," but in all of them we hear that there is a new age of poetry which has a new style inimical to that of Pope. The emphasis and selections of examples vary, but in combination they say that the German influence, the revival of the ballads and the Elizabethans, and the French Revolution were the decisive influences which brought about the change. Thomson, Burns, Cowper, Gray, Collins, and Chatterton are honored as precursors, Percy and the Wartons as initiators. The trio, Wordsworth, Coleridge,

---

[16] *Edinburgh Review*, June 1831 [Wellek's ellipsis]. Reprinted in *Critical and Historical Essays* (Everyman ed.), II, 634–35.

and Southey, are recognized as the founders and, as time progressed, Byron, Shelley, and Keats are added in spite of the fact that this new group of poets denounced the older for political reasons. Clearly, such books as those of Phelps [*The Beginnings of the English Romantic Movement*, 1893] and Beers [*A History of English Romanticism in the Eighteenth Century*, 1898] merely carry out, in a systematic fashion, the suggestions made by the contemporaries and even the actual protagonists of the new age of poetry.

This general scheme is, to my mind, still substantially valid. It seems an unwarranted nominalism to reject it completely and to speak, as Ronald S. Crane does, of "the fairy tales about neoclassicism and romanticism"[17] in the eighteenth century. Not much seems accomplished by George Sherburn when he avoids the term in an excellent summary of what is generally called the romantic tendencies of the late eighteenth century, since he is admittedly confronted with the same problems and facts.[18]

One must grant, of course, that many details of the books of Phelps and Beers are mistaken and out of date. The new understanding of neoclassical theory and the new appreciation of eighteenth-century poetry, especially of Pope, have led to a reversal of the value judgments implied in the older conceptions. Romantic polemics give frequently a totally distorted picture of neoclassical theory, and some modern literary historians seem to have misunderstood the eighteenth-century meaning of such key terms as "Reason," "Nature," and "Imitation." Investigations have shown that the revival of Elizabethan, mediæval, and popular literature began much earlier than has been assumed. Objections against slavish imitation of the classics and strict adherence to the rules were commonplaces of English criticism, even in the seventeenth century. Many supposedly romantic ideas on the role of genius and imagination were perfectly acceptable to the main neoclassical critics. Much evidence has been accumulated to show that many of the precursors of romanticism—Thomson, the Wartons, Percy, Young, Hurd—shared the

---

[17] *Philological Quarterly*, XXII (1943), 143, in a review of an article by Curtis D. Bradford and Stuart Gerry Brown, "On Teaching the Age of Johnson" in *College English*, III (1942), 650–59. [For an attack upon Wellek's procedure and conclusions see Crane's review of this two-part *Comparative Literature* essay in *Philological Quarterly*, XXIX (1950), 257–59.]

[18] In a *Literary History of England*, ed. A. C. Baugh (New York, 1948), p. 971n. The "Part" is called "The Disintegration of Classicism," the chapter "Accentuated Tendencies," terms which give away the argument against preromanticism.

preconceptions of their age and held many basic neoclassical critical convictions, and cannot be called "revolutionaries" or "rebels."

We grant many of these criticisms and corrections of the older view. We may even side with the modern neoclassicists who deplore the dissolution of their creed and the extravagancies of the romantic movement. One should also grant that the hunt for "romantic" elements in the eighteenth century has become a rather tiresome game. A book such as Eric Partridge's *Eighteenth Century English Poetry* (1924) tried to identify "romantic" lines in Pope with great self-assurance. Partridge tells us that "nearly one-fifth of the total number of lines in *Eloisa to Abelard* are indisputably either markedly romantic in themselves or clearly romantic in tendency." He singles out lines in Dyer's *Fleece* as "romantic." There are several German theses which break up an eighteenth-century critic or poet into his wicked pseudoclassical and his virtuous romantic halves.[19]

Nobody has ever suggested that the precursors of romanticism were conscious of being precursors. But their anticipations of romantic views and devices are important, even if it can be shown that these prenouncements, taken in their total context, need to be interpreted differently and were innocuous from a neoclassical point of view. The fact that a later age could fasten on certain passages in Young or Hurd or Warton is relevant—not the intentions of Young, Hurd, or Warton. It is the right of a new age to look for its own ancestors and even to pull passages out of their context. One can prove, as Hoyt Trowbridge has done,[20] that Hurd's total theory was neoclassical; but, in the perspective of a new age, only a few passages from the *Letters on Chivalry and Romance* mattered—Hurd's saying that the *Faerie Queene* "should be read and criticized under the idea of a Gothic, not a classical poem" and his plea for the "pre-eminence of the Gothic manners and fictions as adapted to the end of poetry, above the classic." The argument against the very existence of romanticism in the eighteenth century is based on the prejudice that only the totality of a writer's works is the criterion of judgment, while in the many instances which are constantly being produced to show that individual romantic ideas can be traced to the seventeenth century or beyond, the opposite method is employed

[19] E.g., J. E. Anwander, *Pseudoklassizistisches und Romantisches in Thomsons Seasons* (Leipzig, 1930); Sigyn Christiani, *Samuel Johnson als Kritiker im Lichte von Pseudo-Klassizismus und Romantik* (Leipzig, 1931).

[20] "Bishop Hurd: A Reinterpretation," *PMLA*, LVIII (1943), 450–65.

—an atomistic view which ignores the question of emphasis, place in a system, frequency of occurrence. Both methods have been manipulated interchangeably.

The best solution seems to say that the student of neoclassical literature is right in refusing to see every figure and idea merely in terms of the role it may have played in the preparation of romanticism. But this refusal should not amount to a denial of the problem of the preparation of a new age. One could also study the new age for its survivals of the neoclassical norms,[21] a point of view which could prove illuminating, though it could hardly be considered of equal standing. Time flows in one direction and mankind for some reason (craze for novelty, dynamism, creativity?) is interested more in origins than in residues. If there were no preparations, anticipations, and undercurrents in the eighteenth century which could be described as preromantic, we would have to make the assumption that Wordsworth and Coleridge fell from heaven and that the neoclassical age was unperturbedly solid, unified, and coherent in a way no age has ever been before or since.

An important compromise has been propounded by Northrop Frye.[22] He argues that the second half of the eighteenth century is a "new age" which has "nothing to do with the Age of Reason. It is the age of Collins, Percy, Gray, Cowper, Smart, Chatterton, Burns, Ossian, the Wartons and Blake." "Its chief philosopher is Berkeley and its chief prose writer Sterne." "The age of Blake," he concludes, "has been rather unfairly treated by critics, who have tended to see in it nothing but a transition with all its poets either reacting against Pope or anticipating Wordsworth." Mr. Frye unfortunately ignores the fact that Hume rather than Berkeley dominated the philosophy of the age and that Dr. Johnson was then very much alive. Blake remained totally unknown in his time. In Thomas Warton, certainly, we have a recognition of classical standards and a tempered appreciation of Gothic picturesqueness and sublimity, a theory of a double standard of poetry which apparently was held by him without a feeling of contradiction.[23] Still, the contradictions are inherent in the whole position and it is hard to see what can be objected to calling it "preromantic." One can observe a process

---

[21] Suggested by Louis Landa in *Philological Quarterly*, XXII (1943), 147. Cf. Pierre Moreau, *Le Classicisme des romantiques* (Paris, 1932).

[22] In *Fearful Symmetry: A Study of William Blake* (Princeton, 1947), especially p. 167. [Frye elaborated upon this proposal in his "Towards Defining an Age of Sensibility," *ELH*, XXIII (1956), 144–52. This should be compared to Earl R. Wasserman's "Metaphors for Poetry" in his *The Subtler Language* (Baltimore, 1959).]

[23] Cf. fuller discussion in my *Rise of English Literary History* (Chapel Hill, N.C., 1941), especially pp. 185–86.

by which these scattered and underground tendencies strengthen and collect; some writers become "doubles," houses divided, and thus, seen from the perspective of a later time, can be called "preromantic." We can, it seems, go on speaking of "preromanticism" and romanticism since there are periods of the dominance of a system of ideas and poetic practices which have their anticipations in the preceding decades. The terms "romantic" and "romanticism," though late by the dates of their introduction, were everywhere understood in approximately the same sense and are still useful as terms for the kind of literature produced after neoclassicism.

In the second half of this paper I shall attempt to show that this body of literature forms a unity if we apply a few simple criteria and that the same criteria are valid for all the three major romantic movements—English, French, and German.

II

If we examine the characteristics of the actual literature which called itself or was called "romantic" all over the continent, we find throughout Europe the same conceptions of poetry and of the workings and nature of poetic imagination, the same conception of nature and its relation to man, and basically the same poetic style, with a use of imagery, symbolism, and myth which is clearly distinct from that of eighteenth-century neoclassicism. This conclusion might be strengthened or modified by attention to other frequently discussed elements: subjectivism, mediævalism, folklore, etc. But the following three criteria should be particularly convincing, since each is central for one aspect of the practice of literature: imagination for the view of poetry, nature for the view of the world, and symbol and myth for poetic style.

> [Wellek proceeds here to apply these criteria to the literature of Germany and France; and while German literature "is the clearest case," he finds that the "whole eclectic movement" in France, "fed as it is in part from German sources, especially Schelling, fits into our scheme. . . . "]

Turning to England, we can see complete agreement with the French and Germans on all essential points. The great poets of the English romantic movement constitute a fairly coherent group, with the same view of poetry and the same conception of imagination, the same view of nature and mind. They share also a poetic style, a use of imagery, symbolism, and myth, which is quite distinct from anything that had been practiced by the eighteenth century, and which was felt by their contemporaries to be obscure and almost unintelligible.

The affinity of the concepts of imagination among the English romantic poets scarcely needs demonstration. Blake considers all nature to be "imagination itself." Our highest aim is:

> To see a world in a grain of sand:
> And a Heaven in a Wild Flower,
> Hold Infinity in the palm of your hand
> And Eternity in an hour.

Thus imagination is not merely the power of visualization, somewhere in between sense and reason, which it had been to Aristotle or Addison, nor even the inventive power of the poet, which by Hume and many other eighteenth-century theorists was conceived of as a "combination of innate sensibility, the power of association, and the faculty of conception,"[24] but a creative power by which the mind "gains insight into reality, reads nature as a symbol of something behind or within nature not ordinarily perceived."[25] Thus imagination is the basis of Blake's rejection of the mechanistic world picture, the basis of an idealistic epistemology—

> The Sun's Light, when he unfolds it
> Depends on the Organ that beholds it;

and, of course, the basis of an æsthetics, the justification of art and his own peculiar kind of art. This conception of imagination sufficiently justifies the necessity of myth and of metaphor and symbol as its vehicle.

The concept of the imagination in Wordsworth is fundamentally the same, though Wordsworth draws more heavily on eighteenth-century theories and compromises with naturalism. Still, Wordsworth cannot be explained entirely in Hartley's terms; imagination is for him "creative," an insight into the nature of reality and hence the basic justification of art. The poet becomes a living soul who "sees into the life of things." Imagination is thus an organ of knowledge which trans-

[24] Walter J. Bate's description in *From Classic to Romantic* (Cambridge, Mass., 1946), p. 113. [Bate's last chapter, "The English Romantic Compromise," should be read in relation to a number of essays in the present collection.]

[25] I. A. Richards, *Coleridge on Imagination* (London, 1935), p. 145.

forms objects, sees through them, even if they are only the "meanest flower" or the humble ass, an idiot boy, or simply a child: "mighty prophet, seer blest."

The whole of the *Prelude* is a history of the poet's imagination which, —in a central passage of the last book, is called

> Another name for absolute power
> And clearest insight, amplitude of mind,
> And Reason in her most exalted mood.

In a letter to Landor, Wordsworth tells him that "in poetry it is the imaginative only, i.e., that which is conversant or turns upon Infinity, that powerfully affects me." "All great poets are in this view powerful Religionists."[26]

It is hardly necessary to explain what a central role the imagination plays in Coleridge's theory and practice. There is a book by I. A. Richards, *Coleridge on Imagination*, and recently R. P. Warren has carefully related the theory to the *Rime of the Ancient Mariner*.[27] The key passage in *Biographia Literaria* on primary and secondary imagination is too well known to need quoting. It is Schellingian in its formulation—on the whole, Coleridge's theory is closely dependent on the Germans. His term for "imagination," the "esemplastic power," is a translation of *Einbildungskraft*, based on a fanciful etymology of the German. But, when Coleridge ignores his technical jargon, as in the ode "Dejection" (1802), he still speaks of the "shaping spirit of the imagination," of imagination as a "dim analogue of creation, not all that we believe, but all that we can conceive of creation."[28] If Coleridge had not known the Germans, he would have been able to expound a Neoplatonic theory, just as Shelley did in his *Defence of Poetry*.

Shelley's *Defence of Poetry* is almost identical, in general conception, with Coleridge's theory. Imagination is the "principle of synthesis." Poetry may be defined as the "expression of the imagination." A poet "participates in the eternal, the infinite, and the one." Poetry lifts the veil from the "hidden beauty of the world, and makes familiar objects be as if they were not familiar." "Poetry redeems from decay the visi-

[26] Jan. 21, 1824. In *Letters: Later Years*, ed. E. de Selincourt (Oxford, 1939), I, 134–35.

[27] *The Rime of the Ancient Mariner: With an Essay by Robert Penn Warren* (New York, 1946).

[28] *Letters*, ed. E. H. Coleridge (London, 1890), II, 450.

tations of the divinity in man." To Shelley imagination is creative, and
the poet's imagination is an instrument of knowledge of the real.
Shelley, more sharply than any other English poet with the exception
of Blake, states that the poetic moment is the moment of vision; that the
words are but a "feeble shadow," that the mind in composition is a
"fading coal." In Shelley we find the most radical divorce between the
poetic faculty and will and consciousness.

The affinities and fundamental identities of Keats's views are
obvious, though Keats (under the influence of Hazlitt) has more of the
sensationalist vocabulary than either Coleridge or Shelley. But he also
says: "What the Imagination seizes as Beauty must be Truth whether
it existed before or not." Clarence D. Thorpe, in analyzing all of Keats's
relevant scattered pronouncements, concludes: "Such is the power of
creative imagination, a seeing, reconciling, combining force that seizes
the old, penetrates beneath its surface, disengages the truth slumbering
there, and, building afresh, bodies forth anew a reconstructed universe
in fair forms of artistic power and beauty."[29] This could be a summary of
the theories of imagination of all the romantic poets.

Clearly, such a theory implies a theory of reality and, expecially, of
nature. There are individual differences among the great romantic
poets concerning the conception of nature. But all of them share a
common objection to the mechanistic universe of the eighteenth century—even though Wordsworth admires Newton and accepts him,
at least in the orthodox interpretation. All romantic poets conceived
of nature as an organic whole, on the analogue of man rather than a
concourse of atoms—a nature that is not divorced from æsthetic
values, which are just as real (or rather more real) than the abstractions
of science.

Blake stands somewhat apart. He violently objects to the eighteenth-
century cosmology, personified by Newton.

> May God us keep
> From Single Vision and Newton's sleep!

Blake's writings are also full of condemnations of Locke and Bacon,
atomism, deism, natural religion, and so forth. But he does not share
the romantic deification of nature; he comments expressly on Wordsworth's preface to the *Excursion:* "You shall not bring me down to

---

[29] *The Mind of John Keats* (Oxford, 1926), p. 126.

believe such fitting and fitted." To Blake nature is everywhere fallen. It fell with man; the fall of man and the creation of the physical world were the same event. In the Golden Age to come, nature will (with man) be restored to her pristine glory. Man and nature are, in Blake, not only continuous, but emblematic of each other. . . .

In *Milton* especially, nature appears as man's body turned inside out. The ridges of mountains across the world are Albion's fractured spine. Nothing exists outside Albion; sun, moon, stars, the center of the earth, and the depth of the sea were all within his mind and body. Time even is a pulsation of the artery, and space a globule of blood. The crabbed symbolism, the strident tone have kept these later poems from being widely read; but the books by Damon, Percival, Schorer, and Frye[30] have shown the subtlety and coherence of Blake's speculations which set him in the great tradition of *Naturphilosophie* as it comes down from Plato's *Timaeus* to Paracelsus, Boehme, and Swedenborg.

In Wordsworth's conception of nature there is a shift from something like animistic pantheism to a conception reconcilable with traditional Christianity. Nature is animated, alive, filled with God or the Spirit of the World; it is mysteriously present, it gives a discipline of fear and ministry of pleasure. Nature is also a language, a system of symbols. The rocks, the crags, the streams on Simplon Pass

> Were all like workings of one mind, the features
> Of the same face, blossoms upon one tree;
> Characters of the great Apocalypse,
> The types and symbols of Eternity.

We would misunderstand idealistic epistemology if we questioned the "objectivity" which Wordsworth ascribes to these conceptions. It is a dialectical relation, not a mere subjectivist imposition, in spite of such passages as "from thyself it comes that thou must give, Else never canst receive." The mind must collaborate and it is its very nature that it should be so.

> . . . my voice proclaims
> How exquisitely the individual mind . . .
> to the external world

[30] S. Foster Damon, *William Blake* (Boston, 1924); Milton O. Percival, *William Blake's "Circle of Destiny"* (New York, 1938); Mark Schorer, *William Blake* (New York, 1946); Northrop Frye, *Fearful Symmetry: A Study of William Blake* (Princeton, 1947).

> Is fitted:—and how exquisitely too . . .
> The external world is fitted to the Mind
> And the creation (by no lower name
> Can it be called) which they with blended might
> Accomplish. [Wellek's ellipses]

The ancestry of these ideas in Cudworth, Shaftesbury, Berkeley, and others is obvious; there are certain poetic anticipations in Akenside and Collins; but, in Wordsworth, a natural philosophy, a metaphysical concept of nature, enters poetry and finds a highly individual expression—the brooding presence of the hills, of the firm, eternal forms of nature, combined with a vivid sense of the almost dreamlike unreality of the world.

The general concept of nature he shares with his friend Coleridge. We could easily match all the fundamental concepts of Wordsworth in Coleridge; probably their phrasing is due to the influence of Coleridge, who early was a student of the Cambridge Platonists and of Berkeley.

> The one Life within us and abroad . . .
> And what if all of animated nature . . .
> Plastic and vast, one intellectual breeze.
> At once the Soul of each, and God of all . . . [Wellek's ellipses]

the "eternal language, which thy God utters," "Symbolical, one mighty alphabet," and the conception of subject-object relation:

> We receive but what we give
> And in our life alone does Nature live!

—these are quotations from the early poetry. The later Coleridge developed an elaborate philosophy of nature which leans heavily on Schelling's and Steffens' *Naturphilosophie*. Nature is consistently interpreted by analogy with the progress of man to self-consciousness, and Coleridge indulges in all the contemporary speculative chemistry and physics (electricity, magnetism) to buttress a position which is near to vitalism or panpsychism.

Echoes of this contemporary science also permeate Shelley's conceptions and even images. There are many allusions in his poetry to chemical, electrical, and magnetic theories—to theories expounded by Erasmus Darwin, and Humphrey Davy. But, in general terms, Shelley mainly echoes Wordsworth and Coleridge on the "spirit of nature." There is the same concept of the vitality of nature, its continuity with

man, its emblematic language. There is also the concept of the coopera-
tion and interrelation of subject and object, as in the beginning of
Mont Blanc:

> The everlasting universe of things
> Flows through the mind, and rolls its rapid waves,
> Now dark—now glittering—now reflecting gloom—
> Now lending splendor, where from secret springs
> The source of human thought its tribute brings
> Of waters,—with a sound but half its own.

This seems to say: There is nothing outside the mind of man, but the
receptive function of the stream of consciousness is very much larger
than the tiny active principle in the mind.

> My own, my human mind, which passively
> Now renders and receives fast influencings,
> Holding an unremitting interchange
> With the clear universe of things around.

Here we have, in spite of the stress on the passivity of the mind, a
clear conception of a give and take, of an interchange between its
creative and purely receptive principles. Shelley conceives of nature as
one phenomenal flux; he sings of clouds, wind, and water rather than,
like Wordsworth, of the mountains or the "soul of lonely places."
But he does not, of course, stop with nature, but seeks the higher unity
behind it:

> Life, like a dome of many-colored glass,
> Stains the white radiance of Eternity.

In the highest ecstasy, all individuality and particularity are abolished
by the great harmony of the world. But in Shelley, in contrast to Blake
or Wordsworth who calmly look into the life of things, the ideal itself
dissolves; his voice falters; the highest exaltation becomes a total loss
of personality, an instrument of death and annihilation.

In Keats, the romantic conception of nature occurs, but only in
attenuated form, though it would be hard to deny the poet of *Endymion*
or the "Ode to a Nightingale" an intimate relation to nature and to
the nature mythology of the ancients. "Hyperion" (1820) obscurely
hints at an optimistic evolutionism, as in the speech of Oceanos to his
fellow Titans:

> We fall by course of Nature's laws,
> Not force. . . .
>   As thou wast not the first of powers
> So art thou not the last . . .
> So on our heels a fresh perfection treads.
>   . . . for 'tis the eternal law
> That first in beauty should be first in might. [Wellek's ellipses]

But Keats, possibly because he was a doctor, was least affected by the romantic conception of nature.

This conception occurs, though only fitfully, in Byron, who does *not* share the romantic conception of imagination. It is present especially in the third canto of *Childe Harold* (1818), written in Geneva when Shelley was his constant companion:

> I live not in myself, but I become
> Portion of that around me; and to me
> High mountains are a feeling.

Byron mentions:

>   the feeling infinite, so felt
> In solitude where we are least alone;
> A truth which through our being then doth melt
> And purifies from self.

But generally Byron is rather a deist who believes in the Newtonian world machine and constantly contrasts man's passion and unhappiness with the serene and indifferent beauty of nature. Byron knows the horror of man's isolation, the terrors of the empty spaces, and does not share the fundamental rejection of the eighteenth-century cosmology nor the feeling of continuity and basic at-homeness in the universe of the great romantic poets.

This conception of the nature of poetic imagination and of the universe has obvious consequences for poetic practice. All the great romantic poets are mythopoeic, are symbolists whose practice must be understood in terms of their attempt to give a total mythic interpretation of the world to which the poet holds the key. The contemporaries of Blake began his revival of mythic poetry—which can be seen even in their interest in Spenser, in *Midsummer Night's Dream* and *The Tempest*, in the devils and witches of Burns, in the interest of Collins in Highland superstitions and their value for the poet, in the pseudo-Norse mythology of Gray, and in the antiquarian researches of Jacob Bryant and

Edward Davies. But the first English poet to create a new mythology on a grand scale was Blake.

Blake's mythology is neither classical nor Christian, though it incorporates many Biblical and Miltonic elements. It draws vaguely on some Celtic (Druidical) mythology or rather names, but essentially it is an original (possibly a too original) creation which tries to give both a cosmogony and an apocalypse: a philosophy of history, a psychology, and (as has been recently stressed) a vision of politics and morals. Even the simplest of the *Songs of Innocence* and *Songs of Experience* are permeated by Blake's symbols. His last poems, such as *Jerusalem*, require an effort of interpretation which may not be commensurate to the æsthetic rewards we get; but Northrop Frye has certainly shown convincingly that Blake was an extraordinarily original thinker who had ideas on cycles of culture, metaphysical theories of time, speculations about the universal diffusion throughout primitive society of archetypal myths and rituals—which may be frequently confused and dilettantish, but which should not prove incomprehensible to an age which has acclaimed Toynbee, or Dunne on time, or has developed modern anthropology.

Wordsworth, at first sight, is the romantic poet farthest removed from symbolism and mythology. Josephine Miles in her study, *Wordsworth and the Vocabulary of Emotion*, has taken him as the prime example of the poet who states emotions, names them specifically. But Wordsworth does stress imagery in his theory and is by no means indifferent to mythology. He plays an important part in the new interest in Greek mythology interpreted in terms of animism. There is the sonnet, "The World is too much with us," and there is a passage in the fourth book of the *Excursion* (1814) which celebrates the dim inklings of immortality that the Greek sacrificing a lock in a stream may have had. There is the later turning to classical mythology, "Laodamia" and the "Ode to Lycoris," poems which Wordsworth defended also for their material "which may ally itself with real sentiment."

But, most important, his poetry is not without pervading symbols. Cleanth Brooks has shown convincingly how the "Ode on Intimations" is based on a double, contradictory metaphor of light and how even the sonnet, "Upon Westminster Bridge," conceals an all-pervasive figure.[31] *The White Doe of Rylstone* may be really allegorical, in an almost

---

[31] *The Well Wrought Urn* (New York, 1947). [But see also Brooks's general attack on the romantic conception of metaphor in his essay above.]

mediæval sense (the doe is like an animal in a Bestiary), but even this late piece shows Wordsworth's endeavor to go beyond the anecdotal or the descriptive, beyond the naming and analyzing of emotions and states of mind.

In Coleridge a theory of symbolism is central; the artist discourses to us by symbols, and nature is a symbolic language. The distinction between symbol and allegory is, in Coleridge, related to that between imagination and fancy (which, in some ways, can be described as a theory of imagery), genius and talent, reason and understanding. In a late discussion he says that an allegory is but a translation of abstract notions into a picture language, which is itself nothing but an abstraction from objects of sense. On the other hand, a symbol is characterized by a translucence of the special in the individual, or of the general in the special, or of the universal in the general; above all, a symbol is characterized by the translucence of the eternal through and in the temporal. The faculty of symbols is the imagination. Coleridge condemned classical as distinct from Christian mythology in many early pronouncements; but later he became interested in a symbolically reinterpreted Greek mythology and wrote a queer piece "On the *Prometheus* of Aeschylus" (1825), which is closely dependent on Schelling's treatise, *Über die Gottheiten von Samothrace* (1815).

The early great poetry of Coleridge is certainly symbolic throughout. R. P. Warren has recently given an interpretation of the *Ancient Mariner*, which may go too far in detail, but is convincing in the general thesis—the whole poem implies a concept of "sacramentalism," of the holiness of nature and all natural beings, and is organized on symbols of moon light and sunlight, wind and rain.

That Shelley is a symbolist and mythologist needs no argument. Not only is Shelley's poetry metaphorical through and through, but he aspires to create a new myth of the redemption of the earth which uses classical materials very freely, e.g., in *Prometheus Unbound* (1820), in the *Witch of Atlas*, and in *Adonais* (1821). This last poem can be easily misinterpreted if it is seen merely as a pastoral elegy in the tradition of Bion and Moschus. Through Shelley's poetry runs a fairly consistent system of recurrent symbols: the eagle and the serpent (which has Gnostic antecedents), temples, towers, the boat, the stream, the cave, and, of course, the veil, the cupola of stained glass, and the white radiance of eternity. . . .

In Shelley the ecstasy takes on a hectic, falsetto tone, the voice breaks at the highest points; he swoons, "I faint, I fail!" "I fall upon the thorns of life! I bleed!" Shelley would like us to transcend the boundaries of individuality, to be absorbed into some Nirvana. This craving for unity explains also one pervading characteristic of his style; synæsthesia and the fusing of the spheres of the different senses in Shelley is paralleled in his rapid transitions and fusions of the emotions, from pleasure to pain, from sorrow to joy.

Keats is a mythologist, too. *Endymion* and "Hyperion" are eloquent witnesses. There is in Keats the recurrent symbolism of moon and sleep, temple and nightingale. The great odes are not merely a series of pictures, but symbolic constructions in which the poet tries to state the conflict of artist and society, time and eternity.

Byron also—as Wilson Knight has shown extravagantly in *The Burning Oracle*—can be interpreted in these terms: *Manfred* (1817), *Cain, Heaven and Earth*, and even *Sardanapalus* (1821). The great poets are not alone in their time. Southey wrote his epics, *Thalaba, Madoc* (1805), *The Curse of Kehama* (1810), on mythological themes from ancient Wales and India. Thomas Moore gained fame with the Oriental pseudosplendor of *Lalla Rookh* (1817), Mrs. Tighe's *Psyche* influenced Keats. Finally, in 1821, Carlyle published *Sartor Resartus*, with its philosophy of clothes. Whatever the level of penetration, there is a widespread return to the mythic conception of poetry which had been all but forgotten in the eighteenth century. Pope at most could conceive of burlesque machines such as the Sylphs in the *Rape of the Lock* or the grandiose, semiserious last yawn of Night at the conclusion of the *Dunciad*. . . .[32]

[Wellek here briefly looks at Italian, Spanish, Scandinavian, Slavic, Polish, and Czech romanticism, all or most of which fit his "pattern."]

My conclusion concerning the unity of the romantic movement may be distressingly orthodox and even conventional. But it seems necessary to reassert it, especially in view of Lovejoy's famous attack. "On the Discrimination of Romanticisms" proves, it seems to me, only that Joseph Warton was an early naturalistic preromanticist, that Friedrich Schlegel was a highly sophisticated, self-conscious intellectual, and that Chateaubriand held many classicist views on literary criticism and on Shake-

---

[32] W. K. Wimsatt's excellent "The Structure of Romantic Nature Imagery," in *The Age of Johnson: Essays Presented to C. B. Tinker* (New Haven, 1949), pp. 291–303, was published too late for consideration in the text. It certainly supports my argument. [See Wimsatt's essay below.]

speare. The fact that Chateaubriand was conservative and Hugo ended in liberalism does not disrupt the continuity of French romanticism as a literary movement. On the whole, political criteria seem grossly overrated as a basis for judging a man's basic view of the world and artistic allegiance.

I do not, of course, deny differences between the various romantic movements, differences of emphasis and distribution of elements, differences in the pace of development, in the individualities of the great writers. I am perfectly aware that the three groups of ideas I have selected have their historical ancestry before the age of Enlightenment and in undercurrents during the eighteenth century. The view of an organic nature descends from Neoplatonism through Giordano Bruno, Boehme, the Cambridge Platonists, and some passages in Shaftesbury. The view of imagination as creative and of poetry as prophecy has a similar ancestry. A symbolist, and even mythic, conception of poetry is frequent in history, e.g., in the baroque age with its emblematic art, its view of nature as hieroglyphics which man and especially the poet is destined to read. In a sense, romanticism is the revival of something old, but it is a revival with a difference; these ideas were translated into terms acceptable to men who had undergone the experience of the Enlightenment. It may be difficult to distinguish clearly between a romantic and a baroque symbol, the romantic and the Böhmian view of nature and imagination. But for our problem we need only know that there is a difference between the symbol in Pope and in Shelley. This can be described; the change from the type of imagery and symbolism used by Pope to that used by Shelley is an empirical fact of history. It seems difficult to deny that we are confronted with substantially the same fact in noting the difference between Lessing and Novalis or Voltaire and Victor Hugo.

Lovejoy has argued that the "new ideas of the period were in large part heterogeneous, logically independent and sometimes essentially antithetic to one another in their implications."[33] If we look back on our argument, it will be obvious that this view must be mistaken. There is, on the contrary, a profound coherence and mutual implication between the romantic views of nature, imagination, and symbol. Without such a view of nature we could not believe in the significance of symbol and

[33] "The Meaning of Romanticism for the Historian of Ideas," *Journal of the History of Ideas*, II, (1941), 261.

myth. Without symbol and myth the poet would lack the tools for the insight into reality which he claimed, and without such an epistemology, which believes in the creativity of the human mind, there would not be a living nature and a true symbolism. We may not accept this view of the world for ourselves—few of us can accept it literally today—but we should grant that it is coherent and integrated and, as I hope I have shown, all-pervasive in Europe.

We can then go on speaking of romanticism as one European movement, whose slow rise through the eighteenth century we can describe and examine and even call, if we want to, preromanticism. Clearly there are periods of the dominance of a system of ideas and poetic practices; and clearly they have their anticipations and their survivals. To give up these problems because of the difficulties of terminology seems to me tantamount to giving up the central task of literary history. If literary history is not to be content to remain the usual odd mixture of biography, bibliography, anthology, and disconnected emotive criticism, it has to study the total process of literature. This can be done only by tracing the sequence of periods, the rise, dominance, and disintegration of conventions and norms. The term "romanticism" posits all these questions, and that, to my mind, is its best defense.

BIBLIOGRAPHICAL NOTE: See the bibliographical note to A. O. Lovejoy's essay, p. 81 above, for references to the Lovejoy-Wellek-Peckham controversy. A recent essay taking issue with Wellek is Irving Massey's "The Romantic Movement: Phrase or Fact," *Dalhousie Review*, XLIV (1964), 396–412. See also George Whalley, "Literary Romanticism," *Queens Quarterly*, LXXII (1965), 232–52. Ian Jack, in Vol. X of *The Oxford History of English Literature* (Oxford, 1963) argues that such "schematizations" as Wellek's lead to grave difficulties in studying the literature of the Romantic Period.

Romantic Religion

Hoxie Neale Fairchild

For some years I held the opinion that romanticism could most fruitfully be defined as the attempt to achieve, to retain, or to justify that emotional experience which is produced by an imaginative interfusion of real and ideal, natural and supernatural, finite and infinite, man and God.[1] It might have been simpler to say, "Romanticism means in art what pantheism means in theology." Although "pantheism" is perhaps too slippery a term to be relied upon in explaining a still more slippery one, this shorter version gives a fair equivalent of the original if pantheism be understood as the ascription of numinousness to a feeling of cosmic unity and interfusion. Either ver-

ROMANTIC RELIGION: From *Religious Trends in English Poetry*, Vol. III: *1780–1830, Romantic Faith* (New York: Columbia University Press, 1949), reprinted by permission of the Columbia University Press and Chatto & Windus Ltd.

[1] For an expanded statement of this position see my *Romantic Quest* (New York, 1931) pp. 237–56. [In that work Fairchild defined romanticism as follows: "Romanticism is the endeavour, in the face of growing factual obstacles, to achieve, to retain, or to justify that illusioned view of the universe and of human life which is produced by an imaginative fusion of the familiar and the strange, the known and the unknown, the real and the ideal, the finite and the infinite, the material and the spiritual, the natural and the supernatural."]

sion implies that romanticism, at its deepest and most intense, is essentially a religious experience.

For me this definition remains useful in the study of the romantic spirit and its expression in art. Further reading and thinking, however, have gradually drawn me toward the conclusion that the interfusion-experience is the flower of romanticism but not its root. It is the culminating exploit of that imaginative power which Coleridge describes as "a repetition within the finite mind of the eternal act of creation in the infinite I AM." And the romantic faith in this power stems from a deeper, broader faith in the natural goodness, strength, and creativity of all human energies. The taproot of romanticism, then, is an eternal and universal and primary fact of consciousness: man's desire for self-trust, self-expression, self-expansion. That is why the interfusion-experience is so precious to the romanticist: by effacing all distinctions and boundaries it permits unlimited outward projection of personal energy.

[Fairchild here catalogs various definitions of romanticism—Crane Brinton's in *The Political Ideas of the English Romanticists* (London, 1926), Jacques Barzun's in *Romanticism and the Modern Ego* (Boston, 1943), O. W. Campbell's in *Shelley and the Unromantics* (New York, 1924), J. H. Muirhead's in *Coleridge as Philosopher* (London, 1930), Paul Elmer More's in *The Drift of Romanticism* (Boston, 1913), T. E. Hulme's in *Speculations*, Denis Saurat's in *Blake and Modern Thought* (New York, 1929), and Albert Guerard's in "Prometheus and the Aeolian Lyre," *Yale Review*, XXXIII (1944).]

In the so-called romantic period, human self-confidence totters as it reaches its climax. Man asserts mastery more strongly than ever before—and begins to feel more strongly than ever before that he is the slave of matter and mechanism. Greatly encouraged and greatly threatened, at once triumphant and desperate, the romantic impulse for the first time organizes itself into an *ism*. Prometheus raises his voice in a song of confident power, but he cracks on the top note.

Especially in dealing with the major *English* poets of the period we should avoid exaggerating the romantic elements in their general environment and should duly emphasize those anti-romantic pressures which impelled them to defend their vision—the post-Revolutionary conservative reaction, the mechanistic and materialistic temper of the Industrial Revolution, the Utilitarian-Evangelical compromise, the pervasive pre-Victorian spirit of smug indifference or hostility to art.

The poets to be discussed in this volume are exceptional persons, more influential for later generations than for their own. The historian who examines them is studying the history of great Englishmen rather than the history of the English people between 1780 and 1830. To be sure, the thoughts and feelings of these men may be observed, in varying degrees of dilution, in the verse of their minor contemporaries. But if the present study were as hospitable to bad writing as the two preceding volumes of this series the run-of-the-mill poetry of the 1780–1830 period would reveal, on the whole, a rather timid continuation of eighteenth-century sentimentalism—a romanticism not fully aware of the glory and the peril of its status in a rapidly changing world. More frequently than in the Age of Johnson, however, we should find a blending of sentimental hankerings with a softened, half-romanticized evangelicalism in a poetry which neither boldly affirms nor boldly denies the dominant tendencies of the *milieu*.

The major romantic poets reject this yea-and-nay compromise. "We want the poetry of life." They mean, of course, that they want religion. If human creativity is to elude the threat of mechanism, a downright naturalistic humanism is unthinkable: the pure Renaissance tradition has been taken over by the enemy. Nature—including of course human nature—must be supernaturalized. Some sort of Divine Spirit is therefore a necessity; and while the immanence of this Spirit is of primary importance for the romantic experience, its supernatural status must be safeguarded by ascribing to It some measure of transcendence. Consequently this Spirit of the Universe, or Nature, or Love, or Beauty, may be endowed with several of the traditional attributes of God—creative power, wisdom, benevolence, sometimes even providential care. More or less personified for the uses of poetry, this deity may be loved, worshipped, addressed in prayer, mystically contemplated.

The romantic God, however, exists for the purpose not of transforming a weak and sinful creature into a being worthy of salvation, but of authenticating the natural goodness of man and lending divine sanction to his expansive impulses. "In remembering that one is mortal," says Mrs. Campbell, "there is no romance."[2] More drily, Professor Bush observes that "A romantic has been succinctly defined as a person who does not believe in the fall of man."[3] Although God represents ideals

[2] O. W. Campbell, *Shelley and the Unromantics*, p. 258.
[3] D. N. Bush, *Mythology and the Romantic Tradition in English Poetry* (Cambridge, Mass., 1937), p. 155.

which the romanticist in his less sanguine moments may feel to be unattainable, there can be no essential disharmony between the spirit of God and the spirit of man. The difference is of degree, not of kind. For all his detestation of anthropomorphism, the romantic poet shapes a deity who is the supreme romantic genius, thus erecting a much more formidable rationalization of human self-sufficiency than a flatly nonreligious naturalism could provide.

· · ·

How are Christianity and the romantic religion of self-trust related? The question cannot be answered dogmatically in days when the former term is often applied to anyone who regards the universe with approval and believes in persuading the less attractive young people of the community to dance with one another in drearily wholesome surroundings. For the theologically precise, the problem is simple enough: the religion of Emerson and of the romantic poets is a tissue of heresies. On the other hand, those who interpret Christianity as a religion of human self-sufficiency will naturally assert that romanticism is the embodiment in art of the Christian spirit. Thus Mrs. Campbell describes Jesus as "the great romantic"—greater even than Shelley— because He established that "Christian belief in man" which is the essence of romanticism.[4] Professor Barzun associates romanticism with a more historical conception of Christianity:

> The judgment of Mme. de Staël, aided by Schlegel's, that the romantic view of life is basically Christian seems fully justified, for it combines the infinite worth of the individual soul in its power and weakness, the search for union with God and the gospel of work for one's fellow man.[5]

But here some would plead for a closer analysis of terms, which might show that worth of the soul, power and weakness of the soul, union with God, and human brotherhood do not mean for the romantic quite what they mean for the Christian.

No conclusion can be drawn from what the romantic poets thought of their own beliefs. Burns, Blake, and Coleridge regarded themselves as good Christians. So did Wordsworth throughout most of his long career, though for a brief but important period he probably deemed himself a deist. Shelley and Keats were avowedly non-Christian. Byron at times repudiated Christianity and at other times wished to be

[4] *Op. cit.*, pp. 252, 253.
[5] *Romanticism and the Modern Ego*, p. 133.

thought a better Christian than the shocked readers of *Cain*. Of course anyone can call himself a Christian. On the other hand, if romanticism expresses that pure Christianity toward which the first seventeen centuries of the Christian era had been groping through the fogs of superstition and bigotry, then the more emphatically a poet repudiates traditional Christianity the more strikingly he exemplifies what Christianity *ought* to be. One might suppose that belief in God, not belief in oneself, is the starting-point of the Christian experience. But since Mrs. Campbell regards Christianity and romanticism as equivalent terms for the cult of self-sufficiency, she need not hesitate to describe Shelley as a Christian: "The most important of his beliefs, the motive power of his life and work, was his immense *faith in man*. . . . It seemed to spring in the first place from that sense of his own divinity with which all geniuses are endowed. He extended this to all the world."[6] . . .

The tendency to identify romantic religion with Christianity will be especially strong among those who, brushing aside the distinction between religion and ethics, trace romantic benevolism back to the Sermon on the Mount. It will probably be useless to remind them that there is nothing peculiarly Christian about humanitarianism unless it is the humanitarianism of Christians. The following chapters may indicate that romantic benevolism implies quite as much self-regard as self-sacrifice. The Good Samaritan was not actuated by "that sense of his own divinity with which all geniuses are endowed."

It is at all events a little confusing, for history no less than for theology, to apply the same title to a religion of human insufficiency, which offers redemption at the cost of humility and self-surrender, and to a religion of human sufficiency, which denies the necessity of redemption and offers man limitless self-expansion at no greater cost than the will to affirm his own goodness as part of a good universe; to a religion in which grace descends to man from a great outward Reality completely independent of his desires and imaginings, and to a religion in which grace is the echo of man's pride; to a religion which says, "Be it unto me according to thy word," and to a religion which says, "No law can be sacred to me but that of my own nature." Some will prefer to regard these as two stages in the gradual purification of Christianity. For me, however, the difference is so radical that I must continue to affront certain critics by restricting the term "Christianity" to the former

---

[6] *Op. cit.*, p. 279 [Mrs. Campbell's italics].

kind of religion. The latter I call "religion of sentiment" in its preliminary eighteenth-century phases and "romantic religion" when it comes to full bloom in the period under discussion. Although my personal preference for Christianity is unconcealed, the distinction is drawn not in the spirit of Torquemada but in that of an historian who is trying to avoid muddle.

This terminology by no means denies the possibility of tracing a line of descent from Christian to romantic belief. The spiritual genealogy of Emerson is clear enough: Puritanism sloughs down into Unitarianism; Unitarianism sloughs down into a romantic transcendentalism partly indigenous and partly fabricated from English, German, and Oriental materials. This movement will be familiar to readers of the earlier volumes of this series, which have tried to show that seventeenth-century Protestantism, especially of the Puritan type, is the father of that eighteenth-century sentimentalism which becomes romanticism on attaining maturity. The host of witnesses—some 380 poets of the eighteenth century—cannot be recalled to the stand; but, as above in describing my general conception of romanticism, I shall venture to remind the reader that the thesis is not the unique product of one student's personal bias. The scholars to be cited are not the lobbyists of any single religious faction. In matters of detail their accounts of the historical process sometimes differ widely from mine. We agree, however, on the major point that romantic religion descends from an essential element of the Protestant ethos.

[Fairchild here summarizes several views of the relationship between the course of Puritanism since the seventeenth century and the emergence of romantic "religion"—J. W. Draper's in *The Funeral Elegy and the Rise of Romanticism* (New York, 1929), Louis Cazamian's in *L'évolution psychologique et la litterature en Angleterre 1660–1914* (Paris, 1920), F. C. Gill's in *The Romantic Movement and Methodism* (London, 1937), Umphrey Lee's in *The Historical Backgrounds of Early Methodist Enthusiasm* (New York, 1931), Sister M. Kevin Whelan's in *Enthusiasm in English Poetry of the Eighteenth Century* (Washington, D.C., 1935), and William Haller's in *The Rise of Puritanism* (New York, 1938).]

Of course man's desire to feel self-sufficiently good, strong, and creative is much older than any form of Christianity. It is as old as human nature. In ancient times, it seizes upon selected aspects of Platonism, Stoicism, and Epicureanism—traditions which continue to be directly or indirectly influential throughout the history of the theme.

In the Middle Ages, drawing much encouragement from Neoplatonic thought, it appears most clearly in the Pelagian heresy and in various expressions of "pre-Protestant" mysticism. In the sixteenth century, the romantic impulse is partly encouraged and partly threatened by the Renaissance, by the new science, and by the official formularies of the Reformation; but it draws immense nourishment from deep-rooted elements in Protestant psychology which are soon to transform the theologies of Luther and Calvin—or perhaps to reveal their essential meaning. In the seventeenth century, romantic self-trust becomes the principal factor in the disintegration of Protestant Christianity. Uncurbed by Catholic or classical restraints, it goes far toward substituting a religion of justification by self-esteem for a religion of justification by faith.

In the eighteenth century the romantic urge receives a satisfying rationalization in the sentimental deism of Shaftesbury and in the poetry which flows from it. God, man, and nature are pantheistically interfused. In this system of universal benevolence, man shares immanent divinity with nature. Self-love, social love, and divine love are indistinguishable. Nature's God has confirmed man's longing to find goodness, wisdom, and creative power in the depths of his own heart. With rare exceptions, however, the religion of sentiment as expressed in eighteenth-century poetry retains a considerable amount of neoclassical nothing-too-muchness, common sense, utilitarianism, objectivity, and respect for the mechanical laws of Newtonian science. At last the accelerating tempo of social change renders this compromise inadequate for a few unusually sensitive and perceptive spirits. Then it is that the great poets of the 1780–1830 period, building upon the romantic elements in their eighteenth-century heritage, burst forth in songs of strangely mingled triumph and despair.

[In a series of chapters on the romantic poets Fairchild next demonstrates that each of them, "in his own way, exemplifies the general description of romantic religion" offered above. But, he agrees in his last chapter, "Romantic religion should be judged by its ultimate fruits in art, in the life of the individual, and in social life as a whole. Although such an evaluation must await the completion of this series of studies (i.e., Fairchild's multivolume work, *Religious Trends in English Poetry*), the urgent importance of the problem for our own day perhaps justifies a tentative expression of opinion."]

Those who advocate a revival of romanticism will assert that although our poets were not orthodox Christians they preserved the essentials of Christianity and of all pure religion at a time not unlike our own in that those essentials were in danger of being abandoned along with the outworn creeds which had obscured them. They resisted external dogmas and oppressive ecclesiastical institutions only because they believed so ardently in the free faith of the heart. In the same spirit they championed the rights of the human soul against the crudely mechanistic conception of science and the dehumanizing effects of the Industrial Revolution. Their passionate individualism was not a thing of selfish pride: on the contrary, their highest aspiration was submergence of selfhood in devotion to extrapersonal ideals.

The romantic poets believed in love as the divine creative principle of the universe. They sang of brotherhood, freedom, democracy. They were great liberals and humanitarians. Often, too, they elevated sexual love to a religious level. They believed in nature—not as a mass of matter operating like a soulless machine, but as a beneficent force uniting in a cosmic wholeness of being the divine spirit of love, the love-begotten world of sense-perception, and the loving heart of man. They believed in the creativity of the imagination as the repetition within the human mind of the divine creative act of self-assertion. They believe in the beauty of truth and the truth of beauty. For them poetry was not an elegant amusement, but a prophetic force, a revelation of mystical insight. In a word, they believed in man—in his natural goodness, his spiritual and intellectual energies, his power to see into the life of things, his kinship with divinity.

This, the twentieth-century champion of romanticism will conclude, is the creed of a genuine religion, a religion still available for the reintegration of the modern ego. Romantic religion seems to offer a means of rising above a merely animal or mechanical existence. It promises, furthermore, that in accepting it we shall obtain the higher spiritual values without paying the stiff price exacted by Christianity: discipline, humility, self-surrender, awareness of sin, penitence and penance, the way of the Cross. The romantic faith offers Easter without Good Friday. But if we prefer to identify it with Christianity—Christianity without tears—there is nothing to hinder us from doing so. Coleridge himself has declared that "Christianity at any period" is "the ideal of the Human Soul at that period."

It seems to me, however, that my deliberately flattering sketch has described not what these poets actually believed, but what they vainly longed and struggled to believe. From the utterances of some of our contemporaries we might infer that in shifting our minds backward into the Romantic Period we should be moving from an atmosphere of stultifying doubt into one of vigorous confidence. On the contrary, the final impression made upon us by these poets is that they are desperately striving to retain prerogatives which the three preceding centuries had transferred from God to man but which they now feel to be slipping from their grasp. The extravagance of their most confident moments often sounds over-strained and shrill, and one of their persistent themes is the impossibility of achieving the romantic experience. Sooner or later they all acknowledge the barrenness of their illusions. That Byron does so is obvious. A possible exception is Blake: partly because of his deeper mental eccentricity and partly because he works with his hands as well as with his brain, he holds the vision more firmly and happily than his fellows. Even he, however, is unable to forget the "little curtain of flesh on the bed of our desire." The devotion to "pure" art which characterizes the final phase of his career is in some measure a retreat from the mental fight to which he had originally devoted himself. Burns, after all his glorification of impulse, admits man's weakness and insufficiency. "I have been a fool all my life" is his final judgment of "the religion of the bosom." Wordsworth soon begins to lament the fading of the visionary gleam, and Coleridge the loss of his shaping spirit of imagination. Both poets formally abjure the romantic faith in favor of a religion which remains too romantic to be Christian although it has become too Christian to be romantic. Shelley's iridescent hopes go on and off like a firefly's light, but at the end negation has almost completely triumphed over affirmation. Keats acknowledges that the transforming power of fancy has been overrated, and he is forced to think of death as an "intenser" luxury than beauty or fame. If we wish to draw inspiration from the spectacle of a firm, consistent, sustaining faith in man's intellectual and spiritual potencies, the romantic poets will disappoint us.

•   •   •

Romantic religion deserves much of the credit for the best qualities of romantic poetry. Deprived of their faith, these poets would have had nothing of large human significance to affirm or to deny. Possessing that faith, or struggling to possess it, they had a high hope and a deep sorrow, a style, a cause, a philosophy, and a cult. Obeying the urge toward infinite expansiveness, they "shot their being through earth, sea, and air / Possessing all things with intensest love." To the great benefit of English poetry, they enriched the resources of imagery and rhythm, united man's feelings with external nature and with the glamorous past, revealed the beauty of neglected areas of life, gave a sweet and potent voice to the inmost depths of the human mind.

And yet the religion of the romantics is equally responsible for the deficiencies of their art. The primary business of the poet is not to make a world, but to fashion works of art out of positive or negative responses to the qualities of a world which already exists. The romantic faith in imaginative power, however, can be satisfied only by the creation of a universe. The poems themselves are but confessedly inadequate blueprints of the cosmic mansion. For those who insist with Browning that a man's reach should exceed his grasp the hugeness of the romantics' ambition establishes the greatness of their poetry, but others will object that all this straining to make poetry do the work of metaphysics and theology is damaging not only to religion but to art.

At their best these dreamers are also artists, masters of the technique of their instrument; but too often the joy of the craftsman is hampered by an excessively self-conscious awareness of the priesthood of genius. On the whole they think too much about being poets and not enough about writing poems. They are overly impressed by the powers and duties of the prophetic function. The urgency of their didactic obligation frequently impels them toward symbolism or even toward emotionalized rhetorical discussion. Artists are happier, and they give more happiness to mankind, when they take art a little less solemnly.

Neoromantic scholars who describe these poets as great mystics unwittingly expose one of their most serious shortcomings. Since the religious implications of poetry are not mystical but sacramental, poetry and mysticism represent opposite poles of spiritual life. Admittedly the pinnacle of the romantic faith is a sense of cosmic interfusion. But so far as this experience is genuinely mystical it transcends the utmost powers of speech, while so far as it is laden with the sensuousness of genuine poetry it vitiates the mystical aspiration. Hence the feverish struggle to express the inexpressible through a mixture of concreteness and vagueness which stirs our emotions without completely satisfying the demands either of religion or of art.[7]

•   •   •

For the last time let us remind ourselves of what we have termed the "circularity" of the romantic religious experience. Burns is a warm-hearted soul, but he uses the benevolism enjoined by his "religion of the bosom" as a means of obtaining membershp in a select circle of exceptionally sensitive and enlightened spirits. Hence it becomes an expression of egotism rather than of brotherhood. As a lover of women he is even more obviously self-centered.

Blake, who seems at first glance the most ardently religious of the group, provides the most extreme example of self-deification. "Man can have no idea of anything greater than man. . . . All deities reside in the human breast. . . . Thine own humanity learn to adore." With the deepest reverence he worships a Jesus who is no more than a symbol of his own creative energy. God is man, man in Eternity is imagination, and imagination is the genius of William Blake.

Wordsworth is set somewhat apart from his fellows by his more genuine objectivity and his desire for the security provided by extrapersonal law. It is all the more significant, therefore, that in the last analysis his interfusion-experience should prove to be the exploit of the "absolute power" of the imaginative will, a *fiat* of "the Godhead which is ours." When in revising *The Prelude* he substituted "man's power" for "my power" he made no essential change. Even after he had renounced "That licentious craving of the mind / To act the God amongst external things," he hoped to derive from Christianity a sense of "Submission constituting strength and power." Even his warmest contemporary admirers granted that he was utterly self-willed. Had his reverence always been a subconscious means of obtaining a safe harbor within which his mind could sail about under the illusion of perfect liberty?

There is no need to retrace Coleridge's "religion of I AM" through the mazes of his thought: it is obvious that from Ottery to Highgate he never contemplated anything but the ego which he simultaneously

---

[7] Keats must be regarded as an illustrious exception to these remarks on the limitations of romantic poetry; but even he, as we have observed, often plagues himself with the notion that he *should* resemble his contemporaries in these respects. The romanticism of Burns is so rudimentary that he also should be absolved from these strictures.

adored and loathed. Always he yearns to behold the ultimate reality as

> The whole one Self! Self that no alien knows!
> Self, far diffused as Fancy's wing can travel!
> Self, spreading still! Oblivious of its own,
> Yet all of all possessing!

A finished virtuoso of self-esteem, at the last he can transform even penitence into a source of pride.

The narcissistic quality of Shelley's aspiration was, I believe, sufficiently set forth in the chapter devoted to him. With all his loving soul he sought a reflection of his self-centered goodness in nature, in society, in the heart of woman, and in the Spirit of the Universe. For him as for Blake his imagination is God, and a man precisely like himself is the only conceivable redeemer. In more discouraged moments he can draw almost equal satisfaction from admiration of his blameless sufferings.

In Byron the arc of romantic religion is short-circuited by the very blatancy of his egotism. Because of his special psychological situation he both asserts and denies the impulse which dominates his fellows. He seeks inflation by means of liberalism, pantheism, and the cult of genius; but he is at once too lonely and too cynical to have any strong belief in these disguises of self-regard. He betrays romanticism in deriding his own bluster.

The romantic aspiration of Keats is specialized but intense. Much more of an artist than the others, he tries to elevate sensuous beauty to the level of an object of devotion. But when he thinks of beauty he thinks of the great poets who create it; when he thinks of great poets he thinks of fame; and when he thinks of fame he thinks of his own baffled ambition.

Whatever a romantic poet appears to be devoted to, closer examination reveals that his worship curves backward upon himself. The same may be said of innumerable professors of other religions, but there remains a vast difference between remorsefully failing to surmount a human weakness and making a cult of that weakness. By nature Saint Paul is hardly less egotistic than Blake, but he does not identify his self-esteem with the law of the universe. In his worst moments he says, "I speak as a fool," not "I speak as a genius."

Hence the beginning and the end of romantic religion is what old-fashioned folk call pride. All the loveliness that lies between results from the endeavor to impart some sort of numinous sanction to the craving for independent power. Thus romanticism originates in the deepest primordial subsoil of human nature. Historically speaking, however, the so-called Romantic Movement represents the turning-point of a Titanic assertion of human self-sufficiency which had begun to manifest itself as a dominant movement of mind in the sixteenth century.

The romantic poets show us the crest of the wave just as it shatters itself against the cliffs of reality. But the futility of pride is a lesson that each man must learn for himself, and the devices for evading the repugnant truth are legion.

• • •

BIBLIOGRAPHICAL NOTE: On romanticism and Christianity see H. J. C. Grierson's essay in this collection. See also Irving Babbitt's idea of romanticism as "sham spirituality" and T. E. Hulme's famous charge that it is "spilt religion" (both of these essays are reprinted in this collection.) With Fairchild's interpretation of the "dominant movement of mind in the sixteenth century" that led to "the so-called Romantic Movement," compare such works as Herschel Baker's *The Image of Man* (New York, 1961) and Hiram Hadyn's *The Counter-Renaissance* (New York, 1950). Morse Peckham has attacked Fairchild's "Anglo-Catholic" view of romanticism in *Studies in English Literature*, IV (1963), 596–98.

The Structure
of Romantic
Nature Imagery

W. K. Wimsatt

Students of romantic nature poetry have had a great deal to tell us about the philosophic components of this poetry: the specific blend of deistic theology, Newtonian physics, and pantheistic naturalism which pervades the Wordsworthian landscape in the period of "Tintern Abbey," the theism which sounds in the "Eolian Harp" of Coleridge, the conflict between French atheism and Platonic idealism which even in *Prometheus Unbound* Shelley was not able to resolve. We have been instructed in some of the more purely scientific coloring of the poetry— the images derived from geology, astronomy, and magnetism, and the coruscant green mystery which the electricians contributed to such phenomena as Shelley's Spirit of Earth. We have considered also the "sensibility" of romantic readers, distinct, according to one persuasive interpretation, from that of neoclassic readers. What was exciting to the age of Pope, "Puffs, Powders, Patches, Bibles, Billet-doux" (even about these the age might be loath to admit its excitement), was not, we are told, what was so manifestly exciting to the age of Wordsworth. "High mountains are a feeling, but the hum of cities torture." Lastly, recent

THE STRUCTURE OF ROMANTIC NATURE IMAGERY: From *The Age of Johnson: Essays Presented to Chauncey Brewster Tinker*, Copyright 1949 by Yale University Press. Reprinted by permission of the Yale University Press.

critical history has reinvited attention to the romantic theory of imagination, and especially to the version of that theory which Coleridge
derived from the German metaphysicians, the view of poetic imagination as the *esemplastic* power which reshapes our primary awareness of
the world into symbolic avenues to the theological.

We have, in short, a *subject*—simply considered, the nature of birds
and trees and streams—a *metaphysics* of an animating principle, a special
sensibility, and a *theory* of poetic imagination—the value of the last a
matter of debate. Romantic poetry itself has recently suffered some
disfavor among advanced critics. One interesting question, however,
seems still to want discussion; that is, whether romantic poetry (or more
specifically romantic nature poetry) exhibits any imaginative *structure*
which may be considered a special counterpart of the subject, the philosophy, the sensibility, and the theory—and hence perhaps an explanation of the last. Something like an answer to such a question is what I
would sketch.

For the purpose of providing an antithetic point of departure, I
quote here a part of one of the best known and most toughly reasonable
of all metaphysical images:

> If they be two, they are two so
> As stiff twin compasses are two,
> Thy soul the fixed foot, makes no show
> To move, but doth, if th' other do.

It will be relevant if we remark that this similitude, rather far-fetched
as some might think, is yet unmistakable to interpretation because
quite overtly stated, but again is not, by being stated, precisely defined
or limited in its poetic value. The kind of similarity and the kind of
disparity that ordinarily obtain between a drawing compass and a pair
of parting lovers are things to be attentively considered in reading this
image. And the disparity between living lovers and stiff metal is not least
important to the tone of precision, restraint, and conviction which it is
the triumph of the poem to convey. Though the similitude is cast in the
form of statement, its mood is actually a kind of subimperative. In the
next age the tension of such a severe disparity was relaxed, yet the overt-
ness and crispness of statement remained, and a wit of its own sort.

> 'Tis with our judgments as our watches, none
> Go just alike, yet each believes his own.

We may take this as typical, I believe, of the metaphoric structure in which Pope achieves perfection and which survives a few years later in the couplets of Samuel Johnson or the more agile Churchill. The difference between our judgments and our watches, if noted at all, may be a pleasant epistemological joke for a person who questions the existence of a judgment which is taken out like a watch and consulted by another judgment.

But the "sensibility," as we know, had begun to shift even in the age of Pope.* Examples of a new sensibility, and of a different structure, having something to do with Miltonic verse and a "physico-theological nomenclature," are to be found in Thomson's *Seasons*. Both a new sensibility and a new structure appear in the "hamlets brown and dim-discovered spires" of Collins's early example of the full romantic dream. In several poets of the mid century, in the Wartons, in Grainger, or in Cunningham, one may feel, or rather see stated, a new sensibility, but at the same time one may lament an absence of poetic quality—that is, of a poetic structure adequate to embody or objectify the new feeling. It is as if these harbingers of another era had felt but had not felt strongly enough to work upon the objects of their feelings a pattern of meaning which would speak for itself—and which would hence endure as a poetic monument.

As a central exhibit I shall take two sonnets, that of William Lisle Bowles "To the River Itchin" (1789) and for contrast that of Coleridge "To the River Otter" (1796)—written in confessed imitation of Bowles. Coleridge owed his first poetic inspiration to Bowles (the "father" of English romantic poetry) and continued to express unlimited admiration for him as late as 1796. That is, they shared the same sensibility—as for that matter did Wordsworth and Southey, who too were deeply impressed by the sonnets of Bowles. As a schoolboy Coleridge read eagerly in Bowles's second edition of 1789 (among other sonnets not much superior):

> Itchin, when I behold thy banks again,
> Thy crumbling margin, and thy silver breast,
> On which the self-same tints still seem to rest,
> Why feels my heart the shiv'ring sense of pain?
> Is it—that many a summer's day has past

---

* For a different view of this "shift of sensibility" see Mario Praz's essay in the collection. See also Northrop Frye's "Towards Defining an Age of Sensibility," *ELH* XXIII (1956), 144–52.

> Since, in life's morn, I carol'd on thy side?
> Is it—that oft, since then, my heart has sigh'd,
> As Youth, and Hope's delusive gleams, flew fast?
> Is it—that those, who circled on thy shore,
> Companions of my youth, now meet no more?
> Whate'er the cause, upon thy banks I bend
> Sorrowing, yet feel such solace at my heart,
> As at the meeting of some long-lost friend,
> From whom, in happier hours, we wept to part.

Here is an emotive expression which once appealed to the sensibility of its author and of his more cultivated contemporaries, but which has with the lapse of time gone flat. The speaker was happy as a boy by the banks of the river. Age has brought disillusion and the dispersal of his friends. So a return to the river, in reminding him of the past, brings both sorrow and consolation. The facts are stated in four rhetorical questions and a concluding declaration. There is also something about how the river looks and how its looks might contribute to his feelings— in the metaphoric suggestion of the "crumbling" margin and in the almost illusory tints on the surface of the stream which surprisingly have outlasted the "delusive gleams" of his own hopes. Yet the total impression is one of simple association (by contiguity in time) simply asserted —what might be described in the theory of Hume or Hartley or what Hazlitt talks about in his essay "On the Love of the Country." "It is because natural objects have been associated with the sports of our childhood, . . . with our feelings in solitude . . . that we love them as we do ourselves."

Coleridge himself in his "Lines Written at Elbingerode in 1799" was to speak of a "spot with which the heart associates Holy remembrances of child or friend." His enthusiasm for Hartley in this period is well known. But later, in the *Biographia Literaria* and in the third of his essays on "Genial Criticism," he was to repudiate explicitly the Hartleyan and mechanistic way of shifting back burdens of meaning. And already, in 1796, Coleridge as poet was concerned with the more complex ontological grounds of association (the various levels of sameness, of correspondence and analogy), where mental activity transcends mere "associative response"—where it is in fact the unifying activity known both to later eighteenth century associationists and to romantic poets as "imagination." The "sweet and indissoluble union between the intellectual and the material world" of which Coleridge speaks in the introduction to his pamphlet anthology of sonnets in 1796 must be applied by us in one sense to the sonnets of Bowles, but in another to the best romantic poetry and even to Coleridge's imitation of Bowles. There is an important difference between the kinds of unity. In a letter to Southey of 1802 Coleridge was to say more emphatically: "The poet's heart and intellect should be *combined*, intimately combined and unified with the great appearances of nature, and not merely held in solution and loose mixture with them." In the same paragraph he says of Bowles's later poetry: "Bowles has indeed the *sensibility* of a poet, but he has not the *passion* of a great poet . . . he has no native passion because he is not a thinker."

The sententious melancholy of Bowles's sonnets and the asserted connection between this mood and the appearances of nature are enough to explain the hold of the sonnets upon Coleridge. Doubtless the metaphoric coloring, faint but nonetheless real, which we have remarked in Bowles's descriptive details has also something to do with it. What is of great importance to note is that Coleridge's own sonnet "To the River Otter" (while not a completely successful poem) shows a remarkable intensification of such color.

> Dear native Brook! wild Streamlet of the West!
> How many various-fated years have past,
> What happy and what mournful hours, since last
> I skimmed the smooth thin stone along they breast,
> Numbering its light leaps! yet so deep imprest
> Sink the sweet scenes of childhood, that mine eyes
> I never shut amid the sunny ray,
> But straight with all their tints thy waters rise,
> Thy crossing plank, thy marge with willows grey,
> And bedded sand that veined with various dyes
> Gleamed through thy bright transparence! On my way,
> Visions of Childhood! oft have ye beguiled
> Lone manhood's cares, yet waking fondest sighs:
> Ah! that once more I were a careless Child!

Almost the same statement as that of Bowles's sonnet—the sweet scenes of childhood by the river have only to be remembered to bring both beguilement and melancholy. One notices immediately, however, that the speaker has kept his eye more closely on the object. There are more details. The picture is more vivid, a fact which according to one school of poetics would in itself make the sonnet superior. But a more analytic theory will find it worth remarking also that certain ideas, latent or involved in the description, have much to do with its vividness.

As a child, careless and free, wild like the streamlet, the speaker amused himself with one of the most carefree motions of youth—skimming smooth thin stones which leapt lightly on the breast of the water. One might have thought such experiences would sink no deeper in the child's breast than the stones in the water—"yet so deep imprest"—the very antithesis (though it refers overtly only to the many hours which have intervened) defines imaginatively the depth of the impressions. When he closes his eyes, they *rise* again (the word *rise* may be taken as a trope which hints the whole unstated similitude); they rise like the tinted waters of the stream; they gleam up through the depths of memory— the "various-fated years"—like the "various dyes" which vein the sand of the river bed. In short, there is a rich ground of meaning in Coleridge's sonnet beyond what is overtly stated. The descriptive details of his sonnet gleam brightly because (consciously or unconsciously—it would be fruitless to inquire how deliberately he wrote these meanings into his lines) he has invested them with significance. Here is a special perception, "invention" if one prefers, "imagination," or even "wit." It can be explored and tested by the wit of the reader. In this way it differs from the mere flat announcement of a Hartleian association, which is not open to challenge and hence not susceptible of confirmation. If this romantic wit differs from that of the metaphysicals, it differs for one thing in making less use of the central overt statement of similitude which is so important in all rhetoric stemming from Aristotle and the Renaissance. The metaphor in fact is scarcely noticed by the main statement of the poem. Both tenor and vehicle, furthermore, are wrought in a parallel process out of the same material. The river landscape is both the occasion of reminiscence and the source of the metaphors by which reminiscence is described. A poem of this structure is a signal instance of that kind of fallacy (or strategy) by which death in poetry occurs so often in winter or at night, and sweethearts meet in the spring countryside. The tenor of such a similitude is likely to be subjective—reminiscence or sorrow or beguilement—not an object distinct from the vehicle, as lovers or their souls are distinct from twin compasses. Hence the emphasis of Bowles, Coleridge, and all other romantics on spontaneous feelings and sincerity. Hence the recurrent themes of One Being and Eolian Influence and Wordsworth's "ennobling interchange of action from within and from without." In such a structure again the element of tension in disparity is not so important as for metaphysical wit. The interest derives not from our being aware of disparity where likeness is firmly insisted on, but in an opposite activity of discerning the design which is latent in the multiform sensuous picture.

Let us notice for a moment the "crossing plank" of Coleridge's sonnet, a minor symbol in the poem, a sign of shadowy presences, the lads who had once been there. The technique of this symbol is the same as that which Keats was to employ in a far more brilliant romantic instance, the second stanza of his "Ode to Autumn," where the very seasonal spirit is conjured into reality out of such haunted spots—in which a gesture lingers—the half-reaped furrow, the oozing cider press, the brook where the gleaners have crossed with laden heads. To return to our metaphysics—of an animate, plastic Nature, not transcending but immanent in and breathing through all things—and to discount for the moment such differences as may relate to Wordsworth's naturalism, Coleridge's theology, Shelley's Platonism, or Blake's visions: we may observe that the common feat of the romantic nature poets was to read meanings into the landscape. The meaning might be such as we have seen in Coleridge's sonnet, but it might more characteristically be more profound, concerning the spirit or soul of things—"the one life within us and abroad." And that meaning especially was summoned out of the very surface of nature itself. It was embodied imaginatively and without the explicit religious or philosophic statements which one will find in classical or Christian instances—for example in Pope's "Essay on Man":

> Here then we rest: "The Universal Cause
> Acts to one end, but acts by various laws,"

or in the teleological divines, More, Cudworth, Bentley, and others of the seventeenth and eighteenth centuries, or in Paley during the same era as the romantics. The romantic poets want to have it and not have it too—a spirit which the poet himself as superidealist creates by his own higher reason or esemplastic imagination. Here one may recall Ruskin's chapter of *Modern Painters* on the difference between the Greek gods of rivers and trees and the vaguer suffusions of the romantic vista—"the curious web of hesitating sentiment, pathetic fallacy, and wandering fancy, which form a great part of our modern view of nature." Wordsworth's *Prelude*, from the cliff that "upreared its head" in the night above Ullswater to the "blue chasm" that was the "soul" of the moonlit cloudscape beneath his feet on Snowdon, is the archpoet's testament, both theory and demonstration of this way of reading nature. His "Tintern Abbey" is another classic instance, a whole pantheistic poem woven of the landscape, where God is not once mentioned. After the "soft inland murmur," the "one green hue," the "wreaths of smoke . . . as . . . Of vagrant dwellers in the houseless woods" (always something just out of sight or beyond definition), it is an easy leap to the "still, sad music of humanity," and

> a sense sublime
> Of something far more deeply interfused,
> Whose dwelling is the light of setting suns.

This poem, written as Wordsworth revisited the banks of a familiar stream, the "Sylvan Wye," is the full realization of a poem for which Coleridge and Bowles had drawn slight sketches. In Shelley's "Hymn to Intellectual Beauty" the "awful shadow" of the "unseen Power" is substantiated of "moonbeam" showers of light behind the "piny mountain," of "mist o'er mountains driven." On the Lake of Geneva in the summer of 1816 Byron, with Shelley the evangelist of Wordsworth at his side, spoke of "a living fragrance from the shore," a "floating whisper on the hill." We remark in each of these examples a dramatization of the spiritual through the use of the faint, the shifting, the least tangible and most mysterious parts of nature—a poetic counterpart of the several theories of spirit as subtile matter current in the eighteenth century, Newton's "electric and elastic" active principle, Hartley's "infinitesimal elementary body." The application of this philosophy to poetry by way of direct statement had been made as early as 1735 in Henry Brooke's "Universal Beauty," where an "elastick Flue of fluctuating Air" pervades the universe as "animating Soul." In the high romantic period the most scientific version to appear in poetry was the now well-recognized imagery which Shelley drew from the electricians.

In such a view of spirituality the landscape itself is kept in focus as a literal object of attention. Without it Wordsworth and Byron in the examples just cited would not get a start. And one effect of such a use of natural imagery—an effect implicit in the very philosophy of a World Spirit—is a tendency in the landscape imagery to a curious split. If we have not only the landsape but the spirit which either informs or visits it, and if both of these must be rendered for the sensible imagination, a certain parceling of the landscape may be the result. The most curious illustrations which I know are in two of Blake's early quartet of poems to the seasons. Thus, "To Spring":

> O thou with dewy locks, who lookest down
> Thro' the clear windows of the morning, turn
> Thine angel eyes upon our western isle,
> Which in full choir hails thy approach, O Spring!
>
> The hills tell each other, and the list'ning
> Vallies hear; all our longing eyes are turned
> Up to thy bright pavillions; issue forth,
> And let thy holy feet visit our clime.
>
> Come o'er the eastern hills, and let our winds
> Kiss thy perfumed garments; let us taste
> Thy morn and evening breath; scatter thy pearls
> Upon our love-sick land that mourns for thee.

And "To Summer":

> O thou, who passest thro' our vallies in
> Thy strength, curb thy fierce steeds, allay the heat
> That flames from their large nostrils! thou, O Summer,
> Oft pitched'st here thy golden tent, and oft
> Beneath our oaks hast slept, while we beheld
> With joy thy ruddy limbs and flourishing hair.
>
> Beneath our thickest shades we oft have heard
> Thy voice, when noon upon his fervid car
> Rode o'er the deep of heaven; beside our springs
> Sit down, and in our mossy vallies, on
> Some bank beside a river clear, throw thy
> Silk draperies off, and rush into the stream.

Blake's starting point, it is true, is the opposite of Wordsworth's or Byron's, not the landscape but a spirit personified or allegorized. Nevertheless, this spirit as it approaches the "western isle" takes on certain distinctly terrestial hues. Spring, an oriental bridegroom, lives behind the "clear windows of the morning" and is invited to issue from "bright pavillions," doubtless the sky at dawn. He has "perfumed garments" which when kissed by the winds will smell much like the flowers and leaves of the season. At the same time, his *own* morn and evening breaths are most convincing in their likeness to morning and evening breezes. The pearls scattered by the hand of Spring are, we must suppose, no other than the flowers and buds which literally appear in the landscape at this season. They function as landscape details and simultaneously as properties of the bridegroom and—we note here a further complication—as properties of the land taken as lovesick maiden. We have in fact a double personification conjured from one nature, one landscape, in a wedding which approximates fusion. Even more curious is the case of King Summer, a divided tyrant and victim, who first appears as the source and spirit of heat, his steeds with flaming nostrils, his limbs ruddy, his tent golden, but who arrives in our valleys only to sleep in the shade of the oaks and be invited to rush into the river for a swim. These early romantic poems are examples of the biblical, classical, and Renaissance tradition of allegory as it approaches the romantic condition of landscape naturalism—as Spring and Summer descend into the landscape and are fused with it. Shelley's Alastor is a spirit of this kind, making the "wild his home," a spectral "Spirit of wind," expiring "Like some frail exhalation; which the dawn Robes in its golden beams." Byron's Childe Harold desired that he himself might become a "portion" of that around him, of the tempest and the night. "Be thou, Spirit fierce," said Shelley to the West Wind, "My spirit! Be thou me."

An English student of the arts in the Jacobean era, Henry Peacham, wrote a book on painting in which he gave allegorical prescriptions for representing the months, quoted under the names of months by Dr. Johnson in his *Dictionary:*

> *April* is represented by a young man in green, with a garland of myrtle and hawthorn buds; in one hand primroses and violets, in the other the sign Taurus.

> *July* I would have drawn in a jacket of light yellow, eating cherries, with his face and bosom suburnt.

But that would have been the end of it. April would not have been painted into a puzzle picture where hawthorn buds and primroses were arranged to shadow forth the form of a person. There were probably deep enough reasons why the latter nineteenth century went so far in the development of so trivial a thing as the actual landscape puzzle picture.

In his Preface of 1815 Wordsworth spoke of the *abstracting* and "*modifying* powers of the imagination." He gave as example a passage from his own poem, "Resolution and Independence," where an old leech gatherer is likened to a stone which in turn is likened to a sea beast crawled forth to sun itself. The poems which we have just considered, those of Coleridge, Wordsworth, and Blake especially, with their blurring of literal and figurative, might also be taken, I believe, as excellent examples. In another of his best poems Wordsworth produced an image which shows so strange yet artistic a warping, or modification, of vehicle by tenor that, though not strictly a nature image, it may be quoted here with close relevance. In the ode "Intimations of Immortality":

> Hence, in a season of calm weather,
> Though inland far we be,
> Our souls have sight of that immortal sea
> Which brought us hither;
> Can in a moment travel thither—
> And see the children sport upon the shore,
> And hear the mighty waters rolling evermore.

Or, as one might drably paraphrase, our souls in a calm mood look back to the infinity from which they came, as persons inland on clear days can look back to the sea by which they have voyaged to the land. The tenor concerns souls and age and time. The vehicle concerns travelers and space. The question for the analyst of structure is: Why are the children found on the seashore? In what way do they add to the solemnity or mystery of the sea? Or do they at all? The answer is that they are not strictly parts of the traveler-space vehicle, but of the soul-age-time tenor, attracted over, from tenor to vehicle. The travelers looking back in both space and time see themselves as children on the shore, as if just born like Venus from the foam. This is a sleight of words, an imposition of image upon image, by the *modifying* power of imagination.

Poetic structure is always a fusion of ideas with material, a statement in which the solidity of symbol and the sensory verbal qualities are somehow not washed out by the abstraction. For this effect the iconic or directly imitative powers of language are important—and of these the well-known onomatopoeia or imitation of sound is only one, and one of the simplest. The "stiff twin compasses" of Donne have a kind of iconicity in the very stiffness and odd emphasis of the metrical situation. Neoclassic iconicity is on the whole of a highly ordered, formal, or intellectual sort, that of the "figures of speech" such as antithesis, isocolon, homoeoteleuton, or chiasmus. But romantic nature poetry tends to achieve iconicity by a more direct sensory imitation of something headlong and impassioned, less ordered, nearer perhaps to the subrational. Thus: in Shelley's "Ode to the West Wind" the shifts in imagery of the second stanza, the pell-mell raggedness and confusion of loose clouds, decaying leaves, angels and Mænads with hair uplifted, the dirge, the dome, the vapors, and the enjambment from tercet to tercet combine to give an impression beyond statement of the very wildness, the breath and power which is the vehicle of the poem's radical metaphor. If we think of a scale of structures having at one end logic, the completely reasoned and abstracted, and at the other some form of madness or surrealism, matter or impression unformed and undisciplined (the imitation of disorder by the idiom of disorder), we may see metaphysical and neoclassical poetry as near the extreme of logic (though by no means reduced to that status) and romantic poetry as a step toward the directness of sensory presentation (though by no means sunk into subrationality). As a structure which favors implication rather than overt statement, the romantic is far closer than the metaphysical to symbolist poetry and the varieties of postsymbolist most in vogue today. Both types of structure, the metaphysical and the romantic, are valid. Each has gorgeously enriched the history of English poetry.

BIBLIOGRAPHICAL NOTE: On the nature of romantic metaphor and the structure of romantic imagery see the essays by R. H. Fogle, René Wellek, and Albert Gérard in this collection, Frank Kermode's *Romantic Image* (London, 1957), and E. R. Wasserman's "Metaphors for Poetry" in his *The Subtler Language* (Baltimore, 1959). All of these works should be compared to Cleanth Brooks's view of romantic metaphor in his essay above.

Toward a Theory
of Romanticism

Morse Peckham

Can we hope for a theory of romanticism? The answer, I believe, is, Yes. But before proceeding further, I must make quite clear what it is that I propose to discuss.

First, although the word "romanticism" refers to any number of things, it has two primary referents: (1) a general and permanent characteristic of mind, art, and personality, found in all periods and in all cultures; (2) a specific historical movement in art and ideas which occurred in Europe and America in the late eighteenth and early nineteenth centuries. I am concerned only with the second of these two meanings. There may be a connection between the two, but I doubt it, and at any rate whatever I have to say refers only to historical romanticism.

Second, in this historical sense "romanticism" as a revolution in art and ideas is often considered to be only an expression of a general redirection of European life which included also a political revolution, an industrial revolution, and perhaps several others. There may be a connection between the revolution in ideas and the arts and the more

TOWARD A THEORY OF ROMANTICISM: From *PMLA*, LXVI (1951), 5–23; and *Studies in Romanticism*, I (1961), 1–8. Reprinted by permission of the editors and author.

231

or less contemporary revolutions in other fields of human activities, but for the time being, at any rate, I think it is wise to dissociate the romanticism of ideas and art from these other revolutions. Just as one of our greatest difficulties so far has arisen from assuming an identity between general and historical romanticism, so much of our difficulty in considering the nature of historical romanticism has come from assuming its identity with all of the other more or less contemporary revolutions. Let us first isolate the historical romanticism of ideas and arts before we beg any questions about the nature of history. For example, I think it is at present wiser to consider romanticism as one of the means then available for hindering or helping the early-nine-teenth-century movement for political reform than it is to assume that romanticism and the desire for political reform and its partial achieve-ment are the same thing.

With these two distinctions in mind, I repeat, Can we hope for a theory of the historical romanticism of ideas and art? Such a theory must be able to submit successfully to two tests. First, it must show that Wordsworth and Byron, Goethe and Chateaubriand, were all part of a general European literary movement which had its correspondencies in the music, the painting, the architecture, the philosophy, the theol-ogy, and the science of the eighteenth and early nineteenth centuries. Second, it must be able to get us inside individual works of literature, art, and thought: that is, to tell us not merely that the works are there, to enable us not merely to classify them, but to deliver up to us a key to individual works so that we can penetrate to the principles of their intellectual and æsthetic being. Can we hope for such a theory? *Dare* we hope for such a theory? To this question I answer, "Yes, we can." I feel that we have it almost within our grasp—that one or two steps more and we shall have mastered this highly perplexing literary prob-lem.

Certainly there is no generally accepted theory of romanticism at the present time. Twenty years ago, and for more than twenty years before that the problem of romanticism was debated passionately, not least because of the redoubtable but utterly misdirected attacks of Babbitt and More. In his *Romanticism and the Modern Ego* (1943) Jacques Barzun has made a good collection of some of the definitions that have been more or less widely used in the past fifty years: a return to the Middle Ages, a love of the exotic, the revolt from Reason, a vindication of the individual, a liberation of the unconscious, a reaction against scientific method, a revival of pantheism, a revival of idealism, a revival of Catholicism, a rejection of artistic conventions, a return to emotionalism, a return to nature—and so on. The utmost confusion reigns in the whole field. . . . It is a discouraging situation, but my purpose is to suggest that it is not so discouraging as it appears.

In the last few years there have been signs that some scholars at least are moving toward a common concept of romanticism. In 1943 Jacques Barzun spoke of romanticism as a biological revolution; and in 1949, he defined it as part of "the great revolution which drew the intellect of Europe . . . from the expectation and desire of fixity into desire and expectation of change."[1] Stallknecht, in his fascinating book on Wordsworth, *Strange Seas of Thought* (1945), spoke of how romanticism established the sentiment of being in England, and then, reversing his statement, suggested that the sentiment of being established romanticism. In his admirable introduction to his edition of *Sartor Resartus* (1937) C. Frederick Harrold . . . wrote of Carlyle's ideas about organicism and dynamism. And in his and Templeman's excellent anthology of Victorian prose (1938) there is an appendix "illustrative of nineteenth-century conceptions of growth, development, evolution." But the most recent attempt to tackle the problem, the best yet, though I think not entirely satisfactory, has been René Wellek's two articles, "The Concept of Romanticism," published in 1949 in the first two issues of *Comparative Literature*. There he offered three criteria of romanticism: imagination for the view of poetry, an organic concept of nature for the view of the world, and symbol and myth for poetic style.

Wellek does establish to my mind three things in his article: first, that there *was* a European intellectual and artistic movement with certain intellectual and artistic characteristics, a movement properly known as romanticism; second, that the participators in that movement were quite conscious of their historic and revolutionary significance; and third, that the chief reason for the current skepticism in America about a theory of romanticism was the publication in 1924 of Arthur O. Lovejoy's famous article, "On the Discrimination of Romanticisms." In this article Lovejoy pointed out that the term is used in a fearful variety of ways, and that no common concept can include them all. Indeed, the growth of skepticism about any solid

---

[1] "Romanticism: Definition of a Period," *Magazine of Art*, XLII (1949), 243.

conclusions on romanticism does seem to begin—or at least start to become very powerful and eventually dominant—with the publication of that article. Wellek decries what he calls Lovejoy's excessive nominalism and skepticism, and refuses to be satisfied with it. He also puts in the same category of nominalism and skepticism Lovejoy's 1941 article, "The Meaning of Romanticism for the Historian of Ideas" [*JHI*, II (1941), 237–78]. Here Lovejoy offered three criteria of romanticism, or rather the three basic ideas of romanticism, "heterogeneous, logically independent, and sometimes essentially antithetic to one another in their implications." These ideas are organicism, dynamism, and diversitarianism. Now in discussing Lovejoy's 1941 paper Wellek has made, I think, an error. He seems to have confused the nature of the two articles, because, apparently, he has forgotten about the last three chapters of *The Great Chain of Being* (1936).[2]

Lovejoy's great book is a landmark of scholarship, and also for scholarship. It is a book on which some of the most useful scholarship of our times has been based, and it is as useful to the teacher who uses it with intelligence as it is to the scholar. Twenty-five years from now, scholars of literature will look back on the publication of *The Great Chain of Being* as a turning point in the development of literary scholarship; for it has been of astonishing value in opening up to our understanding in quite unexpected ways the literature of the sixteenth, seventeenth, and eighteenth centuries. But so far as I know, almost no use has been made of the last three chapters, especially of the last two, in explaining romanticism and romantic works. It is a curious situation; for these chapters contain the foundations for a theory of romanticism which will do everything that such a theory must be able to do—place works and authors in relation to each other and illuminate individual works of art as they ought to be illuminated.

By ignoring (at least in his two papers) *The Great Chain of Being*, Wellek concluded that the same kind of skepticism was present in both Lovejoy's 1924 and 1941 articles. Actually *The Great Chain of Being* is an answer to Lovejoy's 1924 article. Without emphasizing the

[2] Wellek's confusion, or apparent confusion, lies in his implication that the "romanticisms" Lovejoy discussed in 1924 are the same as the "romantic ideas" which in 1941 he called "heterogeneous, logically independent, and sometimes essentially antithetic to one another in their implications." As I read the 1941 article, I interpret the latter as these three: organicism, dynamism, and diversitarianism. (See Section II of this essay.) These are not the "romanticisms" of 1924.

fact, Lovejoy *did* in 1933 and 1934, when he delivered the lectures on which the book is based, what in 1924 he said could not be done. To be brief, in 1936 he stated simply that literary romanticism was the manifestation of a change in the way of thinking of European man, that since Plato European man had been thinking according to one sysem of thought—based on the attempted reconciliation of two profoundly different ideas about the nature of reality, both stemming from Plato—and that in the late eighteenth and early nineteenth centuries occidental thought took an entirely different direction, as did occidental art. Furthermore, he says that the change in the way the mind works was the most profound change in the history of occidental thinking, and by implication it involved a similar profound change in the methods and objects of European art.

I

What I wish to do in the rest of this paper is, first, to explain what these new ideas of the late eighteenth century involved, to reconcile Wellek and Lovejoy, and Lovejoy with himsef, and to show the relevance of certain other ideas about romanticism I have mentioned; and second, to make one addition to the theories of Lovejoy and Wellek, an addition which I hope goes far toward clearing up an essential problem which Lovejoy scarcely faced and with which Wellek is unable to come to terms.

It is scarcely necessary in this journal to outline what *The Great Chain of Being* implied. Yet I should like to reduce the concepts involved to what I think to be their essentials. Briefly the shift in European thought was a shift from conceiving the cosmos as a static mechanism to conceiving it as a dynamic organism: static—in that all the possibilities of reality were realized from the beginning of things or were implicit from the beginning, and that these possibilities were arranged in a complete series, a hierarchy from God down to nothingness—including the literary possibilities from epic to Horatian ode, or lyric; a mechanism—in that the universe is a perfectly running machine, a watch usually. (A machine is the most common metaphor of this metaphysic.) Almost as important as these concepts was that of uniformitarianism, implicit both in staticism and in mechanism, whenever these two are separated, as frequently happens. That is, everything that change produces was to be conceived as a part to fit into the already perfectly running machine; for all things conformed to ideal patterns in the mind of God or in the nonmaterial ground of phenomena.

If, in short, you conceive of the universe as a perfectly ordered machine, you will assume that any imperfections you may notice are really things you do not understand. You will think of everything in the universe as fitting perfectly into that machine. You will think that immutable laws govern the formation of every new part of that machine to ensure that it fits the machine's requirements. And, although with delightful inconsistency —as Pope made his "Essay on Man" the basis of his satires—you will judge the success of any individual thing according to its ability to fit into the working of the machine, your inconsistency will be concealed, for a time, by the influence of either original sin, if you are an orthodox Christian, or of the corruptions of civilization, if you are a deist or a sentimentalist—not that there is much difference. Your values will be perfection, changelessness, uniformity, rationalism.

Now this mighty static metaphysic which had governed perilously the thoughts of men since the time of Plato, collapsed of its own internal inconsistencies in the late eighteenth century—or collapsed for some people. For most people it still remains the unrealized base for most of their values, intellectual, moral, social, æsthetic, and religious. But to the finer minds of the eighteenth and nineteenth centuries, it was no longer tenable. There are a number of reasons why this should have been so. The principal cause was that all its implications had been worked out; they stood forth in all their naked inconsistency. It became impossible to accept a theodicy based upon it. More and more, thinkers began searching for a new system of explaining the nature of reality and the duties of men.

I shall omit the development of the new idea. The grand outlines have been magnificently sketched by Lovejoy, and the details are steadily being filled in. Rather, I shall present the new idea in its most radical form. Let us begin with the new metaphor. The new metaphor is not a machine; it is an organism. It is a tree, for example; and a tree is a good example, for a study of nineteenth-century literature reveals the continual recurrence of that image. Hence the new thought is organicism. Now the first quality of an organism is that it is not something made, it is something *being* made or growing. We have a philosophy of becoming, not a philosophy of being. Furthermore, the relation of its component parts is not that of the parts of a machine which have been made separately, i.e., separate entities in the mind of the deity, but the relation of leaves to stem to trunk to root to earth. Entities are an organic part of that which produced them. The existence of each part is made possible only by the existence of every other part. Relationships, not entities, are the object of contemplation and study.

Moreover, an organism has the quality of life. It does not develop additively; it grows organically. The universe is alive. It is not something made, a perfect machine; it grows. Therefore change becomes a positive value, not a negative value; change is not man's punishment, it is his opportunity. Anything that continues to grow, or change qualitatively, is not perfect, can, perhaps, never be perfect. Perfection ceases to be a positive value. Imperfection becomes a positive value. Since the universe is changing and growing, there is consequently a positive and radical intrusion of novelty into the world. That is, with the intrusion of each novelty, the fundamental character of the universe itself changes. We have a universe of emergents. If all these things be true, it therefore follows that there are no pre-existent patterns. Every work of art, for instance, creates a new pattern; each one has its own æsthetic law. It may have resemblances even in principle to previous works of art, but fundamentally it is unique. Hence come two derivative ideas. First, diversitarianism, not uniformitarianism, becomes the principle of both creation and criticism. The romantics, for example, have been accused of confusing the genres of poetry. Why shouldn't they? The whole metaphysical foundation of the genres had been abandoned, or for some authors had simply disappeared. The second derivative is the idea of creative originality. True, the idea of originality had existed before, but in a different sense. Now the artist is original because he is the instrument whereby a genuine novelty, an emergent, is introduced into the world, not because he has come with the aid of genius a little closer to previously existent patterns, natural and divine.

In its radical form, dynamic organicism results in the idea that the history of the universe is the history of God creating himself. Evil is at last accounted for, since the history of the universe—God being imperfect to begin with—is the history of God, whether transcendent or immanent, ridding himself, by the evolutionary process, of evil. Of course, from both the old and the new philosophy, God could be omitted. Either can become a materialism.

In a metaphysical nutshell, the older philosophy grounded itself on the principle that nothing can come from nothing. The new philosophy grounded itself on the principle that something *can* come from nothing, that an excess can come from a deficiency, that nothing succeeds like excess.

II

I have presented these ideas in a radical form to make them as clear as I can and to bring out in the strongest possible colors the contrast between the old and new methods of thought. Now I should like to apply them to Lovejoy and Wellek. Lovejoy stated that the three new ideas of romantic thought and art were organicism, dynamism, and diversitarianism. He says that they are three separate and inconsistent ideas. I agree that they often appear separately, but I am convinced that they are all related to and derived from a basic or root-metaphor, the organic metaphor of the structure of the universe.[3] Strictly speaking, organicism includes dynamism, for an organism must grow or change qualitatively, but I prefer to use the term "dynamic organicism" in order to emphasize the importance of imperfection and change. Diversitarianism, of course, is in these terms a positive value; for the diversity of things and their uniqueness is the proof of the constant intrusion of novelty in the past, the present, and the future.

Turning to Wellek and his three criteria, I have already included one, organicism; the other two are imagination and symbolism. Wellek means the creative imagination, and a little thought will show that the idea of the creative imagination is derived from dynamic organicism. If the universe is constantly in the process of creating itself, the mind of man, his imaginative power, is radically creative. The artist is that man with the power of bringing new artistic concepts into reality, just as the philosopher brings new ideas into reality. And the greatest man is the

[3] I am alarmed at finding myself in disagreement with Lovejoy. Although I think his three ideas are not heterogeneous, but homogeneous or at least derived from a common root-metaphor, the possibility that they really *are* heterogeneous does not deprive them in the least of their value in understanding romanticism, nor does their possible heterogeneity have any effect on my proposal which follows.

philosopher-poet, who supremely gifted simultaneously does both. Furthermore, the artist is the man who creates a symbol of truth. He can think metaphorically, and if the world is an organic structure only a statement with the organic complexity of the work of art can create an adequate symbol of it. And is this not the method of symbolism? In allegory, a symbolic unit preserves its meaning when taken from its context. The Cave of Error *is* the Cave of Error. There is a direct one-to-one relationship between any unit in the world of phenomena and any unit in the world of ideas. But in symbolism, a symbolic unit has power only because of its relationships to everything else in the work of art. Ahab has symbolical value because of the whale, and the whale because of Ahab. In symbolism the interrelationships of the symbolic units involved are equated with the interrelationships of a group of concepts. Let a series of 1, 2, 3, 4, etc., stand for a series of ideas in the mind, and a similar series of a, b, c, d, etc., stand for a series of things in the real world or in the world of the concretizing imagination. Now in allegory, if "a" is a symbolic unit, it stands for "1," "b" for "2," and so on. Thus the Dragon in the *Faerie Queene*, Canto i of Book I, stands for Error, whether the Red Cross Knight is there or not, and the Knight, on one level of interpretation, stands for Holiness, whether the Dragon is there or not. But in symbolism, "a" or "b" or "c" has no direct relation to "1" or "2" or "3." Rather, the interrelationships among the first three have symbolic reference to the interrelationships among the second group of three. Moby Dick has symbolic power only because Ahab is hunting him; in fact, he has symbolic power only because almost everything else in the book has symbolic power as well.

The now current though probably not widely accepted critical principle that a symbolic system is capable of an indefinite number of equally valid interpretations is itself a romantic idea, in the sense that the work of art has no fixed or static meaning but changes with the observer in a relationship between the two which is both dialectical, or dynamic, and organic.

Thus we may conclude that Wellek's three criteria—organicism, imagination, and symbolism—are all three derivable from the basic metaphor or concept of dynamic organicism.

There is yet another profoundly important idea which I have not so far mentioned, the idea of the unconscious mind, which appears in Wordsworth, in Coleridge, in Carlyle, and indeed all over the nineteenth and twentieth centuries. In 1830 in his magnificent essay, "Characteristics," Carlyle says that the two big ideas of the century are dynamism and the unconscious mind. The idea of the unconscious mind goes back to Hartley, to Kant, to Leibniz, and is implicit in Locke. Indeed it goes back to any poet who seriously talks about a muse. But it appears only in full force with the appearance of dynamic organicism. Best known to the English romantics in the mechanistic associationism of Hartley, it became a central part of their thought when they made the mind radically creative. Heretofore the divine had communicated with man either directly through revelation or indirectly through the evidence of his perfect universe. But with God creating himself, with an imperfect but growing universe, with the constant intrusion of novelty into the world, how can there be any apprehension of truth? If reason is inadequate—because it is fixed and because historically it has failed— the truth can only be apprehended intuitively, imaginatively, spontaneously, with the whole personality, from the deep sources of the fountains that are within. The unconscious is really a postulate to the creative imagination, and as such continues today without the divine sanction as part of present-day critical theory.* It is that part of the mind through which novelty enters into the personality and hence into the world in the form of art and ideas. We today conceive of the unconscious spatially as inside and beneath; the earlier romantics conceived of it as outside and above. We descend into the imagination; they rose into it. The last method, of course, is the method of transcendentalism.

Furthermore, as I shall shortly show, not only was the unconscious taken over from Locke and Kant and Hartley and converted into something radically creative, it also became an integral part of dynamic organicism because a number of the early romantics proved it, as it were, empirically, by their own personal experience. It became to them proof of the validity of the new way of thinking. Hence also romantic subjectivism, the artist watching his powers develop and novelty emerging from his unconscious mind.

What then is romanticism? Whether philosophic, theologic, or æsthetic, it is the revolution in the European mind against thinking

---

* Cf., e.g., Mario Praz's essay above. Compare also F. L. Lucas's essay, which sees the unconscious as leading to decadence, and Herbert Read's connecting of romanticism and surrealism via the unconscious.

in terms of static mechanism and the redirection of the mind to thinking in terms of dynamic organicism. Its values are change, imperfection, growth, diversity, the creative imagination, the unconscious.

III

. . .

Dynamic organicism, manifested in literature in its fully developed form with all its main derivative ideas, I have called "radical romanticism." To this term I should now like to add "positive romanticism," as a term useful in describing men and ideas and works of art in which dynamic organicism appears, whether it be incomplete or fully developed. But by itself, "positive romanticism" for the purposes of understanding the romantic movement is not only frequently useless; it is often worse than useless. It is often harmful. If some of my readers have been muttering, "What about Byron?" they are quite right in doing so. Positive romanticism cannot explain Byron; positive romanticism is not enough. To it must be added the term "negative romanticism," and to that I now turn.[4]

It may at first seem that I am here denying my basic aim of reducing the multiplicity of theories of romanticism to a single theory, but this is not really so. Negative romanticism is a necessary complement to positive romanticism, not a parallel or alternative to it, with which it must be reconciled. Briefly, negative romanticism is the expression of the attitudes, the feelings, and the ideas of a man who has left static mechanism but has not yet arrived at a reintegration of his thought and art in terms of dynamic organicism. I am here, of course, using a method of analysis which is now so common that one inhales it with the dust of our libraries, the method of analyzing the works of a man in terms of

[4] Wellek, for instance, says that Byron "does not share the romantic conception of imagination," or does so "only fitfully." He quotes *Childe Harold*, Canto III, written and published in 1816, when Byron was temporarily under Wordsworth's influence through Shelley. Byron's romantic view of nature as an organism with which man is unified organically by the imagination is equally fitful and limited to the period of Shelleyan influence. Wellek's suggestion that Byron is a symbolist, depending as it does on Wilson Knight's *The Burning Oracle*, is not very convincing. Knight strikes me as a weak reed to lean upon, and Wellek himself calls Knight "extravagant," certainly an understatement. In short, I think Wellek's three categories of romanticism are useless, or only very rarely useful, when they are applied to Byron. So are Lovejoy's three romantic ideas; for the same reasons, of course. (See Wellek's second article, *CL*, I, 165 and 168.) To be sure, Byron uses symbols; but he uses them compulsively, as everyone else does, not as a conscious principle of literary organization and creation.

his personal development. Before we study any artist, we begin by establishing his canon and chronology. We *begin*, that is, by *assuming* that there is a development in his art. I hope I am not being merely tedious in pointing out that this method is in itself a particular application of one of the main ideas derived from dynamic organicism, or positive romanticism—the idea of evolution in the nineteenth-century sense. But to show what I mean by negative romanticism, therefore, and how it fits in with positive romanticism, and to show how the theory works in practice, I shall discuss very briefly three works from the earlier years of the Romantic Movement: *The Ancient Mariner*, *The Prelude*, and *Sartor Resartus*.[5]

Briefly, all three works are about spiritual death and rebirth, or secular conversion. In its baldest form, such an experience amounts to this: A man moves from a trust in the universe to a period of doubt and despair of any meaning in the universe, and then to a re-affirmation of faith in cosmic meaning and goodness, or at least meaning. The transition from the first stage to the second, we may call spiritual death; that from the second to the third, we may call spiritual rebirth.

Let us first consider *The Prelude*. The subtitle, not Wordsworth's, is "The Growth of a Poet's Mind." After Wordsworth had started *The Recluse*, he found that in order to explain his ideas he must first explain how he came to have them. This decision is in itself a sign of positive romanticism. If you think in static terms, you will, as Pope did in *The Essay on Man*, present the result of a process of thought and experience. But if you find that you cannot explain your ideas except in terms of the process of how you have arrived at them, your mind is working in a different way, according to the principles of development and growth. The central experience which Wordsworth describes is spiritual death and rebirth. He began by having a complete faith in the principles of the French Revolution as the deistic *philosophes* and constitutionalists explained it. Their basic political principle was that we have only to restore to man his originally pure but now corrupt political organization and social contract, and a perfect society will

[5] In what follows I shall offer an interpretation of *The Ancient Mariner* which I worked out some years ago, but which is substantially that developed from different points of view by Stallknecht, Maud Bodkin, and various other critics. I shall also suggest that all three works are about the same subjective experience. Stallknecht, so far as I know, is the only commentator who has pointed out—in his *Strange Seas of Thought*—that *The Prelude* and *The Ancient Mariner* are about the same thing; and so far as I know, no one has suggested that *Sartor Resartus* is concerned with the same subject.

necessarily result. Wordsworth accepted this as he also accepted the sentimentality, most notably and fully expressed by Shaftesbury, which was the eighteenth-century emotional expression of faith in the perfection and goodness of the universe, a sentimentalism which became more strident and absurd as its basic theodicy became increasingly less acceptable. Any man who is defending an idea in which he is emotionally involved, will become more emotional and passionate in its defense as his opponent shows with increasing clarity that the idea is untenable.

The French Revolution, to Wordsworth, failed. It made men worse instead of better, and from the creation of political and intellectual freedom it turned to tyranny, slaughter, and imperialist expansion. He saw that he had been misled by his emotions into too facile an acceptance. It was then that he rejected sentimentalism and brought all values before the bar of reason, so that reason might sit in judgment. But reason also was not enough. The boasted reason of the enlightenment could neither explain the failure of the French Revolution nor provide a means of acceptance. Then occurred his spiritual death. He had invested heavily in emotion and in reason. Each had betrayed him. He was spiritually bankrupt. Where was a means of acceptance? Moving to Racedown, rejoining Dorothy, coming to know Coleridge, and going to live near him at Nether Stowey, he reorganized all his ideas, with Coleridge's and Dorothy's intellectual and emotional help, and reaffirmed in new terms his faith in the goodness and significance of the universe. He stood, he said, "in Nature's presence a sensitive being, a *creative* soul"; that is, his creative power was a "power like one of Nature's." Nature and the creative soul maintain, he believed, an ennobling and enkindling interchange of action. The voice of nature was a living voice. And there are moods when that living voice can be heard, when "We see into the life of things," when we feel

> a sense sublime
> Of something far more deeply interfused; . . .
> A motion and a spirit, that impels
> All thinking things, all objects of all thought,
> And rolls through all things. [Peckham's ellipsis]

The universe is alive, not dead; living and growing, not a perfect machine; it speaks to us directly through the creative mind and its senses. Its truth cannot be perceived from the "evidences of nature" but only through the unconscious and creative mind. And this is the point of the famous description of the ascent of Mt. Snowdon, in the last book of *The Prelude*. Climbing through the mist, Wordsworth comes to the top of the mountain. Around and below him is a sea of clouds, with the moon shining over all, clear, beautiful, and bright. But through a gap in the clouds comes the roar of the waters in the valleys around the mountains. Thus in the moon he beheld the emblem of a mind

> That feeds upon infinity, that broods
> Over the dark abyss, intent to hear
> Its voices issuing forth to silent light
> In one continuous stream.

This is his symbol of the unconscious mind, both of man and the universe, ultimately identical, both striving to become as well as to be. He has by a profound experience proved to himself the existence and the trustworthiness and the power of the unconscious mind, of the life of the universe, of the continuous creative activity of the cosmos.

• • •

Leaving chronological order aside, I turn now to *Sartor Resartus*. The central chapters of Carlyle's work are "The Everlasting No," "The Centre of Indifference," and "The Everlasting Yea." They obviously present a pattern of spiritual death and rebirth. Carlyle, speaking of himself under the guise of Professor Teufelsdröckh, tells us how he lost his religious belief. "The loss of his religious faith was the loss of everything." "It is all a grim Desert, this once-fair world of his." "Invisible yet impenetrable walls divided me from all living; was there in the wide world, any true bosom I could press trustfully to mine? No, there was none. . . . It was a strange isolation I then lived in. The universe was all void of Life, of Purpose, of Volition, even of Hostility; it was one huge dead immeasurable Steam-engine, rolling on, in its dead indifference, to grind me limb from limb." "The Universe had pealed its Everlasting No authoritatively through all the recesses of his being." But in the moment of Baphometic fire-baptism he stood up and cried out that he would not accept that answer. This was not yet the moment of rebirth, but it was the first step, the step of defiance and rebellion.

There follows the Centre of Indifference, of wandering grimly across the face of Europe, of observing the absurdities and cruelty and wickedness of mankind; he is a wanderer, a pilgrim without any shrine to go to. And then one day, surrounded by a beautiful landscape, in the midst of nature and the tenderness of the natural piety of human beings, came a change. "The heavy dreams rolled gradually away, and I awoke to a new Heaven and a new Earth. . . . What is nature? Ha! Why do I not name thee GOD? Are not thou the 'Living Garment of God'? The universe is not dead and demoniacal, a charnel-house with spectres, but god-like and my Father's." It is alive. Nature—as he tells us later in the book, in the chapter called "Organic Filaments"— —Nature "is not completed, but ever completing. . . . Mankind is a living movement, in progress faster or slower." Here indeed is a positive romanticism so complete that it is almost a radical romanticism, though Carlyle, like Wordsworth, retained an inconsistent static principle in his thought. Like Wordsworth, his nostalgia for a static principle or static ground to the evolving universe was to prove his undoing, but that again is another story.

In *The Ancient Mariner* Coleridge tells us of an experience which is the same as that given by Wordsworth and Carlyle. The mariner, on his journey around the world, or through life, violates the faith of his fellow-man by shooting the albatross, the one thing alive in the world of ice and snow, always symbols of spiritual coldness and death. His fellow mariners reject him, marking him with the sign of his own guilt. From the world of ice and snow they come to the world of fire and heat, again symbols of spiritual death, alienation, and suffering. The soul of the mariner is won by Life-in-Death. He alone remains alive while his fellow sailors, silently and with reproachful eyes, die around him. As Carlyle put it, "it was a strange isolation I lived in then." And Carlyle also uses the symbols of ice and fire to describe his condition. Isolation, alienation, and guilt possess the soul of the mariner. He is alone, in a burning and evil universe. "The very deep did rot," and the slimy and evil watersnakes surround his ship. And as he watches them in the moonlight he is suddenly taken with their beauty, and "I blessed them unaware." From the depths of the unconscious rose an impulse of affirmation, of love, of acceptance. The albatross drops from his neck into the sea. The symbol of guilt and alienation and despair vanishes. The universe comes alive. It rains, and the rain is the water of life. The wind blows; the breath of a living universe wafts the ship across the ocean. The air is filled with voices and the sky is filled with living light. The spirit of the land of ice and snow comes to his aid. (As Carlyle put it, even in his most despairful moments there was within him, unconsciously, a principle of faith and affirmation.) Angels come into the bodies of the dead sailors and work the ship. The whole universe comes to the mariner's aid, and he completes his journey.

And thereafter, though he has been forgiven and reaccepted into man's life by the act of confession, there comes an impulse to tell his story, the creative impulse of the poet rising powerfully from his unconscious mind. Poetry is conceived of as a compulsive but creative act. In a sense Coleridge is more profound than either Wordsworth or Carlyle. He knows that for a romantic, once alienated means always alienated. He cannot join the wedding feast. Edwin Markham put it well:

> He drew a circle that shut me out—
> Heretic, rebel, a thing to flout:
> But Love and I had the wit to win:
> We drew a circle that took him in!

Though a man may create a synthesis that includes the ideas of his fellow men, to those very men he will always be outside the circle of accepted beliefs, even though he blesses all things great and small.

At any rate we see here a highly radical positive romanticism. It is the record of a process; it affirms the unconscious mind and the creative imagination; it affirms the principle of the living universe; it affirms diversitarianism; and it is a fully developed symbolism, an organic symbolism in which the shooting of the albatross is without symbolic power unless it is thought of in terms of the power and the interrelations of the various symbolic units.

These interpretations, to me at least, demonstrate the excellence of Lovejoy's three principles of romanticism—organicism, dynamism, and diversitarianism—to get us inside various works of romantic art and to show us the relationships that tie them together into a single literary movement. And again to me, they show that these ideas are not heterogeneous, independent ideas, but closely associated ideas, all related to a central concept or world-metaphor.

And now to define negative romanticism. I have, of course, taken the term from Carlyle's Everlasting No. As various individuals, according to their natures, and their emotional and intellectual depths, went through the transition from affirming the meaning of the cosmos in terms of static mechanism to affirming it in terms of dynamic organicism, they went through a period of doubt, of despair, of religious and social isolation, of the separation of reason and creative power. It was a period during which they saw neither beauty nor goodness in the universe, nor any significance, nor any rationality, nor indeed any order at all, not even an evil order. This is negative romanticism, the prelim-

inary to positive romanticism, the period of *Sturm und Drang*.* As
the nineteenth century rolled on, the transition became much easier, for
the new ideas were much more widely available. But for the early
romantics the new ideas had to be learned through personal and painful
experience. The typical symbols of negative romanticism are individuals
who are filled with guilt, despair, and cosmic and social alienation.
They are often presented, for instance, as having committed some
horrible and unmentionable and unmentioned crime in the past. They
are often outcasts from men and God, and they are almost always
wanderers over the face of the earth. They are Harolds, they are Man-
freds, they are Cains. They are heroes of such poems as *Alastor*. But
when they begin to get a little more insight into their position, as they
are forced to develop historical consciousness, as they begin to seek
the sources for their negation and guilt and alienation, they become
Don Juans. That is, in *Don Juan*, Byron sought objectivity by means of
satire, and set out to trace in his poem the development of those attitudes that had resulted in himself. As I said earlier, positive romanticism
cannot explain Byron, but negative romanticism can. Byron spent his
life in the situation of Wordsworth after the rejection of Godwin and
before his move to Racedown and Nether Stowey, of the Mariner
alone on the wide, wide sea, of Teufelsdröckh subject to the Everlasting No and wandering through the Centre of Indifference.

It is the lack of this concept that involves Wellek's second article
and much of Barzun's book, for all their admirable insights, in certain
difficulties, in such a foredoomed attempt to find in figures who express
negative romanticism and figures who express positive romanticism a
common and unifying element. Theirs is the same difficulty as that with
which Auden gets involved in *The Enchafed Flood* [New York, 1950].
It is true that both positive and negative romanticism often cause
isolation of the personality, but as Coleridge of these three men alone
realized, negative romanticism causes isolation and despair because
it offers no cosmic explanations, while positive romanticism offers
cosmic explanations which are not shared by the society of which one
is a part. To Arnold, "Not a having and a resting, but a growing and
a becoming, is the character of perfection as culture conceives it."
His ideas isolated him from Barbarians, Philistines, and Populace;

* For another explanation of "negative romanticism" in very nearly the same
terms see Robert Langbaum's *The Poetry of Experience* (New York, 1957).

they were impressed but they did not follow; for they could not comprehend, so far were his fundamental attitudes separated from theirs. Picasso has in his painting expressed profoundly the results of the freedom that romanticism has given to the creative imagination, but he is detested by most people who have seen his cubist or post-cubist paintings—as well as by a great many who have not. He is at home in the universe, but not in his society.[6]

[6] This is perhaps the place to insert a word about preromanticism, a term which I would wholly abandon [Wellek, it will be remembered, justifies the use of the term; see pp. 191–93 above]. Apparently it arose in the first place from a naïve application of Darwinian evolution to literary history. If the great romantics liked nature, any eighteenth-century enjoyment or praise of nature became preromanticism, in spite of the Horatian tradition of neoclassicism. If the romanticists liked emotion, any praise of emotion in the eighteenth century was preromantic, as if any age, including "The Age of Reason," could be without emotional expression. In their youth Wordsworth and Coleridge were sentimentalists; therefore sentimentalism is romantic. And so on. James R. Foster, in his recent *History of the Pre-Romantic Novel in England* (New York, 1949), has shown that sensibility was the emotional expression of deism, just as Lovejoy has demonstrated in various books and articles that deism and neoclassicism were parallel. If it seems odd that sentimentalism, "cosmic Toryism," and deism are all expressions of the same basic attitudes, it must be remembered that the eighteenth century was the period when the mechanistic and static theodicy broke down from its own inconsistencies. Romanticism did not destroy its predecessor. It came into existence to fill a void. . . . I would recommend the total abandonment of the term "preromantic," and the substitution for it of some term such as "neoclassic disintegration." [*A Literary History of England*, ed. A. C. Baugh *et al* (New York, 1948) does precisely this, Part III covering the "preromantics" being titled "The Disintegration of Classicism."] For instance, to refer to Wellek once more, on the first page of his second article he has this to say: "There was the 'Storm and Stress' movement in the seventies which exactly parallels what today is elsewhere called 'preromanticism.'" In a widely used anthology, *The Literature of England*, by G. B. Woods, H. A. Watt, and G. K. Anderson, first published in 1936, the section called "The Approach to Romanticism" includes Thomson, Gray, Collins, Cowper, Burns, and Blake; and in Ernest Bernbaum's *Guide through the Romantic Movement*, another widely known and used work. . . . the "preromantic movement" includes the following, among others: Shaftesbury, Winchilsea, Dyer, Thomson, Richardson, Young, Blair, Akenside, Collins, the Wartons, Hartley, Gray, Goldsmith, MacKenzie, Burns, Darwin, Blake, Godwin, and Radcliffe. Some of these are "Storm and Stress"; others are quite plainly not. To lump all of them together, as a great many teachers and writers do, is to obliterate many highly important distinctions. To my mind, for *some* individuals neoclassicism disintegrated; thereupon what I call "negative romanticism," of which "Storm and Stress" is a very important expression, for *some* individuals ensued. Then *some* individuals, initially a very few, moved into the attitudes which I call "positive romanticism." As it is now used, "preromanticism" confuses the first two of these three stages, just as "romanticism" as it is now generally used confuses the second two and often all three.

IV

My proposal is now complete. This theory does, I firmly believe, what such a theory must do. It gets us inside of various works of art, and it shows the relevance of one work of art to another. . . . [However] I wish to make one final suggestion, to issue a warning to anyone who may be taken enough with these ideas to try to employ them.

Although negative and then positive romanticism developed by reaction out of the static-mechanistic-uniformitarian complex, with its cosmic Toryism, its sentimentalism, and its deism, they were also superimposed upon it. At any point in nineteenth or twentieth-century culture it is possible to take a cross-section and find all three actively at work. The past one hundred and fifty years or so must be conceived as a dramatic struggle, sometimes directly between positive romanticism and static, mechanistic thought, sometimes three-cornered. It is a struggle between minds and within minds. It is seen today in the profound disparity between what is sometimes called high art and popular art; it is expressed in the typical modern cultural phenomena of the *avant-garde*, which is as modern as Wordsworth and Coleridge. It appeared in the struggle over the "packing" of the supreme court, and the wearisome but still vital quarrels about progressive education. It appears in the antagonism between our relativistic critics and our absolutistic critics. It appears in the theological struggle between the theology of such a man as Charles Raven[7] and the proponents of the "theology of crisis." A very pure positive romanticism is at the heart of Ruth Benedict's *Patterns of Culture;* her ideal of a good society is organic, dynamic, and diversitarian. In short, the history of ideas and the arts in the nineteenth and twentieth centuries is the history of the dramatic struggle among three opposing forces: static mechanism, negative romanticism, and positive romanticism. In this drama, to me the hero is dynamic and diversitarian organicism, and I think Goethe and Beethoven and Coleridge and the other founders of the still vital romantic tradition—a tradition often repudiated by those who are at the very heart of it, and understandably—have still much to say to us, are not

---

[7] Raven is both biologist and theologian. See his *Science, Religion, and the Future* (New York, 1943).

mere intellectual and æsthetic curiosities. Nevertheless, I am aware that
to many scholars and thinkers, positive romanticism is the villain,
responsible for all the ills of our century.* The drama may indeed
turn out to be a tragedy, but if it does, it is because static mechanism
persists in staying alive.[8]

Of course the fact that my attitude towards the continuing and future usefulness of positive romanticism may not after all be justified is
not essential to my argument, or even germane to it. I ask only that
my readers take under serious consideration, and test in their studies,
in their reading, and in their classrooms the theories about romanticism
which I have outlined. I trust that many of them will find these ideas
useful, even though they withhold final assent.

V**

. . .

Some five years ago, when I had arrived at the point of thinking
the whole thing purest nonsense, I set out to reconstruct the theory. I
felt that much was sound and worth salvaging, and to an exposition of
my current notions on this maddening subject I shall now turn, only
begging the reader to prefix mentally to each sentence, "At the moment
I find it useful to employ the following proposition in thinking about
romanticism."

If order is perceived as structured into the empirical world—natural
and social, value (i.e., what is variously referred to as "meaning" or
"purpose") and identity are also thus seen. Consequently the perception of order is felt to be interchangeable with the perception of value,
and the perception of both is accompanied by the emergence of identity,
perceived in terms of a socially structured role. Nevertheless, because
of the disparity between an orientation and the data it is called upon
to organize, the individual, if he is to adapt successfully to his environ-

---

* See e.g., the works cited in the final footnote to F. L. Lucas's essay above, pp.
134–35.

[8] The romantic metaphysic does not *necessarily* involve optimism. That is, although
the world is growing in a better direction, the sum of evil may still outweigh the sum
of good. Nor does it *necessarily* involve progressivism. That is, the development from
the simple to the complex may mean development towards the better, or it may mean
development towards the worse, or it may simply mean development without either
improvement or degeneration. However, in the early part of the nineteenth century
and generally since then, it usually implies both optimism and progressivism. . . .

** At this point Peckham's "Reconsiderations" (published ten years after his
first article) begins.

ment, *must* perceive a disparity between the order affirmed by orientation and his actual experience of randomness. In the Western tradition there have been two primary pseudo-explanations for this disparity.
The first is the myth of paradise and the Fall. That it is an emotionally
and pragmatically satisfactory resolution is evidenced by its continuing
vitality. An environment such that the orientation corresponds exactly
with the experienced world v·ould be paradise, a place of pure order,
pure value, and never-threatened identity, that is, salvation. From this
point of view the reason for the Fall is of no importance. The possibilities for explaining it are infinite. The important element is the contrast
between the prelapsarian state and the postlapsarian, between perfect
orientation and the world as we experience it. The Platonic solution,
at least after the Neoplatonists had their way with it, exhibits the same
pattern, nonhistorically. A real word of pure order and value is set
against the experienced, shadowy, imitated world, of disorder and little
or no value. Thus the myth of the Fall and the Neoplatonic epistemological myth can be perfectly synthesized by containing time in eternity.
The Middle Ages were founded on a world-hypothesis according to
which the world of space and time is disordered and of only partial
and occasional value, in which even perceived order can be used as a
temptation by Satan, the spirit that denies value; the moral task is to
maintain as much order and value as possible until death, or the last
judgment, when the individual would either re-enter paradise, a world
of total order, value, and salvation, or identity, or be forever plunged
into its opposite. Since such a scheme embraced orientation and perception, order and disorder, good and evil, in an all-embracing orientation, it exhibited remarkable stability, and continues to do so.

However, the Renaissance brought out a different attitude; in the
older scheme the source of the order was revelation and the means of
its transmission was the Church, through its redemptive power. The
progressive organization and accumulation of knowledge in medieval
science and philosophy led to a situation in which some individuals
began to believe that it was possible to arrive at the vision of order
outside of the Church, and even outside of religion. The human mind,
it was decided by a few, could achieve the truth of revelation without
the instrumentality of ecclesiastical transmission and sanction. A revival
of Neoplatonism was the consequence, or rather the separation of
Neoplatonism from its Judaeo-Christian twin. Recent investigations
have shown the Neoplatonic backgound of both Galileo and Newton;
and Descartes's decision to think through the world, since order was

thought of as discovered and not ascribed, and value and identity as given, led, with the aid of Galileo and Newton, to a wholly new orientation. The sensational results have been admirably described and the roots investigated in the remarkable contributions to the history of science made in the past ten years, and for the literary scholar in Marjorie Nicolson's *Mountain Gloom and Mountain Glory: The Development of the Æsthetics of the Infinite* [Ithaca, N.Y., 1950] and particularly in Ernest Tuveson's *The Imagination as a Means of Grance: Locke and the Æsthetics of Romanticisim* [Berkeley, 1960]. The new orientation was that this is not a fallen world, nor a shadowy world, but that order and value are structured into the perceived world, and that identity is given with the existence of each biological human entity. Society is a natural emergent, not the result of divine fiat. The disparity between the orientation and the experience lies in the fact of our ignorance—a notion easily demonstrated—not in the fact that we are faced with a corrupt world. Man is naturally part of that order; the moral task is to restore his originally perfect adaptation by exploiting his civilization and knowledge. Since the natural order grants perfect adaptation, what has been lost through ignorance can be regained through knowledge. Or—and here was the rub—since man is the product of nature, he is not in fact maladapted at the present time. His task is to adapt himself morally and emotionally to the order in which we now find ourselves. In either case observable order assures that value is structured into the universe. However, in the long run neither perspective offers any means to make moral discriminations. Down one can be seen Soame Jenyns, down the other, Robespierre. Rigorously interpreted, whatever moral decision you make, you cannot be wrong; you can only be ignorant. Whether you wish to persuade people that they are in a perfect world, you are quite justified in your choice of means, since by definition the ends, which will be arrived at by a natural process, have order and value structured in them; and De Sade's frustration emerges: it is impossible to perform an unnatural act. Recent studies in Enlightenment pessimism have shown that as the eighteenth century wore on, more and more Enlightenment figures became aware of the difficulty. An important consequence for students of literature was the steady development in intensity and quantity of sentimentalism. Its original source was the necessity to discharge the tension consequent upon the affirmation that the world is radiant with order and value which any mind free from superstition, tyranny, and priestcraft could arrive at for itself, and the inconsistent perception that it is not. An æsthetic stimulus came to be valued for its power to discharge that tension in tears and enthusiasm. Further, the more the basic instability became apparent, the more necessity there was to fall back upon an emotional affirmation of order, value, and identity, as qualities structured into the real world. From this point of view Ossian was a typical late Enlightenment phenomenon. The enthusiastic poet and the man of feeling dominated the scene. As Professor Tuveson has so well demonstrated, Nature, through the exercise of the imagination, redeemed man. If you wish, as many do, to use the term "romanticism" to refer to this Enlightenment and enthusiasm and sentimentalism and natural redemption, I have no objection. One long tradition has always called it romanticism. But nothing could be more different from what I am talking about when I use that word. When the crash came, when a tiny minority of Enlightenment personalities, themselves a cultural minority, saw through Enlightenment pretensions and saw that it is impossible to maintain them, and when the Enlightenment was put to the test in the French Revolution and its superficiality revealed, a major cultural break occurred.

The logical possibilities of identifying Nature with order and value had been exhausted. If it is not true that order and value once were in this world and no longer are, or that they are outside the world, if it is not true that order and value are in the world, where are they? They do not exist at all, cries in anguish the negative romantic. But it is impossible for people at a high level of culture and civilization to endure for long such total disorientation. In such a situation was (and still is) any individual who enters the negative romantic stage, unless he can turn back to a pre-Enlightenment orientation or successfully repress his doubts about the Enlightenment construct. If he can do neither, he turns the world inside out.

Long ago George Herbert Mead said that romanticism is marked by the separation of the role from the self. With the collapse of the Enlightenment there also collapses the natural social structure, and with it the possibility of playing a role. Hence the social alienation which accompanies the cosmic isolation, or loss of relatedness to the perceived world. The first step at reconstituting value, then, is to strip bare the self, or more accurately, to invent the self, to conceptualize the sense of identity. To survive, one asserts pure identity as the basic datum. As two recent studies have pointed out, Schelling and Wordsworth attempted to assert the self as real and the world as a symbol of value.[9] Wordsworth eventually regressed, for such a position is a compromise. To be sure, there is all the difference between perceiving the world as evidence of divine order and perceiving it as a symbol of divine value, and finding order in the act of perception itself, but the latter, or symbolic, perception is extremely unstable, since it really asserts the existence of two sources of value and order, the self and the world. Rather, the more stable solution is to perceive the world as symbol of the self, and order and value as projected upon the world by the self. I think Professor Tuveson is in error, therefore, when he thinks of eighteenth-century Enlightenment and enthusiastic "early romanticism" as the predecessor of "high romanticism" (*my* romanticism), which is its fulfillment. Rather, *my* romantics used the same words, but sang them to a different tune. Imagination is a means of grace, to be sure, but Nature does not redeem man. Rather, man, through the exercise of the imagination, redeems Nature. Value enters the world through the self, which is not supported by any perceptible social or cosmic order, and the self projects upon the world an order which serves to symbolize that self-generated value. To be sure, for a time, and for some, the self was seen as the portal of the divine, a mythological symbolization for the sense of value. This was the transcendental stage of romanticism; but side by side, and eventually superseding it, was a nonmetaphysical realization that the only conceivable source of value was the necessity for the individual self to create it in order to maintain itself. In short, the self does not emerge through the perception of order and value in the world; rather, order and value emerge from the perception of the self. Nature is not the source of value, but the occasion for projecting it.

Man therefore redeems the world; and since in the poet the imagination is predominant, the poet is the primary source of value, in traditional language, redemption. The romantic poet thus takes upon himself the role of Christ; he becomes Christ, and he is himself his own redeemer and the model for the redemption of mankind. Eventually this task of the artist is extended to every human being. Further, if man is to redeem the world, it is only this world which can be redeemed. After yielding up moral questions in despair, because they are ultimately unsolvable by the Enlightenment orientation, Wordsworth grasped both horns of his dilemma. Nature is the source of both disturb-

[9] David Ferry, *The Limits of Mortality* (Middletown, Conn., 1960) and E. D. Hirsch, Jr., *Wordsworth and Schelling* (New Haven, 1960).

ance and equilibrium, of disorientation and orientation. To see what a gulf has here been crossed it is sufficient to call to mind that to the Enlightenment, Nature was the source of orientation only. Hence the frequent marriages of heaven and hell in the romantic tradition. Kubla Khan's garden includes both. Here or nowhere we find our home. Since it is this world which must be redeemed, the first task of the romantic is to face fully the horror, the brutality, and the evil which before had been either thought away or dismissed or regarded as either temporary or ultimately unreal. The flower of value must be plucked not on the sunny mountaintop, but in the very abyss. The worship of *sorrow* is divine. The world must be redeemed, in its absurdity and ugliness, as well as its order and beauty. Hence romanticism leads directly to the realism of Dickens and Balzac and so down to the present. It is the romantic's tradition that is really tough-minded. To him nothing is so beautiful as fact, nor does anything offer such sweet bones to gnaw on as the empirical world itself, the only world we can know, for the self can only be symbolized, not known. And hence the profoundest way to symbolize it is to recognize and assert its existence in another; and this emphatic assertion is the basis of romantic social morality.

From this fundamental percept of the self as the source of order flows romanticism's essentially antimetaphysical character. With and without the aid of Kant, an orientation is now seen not as a discovery but as a projection. Thus a metaphysical theory is thought of as an instrument, not as a reality, not as something in Nature, but as something imposed upon it. On the one hand it is conceived as an instrument for symbolizing the self or value; on the other it is thought of as an epistemological instrument. Further consequences flow from this. If an orientation is only instrumentally, not constitutively, valid, it is useful only temporarily. But then value, identity, and order can be experienced only temporarily, in moments of illumination, spots of time. Further, the romantic knows from history, his own and man's, that the great human temptation is to regard an orientation as final and that succumbing leads to disaster, for Christianity and the Enlightenment had ultimately collapsed. Consequently his moral task is to break down an orientation once it has been fully realized. His only means is self-disorientation. Hence the judgment often made that the romantic values emotional disturbance for its own sake. Not at all; he values it as a means to break down an orientation which, as a human being, he is tempted to preserve but as a romantic human being, he knows by definition is inadequate. As Browning implied, the only failure is success. Hence throughout the nineteenth century the use of drugs, alcohol, sex, and Asiatic theologies as means of deliberately dislocating the senses so that new worlds may emerge. Only with the breakthrough into modern art did the romantic artist and thinker learn how to break down an orientation without partially disintegrating his personality.

From this perspective it is possible to develop a more adequate explanation of the presence of dynamic organicism in the romantic tradition than the one I proposed twelve years ago. To begin with, it is now apparent—and perhaps was then—though not to me—that organicism is a product of the Enlightenment, that the increasing dependence on the natural world was bound to lead to conceiving the cosmos on the model of an organism rather than of a machine, and did. Further, the values of diversity, change, growth, and uniqueness, derived from organicism, are mainly late Enlightenment values, though, to be sure, relatively rare. From this point of view Herder, for example, appears as an Enlightenment figure, not a romantic one. The organic episode in the development of romanticism occurred partly because it was in the culture and could be used to symbolize the subjective experience of the romantic personality, the emergence of the self, partly because it was a novelty to many romantics, who did not realize its Enlightenment origins. Nevertheless, to the romantic it is always an instrument, while to nineteenth-century Enlightenment thinking it is constitutive. Although it was the most important metaphysical episode in the history of romanticism, it was abandoned, as all romantic world-hypotheses are abandoned, for by definition they are inadequate; and this process continues until romanticism learns that it can do entirely without constitutive metaphysics and can use any metaphysic or world-hypothesis as a supreme fiction.

To conclude with a phrase from Wallace Stevens is, I think, appropriate, for I still believe what I said twelve years ago and what is now, in fact, becoming almost a platitude, that modern art is the triumph of romanticism, that modern culture, in its vital areas, is a romantic culture, and that nothing has yet replaced it. Since the logic of romanticism is that contradictions must be included in a single orientation, but without pseudo-reconciliations, romanticism is a remarkably stable and fruitful orientation. For the past 165 years the romantic has been the tough-minded man, determined to create value and project order to make feasible the pure assertion of identity, determined to assert identity in order to engage with reality simply because it is there and because there is nothing else, and knowing eventually that his orientations are adaptive instruments and that no orientation is or can be final. The romantic artist does not escape from reality: he escapes into it. We may expect that the present revival of interest in nineteenth-century romanticism among younger scholars and artists will continue, for as a consequence of the current widespread breakdown of the Enlightenment tradition, romanticism is at last beginning to receive an adequate response.

BIBLIOGRAPHICAL NOTE: For the Lovejoy-Wellek-Peckham controversy see the bibliographical note to Lovejoy's essay p. 81 above. Peckham has pursued his argument more broadly in *Beyond the Tragic Vision* (New York, 1962) and *Romanticism: The Culture of the Nineteenth Century* (New York, 1965). With these works compare, particularly, Raymond Williams's *Culture and Society 1780–1950* (New York, 1958) and the excerpt from it below; also René Wellek's attack on Peckham's interpretation of cultural history in "Romanticism Re-examined," *Romanticism Reconsidered*, ed. Northrop Frye (New York and London, 1963). A very recent ambitious contribution to the controversy between advocates of "romanticisms" and those of "romanticism" is Lilian R. Furst's *Romanticism in Perspective* (London and New York, 1969), which leans much further toward Lovejoy than toward either Wellek or Peckham.

On the Logic
of Romanticism

Albert Gérard

The final verdict in a case in literary history is normally reached by
a procedure that exactly reverses that of the law courts. Instead of
defence following prosecution, prosecution follows defence. First, the
phase of uncritical enthusiasm that accompanies the discovery of a new
author or the phase of uncritical depreciation that such enthusiasms
necessarily provoke. Phase I, "He was not of an age, but for all time!"
Phase II, Rymer on *Othello*. And it is only when the second depreciatory phase has run its course that a judicial summary, such as that
provided by Johnson and Coleridge on Shakespeare, can prepare the
way for the agreed verdict of history. Note, however, that the third
and final phase is not reached by a compromise that splits the difference between too much enthusiasm and too much contempt. Its
distinguishing character is rather the newness of its approach, a degree

ON THE LOGIC OF ROMANTICISM: From *Essays in Criticism*, VII (1957), 262–73.
Translated by George Watson from an article in *L'Athénée*, XLV (1956). Reprinted
by permission of Basil Blackwell & Mott Ltd. [The first two paragraphs of the essay
were added by the Editor of *Essays in Criticism*. A further development of the point of
view in this essay (incorporating substantial portions of it) may be found in the
chapter entitled "Souls in Ferment: Reality, Knowledge, and Romantic Art" in
Professor Gérard's book, *English Romantic Poetry: Ethos, Structure, and Symbol in Coleridge, Wordsworth, Shelley and Keats* (Berkeley, 1968).]

of reinterpretation that amounts to a difference of critical kind. Johnson and Coleridge in their different but complementary ways had arrived at a completely new and hitherto unsuspected way of looking at Shakespeare, although it is the way that has now become standard and orthodox.

The question of the critical status of romanticism, after passing through its Phases I and II, appears to be emerging today into its third and final phase. And this version is also strikingly different from its predecessors—so much so, indeed, that a preliminary survey, based upon the author's *L'idée romantique de la poésie en Angleterre* (Paris: Les Belles Lettres, 1955), appears to be worth attempting.

We need not linger for the moment on the first, laudatory, phase in the development of a critical attitude towards romanticism. The second phase begins with the appearance in Paris of a bulky volume entitled *Le romantisme francais*, in which the author, Pierre Lasserre, presented an indictment of the new ways of feeling and thinking introduced into France at the beginning of the nineteenth century. It was a vehement piece of writing, impassioned and stimulating, and one which, as academic work goes, was to prove exceptionally influential. Published in 1907, reissued in 1908 and 1919, the book has helped to condition the attitude of our age toward romanticism, not only in France, but in the English-speaking countries as well. For Lasserre transmitted his furiously anti-romantic convictions to Irving Babbitt, who was at that time Professor of French Literature at Harvard. And Babbitt, long before his published attacks on romanticism in such books as *The New Laokoön* (1910), and *Rousseau and Romanticism* (1919), had communicated his ideas to his students, notably to the young T. S. Eliot, who left Harvard in 1910. In 1914, Eliot settled in England; and by way of his essays and his poetry he has spread the reaction against the romantic tradition in this country.

This movement, like any other Phase II, was perfectly justified and healthy. It was high time that English poetry and criticism should turn its back on the bog of syrupy sentiment created by the deliquescence of romanticism. It was only to be expected that Eliot and other modern critics should bypass romanticism to seek models among the Jacobean poets and in Dryden and Pope. After all, a century earlier, Sainte-Beuve in his *Tableau historique et critique* had bypassed classicism in the same way, to find in the Pléiade the first flourishing of a tradition which, according to him, romanticism continued.

In attacking romanticism, the critics of the twentieth century have taken their stand against its sentimentality, subjectivism, and primitivism, against the cult of spontaneity, the deification of self, the contempt for any kind of discipline in thought as well as in form, the escapism, and the lack of contact between poetry and the realities of life today. As is characteristic of Phase II criticism, the points are valid, but overstated. These properties have indeed been part and parcel of the romantic attitude at one time or another. But is one therefore entitled to assert that they are the whole, or even the vital core, of romanticism? Is it really true, as Georg Brandes claimed, that "according to the romantic doctrine the artistic omnipotence of the self and the poet's will should not submit to any law"? Is it correct to state, as F. R. Leavis has done, that the only thing the romantics had in common was "something negative: the absence of anything to replace the very positive tradition (literary, and more than literary— hence its strength) that had prevailed till towards the end of the eighteenth century"? (*The Common Pursuit* [1952], p. 185)

It is such charges, and others of the same sort, that are now being reinvestigated by historians of English romanticism.

That the romantic attitude to life and art has a subjective foundation is not to be denied. Romantic poetry and thought have their starting-point in the poet himself, in his aspirations and in his experience: on the one hand, his aspiration to a certain fulness of being, to a certain purity of spiritual life, to harmony and unity, a yearning toward the absolute, usually known by its German name *Sehnsucht*; on the other hand, a visionary experience which responds to this aspiration, and which assures the soul of the validity of its dream and of its hope. To understand the romantic doctrine, it is therefore necessary to scrutinise the experiences which the romantics thought crucial and from which all their intellectual activity arose. In these germinal experiences, there are many individual differences which cannot delay us here. But there are some common features.

The first of these is that the poetic experience brings the whole personality of the poet into play. It is often disparagingly said that romantic poetry is poetry of feeling. It is indeed surrounded with an aura of emotion. But the "feeling" of which these poets speak so much, the enthusiasm, the joy which possesses them, is more properly the psychological consequence and inner proof of the vital importance of the experience and of all it gives. The experience itself is not only emotional; it is also cognitive; it includes sensory and intellectual elements; it is rich in moral and metaphysical ramifications.

Essentially—and this is the second common feature—the poetic experience is a form of knowledge. It is not a strictly sensory form of knowledge, like that which often inspires the Imagists, since through the particular and the sensuous it aspires to reach to the universal. But it does not reach to the universal by way of abstractions, like the didactic poetry of eighteenth-century neoclassicism. In fact, it is fundamentally the intuition of a cosmic unity: the intuition that the universe is not an unintelligible chaos, nor a well-regulated mechanism, but a living organism, imbued throughout with an idea which endows it with its unity, its life, and its harmony.

It is from the poetic experience so conceived that all romantic thinking on life, art, and the universe ultimately derives.

When they came to interpret this experience on the plane of abstract metaphysical significance, the English poets had recourse to various philosophical traditions. But here again there are common features, of which the principal is that they spontaneously and immediately interpret their experiences in "spiritual" terms. The intuition of unity does not seem to them a subjective phenomenon which would arise from an arbitrary operation of the mind on the intrinsic diversity of things: it bears witness to an actual unity.

Their first impulse is to treat this unity as a unity of substance. In other words, they tend to invest their experience with a mystical colouring and to treat it as an immediate contact with the absolute in all its purity. It is in this sense that we may speak, as is so often the case, of Wordsworth's "pantheism" or Shelley's "idealism."

But what is chiefly worthy of notice is that the English romantics did not remain content with these rather facile philosophies, the amateurish pantheism and Neoplatonism which consist simply in denying the sensuous world or in deifying it. There is, of course, something mystical about many of the metaphors they used to convey their experience: they sometimes seem to imply an immediate contact with the absolute. But often, too, the cosmic unity seems to be felt as a unity not of substance, but of composition. Natural forms are not then presented as an obstacle to vision or as the proper object of the vision: instead, their harmony and vitality are felt as the mark of the action of a superior force which remains transcendent.

As a matter of fact, the romantics, are far less interested in the

nature of this spiritual force than might be inferred from the number
of commentators who have concentrated on this aspect of their thought.
Their phrasing points to diverse and sometimes divergent doctrines,
but they are united in proclaiming vigorously the *existence* of a
spiritual being which constantly leaves its mark on the visible world.
And what most concerns them is less the exact nature of this spiritual
force than its mark, the way it acts on the universe and brings order
into chaos.

The proper object of the romantic poetic experience is, in fact, a
sort of matter-spirit continuum. For the English romantic poets,
nature is not the treasure-house of all that is primitive, chaotic, savage,
or sensational. *It is the archetype and the accomplished model of all creation.*
Their metaphysics may be thought rather woolly: they are not
English for nothing. But they have brought into being what might
be called a *philosophy of creativity*, which is the doctrinal core of their
thought, in the same way as the *experience* in which this philosophy
originates is its vital core.

Such an approach allows us to see the romantic doctrine of nature
in its proper perspective. Nature, as revealed by the poetic experience,
is a *tertium quid* born of the meeting and interpenetration of two
opposite forces: the unity and organising (or plastic) power of the spirit,
and the diversity and chaos of matter. It is in this sense that, for
Shelley, God is "the overruling Spirit of the collective energy of the
moral and material world," "something mysteriously and illimitably
pervading the frame of things" (*Prose Works*, ed. H. B. Forman, II,
341–43); it is in this sense that, according to Coleridge, "Nature . . .
would give us the impression of a work of art, if we could see the thought
which is present at once in the whole and in every part" ("On Poesy
or Art," in *Biographia Literaria*, ed. J. Shawcross, II, 255); again, it is in
this sense that Wordsworth considers the visible world "as ruled by
those fixed laws / Whence spiritual dignity originates" (*Prelude*, XIII,
372–3). For the English romantics, Nature is not that "*quelque chose
d'énorme, de barbare et de sauvage*" which Diderot prized so highly. On
the contrary, it is striking how often they mention the "laws" which
bring order into the universe. For them these laws manifest the divine
thought, which gives to nature its life and its beauty.

The romantics, applying this philosophy of creativity to epistemology,
endeavoured to formulate a general theory of knowledge which would
take the poetic experience into account and justify the extraordinary

importance they attributed to poetry. They rejected the doctrines of rationalism, empiricism, and associationism, and claimed that all true knowledge is an act of creation. Even at the lowest level, perception is a *tertium quid* resulting from the action of the mind on sensory data, i.e., from a merging of subjective and objective. In what Coleridge calls "vital knowledge" an intimate fusion takes place between the consciousness and its object, and the percept becomes an integral part of the percipient's mind. This is why Wordsworth often uses such metaphorical terms as "drink," "eat," "absorb," "nourish," "feed," to describe the relationship of cognition and, above all, of assimilation which is established between the thinking subject and the objective world. Similarly, what Keats calls "sensation" is not an immediate intuition of truth with which the poet alone is favoured: it is the lived experience of reality, on the physical, moral, and metaphysical planes; this experience (in which the personality is totally involved, with its intellectual, emotional, and volitional faculties) is the fundamental act by which the personality of a man deepens and grows towards the fulness of wisdom. This idea of "vital knowledge" results, it is clear, from the conceptualisation of the poetic experience within the framework of the philosophy of creativity which, as we have seen, itself arises from a conception of nature deriving in its turn from the poetic experience.

But it is also clear that such a type of knowledge must belong to a faculty other than the ratiocinative: hence the formidable impulse given by the English romantics to the psychology of the imagination. The notion of imagination was traditionally associated with poetry, generally in a derogatory way. Imagination, in fact, boiled down to invention, a faculty which enables the poet to concoct pleasant fictions or to formulate in ornate language the truths which abstract reason had delivered to him. The romantics, on the contrary, glorify the imagination as the queen of the cognitive faculties and the very organ of truth.

The nature and scope of this development, for which the eighteenth century had prepared the ground, was defined most precisely by Coleridge, who distinguishes two aspects of the imaginative activity. "The primary Imagination," he says, is "the living power and prime agent of all human Perception, and . . . a repetition in the finite mind of the eternal act of creation in the infinite I AM." This, then, is the faculty which gives us vital knowledge. But Coleridge goes on to speak of the "secondary Imagination," which "dissolves, diffuses, dissipates, in order to re-create," which "struggles to idealise and to unify," and which is also "essentially vital" (*Biographia Literaria, op. cit.*, I, 202). This is the poetic imagination, which uses materials provided by the primary imagination, disintegrates them, and recasts the elements to create a *tertium quid*, a work which is an analogue of nature because it reveals the ideal unity underneath the diversity of its sensuous appearances.

The idealising and unifying function of art is, no doubt, something of a commonplace. But for the romantics a poem's unity and ideal quality do not arise out of a strictly intellectual or technical operation; they are not arrived at, as in neoclassicism, by treating general types according to fixed rules. They are, on the contrary, the culmination of an organic process in which the poet creates a work which is a symbol.

The romantic notion of the symbol, in theory if not always in fact, has nothing to do with the vague power of suggestion which Cazamian has describes as "*tout ce qui peut être la source d'un rayonnement significatif indirect*" (*Symbolisme et poésie*, p. 14). For the English romantics, the symbol is something more definite: it is a synthesis, a fusion of polarities. It is characterised, says Coleridge, "by the translucence of the special in the individual, or of the general in the special, or of the universal in the general." In the symbol, the vehicle, which is concrete and singular, and the meaning, which is universal and general, are indissociable and equally essential: they determine each other; their unity is total and indivisible. The symbol, Coleridge writes, "always partakes of the reality which it renders intelligible" (*Statesman's Manual*, Bohn ed., p. 322).

A conception of the symbol as an æsthetic synthesis required a firm psychological foundation. In romantic doctrine, the work of art, like the poetic experience which it expresses, owes its value as synthesis to a concert of the faculties which is orchestrated by the imagination. All the faculties (sensory, emotional, intellectual, imaginative, and moral) contribute to the elaboration of the work of art. They are all necessary for uniting the particular with the universal, the concrete with the ideal, the cognitive with the emotional, and for embodying the parent idea into organic sensuous forms which are both highly individualised and capable of touching the heart of the reader.

There is a widely spread notion that the essential part in romantic poetry and doctrine is played by feeling. But even such an expert dissector of complex words as William Empson has refrained from tackling the task of disentangling the denotative and connotative aspects of that confusing term. One thing, however, should be clearly understood: "feeling," in the romantic sense, is the capacity to be moved, certainly, but to be moved *by some object which deserves it*. The most valuable object, the one most worthy to be used in poetry, is necessarily that given by the poetic experience, that is spiritualised nature, the universe seen as a hieroglyph of the spirit, or, in Baudelaire's phrase, as a *"forêt de symboles."* Consequently, when poetry puts aside the describing of nature and takes man for its theme, the man most worthy to inspire the poet is the one who lives in communion with nature and who submits to the divine impulse that sustains it. This accounts for Wordsworth's temporary interest in rustic life. But in the last analysis, the man most worthy to inspire the poet is the poet himself, who by definition enjoys the supreme vision of a world animated and loaded with meaning by the divine breath. This in its turn accounts for the egotism of the romantics.

Romantic egotism has therefore nothing in common with the egotism of Narcissus. One might almost call it "impersonal egotism." The poet only sees himself as a sample of the human species. Quite simply, he possesses in a higher degree than others this gift of imagination so often called "feeling" out of sheer verbal laziness, which he considers as the divine spark in man.

Although feeling plays a major part in romantic poetry and thought, it is an error to think it the protagonist. And although "Kubla Khan" is naturally a corner-stone for all essays on pure poetry, the romantics never went so far as to recommend total spontaneity. It is the tyrannical *primacy* of reason they attacked, not reason itself. On the contrary, they are deeply conscious of the importance of the ratiocinative faculty in all its aspects.

It is naturally not surprising to hear Coleridge pronounce that "no man was ever yet a great poet, without being at the same time a profound philosopher" (*Biographia Literaria, op. cit.*, II, 19). But Keats himself, long praised or denigrated as the poet of pure sensuality, also recognised the importance of what he called "philosophy," or "wisdom," or "extensive knowledge," or "study," or "application." And for Wordsworth, "general Truths" ranked prominently among the gifts necessary to the poet, second indeed only to imagination (*Prelude*, I, 149–53).

Moreover, the romantics understood that inspiration is not enough for the poet. In their reflections on the technique of their art, in their critical views of other poets, it is clear in every line that they were convinced that *judgment* is necessary to the artist if he is to give adequate form to the visions of his imagination.

One section of the romantic doctrine has been outrageously neglected by historians and commentators; I mean their theory of poetic form. Here again we find the two great lines of reference along which the whole body of romantic thought develops: the poetic experience and the philosophy of creativity. For the finished work is the outcome of a genuine act of creation by which the idea shapes itself organically into adequate sensuous forms. And this idea, in its turn, is nothing other than the vision conveyed by the poetic experience.

No doubt, the romantic poets were fully aware that it is impossible for the poet totally to transmit his experience in words. But they did not yield to the temptation of despair. They have elaborated instead a theory of form based on the notion that in the processes of poetic creation art becomes auxiliary to vision.

The romantic theory of form is at once expressive and functional. What matters is the idea, and the experience from which it arises. Everything which does not derive from the experience, everything which does not help to express the idea, everything ornamental, gratuitous, and superfluous, must be rigorously proscribed. That is why in the sphere of speech the romantics rejected the mechanical conventions of poetic diction dear to their predecessors, with its mythological allegories, beribboned pastorals, and pathetic fallacies. In prosody, they advocate a flexibility which allows metre and rhythm to model themselves directly on the emotion which is their psychological origin. But they add that the rhythm must be controlled, that the metre must have a regularity of its own, because the original emotion issues forth from an intuition of order, harmony, and unity. In the field of imagery, the romantics made detailed literary and psychological analyses. They discovered that the image—metaphor, simile, personification or mere descriptive epithet—is the best instrument for conveying concretely the object of the vision in its complexity and uniqueness, and that it is especially suitable for transmitting the intuition of unity because it is based on analogy. The function of the poetic image is not, therefore, merely decorative. If metaphor is as essential to poetry as Aristotle said it was, it is because it reduces multiplicity to unity.*

* On the issue of romantic metaphor, see Brooks's essay above and the editorial footnote on p. 138.

Now unity, we should recall, is at once the object of the poetic experience and the end of the creative imagination. It must therefore be equally conspicuous in the structure of the finished work. The romantics rejected the classical unities of time and place, because they refer to superficial and adventitious elements. But while retaining the unity of action, they modified it so that we had better speak of a unity of structure: the elements of a work support one another and are subordinated to the whole, thus forming an ordered pattern which, though organic, is none the less rigorous. Being great admirers and practitioners of the sonnet, the romantics accept the laws of composition, not in order to supply the poem with some sort of self-sufficient intrinsic formal unity, but because the laws of composition are the application to art of the universal laws of all creation, so that the work of art becomes in itself a symbol by the simple fact of submitting to them.

It is to this symbolic quality that art owes its high moral significance. It would be surprising indeed if British theorists had overlooked the ethical content of poetry. The romantics lowered themselves at times to the point of courting Puritan prejudices with highly conventional statements. But in general they tried to put the relation between art and morality on a psychological level. Poetry, they say in effect, has a double virtue; on the one hand, it refines our imagination, enlarges the field of our perception and sympathy; on the other hand it strengthens our sense of the unity of the universe and intensifies our feeling for order and harmony. It makes us better fitted for the everyday world. That is why the romantics, borrowing the favorite criterion of their time, assert that poetry is *useful*. And this word, as they use it, is not merely a piece of apologetics.

They passionately wanted to be useful to mankind. They resisted the attractions of the ivory tower. And at their best they did not take refuge in the psuedo-mystical fog of a facile idealism. They were convinced they had apprehended an essential and forgotten truth about the nature of the universe and of life. They had a clear vision of a particular ideal which seemed to them infinitely superior to the prosaic utilitarianism which dominated the thought of their time. They tried strenuously to spread their sense of the absolute and of the spiritual dignity of man and nature. They did not believe there could exist anything that more urgently needed to be spread, or that was more worthy of being spread. But at the same time, they thought that poetry was to fulfil this great task with means appropriate to its own nature. It is clear that in considering the methods of poetry they greatly advanced our understanding of the psychological and æsthetic aspects of art. Nor can it be denied that in devoting themselves to that mission they helped to preserve the spiritual status of man at a moment when it was dangerously threatened.

The romantic doctrine is obviously out of date in numerous ways. In other words, it has become a part of history. But it has at least two permanent merits. The first is that, being loyal to itself, it developed in its own organic unsystematic way, along a path determined by personal experience and inner assent. The second is that, in spite of this, it was distinguished by a remarkable unity which, though hidden within vast masses of unorganised writing, is none the less real. It is this inner unity which accounts for the lasting interest of romanticism. It could not have dominated literature and criticism for more than a century, as it did in its first phase, if it had merely been characterised by the narcissism, intellectual incoherence, mental weakness, and æsthetic laxity which its opponents hold against it. Such criticism, typical of the second or anti-romantic phase, had some measure of justification. The anti-romantic critics have helped us, by their exaggerations and distortions, to see romanticism as in itself it really was. They have driven it out of the agora. It is now, in the third phase of its history, being installed in the pantheon of acknowledged literary classics. But the basis of this acknowledgement, it is now becoming clear, is not, as we have tended to take for granted, an emotional quality, good or bad, so much as a special mode of statement, an original language almost, that comes to flower in the best romantic poetry.

BIBLIOGRAPHICAL NOTE: For other general studies of romanticism see, e.g., C. M. Bowra, *The Romantic Imagination* (Cambridge, Mass., 1949); Herbert Read, *The True Voice of Feeling* (New York, 1953); R. A. Foakes, *The Romantic Assertion* (London, 1958); and David Perkins, "General Introduction," *English Romantic Writers* (New York, 1967). See also M. H. Abrams, *The Mirror and the Lamp* (New York, 1953), and W. J. Bate, *From Classic to Romantic* (Cambridge, Mass., 1946). On "the poetic experience" as "a form of knowledge" see especially E. R. Wasserman's essay in this collection.

The Romantic Artist

Raymond Williams

Than the poets from Blake and Wordsworth to Shelley and Keats there have been few generations of creative writers more deeply interested and more involved in study and criticism of the society of their day. Yet a fact so evident, and so easily capable of confirmation, accords uneasily in our own time with that popular and general conception of the "romantic artist" which, paradoxically, has been primarily derived from study of these same poets. In this conception, the Poet, the Artist, is by nature indifferent to the crude worldliness and materialism of politics and social affairs; he is devoted, rather, to the more substantial spheres of natural beauty and personal feeling. The elements of this paradox can be seen in the work of the romantic poets themselves, but the supposed opposition between attention to natural beauty and attention to government, or between personal feeling and the nature of man in society, is on the whole a later development. What were seen at the end of the nineteenth century as disparate interests, between which a man must choose and in the act

THE ROMANTIC ARTIST: From *Culture and Society 1780–1950* (New York: Columbia University Press, 1958). Reprinted by permission of Columbia University Press and Chatto & Windus Ltd.

269

of choice declare himself poet or sociologist, were, normally, at the beginning of the century, seen as interlocking interests: a conclusion about personal feeling became a conclusion about society, and an observation of natural beauty carried a necessary moral reference to the whole and unified life of man. The subsequent dissociation of interests certainly prevents us from seeing the full significance of this remarkable period, but we must add also that the dissociation is itself in part a product of the nature of the romantic attempt. Meanwhile, as some sort of security against the vestiges of the dissociation we may usefully remind ourselves that Wordsworth wrote political pamphlets, that Blake was a friend of Tom Paine and was tried for sedition, that Coleridge wrote political journalism and social philosophy, that Shelley, in addition to this, distributed pamphlets in the streets, that Southey was a constant political commentator, that Byron spoke on the frame-riots and died as a volunteer in a political war; and, further, as must surely be obvious from the poetry of all the men named, that these activities were neither marginal nor incidental, but were essentially related to a large part of the experience from which the poetry itself was made. It is, moreover, only when we are blinded by the prejudice of the dissociation that we find such a complex of activities in any way surprising. For these two generations of poets lived through the crucial period in which the rise both of democracy and of industry was effecting qualitative changes in society: changes which by their nature were felt in a personal as well as in a general way. In the year of the French Revolution, Blake was 32, Wordsworth 19, Coleridge 17, and Southey 15. In the year of Waterloo, Byron was 31, Shelley 27, Keats 24. The dates are sufficient reminder of a period of political turmoil and controversy fierce enough to make it very difficult for even the least sensitive to be indifferent. Of the slower, wider, less observable changes that we call the Industrial Revolution, the landmarks are less obvious; but the lifetime of Blake, 1757 to 1827, is, in general, the decisive period. The changes that we receive as record were experienced, in these years, on the senses: hunger, suffering, conflict, dislocation; hope, energy, vision, dedication. The pattern of change was not background, as we may now be inclined to study it; it was, rather, the mould in which general experience was cast.

It is possible to abstract a political commentary from the writings of these poets, but this is not particularly important.* The development of Wordsworth, Coleridge, and Southey from differing degrees of revolutionary ardour in their youth to differing degrees of Burkean conservatism in their maturity is interesting. A distinction betwen the revolutionary principles of Shelley and the fine libertarian opportunism of Byron is useful. A reminder that Blake and Keats cannot be weakened to some ideal vagueness, but were, as men and poets, passionately committed to the tragedy of their period, is timely. In every case, however, the political criticism is now less interesting than the wider social criticism: those first apprehensions of the essential significance of the Industrial Revolution, which all felt and none revoked. Beyond this, again, is a different kind of response, which is a main root of the idea of culture. At this very time of political, social, and economic change there is a radical change also in ideas of art, of the artist, and of their place in society. It is this significant change that I wish to adduce.

There are five main points: first, that a major change was taking place in the nature of the relationship between a writer and his readers; second, that a different habitual attitude towards the "public" was establishing itself; third, that the production of art was coming to be regarded as one of a number of specialised kinds of production, subject to much the same conditions as general production; fourth, that a theory of the "superior reality" of art, as the seat of imaginative truth, was receiving increasing emphasis; fifth, that the idea of the independent creative writer, the autonomous genius, was becoming a kind of rule. In naming these points, it is of course necessary to add at once that they are clearly very closely interrelated, and that some might be named as causes, and some as effects, were not the historical process so complex as to render a clear division impossible.

The first characteristic is clearly a very important one. From the third and fourth decades of the eighteenth century there had been

---

* Cf., e.g., Crane Brinton, *The Political Ideas of the English Romanticists* (Oxford, 1926); Alfred Cobban, *Edmund Burke and the Revolt against the Eighteenth Century* (London, 1929); H. N. Brailsford, *Shelley, Godwin and Their Circle* (Toronto 1952); and Jacques Barzun, *Romanticism and the Modern Ego* (Boston, 1943), revised in 1962 and issued as *Classic, Romantic, and Modern*.

growing up a large new middle-class reading public, the rise in which corresponds very closely with the rise to influence and power of the same class. As a result, the system of patronage had passed into subscription-publishing, and thence into general commercial publishing of the modern kind. These developments affected writers in several ways. There was an advance, for the fortunate ones, in independence and social status—the writer became a fully-fledged "professional man." But the change also meant the institution of "the market" as the type of a writer's actual relations with society. Under patronage, the writer had at least a direct relationship with an immediate circle of readers, from whom, whether prudentially or willingly, as mark or as matter of respect, he was accustomed to accept and at times to act on criticism. It is possible to argue that this system gave the writer a more relevant freedom than that to which he succeeded. In any event, against the dependence, the occasional servility, and the subjection to patronal caprice had to be set the direct relation of the act of writing with at least some part of society, personally known, and the sense, when relations were fortunate, that the writer "belonged." On the other hand, against the independence and the raised social status which success on the market commanded had to be set similar liabilities to caprice and similar obligations to please, but now, not liabilities to individuals personally known, but to the workings of an institution which seemed largely impersonal. The growth of the "literary market" as the type of a writer's relations with his readers has been responsible for many fundamental changes of attitude. But one must add, of course, that such a growth is always uneven, both in its operations and in its effects. It is not perhaps until our own century that it is so nearly universal as to be almost dominant. By the beginning of the nineteenth century the institution was established, but it was nevertheless modified by many kinds of survival of earlier conditions. The important reactions to it were, however, laid down at this time.

One such reaction, evidently, is that named as the second point: the growth of a different habitual attitude towards the "public." Writers had, of course, often expressed, before this time, a feeling of dissatisfaction with the "public," but in the early nineteenth century this feeling became acute and general. One finds it in Keats: "I have not the slightest feel of humility towards the Public"; in Shelley: "Accept no counsel from the simple-minded. Time reverses the judgment of the foolish crowd. Contemporary criticism is no more than the sum of the folly with which genius has to wrestle." One finds it, most notably and most extensively, in Wordsworth:

> Still more lamentable is his error who can believe that there is anything of divine infallibility in the clamour of that small though loud portion of the community, ever governed by factitious influence, which, under the name of the PUBLIC, passes itself upon the unthinking, for the PEOPLE. Towards the Public, the Writer hopes that he feels as much deference as it is entitled to; but to the People, philosophically characterised, and to the embodied spirit of their knowledge . . . his devout respect, his reverence, is due [Williams's ellipsis].

It is, of course, easier to be respectful and reverent to "the People, philosophically characterised," than to a Public, which noisily identifies itself. Wordsworth, in his conception of the People, is drawing heavily on the social theory of Burke, and for not dissimilar reasons. However the immediate argument went, whatever the reactions of actual readers, there was thus available a final appeal to "the embodied spirit . . . of the People": that is to say, to an Idea, an Ideal Reader, a standard that might be set above the clamor of the writer's actual relations with society. The "embodied spirit," naturally enough, was a very welcome alternative to the market. Obviously, such an attitude then affects the writer's own attitude to his work. He will not accept the market quotation of popularity. . . . He will continue to insist, in fact, on an Idea, a standard of excellence, the "embodied spirit" of a People's knowledge, as something superior to the actual course of events, the actual run of the market. This insistence, it is worth emphasizing, is one of the primary sources of the idea of Culture. Culture, the "embodied spirit of a People," the true standard of excellence, became available, in the progress of the century, as the court of appeal in which real values were determined, usually in opposition to the "factitious" values thrown up by the market and similar operations of society.

The subjection of art to the laws of the market, and its consideration as a specialized form of production subject to much the same conditions as other forms of production, had been prefigured in much late-eighteenth-century thinking. Adam Smith had written:

> In opulent and commercial societies to think or to reason comes to be, like every other employment, a particular business, which is carried on by a very few people, who furnish the public with all the thought and reason possessed by the vast multitudes that labour.

This is significant as a description of that special class of persons who from the 1820's were to be called "intellectuals." It describes, also, the new conditions of specialization of the artist, whose work, as Adam Smith had said of knowledge, was not in fact "purchased, in the same manner as shoes or stockings, from those whose business it is to make up and prepare for the market that particular species of goods." Such a position, and such a specialization of function, followed inevitably from the institution of commercial publishing. The novel, in particular, had quickly become a commodity; its main history as a literary form follows, as is well known, precisely the growth of these new conditions. But the effects were also obvious in poetry, on which the impact of a market relationship was inevitably severe. Alongside the rejection of the Public and of Popularity as standards of worth, increasing complaint was made that literature had become a trade. The two things, in fact, were normally treated together. Sir Egerton Brydges wrote in the 1820's:

> It is a vile evil that literature is become so much a trade all over Europe. Nothing has gone so far to nurture a corrupt taste, and to give the unintellectual power over the intellectual. Merit is now universally esteemed by the multitude of readers that an author can attract. . . . Will the uncultivated mind admire what delights the cultivated? [Williams's ellipsis]

Similarly in 1834 Tom Moore spoke of the "lowering of standards that must necessarily arise from the extending of the circle of judges; from letting the mob in to vote, particularly at a period when the market is such an object to authors." He went on to distinguish between the "mob" and the "cultivated few." It is obvious, here, how the adjective "cultivated" contributed to the newly necessary abstractions, "cultivation" and "culture." In this kind of argument, "culture" became the normal antithesis to the market.

I have emphasized this new type of an author's relationship to his readers because I believe that such matters are always central in any kind of literary activity. I turn now to what is clearly a related matter, but one which raises the most difficult issues of interpretation. It is a fact that in this same period in which the market and the idea of specialist production received increasing emphasis there grew up, also, a system of thinking about the arts of which the most important elements are, first, an emphasis on the special nature of art-activity as a means to "imaginative truth," and, second, an emphasis on the artist as a special kind of person. It is tempting to see these theories as a direct response to the actual change in relations between artist and society. Certainly, in the documents, there are some obvious elements of compensation: at a time when the artist is being described as just one more producer of a commodity for the market, he is describing himself as a specially endowed person, the guiding light of the common life. Yet, undoubtedly, this is to simplify the matter, for the response is not merely a professional one. It is also (and this has been of the greatest subsequent importance) an emphasis on the embodiment in art of certain human values, capacities, energies, which the development of society towards an industrial civilization was felt to be threatening or even destroying. The element of professional protest is undoubtedly there, but the larger issue is the opposition on general human grounds to the kind of civilization that was being inaugurated.

Romanticism is a general European movement,* and it is possible to relate the new ideas, as they arise, solely to a larger system of ideas in European thinking as a whole. The influence of Rousseau, of Goethe, of Schiller, and of Chateaubriand can certainly be traced. Indeed, if we consider the ideas in abstraction, we can take the idea of the artist as a special kind of person, and of the "wild" genius, as far back as the Socratic definition of a poet in Plato's *Ion*. The "superior reality" of art has a multitude of classical texts, and, within our period, is in obvious relation with the German idealist school of philosophy and its English dilution through Coleridge and Carlyle. These relations are important, yet an idea can perhaps only be weighed, only understood, in a particular mind and a particular situation. In England, these ideas that we call romantic have to be understood in terms of the problems in experience with which they were advanced to deal.

A good example is a definition in one of the early documents of English romanticism, Young's *Conjectures on Original Composition* (1759):

> An Original may be said to be of a *vegetable* nature; it rises spontaneously from the vital root of genius; it *grows*, it is not *made*; Imitations are often a sort of *manufacture*, wrought up by those *mechanics*, art and *labour*, out of pre-existent materials not their own.

* This thesis has been ably documented by René Wellek in his essay above.

This is a piece of very familiar romantic literary theory: contrasting the spontaneous work of genius with the formal imitative work bound by a set of rules. As Young also writes: "Modern writers have a *choice* to make . . . they may soar in the regions of *liberty*, or move in the soft fetters of easy *imitation*." But what Young is saying when he defines an "original" is, if we look at his terms, very closely linked with a whole general movement of society. It is certainly literary theory, but as certainly it is not being formulated in isolation. When he says of an original that "it grows, it is not made," he is using the exact terms on which Burke based his whole philosophical criticism of the new politics. The contrast between "grows" and "made" was to become the contrast between "organic" and "mechanical" which lies at the very centre of a tradition which has continued to our own day. Again, when he defines an "imitation," Young condemns it in terms of the very industrial processes which were about to transform English society: "a sort of *manufacture, wrought up* by those *mechanics . . . out of pre-existent materials not their own*." The point may or may not hold in literary theory; but these are certainly the terms and the implied values by which the coming industrial civilization was to be condemned.

Burke condemned the new society in terms of his experience (or his idealization) of the earlier society. But increasingly as the huge changes manifested themselves the condemnation became specialized, and, in a sense, abstract. One part of the specialization was the growth of the standard of Cultivation or Culture; another part, closely related to this and later in fact to combine with it, was the growth of the new idea of Art. This new idea of a superior reality, and even of a superior power, is strikingly expressed by Blake:

> "Now Art has lost its mental charms
> France shall subdue the World in Arms."
> So spoke an Angel at my birth,
> Then said, "Descend thou upon Earth.
> Renew the Arts on Britain's Shore,
> And France shall fall down and adore.
> With works of Art their armies meet,
> And War shall sink beneath thy feet.
> But if thy Nation Arts refuse,
> And if they scorn the immortal Muse,
> France shall the arts of Peace restore,
> And save thee from the Ungrateful shore."
> Spirit, who lov'st Britannia's Isle,
> Round which the Fiends of Commerce smile. . . .

In Blake, the professional pressures can be easily discerned, for he suffered badly in "the desolate market where none come to buy." He reminds us of Young, when he attacks "the interest of the Monopolising Trader who Manufactures Art by the Hands of Ignorant Journeymen till . . . he is Counted the Greatest Genius who can sell a Good-for-Nothing Commodity for a Great Price." But equally, Blake's criticism goes far beyond the professional complaint: the Imagination which, for him, Art embodies is no commodity, but "a Representation of what Eternally Exists, Really and Unchangeably." It is in such a light that the inadequacies of existing society and of the quality of life which it promotes are to be seen and condemned.

It is important to measure the strength of this claim, for we shall misunderstand it if we look only at some of the later divagations of the idea of Genius. The ambiguous word in Young's definition is "imitation," which in nearly all romantic theory acquired a heavily derogatory sense. This is because "imitation" was understood to mean imitation of works already done, that is to say conformity to a given set of rules. The eloquence deployed against the set of rules is both remarkable and, in the end, tedious. What was happening, technically, was no more than a change of convention, which when it is of any magnitude normally carries such eloquence as a by-product. To the degree that the change is more than a change in convention—and changes in convention only occur when there are radical changes in the general structure of feeling—the word "Imitation" is particularly confusing. For indeed, in the best "classicist" theory, Imitation is the term normally used to describe what Blake has just described, and what all the romantic writers emphasized: "a Representation of what Eternally Exists, Really and Unchangeably." Imitation, at its best, was not understood as adherence to somebody else's rules; it was, rather, "imitation of the universal reality." An artist's precepts were not so much previous works of art as the "universals" (in Aristotle's term) or permanent realities. This argument, really, had been completed in the writings of the Renaissance.

The tendency of romanticism is towards a vehement rejection of dogmas of method in art, but it is also, very clearly, towards a claim which all good classical theory would have recognized: the claim that the artist's business is to "read the open secret of the universe." A "romantic" critic like Ruskin, for example, bases his whole theory of art on just this "classicist" doctrine. The artist perceives and represents Essential Reality, and he does so by virtue of his master faculty Imagination. In fact, the doctrines of "the genius" (the autonomous creative artist) and of the "superior reality of art" (penetration to a sphere of universal truth) were in romantic thinking two sides of the same claim. Both romanticism and classicism are in this sense idealist theories of art; they are really opposed not so much by each other as by naturalism.*

What was important at this time was the stress given to a mode of human experience and activity which the progress of society seemed increasingly to deny. Wordsworth might hold with particular conviction the idea of the persecuted genius, but there is a more general significance in his attitudes to poetry, and indeed to art as a whole:

> High is our calling, Friend!—Creative Art . . .
> Demands the service of a mind and heart
> Though sensitive, yet in their weakest part
> Heroically fashioned—to infuse
> Faith in the whispers of the lonely Muse
> While the whole world seems adverse to desert.

These are the lines to the painter Haydon, in December 1815. They are significant for the additional reason that they mark the fusing into the common "sphere of imaginative truth" of the two separate *arts*, or skills, of poetry and painting. While in one sense the market was specializing the artist, artists themselves were seeking to generalize their skills into the common property of imaginative truth. Always, this kind of emphasis is to be seen as a mode of defence: the defensive tone in Wordsworth's lines is very obvious, and in this they are entirely characteristic. At one level the defence is evidently compensatory: the height of the artists' claim is also the height of their despair. They defined, emphatically, their high calling, but they came to define and to emphasize because they were convinced that the principles on which the new society was being organized were actively hostile to the necessary principles of art. Yet, while to see the matter in this way is to explain the new emphasis, it is not to explain it away. What was laid down as a defensive reaction became in the course of the century a most important positive principle, which in its full implications was deeply and generally humane.

---

* Cf. Lascelles Abercrombie, *Romanticism* (London, 1926), and F. L. Lucas, pp. 126–27 above, both of whom oppose romanticism to realism. See also Georg Brandes's *Naturalism in Nineteenth Century English Literature* (London, 1905).

There are many texts from which this principle can be illustrated, but the most characteristic, as it is also among the best known, is Wordsworth's Preface of 1800 to the *Lyrical Ballads*. Here it is not only the truth but the general humanity of poetry which Wordsworth emphasizes: first, by attacking those "who talk of Poetry as of a matter of amusement and idle pleasure; who will converse with us as gravely about a *taste* for poetry, as they express it, as if it were a thing as indifferent as a taste for rope-dancing, or Frontiniac or Sherry." The concept of *taste*—which implies one kind of relationship between writer and reader—is inadequate because

> it is a metaphor, taken from a *passive* sense of the human body, and transferred to things which are in their essence *not* passive—to intellectual *acts* and *operations*. . . . But the profound and the exquisite in feeling, the lofty and universal in thought and imagination . . . are neither of them, accurately speaking, objects of a faculty which could ever without a sinking in the spirit of Nations have been designated by the metaphor *Taste*. And why? Because without the exertion of a cooperating *power* in the mind of the Reader, there can be no adequate sympathy with either of these emotions: without this auxiliary impulse, elevated or profound passion cannot exist.

This states in another way an important criticism of the new kind of social relationships of art: when art is a commodity, taste is adequate, but when it is something more, a more active relationship is essential. The "something more" is commonly defined:

> Aristotle, I have been told, has said, that Poetry is the most philosophic of all writing; it is so: its object is truth, not individual and local, but general and operative; not standing upon external testimony, but carried alive into the heart by passion; truth which is its own testimony, which gives competence and confidence to the tribunal to which it appeals, and receives them from the same tribunal. . . . The Poet writes under one restriction only, namely, the necessity of giving immediate pleasure to a human Being possessed of that information which may be expected from him, not as a lawyer, a physician, a mariner, an astronomer, or a natural philosopher, but as a Man. . . . To this knowledge which all men carry about with them, and to these sympathies in which, without any other discipline than that of our daily life, we are fitted to take delight, the Poet principally directs his attention. . . . He is the rock of defence for human nature; an upholder and preserver, carrying everywhere with him relationship and love. In spite of difference of soil and climate, of language and manners, of laws and customs: in spite of

things silently gone out of mind, and things violently destroyed; the Poet binds together by passion and knowledge the vast empire of human society, as it is spread over the whole earth, and over all time.

This is the case which, in its essentials, was to be eloquently restated by Shelley in his *Defence of Poetry*. It is the case which extends through Ruskin and Morris into our own century, when Poetry, as Wordsworth would have approved, has been widened to Art in general. The whole tradition can be summed up in one striking phrase used by Wordsworth, where the poet, the artist in general, is seen as "an upholder and preserver, carrying everywhere with him relationship and love." Artists, in this mood, came to see themselves as agents of the "revolution for life," in their capacity as bearers of the creative imagination. Here, again, is one of the principal sources of the idea of Culture; it was on this basis that the association of the idea of the general perfection of humanity with the practice and study of the arts was to be made. For here, in the work of artists—"the first and last of all knowledge . . . as immortal as the heart of man"—was a practicable mode of access to that ideal of human perfection which was to be the center of defence against the disintegrating tendencies of the age.

The emphasis on a general common humanity was evidently necessary in a period in which a new kind of society was coming to think of man as merely a specialized instrument of production. The emphasis on love and relationship was necessary not only within the immediate suffering but against the aggressive individualism and the primarily economic relationships which the new society embodied. Emphasis on the creative imagination, similarly, may be seen as an alternative construction of human motive and energy, in contrast with the assumptions of the prevailing political economy. This point is indeed the most interesting part of Shelley's *Defence*:

> Whilst the mechanist abridges, and the political economist combines, labour, let them beware that their speculations, for want of correspondence with those first principles which belong to the imagination, do not tend, as they have in modern England, to exasperate at once the extremes of luxury and want. . . . The rich have become richer, and the poor have become poorer; and the vessel of the state is driven between the Scylla and Charybdis of anarchy and despotism. Such are the effects which must ever flow from an unmitigated exercise of the calculating faculty.

This is the general indictment which we can see already forming as a tradition, and the remedy is in the same terms:

> There is no want of knowledge respecting what is wisest and best in morals, government, and political economy, or at least, what is wiser and better than what men now practise or endure. But . . . we want the creative faculty to imagine that which we know; we want the generous impulse to act that which we imagine; we want the poetry of life: our calculations have outrun conception; we have eaten more than we can digest. . . . Poetry, and the Principle of Self, of which Money is the visible incarnation, are the God and Mammon of the world.

The most obvious criticism of such a position as Shelley's is that, while it is wholly valuable to present a wider and more substantial account of human motive and energy than was contained in the philosophy of industrialism, there are corresponding dangers in specializing this more substantial energy to the act of poetry, or of art in general. It is this specialization which, later, made much of this criticism ineffectual. The point will become clearer in the later stages of our enquiry, where it will be a question of distinguishing between the idea of culture as art and the idea of culture as a whole way of life. The positive consequence of the idea of art as a superior reality was that it offered an immediate basis for an important criticism of industrialism. The negative consequence was that it tended, as both the situation and the opposition hardened, to isolate art, to specialize the imaginative faculty to this one kind of activity, and thus to weaken the dynamic function which Shelley proposed for it. We have already examined certain of the factors which tended towards this specialization; it remains now to examine the growth of the idea of the artist as a "special kind of person."

The word *Art*, which had commonly meant "skill," became specialized during the course of the eighteenth century, first to "painting," and then to the imaginative arts generally. *Artist*, similarly, from the general sense of a skilled person, in either the "liberal" or the "useful" arts, had become specialized in the same direction, and had distinguished itself from *artisan* (formerly equivalent with *artist*, but later becoming what we still call, in the opposite specialized sense, a "skilled worker"), and of course from *craftsman*. The emphasis on skill, in the word, was gradually replaced by an emphasis on sensibility; and this replacement was supported by the parallel changes in such words as *creative* (a word which could not have been applied to art until the idea of the "superior reality" was forming), *original* (with its important implications of spontaneity and vitalism; a word, we remember, that Young virtually contrasted with *art* in the sense of skill), and *genius* (which, because of its root association with the idea of *inspiration*, had changed from "characteristic disposition" to "exalted special ability," and took its tone in this from the other affective words). From *artist* in the new sense there were formed *artistic* and *artistical*, and these, by the end of the nineteenth century, had certainly more reference to "temperament" than to skill or practice. *Æsthetics*, itself a new word, and a product of the specialization, similarly stood parent to *æsthete*, which again indicated a "special kind of person."

The claim that the artist revealed a higher kind of truth is, as we have seen, not new in the romantic period, although it received significant additional emphasis. The important corollary of the idea was, however, the conception of the artist's autonomy in this kind of revelation; his substantive element, for example, was now not faith but genius. In its opposition to the "set of rules," the autonomous claim is of course attractive. Keats puts it finely: "The Genius of Poetry must work out its own salvation in a man: It cannot be matured by law and precept, but by sensation and watchfulness in itself. That which is creative must create itself." Our sympathy with this rests on the emphasis on a personal discipline, which is very far removed from talk of the "wild" or "lawless" genius. The difference is there, in Keats, in the emphasis on "the Genius of Poetry," which is impersonal as compared with the personal "genius." Coleridge put the same emphasis on law, with the same corresponding emphasis on autonomy:

> No work of true genius dares want its appropriate form, neither indeed is there any danger of this. As it must not, so genius cannot, be lawless; for it is even this that constitutes it genius—the power of acting creatively under laws of its own origination.

This is at once more rational and more useful for the making of art than the emphasis, at least as common in romantic pamphleteering, on an "artless spontaneity." Of the Art (sensibility) which claims that it can dispense with art (skill) the subsequent years hold more than enough examples.

As literary theory, the emphases of Keats and Coleridge are valuable. The difficulty is that this kind of statement became entangled with other kinds of reaction to the problem of the artist's relations with society. The instance of Keats is most significant, in that the entanglement is less and the concentration more. If we complete the sentence earlier quoted from him we find: "I have not the slightest feel of humility towards the public, or to anything in existence,—but the eternal Being, the Principle of Beauty, and the Memory of Great Men." This is characteristic, as is the famous affirmation:

> I am certain of nothing but of the holiness of the Heart's affections, and the truth of Imagination. What the Imagination seizes as Beauty must be truth—whether it existed before or not—for I have the same idea of all our passions as of Love; they are all, in their sublime, creative of essential Beauty. . . . The Imagination may be compared to Adam's dream—he awoke and found it truth.

But the account of the artist's personality which Keats then gives is, in his famous phrase, that of "Negative Capability . . . when a man is capable of being in uncertainties, mysteries, doubts, without any irritable reaching after fact and reason." Or again:

> Men of Genius are great as certain ethereal Chemicals operating on the Mass of neutral intellect—but they have not any individuality, any determined Character—I would call the top and head of those who have a proper self, Men of Power.

It is certainly possible to see this emphasis on passivity as a compensatory reaction, but this is less important than the fact that Keats's emphasis is on the poetic *process* rather than on the poetic *personality*. The theory of Negative Capability could degenerate into the wider and more popular theory of the poet as "dreamer," but Keats himself worked finely, in experience, to distinguish between "dreamer" and "poet," and if in the second *Hyperion* his formal conclusion is uncertain, it is at least clear that what he means by "dream" is something as hard and positive as his own skill. It is not from the fine discipline of a Keats that the loose conception of the romantic artist can be drawn.

Wordsworth, in the *Preface to Lyrical Ballads*, shows us most clearly how consideration of the poetic process became entangled with more general questions of the artist and society. In discussing his own theory of poetic language, he is in fact discussing communication. He asserts, reasonably and moderately, the familiar attitude to the Public:

> Such faulty expressions, were I convinced they were faulty at present, and that they must necessarily continue to be so, I would willingly take all reasonable pains to correct. But it is dangerous to make these alterations on the simple authority of a few individuals, or even of certain classes of men; for where the understanding of an Author is not convinced, or his feelings altered, this cannot be done without great injury to himself: for his own feelings are his stay and support.

This has to be said on the one side, while at the same time Wordsworth is saying: "The Poet thinks and feels in the spirit of human passions. How, then, can his language differ in any material degree from that of all other men who feel vividly and see clearly?" And so:

> Among the qualities . . . enumerated as principally conducing to form a Poet, is implied nothing differing in kind from other men, but only in degree. . . . The Poet is chiefly distinguished from other men by a greater promptness to think and feel without immediate external excitement, and a greater power in expressing such thoughts and feelings as are produced in him in that manner. But these passions and thoughts and feelings are the general passions and thoughts and feelings of men.

Of these chief distinctions, while the first is a description of a psychological type, the second is a description of a skill. While the two are held in combination, the argument is plausible. But in fact, under the tensions of the general situation, it became possible to dissociate them, and so to isolate the "artistic sensibility."

The matter is exceptionally complex, and what happened, under the stress of events, was a series of simplifications. The obstruction of a certain kind of experience was simplified to the obstruction of poetry, which was then identified with it and even made to stand for it as a whole. Under pressure, art became a symbolic abstraction for a whole range of general human experience: a valuable abstraction, because indeed great art has this ultimate power; yet an abstraction nevertheless, because a general social activity was forced into the status of a department or province, and actual works of art were in part converted into a self-pleading ideology. This description is not offered for purposes of censure; it is a fact, rather, with which we have to learn to come to terms. There is high courage, and actual utility, if also simplification, in romantic claims for the imagination. There is courage, also, in the very weakness which, ultimately, we find in the special pleading of personality. In practice there were deep insights, and great works of art; but, in the continuous pressure of living, the free play of genius found it increasingly difficult to consort with the free play of the market, and the difficulty was not solved, but cushioned, by an idealization. The last pages of Shelley's *Defence of Poetry* are painful to read. The bearers of a high imaginative skill become suddenly the "legislators," at the very moment when they were being forced into practical exile; their description as "unacknowledged," which, on the theory, ought only to be a fact to be accepted, carries with it also the felt helplessness of a generation. Then Shelley at the same time claims that the Poet "ought personally to be the happiest, the best, the wisest, and the most illustrious of men"; where the emphasis, inescapably, falls painfully on the *ought*. The pressures, here personal as well as general, create, as a defensive reaction, the separation of poets from other men, and their classification into an idealized general person, "Poet" or "Artist," which was to be so widely and so damagingly received. The appeal, as it had to be, is beyond the living community, to the "mediator and . . . redeemer, Time." Over the England of 1821 there had, after all, to be some higher Court of Appeal. We are not likely, when we remember the lives of any of these men, to be betrayed into the irritability of prosecution, but it is well, also, if we can avoid the irritability of defence. The whole action has passed into our common experience, to lie there, formulated and unformulated, to move and to be examined. "For it is less their spirit, than the spirit of the age" [Shelley, *Defence of Poetry*].

BIBLIOGRAPHICAL NOTE: Other works that deal with the romantic artist in relation to society and to culture are Morse Peckham's *Beyond the Tragic Vision* (New York, 1962) and *Romanticism: The Culture of the Nineteenth Century* (New York, 1965). See also the essays listed in the bibliographical note to Christopher Caudwell's essay above, pp. 123–24.

Romanticism and Antiself-consciousness

Geoffrey H. Hartman

I

The dejection afflicting John Stuart Mill in his twentieth year was alleviated by two important events. He read Wordsworth, and he discovered for himself a view of life resembling the "antiself-consciousness theory" of Carlyle. Mill describes this strangely named theory in his *Autobiography*: "Ask yourself whether you are happy, and you cease to be so. The only chance is to treat, not happiness, but some end external to it as the purpose of life. Let your self-consciousness, your scrutiny, your self-interrogation exhaust themselves on that."[1]

It is not surprising that Wordsworth's poetry should also have served to protect Mill from the morbidity of his intellect. Like many

---

ROMANTICISM AND ANTISELF-CONSCIOUSNESS: From *Centennial Review*, VI, No. 4 (Fall 1962), 553–65, revised by the author for this edition. Reprinted by permission of the Editor of *Centennial Review* and the author.

[1] *Autobiography* (1873), Ch. 5. Mill says that he had not heard, at the time, of Carlyle's theory. The first meeting between the writers took place in 1831; Mill's depression lasted, approximately, from Autumn 1826 to Autumn 1828. Mill called self-consciousness "that demon of the men of genius of our time from Wordsworth to Byron, from Goethe to Chateaubriand." See Wayne Shumaker, *English Autobiography* (Berkeley and Los Angeles, 1954), Ch. 4.

romantics, Wordsworth had passed through a depression clearly linked to the ravage of self-consciousness and the "strong disease" of self-analysis.[2] Book XI of the *Prelude*, Chapter 5 of Mill's *Autobiography*, Carlyle's *Sartor Resartus*, and other great confessional works of the romantic period, show how crucial these "maladies" are for the adolescent mind. Endemic, perhaps, to every stage of life, they especially affect the transition from adolescence to maturity; and it is interesting to observe how man's attention has shifted from the fact of death and its *rites de passage*, to these trials in what Keats called "the Chamber of Maiden-Thought," and more recently still, to the perils of childhood. We can say, taking a metaphor from Donne, that "streights, and none but streights" are ways to whatever changes the mind must undergo; and that it is the romantics who first explored the dangerous passageways of maturation.

Two trials or perils of the soul deserve special mention. We learn that every increase in consciousness is accompanied by an increase in self-consciousness, and that analysis can easily become a passion that "murders to dissect." These difficulties of thought in its strength question the ideal of absolute lucidity. The issue is raised of whether there exist what might be called *remedia intellectus*: remedies for the corrosive power of analysis and the fixated self-consciousness.

There is one remedy of great importance and which is almost coterminous with art itself in the romantic period. This remedy differs from certain traditional proposals linked to the religious control of the intellect—the wild, living intellect of man, as Newman calls it in his *Apologia*.[3] A particularly romantic remedy, it is nonlimiting with respect to the mind. It seeks to draw the antidote to self-consciousness from consciousness itself. A way is to be found not to escape from or limit

---

[2] Thought as a disease is an open as well as submerged metaphor among the romantics. There are many hints in Novalis; Schelling pronounces naked reflection (analysis) to be a spiritual sickness of man (*Schellings Sämtliche Werke*, ed. K. F. Schelling, [Stuttgart, 1856–61], II 13–14); the metaphor is explicit in Carlyle's *Characteristics* (1831), and commonplace by the time that E. S. Dallas in *The Gay Science* (1866) lays the "modern disease" to ". . . excessive civilization and overstrained consciousness." The *mal du siecle* is not unrelated to the malady we are describing. Goethe's *Die Leiden des Jungen Werthers* (1774) may be seen as its *terminus a quo*, and Kierkegaard's *Sickness unto Death* (1849) as its noonday point clarity.

[3] *Apologia Pro Vita Sua* (1864), Ch. 5. In the same chapter Newman calls reason "that universal solvent." Concerning Victorian remedies for "this disease/My Self" (Marianne Moore), see also A. Dwight Culler, *The Imperial Intellect* (New Haven, 1955), pp. 234–37.

knowledge but to convert it into an energy finer than intellectual. It
is some such thought which makes Wordsworth in the preface to *Lyrical
Ballads* describe poetry as the "breath and finer spirit of all knowledge,"
and as able to carry sensation into the midst of the most abstract or
remotest objects of science. A more absolute figure for this cure, which
is, strictly speaking, less a cure than a paradoxical faith, is given by
Kleist. "Paradise is locked," says Kleist, ". . . yet to return to the state
of innocence we must eat once more of the tree of knowledge." It is not
by accident that Kleist is quoted by Adrian at a significant point in
Mann's *Doktor Faustus*, which is *the* novel about self-consciousness and
its relation to art.

This idea of a return, via knowledge, to naïvete—to a second
naïvete—is a commonplace among the German romantics. Yet its
presence is perhaps more exciting, because suitably oblique, among the
English and French romantics. A. O. Lovejoy, of course, in his famous
essay on the "Discrimination of Romanticisms" (1924) questions the
posssibility of unifying the various national movements. He rightly
points out that the German romantics insist on an art that rises from the
plenitude of consciousness to absorb progressively the most sophisticated
as well as naïvest experience. But his claim that English romanticism
is marked by a more primitivistic "return to nature" is weakened by
his use of second-rate poetry and isolated passages. One can show that
the practice of the greater English romantics is involved with a problematical self-consciousness similar to that of the Germans; and that, in
the main, no primitivism or "sacrifice of intellect" is found. I do not
mean to deny the obvious, that there are "primitivistic" passages in
Chateaubriand and even Wordsworth; but the primary tendency
should be distinguished from errors and epiphenomena. The desire of
the romantics is perhaps for what Blake calls "organized innocence"
but never for a mere return to the state of nature. The German romantics, however, for a reason mentioned later, and because of the con-
temporaneous philosophical tradition, which centered on the relations
between consciousness and consciousness of self (Fichte, Schelling,
Hegel), gained in some respects a clearer though not more fruitful
understanding of the problem. I cannot consider in detail the case of
French romanticism; but Shelley's visionary despair, Keats' understanding of the poetical character, and Blake's doctrine of the contraries, reveal that self-consciousness cannot be overcome; and the very
desire to overcome it, which poetry and imagination encourage, is part
of a vital, dialectical movement of "soul-making."

The link between consciousness and self-consciousness, or knowledge and guilt, is already expressed in the story of the expulsion from Eden. Having tasted knowledge, man realizes his nakedness, his sheer separateness of self. I have quoted Kleist's reflection; and Hegel, in his interpretation of the Fall, argues that the way back to Eden is via contraries: the naïvely sensuous mind must pass through separation and selfhood to become spiritually perfect. It is the destiny of consciousness, or as the English romantics would have said, of Imagination, to separate from nature, so that it can finally transcend not only nature but also its own lesser forms. Hegel in his *Logic* puts it as follows:

> The first reflection of awakened consciousness in men told them they were naked. . . . The hour that man leaves the path of mere natural being marks the difference between him, a self-conscious agent, and the natural world. The spiritual is distinguished from the natural . . . in that it does not continue a mere stream of tendency, but sunders itself to self-realization. But this position of severed life has in its turn to be overcome, and the spirit must, by its own act, achieve concord once more. . . . The principle of restoration is found in thought, and thought only: the hand that inflicts the wound is also the hand that heals it.

The last sentence states unequivocally where the remedy lies. Hegel, however, does not honor the fact that the meaning he derives from the Fall was originally in the form of myth. And the attempt to think mythically is itself part of a crucial defense against the self-conscious intellect. Bergson in *The Two Sources of Morality and Religion* sees both myth and religion as products of an intellectual instinct created by nature itself to oppose the analytic intellect, to preserve human spontaneities despite the hesitant and complicated mind.[4] Whether myth-making is still possible, whether the mind can find an unself-conscious medium for itself, or maintain something of the interacting unity of self and life, is a central concern of the romantic poets.

Romantic art as myth-making has been discussed convincingly in recent years,* and Friedrich Schlegel's call in *Rede über die Mythologie*

---

[4] *Les Deux Sources de la Morale et de la Religion* (1933), Ch. 2. Both religion and "*la function fabulatrice*" are "*une reaction défensive de la nature contre le pouvoir dissolvant de l'intelligence.*" (Cf. Newman calling the intellect "that universal solvent.") As romanticism shades into modernism, a third peril of overconsciousness comes strongly to the fore—that it leads to a (Hamlet-like) incapacity for action. Bergson, like Kierkegaard, tries to counter this aspect especially.

* See, e.g., Northrop Frye's essay below and his more recent "The Romantic Myth" in *A Study of English Romanticism* (New York, 1968). See also Harold Bloom's *Shelley's Mythmaking* (New Haven, 1959) and *The Visionary Company: A Reading of English Romantic Poetry* (Garden City, N.Y., 1961).

(1800) for a modern mythology is well-known. The question of the renewal of myth is, nevertheless, a rather special response to the larger perplexities of reflective thought. "The poet," says Wallace Stevens in "Adagia," "represents the mind in the act of defending us against itself." Starting with the romantics, this act is clearly focused, and poetry begins to be valued in contradistinction to directly analytic or purely conceptual modes of thought. The intelligence is seen as a perverse though necessary specialization of the whole soul of man, and art as a means to resist the intelligence intelligently.

It must be admitted, at the same time, that the romantics themselves do not give (in their conceptual moments) an adequate definition of the function of art. Their criterion of pleasure or expressive emotion leads to some kind of art for art's sake formula, or to the sentimentalism which Mill still shared, and which marks the shift in sensibility from neoclassic to romantic. That Mill wept over the memoirs of Marmontel, and felt his selfhood lightened by this evidence of his ability to feel, or that Lamartine saw the life of the poet as "tears and love," suggests that the *larmoyant* vein of the later eighteenth century persisted for some time; but also helped, when tears were translated into theory, or even when joy was so translated, to falsify the romantic achievement and make Irving Babbitt's criticism possible.

The *art* of the romantics, on the other hand, is often in advance of even their best thoughts. Neither a mere increase in sensibility nor a mere widening of self-knowledge constitutes its purpose. The romantic poets do not exalt consciousness per se. They have recognized it as a kind of death-in-life, as the product of a division in the self. The mind which acknowledges the existence or past existence of immediate life knows that its present strength is based on a separation from that life. A creative mind desires not mere increase of knowledge, but "knowledge not purchased by the loss of power" (*Prelude*, V). Life, says Ruskin, is the only wealth; yet childhood, or certain irrevocable moments, confront the poet sharply, and give him the sense of having purchased with death the life of the mind. Constructing what Yeats calls an anti-self, or recovering deeply buried experience, the poet seeks a return to "Unity of Being." Consciousness is only a middle-term, the strait through which everything must pass; and the artist plots to have everything pass through whole, without sacrifice to abstraction.

One of the themes which best expresses this perilous nature of consciousness, and which has haunted literature since the romantic period, is that of the Solitary, or Wandering Jew. He may appear as Cain, Ahasuerus, Ancient Mariner, and even Faust. He also resembles the later (and more static) figures of Tithonus, Gerontion, and *poète maudit*. These solitaries are separated from life in the midst of life, yet cannot die. They are doomed to live a middle or purgatorial existence which is neither life nor death, and as their knowledge increases so does their solitude.[5] It is, ultimately, consciousness that alienates them from life and imposes the burden of a self which religion or death or a return to the state of nature might dissolve. Yet their heroism, or else their doom, is not to obtain this release. Rebels against God, like Cain, and men of God, like Vigny's Moses, are equally denied *le sommeil de la terre*, and are show to suffer the same despair, namely, "the self . . . whose worm dieth not, and whose fire is not quenched" (Kierkegaard). And in Coleridge's Mariner, as in Conrad's Marlow, the figure of the Wanderer approaches that of the Poet. Both are storytellers who resubmit themselves to temporality and are compelled to repeat their experiences in the purgatorial form of words. Yeats, deeply affected by the theme of the Wandering Jew, records a marvelous comment of Mme. Blavatsky's. "I write, write, write," said Mme. Blavatsky, "as the Wandering Jew walks, walks, walks."

The Solitary may also be said to create his own, peculiarly romantic genre of poetry. In "Tintern Abbey," or "X Revisited," the poet looks back at a transcended stage and comes to grips with the fact of self-alienation. The retrospective movement may be visionary, as often in Hölderlin, or antiquarian, as in Scott, or deeply oblique, as in lyrical ballad and monologue. In every case, however, there is some confrontation of person with shadow or self with self. The intense lyricism of the romantics may well be related to this confrontation.

---

[5] "I lost the love of heaven above, / I spurned the lust of earth below . . . ," John Clare, "A Vision." By this double exile, and their final madness, two poets as different as Clare and Hölderlin are joined. See Coleridge's intense realization of man's "between-ness," which increases rather than chastens the apocalyptic passion: "O Nature! I would rather not have been—let that which is to come so soon, come now— for what is all the intermediate space, but sense of utter worthlessness? . . . Man is truly and solely an immortal series of conscious mortalities and inherent Disappointments" (*Inquiring Spirit*, ed. K. Coburn [London, 1951], p. 142). But to ask death instead of life of Nature is still to ask for finality, for some mental quietus: it is the bitter obverse, also met at the beginning of Goethe's *Faust*, of the quest for absolute truth.

For the romantic "I" emerges nostalgically when certainty and simplicity of self are lost. In a lyric poem it is clearly not the first-person form that moves us (the poem need not be in the first person) but rather the "I" toward which that "I" reaches. The very confusion in modern literary theory concerning the fictive "I," whether it represents the writer as person or only as persona, may reflect a dialectic inherent in poetry between the relatively self-conscious self, and that self within the self which resembles Blake's "emanation" and Shelley's "epipsyche."

It is true, of course, that this dialectic is found in every age and not restricted to the romantic. The notion of man (as of history) seems to presuppose that of self-consciousness, and art is not the only major reaction to it. Mircea Eliade, following Nietzsche, has recently linked art to religion by interpreting the latter as originating in a periodic and ritually controlled abolition of the burden of self, or rather of this burden in the form of a nascent historical sense. It is not true, according to Eliade, that "primitive man" has no sense of history; on the contrary, his sense of it is too acute; he cannot tolerate the weight of responsibility accruing through memory and individuation; and only gradually does religious myth, and especially the Judaeo-Christian revelation, teach him to become a more conscious historical being. The question, therefore, is why the romantic reaction to the problem of self-consciousness should be in the form of an aggrandizement of art, and why the entire issue should now achieve an urgency and explicitness previously lacking.

The answer requires a distinction between religion and art. This distinction can take a purely historical form. There clearly comes a time when art frees itself from its subordination to religion or religiously inspired myth, and continues or even replaces them. This time seems to coincide with what is generally called the romantic period: the latter, at least, is a good *terminus a quo*. Though every age may find its own means to convert self-consciousness into the larger energy of "imagination," in the romantic period it is primarily art on which this crucial function devolves. Thus, for Blake, all religion is a derivation of the Poetic Genius; and Matthew Arnold is already matter-of-fact rather than prophetic about a new age in which the religious passion is preserved chiefly by poetry. If romantic poetry appears to the orthodox as misplaced religious feeling (spilt religion),* to the romantics themselves it *redeems* religion.[6]

II

Yet as soon as poetry is separated from imposed religious or communal ends it becomes as problematic as the individual himself. The question, how is art possible, though postromantic in its explicitness, has its origin here, for the artist is caught up in a serious paradox. His art is linked to the autonomous and individual; yet that same art, in the absence of an authoritative myth, must bear the entire weight of having to transcend or ritually limit these tendencies. No wonder that the problem of the subjective, the isolated, the individual, grows particularly acute. Subjectivity—even solipsism—becomes the subject of poems which qua poetry seek to transmute it.

This paradox seems to inhere in all the seminal works of the romantic period. "Thus my days are passed / In contradiction," Wordsworth writes sadly at the beginning of *The Prelude*. He cannot decide whether he is fit to be a poet on an epic scale. The great longing is there; the great (objective) theme eludes him. Wordsworth cannot find his theme because he already has it: himself. Yet he knows self-consciousness to be at once necessary *and* opposed to poetry. It will take him the whole of *The Prelude* to be satisfied *in actu* that he is a poet. His poem, beginning in the vortex of self-consciousness, is carried to epic length in the desire to prove that his former imaginative powers are not dead.

I have already confessed to understanding the *Ancient Mariner* as a poem that depicts the soul after its birth to the sense of separate (and

---

* The phrase is T. E. Hulme's; see above, p. 58.

[6] I have omitted here the important role played by the French Revolution. The aggrandizement of art is due in no small measure to the fact that poets like Wordsworth and Blake cannot give up one hope raised by the Revolution—that a *terrestrial* paradise is possible—yet are eventually forced to give up a second hope—that it can be attained by direct political action. The shift from faith in the reformation of man through the prior reformation of society, to that in the prior reformation of man through vision and art, has often been noted. The "failure" of the French Revolution anchors the romantic movement, or is the consolidating rather than primary cause. It closes, perhaps until the advent of communism, the possibility that politics rather than art should be invested with a passion previously subsumed by religion.

segregated) being. In one of the really magical and hypnotic poems in the language, which, generically, converts self-consciousness into imagination, Coleridge describes the travail of a soul passing from self-consciousness to imagination. The slaying of an innocent creature, the horror of stasis, the weight of conscience or of the vertical eye (the sun), the appearance of the theme of deathlessness, and the terrible repetitive process of penitence, whereby the Wanderer becomes aware through the spirits above and the creatures below of his focal solitude between both—these point with archetypal force to the burden of selfhood, the straits of solitude, and the compensating plenary imagination that grows inwardly. The poem opens by evoking that *rite de passage* we call a wedding, and which leads to full human communion; but the Mariner's story interposes itself as a reminder of human separateness, and of the intellectual love (in Spinoza's sense) made possible by it.

To explore the transition from self-consciousness to imagination, and to achieve that transition while exploring it (and so to prove it still possible) is the romantic purpose I find most crucial. The precariousness of that transition naturally evokes the idea of a journey; and in some later poets, like Rimbaud and Hart Crane, the motif of the journey has actually become a sustained metaphor for the experience of the artist during creation. This journey, of course, does not lead to what is generally called a *truth*: some final station for the mind. It remains as problematic a crossing as that from death to second life or from exile to redemption. These religious concepts, moreover, are often blended in, and remind us that romantic art has a function analogous to that of religion. The traditional scheme of Eden, Fall, and Redemption merges with the new triad of Nature, Self-Consciousness, Imagination; while the last term in both involves a kind of return to the first.

Yet everything depends on whether it is the right and fruitful return. For the journey beyond self-consciousness is shadowed by cyclicity, by paralysis before the endlessness of introspection, and by the lure of false ultimates. Blake's "Mental Traveller," Browning's "Childe Roland to the Dark Tower Came," and Emily Dickinson's "Our journey had advanced" show these dangers in some of their forms. Nature in its childhood or sensuous radiance (Blake's "Beulah") exerts an expecially deceptive lure. The desire to gain truth, finality, or revelation generates a thousand such enchantments. Mind has its blissful islands as well as its mountains, its deeps, and treacherous crossroads. Depicting these trials by horror and by enchantment romanticism is genuinely a rebirth of romance.

III

In the years following World War I, it became customary to see classicism and romanticism as two radically different philosophies of life, and to place modernism on the side of the antiromantic. André Malraux defined the classical element in modern art as a "lucid horror of seduction." Today it is clear that romantic art shared that lucidity. Romanticism, at its profoundest, reveals the depth of the enchantment in which we live. We dream, we wake on the cold hillside, and our "sole self" pursues the dream once more. In the beginning was the dream; and the task of disenchantment never ends.

The nature poetry of the romantics is a case in point. Far from being an indulgence in dewy moments, it is the exploration of enchanted ground. The romantic poets, like the Impressionist painters, refuse to "simplify the ghost" of Nature. They begin to look steadfastly at all sensuous experience, penetrating its veils and facing its seductions. Shelley's *Mont Blanc* is not an enthusiastic nature poem but a spirit-drama in which the poet's mind seeks to release itself from an over-whelming impression and to reaffirm its autonomy vis-a-vis Nature. Keats also goes far in respecting illusions without being deluded. His starting-point is the dream of Nature fostered by romance; he agrees to this as consciously as we lie down to sleep. But he intends such dreaming "beyond self" to unfold its own progressions, and to wake into truth. To this end he passes from a gentler to a severer dream-mode: from the romance of *Endymion* to the more austere *Hyperions*. Yet he is forced to give up the *Hyperions* because Saturn, Apollo and others behave like quest-heroes instead of gods. Having stepped beyond romance into a sublimer mode, Keats finds the quest for self-identity elated rather than effaced. It has merely raised itself to a "divine" level. He cannot reconcile Miltonic sublimity with the utterly human pathos that keeps breaking through. The "egotistical sublime" remains.

It was Wordsworth, of course, whose poetry Keats had tried to escape by adhering to a less self-centered kind of sublimity: "Let us have the old Poets, and Robin Hood." Wordsworth had subdued poetry to the theme of nature's role in the growth of the individual mind. The dream of Nature, in Wordsworth, does not lead to formal romance but is an early, developmental step in converting the solipsistic into the sympathetic imagination. It entices the brooding soul out of itself, toward nature first, then toward humanity. Wordsworth knew the weight of self-consciousness:

> It seemed the very garments that I wore
> Preyed on my strength, and stopped the quiet stream
> Of self-forgetfulness. (1850 *Prelude*, V., 294ff.)

The wound of self is healed, however, by "unconscious intercourse" with a Nature "old as creation." Nature makes the "quiet stream" flow on. Wordsworth evokes a type of consciousness more integrated than ordinary consciousness, though deeply dependent on its early— and continuing—life in rural surroundings.[7]

The romantic emphasis on "unconsciousness" and "organic form" is significant in this light. Unconsciousness remains an ambiguous term in the romantic and Victorian periods, referring to a state distinctly other than consciousness or simply to un*self*-consciousness. The characteristic of right performance, says Carlyle in "Characteristics" (1831), is an *unconsciousness*— "the healthy know not of their health, but only the sick." The term clearly approaches here its alternate meaning of unself-consciousness, and it is to such statements that Mill must be indebted when he mentions the "antiself-consciousness theory" of Carlyle. In America, Thoreau perpetuates the ambiguity. He also prescribes "unconsciousness" for his sophisticated age, and uses the word as an equivalent of vision: "the absence of the speaker from his speech." It does seem to me that the personal and expressive theory of poetry, ascribed to the romantics,* and the impersonal theory of poetry, claimed in reaction by the moderns, answer to the same problem and are quietly linked by the ambiguity in "unconsciousness." Both theories value art as thought recreated into feeling or self-consciousness into a more communal power of vision. Yet can the modern poet, whom Schiller called "sentimental" and whom we would describe as "alienated," achieve the immediacy of all great verse whatever its personal or historical source?

---

[7] Mill, Hazlitt, and Arnold came to approximately the same estimate of Wordsworth's poetry. Comparing it to Byron's they found that the latter had too much fever of self in it to be remedial; they did not want their image cast back at them magnified. Carlyle prefers to compare Goethe and Byron ("Close your Byron, open your Goethe"), yet his point is the same: Goethe retains a strong simplicity in a tormented and divided age, while Byron seems to him a "spasmodically bellowing self-worshipper."

* See, e.g., M. H. Abrams, *The Mirror and the Lamp* (New York, 1953).

This is as crucial a matter today as when Wordsworth and Coleridge wrote *Lyrical Ballads* and Hölderlin pondered the fate of poetry in "Der Rhein." Is visionary poetry a thing of the past, or can it coexist with the modern temper? Is it an archaic revelation or a universal mode springing from every real contact with Nature? "To interest or benefit us," says a Victorian writer, "poetry must be reflective, sentimental, subjective; it must accord with the conscious, analytical spirit of present men." The difficulties surrounding a modern poetry of vision vary with each national literature. In England the loss of "poesy" is laid by most romantics to a historical though not irreversible fact— to the preceding century's infidelity to the line of Chaucer, Spenser, Shakespeare and Milton. "Let us have the old Poets, and Robin Hood," as Keats said. Yet for the German and the French there was no easy return to a tradition deriving its strength from both learned and popular sources. "How much further along we would be," Herder remarks, "if we had used popular beliefs and myths like the British, if our poetry had built upon them as wholeheartedly as Chaucer, Spenser and Shakespeare did." In the absence of this English kind of literary mediation, the gap between medieval romance and the modern spirit seemed too great. Goethe's *Faust* tried to bridge it, but, like *Wilhelm Meister*, anticipated a new type of literature which subsumed the philosophical character of the age and merged myth and irony into a "progressive" mode. The future belonged to the analytic spirit, to irony, to prose. The death of poetry had certainly occurred to the romantics in idea, and Hegel's prediction of it was simply the overt expression of their own despair. Yet against this despair the greater romantic poets staked their art, and often their sanity.

BIBLIOGRAPHICAL NOTE: Hartman's interpretation of the romantic self should be compared with Morse Peckham's above and with Robert Langbaum's in *The Poetry of Experience* (New York, 1957). See also George Boas, "The Romantic Self: An Historical Sketch," *Studies in Romanticism*, IV (1964), 1–16; and the section entitled "Romantic" in Peckham's *Man's Rage for Chaos* (Philadelphia and New York, 1965). On the romantic self and sincerity see Henri Peyre's chapter, "Romanticism and Sincerity," in his *Literature and Sincerity* (New Haven and London, 1963); and, more specialized, David Perkins, *Wordsworth and the Poetry of Sincerity* (Cambridge, Mass., 1964). On the self as both "center and circumference" see Georges Poulet, "Romanticism," in *The Metaphorphoses of the Circle*, tr. C. Dawson and E. Coleman (Baltimore, 1967; orig. French ed. Paris, 1961).

The Drunken Boat:
The Revolutionary
Element in Romanticism

Northrop Frye

Any such conception as "romanticism" is at one or more removes from actual literary experience, in an inner world where ten thousand different things flash upon the inward eye with all the bliss of oversimplification. Some things about it, however, are generally accepted, and we may start with them. First, romanticism has a historical center of gravity, which falls somewhere around the 1790–1830 period. This gets us at once out of the fallacy of timeless characterization,* where we say that romanticism has certain qualities, not found in the age of Pope, of sympathy with nature or what not, only to have someone produce a poem of Propertius or Kalidasa, or, eventually, Pope himself, and demand to know if the same qualities are not there. Second, romanticism is not a general historical term like "medieval": it appears

THE DRUNKEN BOAT: THE REVOLUTIONARY ELEMENT IN ROMANTICISM: From *Romanticism Reconsidered: Selected Papers from the English Institute*, ed. N. Frye (New York and London: Columbia University Press, 1963), pp. 1–25. Reprinted by permission of Columbia University Press.

* See, e.g., the essays by Grierson, Lucas, and Comfort in this collection. Frye's acceptance of "a historical center of gravity" for romanticism should be compared to similar acceptances by such literary historians as Wellek (see his essay) and Ian Jack, *English Literature: 1815–1832* (Oxford, 1963).

to have another center of gravity in the creative arts. We speak most naturally of romantic literature, painting, and music. . . .

•   •   •

Third, even in its application to the creative arts romanticism is a selective term, more selective even than "baroque" appears to be becoming. We think of it as including Keats, but not, on the whole, Crabbe; Scott, but not, in general, Jane Austen; Wordsworth, but not, on any account, James Mill. As generally used, "romantic" is contrasted with two other terms, "classical" and "realistic."* Neither contrast seems satisfactory. We could hardly call Wordsworth's Preface to the *Lyrical Ballads* antirealistic, or ignore the fact that Shelley was a better classical scholar than, say, Dryden, who, according to Samuel Johnson, translated the first book of the *Iliad* without knowing what was in the second. Still, the pairings exist, and we shall have to examine them. And yet, fourth, though selective, romanticism is not a voluntary category. It does not see Byron as the successor to Pope or Wordsworth as the successor to Milton, which would have been acceptable enough to both poets: it associates Byron and Wordsworth, to their mutual disgust, with each other.

Accepting all this, we must also avoid the two traps in the phrase "history of ideas." First, an idea, as such, is independent of time and can be argued about; an historical event is not and cannot be. If romanticism is in part an historical event, as it clearly is, then to say with T. E. Hulme: "I object to even the best of the romantics" is much like saying: "I object to even the best battles of the Napoleonic War." Most general value-judgments on romanticism as a whole are rationalizations of an agreement or disagreement with some belief of which romantic poetry is supposed to form the objective correlative.

This latter is the second or Hegelian trap in the history of ideas, which we fall into when we assume that around 1790 or earlier some kind of thesis arose in history and embodied itself in the romantic movement. Such an assumption leads us to examining all the cultural products we call romantic as allegories of that thesis. These have a way of disagreeing with each other, and if we try to think of romanticism as some kind of single "idea," all we can do with it is what Lovejoy did: break it down into a number of contradictory ideas with nothing

---

* On these contrasts see the bibliographical note to H. J. C. Grierson's essay above and the footnotes to pp. 126–27 of the F. L. Lucas essay above.

significant in common. In literature, and more particularly poetry, ideas are subordinated to imagery, to a language more "simple, sensuous, and passionate" than the language of philosophy. Hence it may be possible for two poets to be related by common qualities of imagery even when they do not agree on a single thesis in religion, politics, or the theory of art itself.

The history of imagery, unlike the history of ideas, appears to be for the most part a domain where, in the words of a fictional Canadian poetess, "the hand of man hath never trod." Yet we seem inexorably led to it by our own argument, and perhaps the defects in what follows may be in part excused by the novelty of the subject, to me at least. After making every allowance for a prodigious variety of technique and approach, it is still possible to see a consistent framework (I wish the English language had a better equivalent for the French word *cadre*) in the imagery of both medieval and Renaissance poetry. The most remarkable and obvious feature of this framework is the division of being into four levels. The highest level is heaven, the place of the presence of God. Next come the two levels of the order of nature, the human level and the physical level. The order of human nature, or man's proper home, is represented by the story of the Garden of Eden in the Bible and the myth of the Golden Age in Boethius and elsewhere. Man is no longer in it, but the end of all his religious, moral, and social cultivation is to raise him into something resembling it. Physical nature, the world of animals and plants, is the world man is now in, but unlike the animals and plants he is not adjusted to it. He is confronted from birth with a moral dialectic, and must either rise above it to his proper human home or sink below it into the fourth level of sin, death, and hell. This last level is not part of the order of nature, but its existence is what at present corrupts nature. A very similar framework can be found in classical poetry, and the alliance of the two, in what is so often called Christian humanism, accounts for the sense of an antagonism between the romantic movement and the classical tradition, in spite of its many and remarkable affinities with that tradition.

Such a framework of images, however closely related in practice to belief, is not in itself a belief or an expression of belief: it is in itself simply a way of arranging images and providing for metaphors. At the same time the word "framework" itself is a spatial metaphor, and any framework is likely to be projected in space, even confused or identified with its spatial projection. In Dante Eden is a long way up, on top of the mountain of purgatory; heaven is much further up, and hell is down, at the center of the earth. We may know that such conceptions as heaven and hell do not depend on spatial metaphors of up and down, but a cosmological poet, dealing with them as images, has to put them somewhere. To Dante it was simple enough to put them at the top and bottom of the natural order, because he knew of no alternative to the Ptolemaic picture of the world. To Milton, who did know of an alternative, the problem was more complex, and Milton's heaven and hell are outside the cosmos, in a kind of absolute up and down. After Milton comes Newton, and after Newton ups and downs become hopelessly confused.

What I see first of all in romanticism is the effect of a profound change, not primarily in belief, but in the spatial projection of reality. This in turn leads to a different localizing of the various levels of that reality. Such a change in the localizing of images is bound to be accompanied by, or even cause, changes in belief and attitude, and changes of this latter sort are exhibited by the romantic poets. But the change itself is not in belief or attitude, and may be found in, or at least affecting, poets of a great variety of beliefs.

In the earlier framework, the disorder of sin, death, and corruption was restricted to the sublunary world of four elements. Above the moon was all that was left of nature as God had originally planned it before the fall. The planets, with their angel-guided spheres, are images of a divinely sanctioned order of nature which is also the true home of man. Hence there was no poetic incongruity in Dante's locating his Paradiso in the planetary spheres, nor in Milton's associating the music of the spheres with the song of the angels in the "Nativity Ode," nor in using the same word "heaven" for both the kingdom of God and the sky. A post-Newtonian poet has to think of gravitation and the solar system. Newton, Miss Nicolson has reminded us, demanded the muse, but the appropriate muse was Urania, and Urania had already been requested by Milton to descend to a safer position on earth for the second half of *Paradise Lost*.

· · ·

Blake's view . . . is that the universe of modern astronomy, as revealed in Newton, exhibits only a blind, mechanical, subhuman order, not the personal presence of a deity. Newton himself tended to think of God still as "up there," even to the extent of suggesting that space was the divine sensorium: but *what* was up there, according to Blake, is only a set of interlocking geometrical diagrams, and God, Blake says, is not a mathematical diagram. Newtonism leads to what for Blake are intellectual errors, such as a sense of the superiority of abstractions to actual things and the notion that the real world is a measurable but invisible world of primary qualities. But Blake's main point is that admiring the mechanisms of the sky leads to establishing human life in mechanical patterns too. In other words, Blake's myth of Urizen is a fuller and more sophisticated version of the myth of Frankenstein.

Blake's evil, sinister, or merely complacent sky-gods, Urizen, Nobodaddy, Enitharmon, Satan, remind us of similar beings in other romantics: Shelley's Jupiter, Byron's Arimanes, the Lord in the Prologue to *Faust*. They in their turn beget later romantic gods and goddesses, such as Baudelaire's female *froide majesté*, Hardy's Immanent Will, or the God of Housman's "The chestnut casts his flambeaux," who is a brute and blackguard because he is a sky-god in control of the weather, and sends his rain on the just and on the unjust. The association of sinister or unconscious mechanism with what we now call outer space is a commonplace of popular literature today which is a romantic inheritance. Perhaps Orwell's *1984*, a vision of a mechanical tyranny informed by the shadow of a Big Brother who can never die, is the terminal point of a development of imagery that began with Blake's Ancient of Days. Not every poet, naturally, associates mechanism with the movements of the stars as Blake does, or sees it as a human imitation of the wrong kind of divine creativity. But the contrast between the mechanical and the organic is deeply rooted in romantic thinking, and the tendency is to associate the mechanical with ordinary consciousness, as we see in the account of the associative fancy in Coleridge's *Biographia* or of discursive thought in Shelley's *Defence of Poetry*. This is in striking contrast to the Cartesian tradition, where the mechanical is of course associated with the subconscious. The mechanical being characteristic of ordinary experience, it is found particularly in the world "outside"; the superior or organic world is consequently "inside," and although it is still called superior or higher, the natural metaphorical direction of the inside world is downward, into the profounder depths of consciousness.

If a romantic poet, therefore, wishes to write of God, he has more difficulty in finding a place to put him than Dante or even Milton had, and on the whole he prefers to do without a place, or finds "within" metaphors more reassuring than "up there" metaphors. When Wordsworth speaks, in *The Prelude* and elsewhere, of feeling the presence of deity through a sense of interpenetration of the human mind and natural powers, one feels that his huge and mighty forms, like the spirits of Yeats, have come to bring him the right metaphors for his poetry. In the second book of *The Excursion* we have a remarkable vision of what has been called the heavenly city of the eighteenth-century philosophers, cast in the form of an ascent up a mountain, where the city is seen at the top. The symbolism, I think, is modeled on the vision of Cleopolis in the first book of *The Faerie Queene*, and its technique is admirably controlled and precise. Yet surely this is not the real Wordsworth. The spirits have brought him the wrong metaphors; metaphors that Spenser used with full imaginative conviction, but which affect only the surface of Wordsworth's mind.

The second level of the older construct was the world of original human nature, now a lost paradise or golden age. It is conceived as a better and more appropriate home for man than his present environment, whether man can regain it or not. But in the older construct this world was ordinarily not thought of as human in origin or conception. Adam awoke in a garden not of his planting, in a fresh-air suburb of the City of God, and when the descendants of Cain began to build cities on earth, they were building to models already existing in both heaven and hell. In the Middle Ages and the Renaissance the agencies which helped to raise man from the physical to the human world were such things as the sacraments of religion, the moral law, and the habit of virtue, none of them strictly human inventions. These were the safe and unquestioned agencies, the genuinely educational media. Whether the human arts of poetry and painting and music were genuinely educational in this sense could be and was disputed or denied; and the poets themselves, when they wrote apologies for poetry, seldom claimed equality with religion or law, beyond pointing out that the earliest major poets were prophets and lawgivers.

For the modern mind there are two poles of mental activity. One may be described as sense, by which I mean the recognition of what is presented by experience: the empirical, observant habit of mind in which, among other things, the inductive sciences begin. In this attitude reality is, first of all, "out there," whatever happens to it afterwards. The other pole is the purely formalizing or constructive aspect of the mind, where reality is something brought into being by the act of

construction. It is obvious that in preromantic poetry there is a strong
affinity with the attitude that we have called sense. The poet, in all
ages and cultures, prefers images to abstractions, the sensational to the
conceptual. But the preromantic structure of imagery belonged to a
nature which was the work of God; the design in nature was, as Sir
Thomas Browne calls it, the art of God; nature is thus an objective
structure or system for the poet to follow. The appropriate metaphors
of imitation are visual and physical ones, and the creative powers of the
poet have models outside him.*

It is generally recognized that Rousseau represents, and to some
extent made, a revolutionary change in the modern attitude. The
primary reason for his impact was, I think, not in his political or
educational views as such, but in his assumption that civilization was
a purely human artifact, something that man had made, could unmake,
could subject to his own criticism, and was at all times entirely responsible for. Above all, it was something for which the only known model
was in the human mind. This kind of assumption is so penetrating that
it affects those who detest Rousseau, or have never heard of him,
equally with the small minority of his admirers. Also, it gets into the
mind at once, whereas the fading out of such counter assumptions as the
literal and historical nature of the Garden of Eden story is very gradual.
The effect of such an assumption is twofold. First, it puts the arts in the
center of civilization. The basis of civilization is now the creative power
of man; its model is the human vision revealed in the arts. Second, this
model, as well as the sources of creative power, is now located in the
mind's internal heaven, the external world being seen as a mirror
reflecting and making visible what is within. Thus the "outside" world,
most of which is "up there," yields importance and priority to the inner
world, in fact derives its poetic significance at least from it. "In looking
at objects of Nature," says Coleridge in the Notebooks, "I seem rather
to be seeking, as it were *asking* for, a symbolical language for something
within me that already and forever exists, than observing anything
new." This principle extends both to the immediate surrounding world
which is the emblem of the music of humanity in Wordsworth and to
the starry heavens on which Keats read "Huge cloudy symbols of a
high romance."

Hence in romantic poetry the emphasis is not on what we have called

* Cf. W. K. Wimsatt's essay on "The Structure of Romantic Nature Imagery"
above.

sense, but on the constructive power of the mind, where reality is brought into being by experience. There is a contrast in popular speech between the romantic and the realist, where the word "romantic" implies a sentimentalized or rose-colored view of reality. This vulgar sense of the word may throw some light on the intensity with which the romantic poets sought to defy external reality by creating a uniformity of tone and mood. The establishing of this uniformity, and the careful excluding of anything that would dispel it, is one of the constant and typical features of the best romantic poetry, though we may call it a dissociation of sensibility if we happen not to like it. Such a poetic technique is, psychologically, akin to magic, which also aims at bringing spiritual forces into reality through concentration on a certain type of experience. Such words as "charm" or "spell" suggest uniformity of mood as well as a magician's repertoire. Historically and generically, it is akin to romance, with its effort to maintain a self-consistent idealized world without the intrusions of realism or irony.

For these reasons romanticism is difficult to adapt to the novel, which demands an empirical and observant attitude; its contribution to prose fiction is rather, appropriately enough, a form of romance. In the romance the characters tend to become psychological projections, and the setting a period in a past just remote enough to be recreated rather than empirically studied. We think of Scott as within the romantic movement; Jane Austen as related to it chiefly by her parodies of the kind of sensibility that tries to live in a self-created world instead of adapting to the one that is there. Marianne in *Sense and Sensibility*, Catherine in *Northanger Abbey*, and of course everybody in *Love and Friendship*, are examples. Crabbe's naturalistic manifesto in the opening of *The Village* expresses an attitude which in itself is not far from Wordsworth's. But Crabbe is a metrical novelist in a way that Wordsworth is not. The soldier in *The Prelude* and the leech-gatherer in "Resolution and Independence" are purely romantic characters in the sense just given of psychological projections; that is, they become temporary or epiphanic myths. We should also notice that the internalizing of reality in romanticism proper develops a contrast between it and a contemporary realism which descends from the preromantic tradition but acquires a more purely empirical attitude to the external world.

The third level of the older construct was the physical world, theologically fallen, which man is born into but which is not the real world of human nature. Man's primary attitude to external physical nature is thus one of detachment. The kind of temptation represented by Spenser's Bower of Bliss or Milton's Comus is based on the false suggestion that physical nature, with its relatively innocent moral freedom, can be the model for human nature. The resemblances between the poetic techniques used in the Bower of Bliss episode and some of the techniques of the romantics are superficial: Spenser, unlike the romantics, is consciously producing a rhetorical set piece, designed to show that the Bower of Bliss is not natural but artificial in the modern sense. Man for preromantic poets is not a child of Nature in the sense that he was originally a primitive. Milton's Adam becomes a noble savage immediately after his fall; but that is not his original nature. In romanticism the cult of the primitive is a by-product of the internalizing of the creative impulse. The poet has always been supposed to be imitating nature, but if the model of his creative power is in his mind, the nature that he is to imitate is now inside him, even if it is also outside.

The original form of human society also is hidden "within." Keats refers to this hidden society when he says in a letter to Reynolds: "Man should not dispute or assert but whisper results to his neighbour . . . and Humanity . . . would become a grand democracy of Forest Trees!" Coleridge refers to it in the *Biographia* when he says: "The medium, by which spirits understand each other, is not the surrounding air; but the *freedom* which they possess in common." Whether the romantic poet is revolutionary or conservative depends on whether he regards this original society as concealed by or as manifested in existing society. If the former, he will think of true society as a primitive structure of nature and reason, and will admire the popular, simple, or even the barbaric more than the sophisticated. If the latter, he will find his true inner society manifested by a sacramental church or by the instinctive manners of an aristocracy. The search for a visible ideal society in history leads to a good deal of admiration for the Middle Ages, which on the Continent was sometimes regarded as the essential feature of romanticism. The affinity between the more extreme romantic conservatism and the subversive revolutionary movements of fascism and nazism in our day has been often pointed out.* The present significance for us of this fact is that the notion of the inwardness of creative power is inherently revolutionary, just as the preromantic construct was inherently conservative, even for poets as revolutionary as Milton.

---

* See, e.g., the works cited in the footnote to F. L. Lucas's essay p. 135 above.

The self-identifying admiration which so many romantics expressed for Napoleon has much to do with the association of natural force, creative power, and revolutionary outbreak. As Carlyle says, in an uncharacteristically cautious assessment of Napoleon: "What Napoleon *did* will in the long-run amount to what he did *justly*; what Nature with her laws will sanction."

Further, the romantic poet is a part of a total process, engaged with and united to a creative power greater than his own because it includes his own. This greater creative power has a relation to him which we may call, adapting a term of Blake's, his vehicular form. The sense of identity with a larger power of creative energy meets us everywhere in romantic culture, I think even in the crowded excited canvases of Delacroix and the tremendous will-to-power finales of Beethoven. The symbolism of it in literature has been too thoroughly studied in Professor Abrams's *The Mirror and the Lamp* and in Professor Wasserman's *The Subtler Language** for me to add more than a foonote or two at this point. Sometimes the greater power of this vehicular form is a rushing wind, as in Shelley's Ode and in the figure of the "correspondent breeze" studied by Professor Abrams.** The image of the Aeolian harp, or lyre—romantic poets are apt to be sketchy in their orchestration—belongs here. Sometimes it is a boat driven by a beeze or current, or by more efficient magical forces in the *Ancient Mariner*. This image occurs so often in Shelley that it has helped to suggest my title; the introduction to Wordsworth's *Peter Bell* has a flying boat closely associated with the moon. Those poems of Wordsworth in which we feel driven along by a propelling metrical energy, *Peter Bell*, "The Idiot Boy," *The Waggoner*, and others, seem to me to be among Wordsworth's most central poems. Sometimes the vehicular form is a heightened state of consciousness in which we feel that we are greater than we know, or an intense feeling of communion, as in the sacramental corn-and-wine images of the great Keats odes.

The sense of unity with a greater power is surely one of the reasons why so much of the best romantic poetry is mythopoeic. The myth is typically the story of the god, whose form and character are human but who is also a sun-god or tree-god or ocean-god. It identifies the human

* See particularly Wasserman's chapter entitled "Metaphors for Poetry."
** "The Correspondent Breeze: A Romantic Metaphor," *Kenyon Review*, XIX (1957), 113–30; revised version in *English Romantic Poets: Modern Essays in Criticism* (New York, 1960), pp. 37–54.

with the nonhuman world, an identification which is also one of the major functions of poetry itself. Coleridge makes it a part of the primary as well as the secondary imagination. "This I call *I*," he says in the Notebooks, "identifying the percipient and the perceived." The "Giant Forms" of Blake's prophecies are states of being and feeling in which we have our own being and feeling; the huge and mighty forms of Wordsworth's *Prelude* have similar affinities; even the dreams of De Quincey seem vehicular in the same sense. It is curious that there seems to be so little mythopoeic theory in romantic poets, considering that the more expendable critics of the time complained as much about the obscurity of myth as their counterparts of today do now.

• • •

We have found, then, that the metaphorical structure of romantic poetry tends to move inside and downward instead of outside and upward, hence the creative world is deep within, and so is heaven or the place of the presence of God. Blake's Orc and Shelley's Prometheus are Titans imprisoned underneath experience; the Gardens of Adonis are down in *Endymion*, whereas they are up in *The Faerie Queene* and *Comus;* in *Prometheus Unbound* everything that aids mankind comes from below, associated with volcanoes and fountains. In *The Revolt of Islam* there is a curious collision with an older habit of metaphor when Shelley speaks of

> A power, a thirst, a knowledge ... below
> All thoughts, like light beyond the atmosphere.

The "Kubla Khan" geography of caves and underground streams haunts all of Shelley's language about creative processes: in *Speculations on Metaphysics*, for instance, he says: "But thought can with difficulty visit the intricate and winding chambers which it inhabits. It is like a river whose rapid and perpetual stream flows outwards. . . . The caverns of the mind are obscure, and shadowy, or pervaded with a lustre, beautifully bright indeed, but shining not beyond their portals."

In preromantic poetry heaven is the order of grace, and grace is normally thought of as descending from above into the soul. In the romantic construct there is a center where inward and outward manifestations of a common motion and spirit are unified, where the ego is identified as itself because it is also identified with something which is not itself. In Blake this world at the deep center is Jerusalem, the City of God that mankind, or Albion, has sought all through history without success because he has been looking in the wrong direction, outside. Jerusalem is also the garden of Eden where the Holy Word walked among the ancient trees; Eden in the unfallen world would be the same place as England's green and pleasant land where Christ also walked; and England's green and pleasant land is also Atlantis, the sunken island kingdom which we can rediscover by draining the "Sea of Time and Space" off the top of the mind. In *Prometheus Unbound* Atlantis reappears when Prometheus is liberated, and the one great flash of vision which is all that is left to us of Wordsworth's *Recluse* uses the same imagery.

> Paradise, and groves
> Elysian, Fortunate Fields—like those of old
> Sought in the Atlantic Main—why should they be
> A history only of departed things,
> Or a mere fiction of what never was? . . .
> —I, long before the blissful hour arrives,
> Would chant, in lonely peace, the spousal verse
> Of this great consummation.

The Atlantis theme is in many other romantic myths: in the Glaucus episode of *Endymion* and in De Quincey's *Savannah-la-Mar*, which speaks of "human life still subsisting in submarine asylums sacred from the storms that torment our upper air." The theme of land reclaimed from the ocean plays also a somewhat curious role in Goethe's *Faust*. We find the same imagery in later writers who continue the romantic tradition, such as D. H. Lawrence in the "Song of a Man Who Has Come Through":

> If only I am keen and hard like the sheer tip of a wedge
> Driven by invisible blows,
> The rock will split, we shall come at the wonder, we shall find
>   the Hesperides.

In *The Pilgrim's Progress* Ignorance is sent to hell from the very gates of heaven. The inference seems to be that only Ignorance knows the precise location of both kingdoms. For knowledge, and still more for imagination, the journey within to the happy island garden or the city of light is a perilous quest, equally likely to terminate in the blasted ruin of Byron's *Darkness* or Beddoes's *Subterranean City*. In many romantic poems, including Keats's nightingale ode, it is suggested that the final identification of and with reality may be or at least include death. The suggestion that death may lead to the highest knowledge, dropped by Lucifer in Byron's *Cain*, haunts Shelley continually. A famous passage in *Prometheus Unbound* associates the worlds of creation and death in the same inner area, where Zoroaster meets his image in a garden. Just as the sun is the means but not a tolerable object of sight, so the attempt to turn around and see the source of one's vision may be destructive, as the Lady of Shalott found when she turned away from the mirror. Thus the world of the deep interior in romantic poetry is morally ambivalent, retaining some of the demonic qualities that the corresponding preromantic lowest level had.

This sense that the source of genius is beyond good and evil, that the possession of genius may be a curse, that the only real knowledge given to Adam in Paradise, however disastrous, came to him from the devil—all this is part of the contribution of Byron to modern sensibility, and part of the irrevocable change that he made in it. Of his Lara Byron says:

> He stood a stranger in this breathing world,
> An erring spirit from another hurl'd;
> A thing of dark imaginings, that shaped
> By choice the perils he by chance escaped;
> But 'scaped in vain, for in their memory yet
>
> His mind would half exult and half regret . . .
> But haughty still and loth himself to blame,
> He call'd on Nature's self to share the shame,
> And charged all faults upon the fleshly form
> She gave to clog the soul, and feast the worm;
> Till he at last confounded good and ill,
> And half mistook for fate the acts of will.

It would be wrong to regard this as Byronic hokum, for the wording is very precise. Lara looks demonic to a nervous and conforming society, as the dragon does to the tame villatic fowl in Milton. But there is a genuinely demonic quality in him which arises from his being nearer than other men to the unity of subjective and objective worlds. To be in such a place might make a poet more creative; it makes other types of superior beings, including Lara, more destructive.

We said earlier that a romantic poet's political views would depend partly on whether he saw his inner society as concealed by or as mani-

fested in actual society. A romantic poet's moral attitude depends on
a similar ambivalence in the conception of nature. Nature to Wordsworth is a mother-goddess who teaches the soul serenity and joy, and
never betrays the heart that loves her; to the Marquis de Sade nature
is the source of all the perverse pleasures that an earlier age had classified as "unnatural." For Wordsworth the reality of Nature is manifested by its reflection of moral values; for De Sade the reality is
concealed by that reflection. It is this ambivalent sense (for it is
ambivalent, and not simply ambiguous) of appearance as at the same
time revealing and concealing reality, as clothes simultaneously reveal
and conceal the naked body, that makes *Sartor Resartus* so central a
document of the romantic movement. We spoke of Wordsworth's
Nature as a mother-goddess, and her psychological descent from mother-
figures is clearly traced in *The Prelude*. The corn-goddess in Keats's
"To Autumm," the parallel figure identified with Ruth in the "Ode to a
Nightingale," the still unravished bride of the Grecian urn, Psyche,
even the veiled Melancholy, are all emblems of a revealed Nature.
Elusive nymphs or teasing and mocking female figures who refuse to
take definite form, like the figure in *Alastor* or Blake's "female will"
types; terrible and sinister white goddesses like *La Belle Dame sans
Merci*, or females associated with something forbidden or demonic,
like the sister-lovers of Byron and Shelley, belong to the concealed
aspect.

For Wordsworth, who still has a good deal of the preromantic
sense of nature as an objective order, nature is a landscape nature,
and from it, as in Baudelaire's *Correspondances*, mysterious oracles seep
into the mind through eye or ear, even a bird with so predictable a
song as the cuckoo being an oracular wandering voice. This landscape is a veil dropped over the naked nature of screaming rabbits
and gasping stags, the nature red in tooth and claw which haunted a
later generation. Even the episode of the dog and the hedgehog in
The Prelude is told from the point of view of the dog and not of the
hedgehog. But the more pessimistic, and perhaps more realistic,
conception of nature in which it can be a source of evil or suffering as
well as good is the one that gains ascendancy in the later period of
romanticism, and its later period extends to our own day.

· · ·

In romanticism proper a prominent place in sense experience is given to the ear, an excellent receiver of oracles but poor in locating things accurately in space. This latter power, which is primarily visual, is associated with the fancy in Wordsworth's 1815 preface, and given the subordinate position appropriate to fancy. In later poetry, beginning with *symbolisme* in France, when there is a good deal of reaction against earlier romanticism, more emphasis is thrown on vision. In Rimbaud, though his *Bateau Ivre* has given me my title, the poet is to *se faire voyant*, the *illuminations* are thought of pictorially; even the vowels must be visually colored. Such an emphasis has nothing to do with the preromantic sense of an objective structure in nature: on the contrary, the purpose of it is to intensify the romantic sense of oracular significance into a kind of autohypnosis. (The association of autohypnosis and the visual sense is discussed in Professor Marshall McLuhan's new book, *The Gutenberg Galaxy*.) Such an emphasis leads to a technique of fragmentation. Poe's attack on the long poem is not a romantic but an antiromantic manifesto, as the direction of its influence indicates. The tradition of *symbolisme* is present in imagism, where the primacy of visual values is so strongly stated in theory and so cheerfully ignored in practice, in Pound's emphasis on the spatial juxtaposing of metaphor, in Eliot's insistence on the superiority of poets who present the "clear visual images" of Dante. T. E. Hulme's attack on the romantic tradition is consistent in preferring fancy to imagination and in stressing the objectivity of the nature to be imitated. . . .

What this antiromantic movement did not do was to create a third framework of imagery. Nor did it return to the older construct, though Eliot, by sticking closely to Dante and by deprecating the importance of the prophetic element in art, gives some illusion of doing so. The charge of subjectivity, brought against the romantics by Arnold and often repeated later, assumes that objectivity is a higher attribute of poetry, but this is itself a romantic conception, and came into English criticism with Coleridge. Antiromanticism, in short, had no resources for becoming anything more than a postromantic movement. . . . All we need do . . . is to examine romanticism by its own standards and canons. We should not look for precision where vagueness is wanted; not extol the virtues of constipation when the romantics were exuberant; not insist on visual values when the poet listens darkling to a nightingale. Then, perhaps, we may see in romanticism also the quality that Melville found in Greek architecture:

> Not innovating wilfulness,
> But reverence for the Archetype.

BIBLIOGRAPHICAL NOTE: With Frye's essay should be compared his more recent *A Study of English Romanticism* (New York, 1968), the first chapter of which, "The Romantic Myth," Frye says grew out of the essay reprinted here. Robert Langbaum deals with "the new Mythus" in his *The Poetry of Experience* (New York, 1957). See also Douglas Bush, *Mythology and the Romantic Tradition in English Poetry* (New York, 1963; 1st ed. 1937); E. B. Hungerford, *Shores of Darkness* (Cleveland and New York, 1963; 1st ed. 1941); D. G. James, *The Romantic Comedy: An Essay on English Romanticism* (New York, 1948); and Harold Bloom's *Shelley's Mythmaking* (New Haven, 1959) and *The Visionary Company* (Garden City, N.Y., 1961).

English Romanticism:
The Spirit Of The Age

M. H. Abrams

My title echoes that of William Hazlitt's remarkable book of 1825, which set out to represent what we now call the climate of opinion among the leading men of his time. In his abrupt way Hazlitt did not stay to theorize, plunging into the middle of things with a sketch of Jeremy Bentham. But from these essays emerges plainly his view that the crucial occurrence for his generation had been the French Revolution. In that event and its repercussions, political, intellectual, and imaginative, and in the resulting waves of hope and gloom, revolutionary loyalty and recreancy, he saw both the promise and the failures of his violent and contradictory era.

The span covered by the active life of Hazlitt's subjects—approximately the early 1790s to 1825—coincides with what literary historians now call the romantic period; and it is Hazlitt's contention that the

ENGLISH ROMANTICISM: THE SPIRIT OF THE AGE: From *Romanticism Reconsidered: Selected Papers from the English Institute*, ed. Northrop Frye (New York and London: Columbia University Press, 1963), pp. 26–72. Reprinted by permission of Columbia University Press.

characteristic poetry of the age took its shape from the form and pressure of revolution and reaction.

• • •

It seems to me that Hazlitt and his contemporary viewers of the literary scene were, in their general claim, manifestly right: the romantic period was eminently an age obsessed with the fact of violent and inclusive change, and romantic poetry cannot be understood, historically, without awareness of the degree to which this preoccupation affected its substance and form. The phenomenon is too obvious to have escaped notice, in monographs devoted to the French Revolution and the English poets, singly and collectively. But when critics and historians turn to the general task of defining the distinctive qualities of "romanticism," or of the English romantic movement, they usually ignore its relations to the revolutionary climate of the time. For example, in an anthology of "the 'classic' statements" on romanticism, especially in England, which came out in 1962, the few essays which give more than passing mention to the French Revolution do so to reduce the particularity of romantic poems mainly to a distant reflection of an underlying economic reality, and to an unconscious rationalization of the bourgeois illusion of "freedom."[1]

It may be useful, then, to have a new look at the obvious as it appeared, not to post-Marxist historians, but to intelligent observers at the time. I shall try to indicate briefly some of the ways in which the political, intellectual, and emotional circumstances of a period of revolutionary upheaval affected the scope, subject-matter, themes, values, and even language of a number of romantic poems. I hope to avoid easy and empty generalizations about the *Zeitgeist*, and I do not propose the electrifying proposition that *"le romantisme, c'est la révolution."* Romanticism is no one thing. It is many very individual poets, who wrote poems manifesting a greater diversity of qualities, it seems to me, than those of any preceding age. But some prominent qualities a number of these poems share, and certain of these shared qualities form a distinctive complex which may, with a high degree of probability, be related to the events and ideas of the cataclysmic

---

[1] *Romanticism: Points of View*, ed. Robert F. Gleckner and Gerald E. Enscoe (Englewood Cliffs, N. J., 1962).

coming-into-being of the world to which we are by now becoming
fairly accustomed.

I. THE SPIRIT OF THE 1790s

By force of chronological habit we think of English romanticism
as a nineteenth-century phenomenon, overlooking how many of its
distinctive features had been established by the end of the century
before. The last decade of the eighteenth century included the complete
cycle of the Revolution in France, from what De Quincey called its
"gorgeous festival era" to the *coup d'état* of November 10, 1799, when to
all but a few stubborn sympathizers it seemed betrayed from without
and within, and the portent of Napoleon loomed over Europe. That
same decade was the period in which the poets of the first romantic
generation reached their literary maturity and had either completed,
or laid out and begun, the greater number of what we now account
their major achievements.

•   •   •

"Few persons but those who have lived in it," Southey reminisced
in his Tory middle age, "can conceive or comprehend what the memory
of the French Revolution was, nor what a visionary world seemed to
open upon those who were just entering it. Old things seemed passing
away, and nothing was dreamt of but the regeneration of the human
race." The early years of the Revolution, a modern commentator has
remarked, were "perhaps the happiest in the memory of civilized
man,"[2] and his estimate is justified by the ecstasy described by Wordsworth in *The Prelude*—"bliss was it in that dawn to be alive"—and
expressed by many observers of France in its glad dawn. Samuel
Romilly exclaimed in May, 1792: "It is the most glorious event, and
the happiest for mankind, that has ever taken place since human
affairs have been recorded." Charles James Fox was less restrained in
his evaluation: "How much the greatest event it is that ever happened
in the world! and how much the best!" A generation earlier Dr.
Johnson had written a concluding passage for Goldsmith's *The
Traveller* which summed up prevailing opinion:

[2] M. Ray Adams, *Studies in the Literary Backgrounds of English Radicalism* (Lancaster,
Pa., 1947), p. 7.

> How small, of all that human hearts endure,
> That part which laws or kings can cause or cure!
> Still to ourselves in every place consigned,
> Our own felicity we make or find.

But now it seemed to many . . . that the revolution against the king and the old laws would cure everything and establish felicity for everyone, everywhere. . . . In 1793, Hazlitt said, schemes for a new society "of virtue and happiness" had been published "in plays, poems, songs, and romances—made their way to the bar, crept into the church . . . got into the hearts of poets and the brains of metaphysicians . . . and turned the heads of almost the whole kingdom." Anyone who has looked into the poems, the sermons, the novels, and the plays of the early 1790s will know that this is not a gross exaggeration. Man regenerate in world made new; this was the theme of a multitude of writers notable, forgotten, or anonymous. In the Prologue to his highly successful play, *The Road to Ruin* (1792), Thomas Holcroft took the occasion to predict that the Revolution in France had set the torrent of freedom spreading,

> To ease, happiness, art, science, wit, and genius to give birth;
> Ay, to fertilize a world, and renovate old earth!

"Renovate old earth," "the regeneration of the human race"—the phrases reflect their origin, and indicate a characteristic difference between French and English radicalism. Most French philosophers of perfectibility (and Godwin, their representative in England) were anticlerical skeptics or downright atheists, who claimed that they based their predictions on an inductive science of history and a Lockian science of man. The chief strength and momentum of English radicalism, on the other hand, came from the religious Nonconformists who, as true heirs of their embattled ancestors in the English Civil War, looked upon contemporary politics through the perspective of biblical prophecy. In a sermon on the French Revolution preached in 1791 the Reverend Mark Wilks proclaimed: "Jesus Christ was a Revolutionist; and the Revolution he came to effect was foretold in these words, 'He hath sent me to proclaim liberty to the captives.'" The Unitarians—influential beyond their numbers because they included so large a proportion of scientists, literary men, and powerful pulpit orators—were especially given to projecting on the empirical science of human progress the pattern and detail of biblical prophecies, Messianic, millennial, and apocalyptic. "Hey for the New Jerusalem! The millennium!" Thomas Holcroft cried out, in the intoxication of first reading Paine's *The Rights of Man* (1791); what this notorious atheist uttered lightly was the fervent but considered opinion of a number of his pious contemporaries. . . . By 1793 the increasingly violent course of the Revolution inspired the prophets to turn from Isaiah's relatively mild prelude to the peaceable kingdom and "the new heavens and the new earth" to the classic text of apocalyptic violence, the Book of Revelation. In February of that year Elhanan Winchester's *The Three Woe Trumpets* interpreted the Revolution in France as the precise fulfillment of those prophecies, with the seventh trumpet just about to sound (Rev. II) to bring on the final cataclysm and announce the Second Advent of Christ, in a Kingdom which should be "the greatest blessing to mankind that ever they enjoyed, or even found an idea of." In 1791 Joseph Priestley, scientist, radical philosopher, and a founder of the Unitarian Society, had written his *Letters* in reply to Burke's *Reflections*, in which he pronounced the American and French revolutions to be the inauguration of the state of universal happiness and peace "distinctly and repeatedly foretold in many prophecies, delivered more than two thousand years ago." Three years later he expanded his views in *The Present State of Europe Compared with Ancient Prophecies*. Combining philosophical empiricism with biblical fundamentalism, he related the convulsions of the time to the Messianic prophecies in Isaiah and Daniel, the apocalyptic passages in various books of the New Testament and especially to the Book of Revelation, as a ground for confronting "the great scene, that seems now to be opening upon us . . . with tranquillity, and even with satisfaction," in the persuasion that its "termination will be glorious and happy," in the advent of "the millennium, or the future peaceable and happy state of the world." Wordsworth's Solitary, in *The Excursion*, no doubt reflects an aspect of Wordsworth's own temperament, but the chief model for his earlier career was Joseph Fawcett, famous Unitarian preacher at the Old Jewry, and a poet as well. In Wordsworth's rendering, we find him, in both song and sermon, projecting a dazzling vision of the French Revolution which fuses classical myth with Christian prophecy:

> I beheld
> Glory—beyond all glory ever seen,
> Confusion infinite of heaven and earth,
> Dazzling the soul. Meanwhile, prophetic harps
> In every grove were ringing, "War shall cease."
>   . . . I sang Saturnian rule
> Returned,—a progeny of golden years
> Permitted to descend and bless mankind.
> —With promises the Hebrew Scriptures teem.
>   . . . the glowing phrase
> Of ancient inspiration serving me,
> I promised also,—with undaunted trust
> Foretold, and added prayer to prophecy. (*The Excursion*,
>   III, 719–65)

The formative age of romantic poetry was clearly one of apocalyptic expectations, or at least apocalyptic imaginings, which endowed the promise of France with the form and impetus of one of the deepest rooted and most compelling myths in the culture of Christian Europe.

II. THE VOICE OF THE BARD

In a verse-letter of 1800 Blake identified the crucial influences in his spiritual history as a series beginning with Milton and the Old Testament prophets and ending with the American War and the French Revolution. Since Blake is the only major romantic old enough to have published poems before the Revolution, his writings provide a convenient indication of the effects of that event and of the intellectual and emotional atmosphere that it generated.

As Northrop Frye has said in his fine book on Blake, his *Poetical Sketches* of 1783 associate him with Collins, Gray, the Wartons, and other writers of what Frye later called "The Age of Sensibility."[3] As early as the 1740s this school had mounted a literary revolution against the acknowledged tradition of Waller-Denham-Pope—a tradition of civilized and urbane verse, controlled by "good sense and judgment," addressed to a closely integrated upper class, in which the triumphs, as Joseph Warton pointed out, were mainly in "the didactic, moral,

---

[3] *Fearful Symmetry* (Princeton, 1947), pp. 167ff.; "Towards Defining an Age of Sensibility," in *Eighteenth-Century English Literature: Modern Essays in Criticism*, ed. James L. Clifford (New York, 1959), pp. 311–18.

and satiric kind." Against this tradition, the new poets raised the claim of a more daring, "sublime," and "primitive" poetry, represented in England by Spenser, Shakespeare, Milton, who exhibit the supreme virtues of spontaneity, invention, and an "enthusiastic" and "creative" imagination—by which was signified a poetry of inspired vision, related to divinity, and populated by allegorical and supernatural characters such as do not exist "in nature."[4]

Prominent in this literature of revolt, however, was a timidity, a sense of frustration very different from the assurance of power and of an accomplished and continuing literary renascence expressed by a number of their romantic successors: Coleridge's unhesitating judgment that Wordsworth's genius measured up to Milton's, and Wordsworth's solemn concurrence in this judgment; Leigh Hunt's opinion that, for all his errors, Wordsworth is "at the head of a new and great age of poetry"; Keats's conviction that "Great spirits now on earth are sojourning"; Shelley's confidence that "the literature of England . . . has arisen, as it were, from a new birth." The poets of sensibility, on the contrary, had felt that they and all future writers were fated to be epigones of a tradition of unrecapturable magnificence. . . . So, in 1783, Blake complained to the Muses:

> How have you left the ancient love
> That bards of old enjoy'd in you!

Besides *Poetical Sketches*, Blake's main achievements before the French Revolution were *Songs of Innocence* and *The Book of Thel*, which represent dwellers in an Eden trembling on the verge of experience. Suddenly in 1790 came *The Marriage of Heaven and Hell*, boisterously promulgating "Energy" in opposition to all inherited limits on human possibilities; to point the contemporary relevance, Blake appended a "Song of Liberty," which represents Energy as a revolutionary "son of fire," moving from America to France and crying the advent of an Isaian millennium: "EMPIRE IS NO MORE! AND NOW THE LION AND WOLF SHALL CEASE." In 1791 appeared Blake's *The French Revolution*, in the form of a Miltonic epic. Of the seven books announced, only the first is extant, but this is enough to demonstrate that Blake, like Priestley and other

[4] See M. H. Abrams, *The Mirror and the Lamp* (New York, 1953), pp. 274–76 and notes.

religious radicals of the day, envisioned the Revolution as the portent of apocalypse. After five thousand years "the ancient dawn calls us / To awake," the Abbé de Sieyés pleads for a peace, freedom, and equality which will effect a regained Eden—"the happy earth sing in its course, / The mild peaceable nations be opened to heav'n, and men walk with their fathers in bliss"; when his plea is ignored, there are rumblings of a gathering Armageddon, and the book ends with the portent of a first resurrection: "And the bottoms of the world were open'd, and the graves of arch-angels unseal'd."

The "Introduction" to *Songs of Experience* (1794) calls on us to attend the voice which will sing all Blake's poems from now on: "Hear the voice of the Bard! / Who Present, Past, & Future, sees," who calls to the lapsèd Soul and enjoins the earth to cease her cycle and turn to the eternal day. This voice is that of the poet-prophets of the Old and New Testaments, now descending on Blake from its specifically British embodiment in that "bard of old," John Milton. In his "minor prophecies," ending in 1795, Blake develops, out of the heroic-scaled but still historical agents of his *French Revolution*, the Giant Forms of his later mythical system. The Bard becomes Los, the "Eternal Prophet" and father of "red Orc," who is the spirit of Energy bursting out in total spiritual, physical, and political revolution; the argument of the song sung by Los, however, remains that announced in *The French Revolution*. As David Erdman has said, *Europe: A Prophecy* (1794) was written at about the time Blake was illustrating Milton's "On the Morning of Christ's Nativity," and reinterprets that poem for his own times.[5] Orc, here identified with Christ the revolutionary, comes with the blare of the apocalyptic trumpet to vex nature out of her sleep of 1,800 years, in a cataclysmic Second Coming in "the vineyards of Red France" which, however, heralds the day when both the earth and its inhabitants will be resurrected in a joyous burst of unbounded and lustful energy.

By the year 1797 Blake launched out into the "strong heroic Verse" of *Vala, or The Four Zoas*, the first of his three full-scale epics, which recounts the total history of "The Universal Man" from the beginning, through "His fall into Division," to a future that explodes into the most spectacular and sustained apocalyptic set-piece since the Book

---

[5] *Blake, Prophet Against Empire* (Princeton, 1954), pp. 246ff.; and see Frye, *Fearful Symmetry*, p. 262.

of Revelation; in this holocaust "the evil is all consum'd" and "all things are chang'd, even as in ancient times."

III. ROMANTIC ORACLES

No amount of historical explanation can make Blake out to be other than a phoenix among poets; but if we put his work into its historical and intellectual context, and alongside that of his poetic contemporaries of the 1790s, we find at least that he is not a freak without historical causes but that he responded to the common circumstances in ways markedly similar, sometimes even to odd details. But while fellow-poets soon left off their tentative efforts to evolve a system of "machinery" by which to come to terms with the epic events of their revolutionary era, Blake carried undauntedly on.

What, then, were the attributes shared by the chief poets of the 1790s, Blake, Wordsworth, Southey, Coleridge?—to whom I shall add, Shelley. Byron and Keats also had elements in common with their older contemporaries, but these lie outside the immediate scope of my paper. Shelley, however, though he matured in the cynical era of Napoleon and the English Regency, reiterated remarkably the pattern of his predecessors. By temperament he was more inclusively and extremely radical than anyone but Blake, and his early "principles," as he himself said, had "their origin from the discoveries which preceded and occasioned the revolutions of America and France." That is, he had formed his mind on those writers, from Rousseau through Condorcet, Volney, Paine, and Godwin, whose ideas made up the climate of the 1790s—and also, it should be emphasized, on the King James Bible and *Paradise Lost*.

1. First, these were all centrally political and social poets. It is by a peculiar injustice that romanticism is often described as a mode of escapism, an evasion of the shocking changes, violence, and ugliness attending the emergence of the modern industrial and political world. The fact is that to a degree without parallel, even among major Victorian poets, these writers were obsessed with the realities of their era. Blake's wife mildly complained that her husband was always in Paradise; but from this vantage point he managed to keep so thoroughly in touch with mundane reality that, as David Erdman has demonstrated, his epics are hardly less steeped in the scenes and events of

the day than is that latter-day epic, the *Ulysses* of James Joyce. Words-worth said that he "had given twelve hours thought to the conditions and prospects of society, for one to poetry"; Coleridge, Southey, and Shelley could have made a claim similarly extravagant; all these poets delivered themselves of political and social commentary in the form of prose-pamphlets, essays, speeches, editorials, or sermons; and all exhibit an explicit or submerged concern with the contemporary historical and intellectual situation in the greater part of their verses, narrative, dramatic, and lyric, long and short.

2. What obscures this concern is that in many poems the romantics do not write direct political and moral commentary but (in Schorer's apt phrase for Blake) "the politics of vision," uttered in the persona of the inspired prophet-priest. Neoclassic poets had invoked the muse as a formality of the poetic ritual, and the school of sensibility had expressed nostalgia for the "diviner inspiration" of Spenser, Shakespeare, and Milton. But when the romantic poet asserts inspiration and revelation by a power beyond himself—as Blake did repeatedly, or Shelley in his claim that the great poets of his age are "the priests of an unappre-hended inspiration, the mirrors of gigantic shadows which futurity casts upon the present"—he means it. And when Wordsworth called himself "A youthful Druid taught . . . Primeval mysteries, a Bard elect . . . a chosen Son," and Coleridge characterized *The Prelude* as "More than historic, that prophetic Lay," "An Orphic song" uttered by a "great Bard," in an important sense they meant it too, and we must believe that they meant it if we are to read them aright.

The romantics, then, often spoke confidently as elected members of what Harold Bloom calls "The Visionary Company," the inspired line of singers from the prophets of the Old and New Testaments through Dante, Spenser, and above all Milton. For Milton had an exemplary role in this tradition as the native British (or Druidic) Bard who was a thorough political, social, and religious revolutionary, who claimed inspiration both from a Heavenly Muse and from the Holy Spirit that had supervised the Creation and inspired the biblical prophets, and who, after the failure of his millennial expectations from the English Revolution, had kept his singing voice and salvaged his hope for mankind in an epic poem.

3. Following the Miltonic example, the romantic poet of the 1790s tried to incorporate what he regarded as the stupendous events of the age in the suitably great poetic forms. He wrote, or planned to write

an epic, or (like Milton in *Samson Agonistes*) emulated Aeschylean tragedy or uttered visions combining the mode of biblical prophecy with the loose Pindaric, "the sublime" or "greater Ode,"* which by his eighteenth-century predecessors had been accorded a status next to epic, as peculiarily adapted to an enthusiastic and visionary imagination. Whatever the form, the romantic bard is one "who present, past, and future sees"; so that in dealing with current affairs his procedure is often panoramic, his stage cosmic, his agents quasi-mythological, and his logic of events apocalyptic. Typically this mode of romantic vision fuses history, politics, philosophy, and religion into one grand design, by asserting Providence—or some form of natural teleology—to operate in the seeming chaos of human history so as to effect from present evil a greater good; and through the mid-1790s the French Revolution functions as the symptom or early stage of the abrupt culmination of this design, from which will emerge a new man on a new earth which is a restored Paradise.

> [Abrams here adduces "support (for) these large generalizations" by reference to Southey's *Joan of Arc*, Coleridge's *The Destiny of Nations* and *Religious Musings* (the latter of which he compares to Blake's *Europe: A Prophecy*), Wordsworth's conclusion to *Descriptive Sketches*, Shelley's *Queen Mab*, several of Hölderlin's odes—all of which he sees as evidence of "the epomania of the age."]

IV. THE APOCALYPSE OF IMAGINATION

The visionary poems of the earlier 1790s and Shelley's earlier prophecies show imaginative audacity and invention, but they are not, it must be confessed, very good poems. The great romantic poems were written not in the mood of revolutionary exaltation but in the later mood of revolutionary disillusionment or despair. Many of the great poems, however, do not break with the formative past, but continue to exhibit, in a transformed but recognizable fashion, the scope, the poetic voice, the design, the ideas, and the imagery developed in the earlier period. This continuity of tradition converts what would otherwise be a literary curiosity into a matter of considerable historical

---

* See Abrams's essay, "Structure and Style in the Greater Romantic Lyric," in *From Sensibility to Romanticism*, ed. F. W. Hilles and H. Bloom (New York, 1965), pp. 527–60.

interest, and helps us to identify and interpret some of the strange but characteristic elements in later romantic enterprises.

Here is one out of many available instances. . . . Certain terms, images, and quasi-mythical agents tend to recur and to assume a specialized reference to revolutionary events and expectations: the earthquake and the volcano, the purging fire, the emerging sun, the dawn of glad day, the awakening earth in springtime, the Dionysian figure of revolutionary destruction and the Apollonian figure of the promise of a bright new order. Prominent among these is a term which functions as one of the principal leitmotifs of romantic literature. To Europe at the end of the eighteenth century the French Revolution brought what St. Augustine said Christianity had brought to the ancient world: hope. As Coleridge wrote, on first hearing Wordsworth's *Prelude* read aloud, the poet sang of his experience "Amid the tremor of a realm aglow,"

> When from the general heart of human kind
> Hope sprang forth like a full-born Deity!

and afterward, "Of that dear Hope afflicted and struck down. . . ." This is no ordinary human hope, but a universal, absolute, and novel hope which sprang forth from the Revolutionary events sudden and complete, like Minerva. Pervasively in both the verse and prose of the period, "hope," with its associated term, "joy," and its opposites, "dejection," "despondency," and "despair," are used in a special application, as shorthand for the limitless faith in human and social possibility aroused by the Revolution, and its reflex, the nadir of feeling caused by its seeming failure—as Wordsworth had put it, the "utter loss of hope itself / And things to hope for."

It is not irrelevant, I believe, that many seemingly apolitical poems of the later romantic period turn on the theme of hope and joy and the temptation to abandon all hope and fall into dejection and despair; the recurrent emotional pattern is that of the key books of *The Excursion*, labeled "Despondency" and "Despondency Corrected," which apply specifically to the failure of millennial hope in the Revolution. But I want to apply this observation to one of those passages in *The Prelude* where Wordsworth suddenly breaks through to a prophetic vision of the hidden significance of the literal narrative. In the sixth book Wordsworth describes his first tour of France with Robert Jones in the summer of 1790, the brightest period of the Revolution. The mighty forms of

Nature, "seizing a youthful fancy," had already "given a charter to irregular hopes," but now all Europe

> was thrilled with joy,
> France standing on the top of golden hours,
> And human nature seeming born again.

Sharing the universal intoxication, "when joy of one" was "joy for tens of millions," they join in feasting and dance with a "blithe host / Of Travellers" returning from the Federation Festival at Paris, "the great spousals newly solemnised / At their chief city, in the sight of Heaven." In his revisions of the 1805 version of *The Prelude*, Wordsworth inserted at this point a passage in which he sees, with anguished foreboding, the desecration by French troops of the Convent of the Chartreuse (an event which did not take place until two years later, in 1792). The travelers' way then brings them to the Simplon Pass.

Wordsworth's earlier account of this tour in the *Descriptive Sketches*, written mainly in 1791–92, had ended with the prophecy of a new earth emerging from apocalyptic fires, and a return to the golden age. Now, however, he describes a strange access of sadness, a "melancholy slackening." On the Simplon road they had left their guide and climbed ever upward, until a peasant told them that they had missed their way and that the course now lay downwards.

> Loth to believe what we so grieved to hear,
> For still we had hopes that pointed to the clouds,
> We questioned him again, and yet again;

but every reply "Ended in this,—*that we had crossed the Alps.*"

> Imagination . . .
> That awful Power rose from the mind's abyss
> Like an unfathered vapour that enwraps,
> At once, some lonely traveller; I was lost;
> Halted without an effort to break through;
> But to my conscious soul I now can say—
> "I recognise thy glory". . . .

Only now, in retrospect, does he recognize that his imagination had penetrated to the emblematic quality of the literal climb, in a revelation proleptic of the experience he was to recount in all the remainder of *The Prelude*. Man's infinite hopes can never be matched by the world as it is and man as he is, for these exhibit a discrepancy no less than that

between his "hopes that pointed to the clouds" and the finite height of
the Alpine pass. But in the magnitude of the disappointment lies its
consolation; for the flash of vision also reveals that infinite longings
are inherent in the human spirit, and that the gap between the
inordinacy of his hope and the limits of possibility is the measure of
man's dignity and greatness:

> Our destiny, our being's heart and home,
> Is with infinitude, and only there;
> With hope it is, hope that can never die,
> Effort, and expectation, and desire,
> And something evermore about to be.

In short, Wordsworth evokes from the unbounded and hence
impossible hopes in the French Revolution a central romantic doctrine;
one which reverses the cardinal neoclassic ideal of setting only accessible
goals, by converting what had been man's tragic error—the inordinacy
of his "pride" that persists in setting infinite aims for finite man—into
his specific glory and his triumph. Wordsworth shares the recognition
of his fellow-romantics, German and English, of the greatness of man's
infinite *Sehnsucht,**his saving insatiability, Blake's "I want! I want!"
Shelley's "the desire of the moth for the star"; but with a characteristic
and unique difference, as he goes on at once to reveal:

> Under such banners militant, the soul
> Seeks for no trophies, struggles for no spoils
> That may attest her prowess, blest in thoughts
> That are their own perfection and reward. . . .

The militancy of overt political action has been transformed into the
paradox of spiritual quietism: under such militant banners is no march,
but a wise passiveness. This truth having been revealed to him, Wordsworth at once goes on to his apocalypse of nature in the Simplon Pass,
where the *coincidentia oppositorum* of its physical attributes become the
symbols of the biblical Book of Revelation:

> Characters of the great Apocalypse,
> The types and symbols of Eternity,
> Of first, and last, and midst, and without end.

This and its companion passages in *The Prelude* enlighten the orphic
darkness of Wordsworth's "Prospectus" for *The Recluse*, drafted as

* On the romantics' *Sehnsucht*, see also Albert Gérard's essay above.

early as 1800, when *The Prelude* had not yet been differentiated from
the larger poem. Wordsworth's aim, he there reveals, is still that of
the earlier period of millennial hope in revolution, still expressed in a
fusion of biblical and classical imagery. Evil is to be redeemed by a
regained Paradise, or Elysium: "Paradise," he says, "and groves /
Elysian, Fortunate Fields . . . why should they be / A history only of
departed things?" And the restoration of Paradise, as in the Book of
Revelation, is still symbolized by a sacred marriage. But the hope has
been shifted from the history of mankind to the mind of the single
individual, from militant external action to an imaginative act; and
the marriage between the Lamb and the New Jerusalem has been
converted into a marriage between subject and object,* mind and nature
which creates a new world out of the old world of sense:

> For the discerning intellect of Man,
> When wedded to this goodly universe
> In love and holy passion, shall find these
> A simple produce of the common day.
> —I, long before the blissful hour arrives,
> Would chant, in lonely peace, the spousal verse
> Of this great consummation . . .
> And the creation (by no lower name
> Can it be called) which they with blended might
> Accomplish:—this is our high argument. [Abrams's ellipses]

In the other romantic visionaries, as in Wordsworth, naïve mil-
lennialism produced mainly declamation, but the shattered trust in
premature political revolution and the need to reconstitute the grounds
of hope lay behind the major achievements. And something close to
Wordsworth's evolution—the shift to a spiritual and moral revolution
which will transform our experience of the old world—is also the argument of a number of the later writings of Blake, Coleridge, Shelley,
and, with all his differences, Hölderlin. An example from Shelley must
suffice. Most of Shelley's large enterprises after *Queen Mab—The
Revolt of Islam, Prometheus Unbound, Hellas*—were inspired by a later
recrudescence of the European revolutionary movement. Shelley's
view of human motives and possibilities became more and more
tragic, and, like Blake after his *French Revolution*, he moved from the
bald literalism of *Queen Mab* to an imaginative form increasingly biblical, symbolic, and mythic; but the theme continues to be the ultimate

* On this point compare, especially, Earl R. Wasserman's essay below.

promise of a renovation in human nature and circumstances. In *Prometheus Unbound* this event is symbolized by the reunion of Prometheus and Asia in a joyous ceremony in which all the cosmos participates. But this new world is one which reveals itself to the purged imagination of Man when he has reformed his moral nature at its deep and twisted roots; and the last words of Demogorgon, the inscrutable agent of this apocalypse, describe a revolution of spirit whose sole agencies are the cardinal virtues of endurance, forgiveness, love, and, above all, hope—though a hope that is now hard to distinguish from despair:

> To suffer woes which Hope thinks infinite . . .
> To love, and bear; to hope till Hope creates
> From its own wreck the thing it contemplates . . .
> This is alone Life, Joy, Empire, and Victory! [Abrams's ellipses]

[Abrams then makes a detailed analysis of the *Lyrical Ballads*, in which he sees Wordsworth as having "turned away from Man as he exists only in the hopes of naïve millennialists or the abstraction of the philosophers of perfectibility . . . to the humble and obscure men of the lower and rural classes." After tracing the origins of Wordsworth's plain style back to the Bible, Abrams illustrates from the "Essay Supplementary to the Preface" of 1815 that, having "given up the hope of revolutionizing the social and political structure," Wordsworth discovered a "new calling"—"to effect through his poetry an egalitarian revolution of the spirit" so that his upper-class readers "may share his revelation of the equivalence of souls, the heroic dimensions of common life, and the grandeur of the ordinary and the trivial in Nature."]

Wordsworth, then, in the period beginning about 1759, came to see his destiny to lie in spiritual rather than in overt action and adventure, and to conceive his radical poetic vocation to consist in communicating his unique and paradoxical, hence inevitably misunderstood, revelation of the more-than-heroic grandeur of the humble, the contemned, the ordinary, and the trivial, whether in the plain style of direct ballad-like representation, or in the elevated voice in which he presents himself in his office as recipient of this gift of vision. In either case, the mode in which Wordsworth conceived his mission evolved out of the ambition to participate in the renovation of the world and of man which he had shared with his fellow-poets during the period of revolutionary enthusiasm.

•　•　•

BIBLIOGRAPHICAL NOTE: Other works dealing with the politics of the romantics are Crane Brinton, *The Political Ideas of the English Romanticists* (Oxford, 1926); Alfred Cobban, *Edmund Burke and the Revolt Against the Eighteenth Century* (London, 1929); R. W. Harris, *Romanticism and the Social Order 1780–1830* (London, 1969); and H. N. Brailsford, *Shelley, Godwin, and Their Circle* (Oxford, 1913). For more specialized studies see, e.g., F. M. Todd, *Politics and the Poet: A Study of Wordsworth* (London, 1958); K. N. Cameron, *The Young Shelley: Genesis of a Radical* (New York, 1950); and C. R. Woodring, *Politics in the Poetry of Coleridge* (Madison, 1961).

The English Romantics:
The Grounds of Knowledge

Earl R. Wasserman

According to the Humpty Dumpty principle of semantic wages we owe the word "romanticism" a good deal of extra pay; we have made it do such a lot of overtime work by meaning so many things. We even insist that, since the word exists, it must stand for something real prior to our isolation of that something, and we have labored to divine that arcane meaning. We generally lop off a period of time, variously and arbitrarily determined, presuming it to be infused with some identifying quality whose name is "romanticism"; and we then set out, in fact, to constitute the *a priori* phantom by defining it, with little resulting agreement, usually by naming the common features in manifestations of what we assume must be "romantic." The logic is that of the vicious circle: the definition assumes as existent and understood that which is to be defined and proved to exist. Since, like Humpty Dumpty, I'd rather not have the word come round of a Saturday night to exact such heavy wages of me, I ask permission to sack it. My subject, then, is Wordsworth, Coleridge, Keats, and Shelley. They share, of course, many features, but a catalogue of these would merely melt the four

THE ENGLISH ROMANTICS: THE GROUNDS OF KNOWLEDGE: From *Studies in Romanticism*, IV (1964), 17–34. Reprinted by permission of the editor and author.

poets into an anonymous confection and filter out what is idiosyncratic; that is, it would destroy our essential reason for reading them and disregard their poetic motives. On the other hand, since the four belong to approximately the same era, what they obviously share is access to facets of a common culture. Ideally, therefore, it should be possible to relate them to that culture in such a way as not merely to preserve their individual uniqueness but indeed to locate it with some precision, for if anything is palpable it is that they vigorously disagreed on central issues and that their works differ in vastly more essential and interesting ways than they are similar.

The bulk of eighteenth-century descriptive poetry is so large as to suggest that the poets must have had a significant apprehension of the external world, or at any rate came to grips with it in profound ways. In point of fact nearly all this verse is, in these terms, trivial, and most of it betrays an uncertain or ineffectual conception of how one experiences the external nature which is its subject matter. Clearly the external world counted for much in that culture, and poetic representation of landscape was thought vaguely significant. But the problem of the transaction between the perceiving mind and the perceived world was either evaded or left uneasily indecisive in descriptive verse, where one might reasonably expect it to demand attention.

If eighteenth-century poetry hedged on this question, which I shall —very loosely—call epistemological, contemporary philosophy certainly did not, and it is highly likely that the subtleties of eighteenth-century epistemology both drove the poets to confront the external world and deterred them from confronting it in any important way. By its very nature British empiricism had long tended to unsettle any assurance of an external world whose existence and qualities are exactly as the senses report. Hobbes had recognized the disparity between sensible qualities and the object being perceived. Locke, building on Boyle's distinction, divided qualities into those which are attributes of the object and those in the perceiver's mind, such as sound and color; and by locating the former in a pure "substance," which is unknowable in itself, he left man convinced of the reality of his own mental impressions, but highly uncertain about the nature or reality of the external world. Berkeley then located both sets of qualities in the perceiver's mind and, destroying Locke's "substance," made God the cause of our perceptions and assigned the reality of the external world to the act of its being perceived: natural science becomes merely a study of the principles governing the uniform relations of our sensations. Hume then completed Berkeley's subversion of the "external" by skeptically concluding that we can have no real knowledge of the existence or nature of the external causes of our impressions. Well might a landscape poet like Richard Jago be uneasy lest "all this outward Frame of Things" be "unsubstantial Air, / Ideal Vision, or a waking Dream" (*Edge-Hill*). Meanwhile, the mechanists like Hartley and the French school tried to cut the epistemological knot by explaining both mind and nature as matter and motion; and the Scottish School took the coward's way out by eschewing theory and limiting itself to description of mental phenomena on the basis of unassailable, God-given common sense. The stage was set for Kant and the epistemology of transcendentalism.

To these whirlwinds of eighteenth-century epistemology the poets, outwardly, remained rather indifferent, as though their poetic valuing of the external world guaranteed it against philosophic doubts. . . . This lack of any significant epistemology can be taken as typical of the hundreds of eighteenth-century meditative-descriptive poems. When the poet is not merely organizing sense data into some picturesque, sublime, or beautiful distribution, he usually devotes himself to humanizing the external scene by associating it with some emotion, moral theme, historical episode, moving narrative, or autobiographical experience. The scene becomes significant only by stimulating the poet to link it with man by some loose association. Even when he directly considers the relation of the objective and subjective worlds he usually postulates nothing more intimate than analogy.* According to Akenside, the imagination, working with sense data, gives the mind "ideas analogous to those of moral approbation and dislike." Almost all the "ornaments of poetic diction," he thought, arise from the analogy between the material and immaterial worlds and between "lifeless things" and man's thought and passion. Accordingly, the eighteenth-century poet is forever interrupting his scene-painting to find its moral or emotional analogue. A description of flickering sunlight must be paired with a note on the analogous emotion of gaiety; if the poet observes that "Those thorns protect the forest's hopes: / That tree the slender ivy props," he must add, "Thus rise the mighty on the mean! / Thus on the strong the feeble lean!" (F. N. C. Munday, *Needwood Forest*, 1776). Does a river spill into a cataract? Then

---

* Cf. Wasserman's "Nature Moralized: the Divine Analogy in the Eighteenth Century," *ELH*, XX (1953), 39–76.

Thus man, the harpy of his own content,
With blust'ring passions, phrensically bent,
Wild in the windy vortex, whirls the soul,
Till Reason bursts, nor can herself controul.
                                (Thomas Maude, *Wensleydale*, 1771)

Such tenous, inorganic bonds between inner man and outer world
betray the impotence of later eighteenth-century poetic epistemology,
just as the ubiquitous urge to find some moral or subjective analogue
to the scene reveals the anxiety to internalize the external and integrate
the spiritual with the phenomenal. The resort to analogy only dodges
the problem, since it both pretends to a relation between subject and
object and yet keeps them categorically apart. In 1802 Coleridge could
justifiably complain of poetry in which

> There reigns . . . such a perpetual trick of *moralizing* every thing . . .
> never to see or describe any interesting appearance in nature, without
> connecting it by dim analogies with the moral world proves faintness
> of Impression. Nature has her proper interest; & he will know what it is,
> who believes & feels, that every Thing has a Life of it's own, & that we
> are all *one Life*. A Poet's *Heart* & *Intellect* should be *combined, intimately*
> combined & *unified*, with the great appearances in Nature—& not
> merely held in solution & loose mixture with them, in the shape of for-
> mal Similies. (Letter to Sotheby, September 10, 1802)

Though the eighteenth-century poets bid us behold nearly every hill
and plain, their reasons and those of the aestheticians are largely adventitious and extrinsic to the unmediated encounter with the object. For
example, Archibald Alison at the end of the century seems to promise a
poetically viable epistemology by proposing that "As it is only . . .
through the medium of matter, that, in the present condition of our
being, the qualities of mind are known to us, the qualities of matter
become necessarily expressive to us of all the qualities of mind they
signify" (*Essays on the Nature and Principles of Taste*, 1790). What we might
then expect is a system identifying perception with significant cognition
and resolving the divorce between subject and object by making perception an act of self-knowledge.* But the subject-object relations Alison
develops are in fact no more than those employed by the descriptive
poets: matter is the immediate sign of mental powers and affections; or

---

* For an interesting discussion of perception and cognition, see A. N. Whitehead's
"The Romantic Reaction" in *Science and the Modern World* (New York, 1925).

it is the sign of mental qualities as a consequence of experience, analogy, and association. In sum, our "minds, instead of being governed by the character of external objects, are enabled to bestow upon them a character which does not belong to them" and to connect with the appearances of nature "feelings of a nobler or more interesting kind, than any that the mere influences of matter can ever convey"; and Alison's system implies little more than the characteristic poetry in which the scene is understood as an independent entity that becomes significant through equally independent subjective values loosely linked to it. His theory of matter as aesthetic sign merely offers a fuzzy rationale for the established eighteenth-century descriptive mode instead of healing the dualism and leading to a more organic poetry. The unresolved dualism of the poets and aestheticians results in a dualistic poetry: the scene is perceived and then felt or associated or thought, but seldom, if ever, apprehended *in* the perception. It is therefore a poetry of hobbling simile, rather than symbol. And it is a poetry that never fulfills itself to allow the poet to withdraw from a self-supporting creation; rather, it ends only when the poet has spent himself, the poem being sustained as long as he continues to annotate his sensory data with significances.

One radical heritage of the early nineteenth century, then, was a deal of revolutionary epistemological speculation and a literary tradition to which these speculations should have been important, but were not. What Wordsworth, Coleridge, Keats, and Shelley chose to confront more centrally and to a degree unprecedented in English literature is a nagging problem in their literary culture: How do subject and object meet in a meaningful relationship? By what means do we have a *significant* awareness of the world? Each of these poets offers a different answer, and each is unique as poet in proportion as his answer is special; but all share the necessity to resolve the question their predecessors had made so pressing through philosophic and aesthetic concern and poetic neglect or incompetence. Even in 1796, when Coleridge had not advanced beyond a poetics in which "moral Sentiments, Affections, or Feelings, are deduced from, and associated with, the Scenery of Nature," he was conscious of a pressure to "create . . . [an] indissoluble union between the intellectual and the material world." Of course epistemologies involve ontologies and can, and did, interconnect with theologies; but the epistemological problem is radical to this poetry as poetry, since it determines the role the poet will assign his raw materials, how he will confront them, and how he will mold them into a poem. Nothing I have to say about each of the poets is less than familiar; but I believe it has not been customary to view them collectively in terms of what I have called epistemology or to see it as the common base on which their poetry rests.

Wordsworth's earliest descriptive poems, *An Evening Walk* and *Descriptive Sketches*, are strictly in the eighteenth-century mode and are dull in proportion as they merely organize images into picturesque and sublime configurations and propose moral analogues. The emergence of the radically different Wordsworth is marked by a primitive, child-like wonderment that he experiences the outer world *at all*. In a sense he is an ur-romantic, celebrating unphilosophically the forgotten basic miracle that the self may possess the outer world in some telling way, and making fresh the wonder of the act. He seeks to convey, for example, the awe with which, when the boy of Winander tensely waited in the silence for the owls to return his hoot,

> a gentle shock of mild surprise
> Has carried far into his heart the voice
> Of mountain-torrents; or the visible scene
> Would enter unawares into his mind
> With all its solemn imagery, its rocks,
> Its woods, and that uncertain heaven received
> Into the bosom of the steady lake.
>
> (*Prelude*, v. 381–388)

Many poems, such as "Expostulation and Reply," are essentially delighted responses to the discovery that the external world *can* move into the consciousness. Stale and negligible as this fact had been to his predecessors, Wordsworth, by responding to it with almost naïve amazement, cleared the ground for fresh poetic considerations of the transactions betwen things and mind. His "To a Highland Girl," for example, progressively transfers the perceived scene and girl into the poet's mind and memory, starting with the paradox, "Thee, neither know I, nor thy peers; / And yet my eyes are filled with tears." Subject is affected by object and yet is unrelated to it. Progressively the poet proposes more binding relationships: to pray for the girl after he is gone, to make a garland for her, to dwell beside her and adopt her ways, to share a common neighborhood, to be her brother, her father. For as an external object, finite and fixed in space, she is to him "but as a wave / Of the wild sea," a transient image on his senses and unrelated to his being. The poet's plea is, "I would have / Some claim upon thee," the subject yearning to possess the object in some absolute relationship, not merely to be transiently touched by it. How the object is transformed into the stuff of the mind Wordsworth does not here say; but it is incorporated into the memory so that he may part from the girl in space and time, and yet,

> till I grow old,
> As fair before me shall behold,
> As I do now, the cabin small,
> The lake, the bay, the waterfall;
> And Thee, the Spirit of them all!

Whereas the eighteenth-century poet took it for granted that we perceive and sought by collateral accretions to give percepts value, Wordsworth invested with value the very act of experience.

That Wordsworth had no philosophy in him has been widely suspected, and it is likely that Coleridge foisted on him the burden of appearing a systematic thinker. At any rate, formal epistemology was of prime importance to Coleridge; and Wordsworth, trying to look like the philosophic poet Coleridge urged him to be, offers almost every variety of epistemological hypothesis. Associationism and analogy are there, and so, too, is mutual interdependence:

> an ennobling interchange
> Of action from without and from within;
> The excellence, pure function, and best power
> Both of the objects seen and eye that sees.
> (*Prelude*, XIII. 375–378)

So, too, is something of Coleridge's position: "thou must give, / Else never canst receive" (*Prelude*, XII, 276–277). Or he can postulate, to Blake's annoyance, the old teleological doctrine of the exquisite fittingness of subject and object, speaking of the relation, however, not as a meeting but as a wedding and of its result as a kind of biological creation, "which they with blended might / Accomplish" (*Recluse*). The power of the senses "to own / An intellectual charm" he attributed to "Those first-born affinities that fit / Our new existence to existing things" (*Prelude*, I, 552–556).

Varied and inconsistent though his many explanations are, they at least reveal how recurrently the poetic enterprise of the romantic required attention to the negotiations between the senses and the mind.

It was inescapable for a poet whose plan, as Coleridge outlined it, was "to treat of man as . . . a subject of eye, ear, touch, and taste, in contact with external nature, and informing the senses from the mind, and not compounding a mind out of the senses." But Wordsworth was honest enough to admit his tolerance for multiple views: "To every natural form, rock, fruit, or flower . . . I gave a moral life: I saw them feel, or linked them to some feeling" (*Prelude*, III, 127–130). Coleridge might well have thought of him as Dr. Johnson did of pliant Poll Carmichael: "I had some hopes for her at first, . . . but she was wiggle-waggle, and I could never persuade her to be categorical."

But when Wordsworth set about to shape a poetic union of the world and the mind, instead of theorizing about it, there tends to appear one dominant mode, which can be described by the following among his many formulations:

> . . . by contemplating these Forms [i.e., of nature]
> In the relations which they bear to man,
> He shall discern, how, through the various means
> Which silently they yield, are multiplied
> The *spiritual* presences of absent things.
>
> (*Excursion*, IV. 1230–1234)

"The Solitary Reaper," for example, ends with approximately the same detailed description of the singing reaper with which it began— but with an essential difference. In the intervening stanzas the girl's song is stretched out in space (by comparison with song among Arabian sands and in the farthest Hebrides) and in time (perhaps its burden is of long ago, today, or the future); and, by virtue of its being in a strange tongue, its content has no specificity. The boundaries around the specific song have been stretched thin, and when we return at length to the original scene the song, having nearly lost its finitude and become quasi-spiritual, has made its way into the poet's inner consciousness.

Perhaps the best account of such a process of experiences is Coleridge's analysis of a partial, inadequate form of his own epistemology. Since Coleridge, adapting Schelling, held that in knowledge object and subject "are identical, each involving, and supposing the other" (*Biographia Literaria*), he rejected the possibility that either has precedence. Were the objective taken as prior, then we would "have to account for the supervention of the subjective, which coalesces with it." If the object were prior, as it is for Wordsworth, then it must "grow into intelligence." "The phaenomena (*the material*) must wholly disappear, and the laws alone (*the formal*) must remain. Thence it comes, that in nature itself the more the principle of law breaks forth, the more does the *husk* drop off, the phaenomena themselves become more spiritual and at length cease altogether in our consciousness." Coleridge rejected this position, but Wordsworth's poetic instincts led him to it: the object is perceived vividly, usually with great specificity; the husk is then dissolved; and when the phenomenon has at last become "spiritualized" it passes into the core of the subjective intelligence. Lucy Gray slips away from her defining surroundings, evaporates into footprints in the snow, which, in turn, vanish at the middle of the bridge between the phenomenal and spiritual worlds; and she becomes the living spirit of solitude. Of the cuckoo's twofold voice, "At once far off, and near," the song to the nearby is addressed to the physical scene, and first becomes subordinate to the far-off one that brings "a tale / Of visionary hours" and then is lost in it, so that the bird may be "No bird, but an invisible thing, / A voice, a mystery," a spirit in nature that binds the poet's past with his present, his far-off with his near. Or, in "Resolution and Independence" the poet oscillates between perception of the leech-gatherer and a dreamlike inner vision of him until at length the leech-gatherer has become an object of the "mind's eye" and moves into the poet's spirit as a moral force, instead of being only a visible exemplum.

To Coleridge the goal of art is "To make the external internal, the internal external, to make Nature thought and thought Nature" ("On Poesy or Art"); and Wordsworth occasionally echoed him: "All things shall live in us and we shall live / In all things that surround us." But in fact only the first half of this statement truly describes his poetic processes, and he was closer to the mark when he wrote that the imagination, "either by conferring additional properties upon an object, or abstracting from it some of those which it actually possesses," enables it to "re-act upon the mind which hath performed the process, like a new existence" (1815 Preface). The senses shuck off or greatly attenuate the materiality of the image, or the imagination transmutes sensory data into something quasi-immaterial so that, for Wordsworth, sound was "Most audible . . . when the fleshly ear . . . Forgot her functions, and slept undisturbed" (*Prelude*, II, 415–418): when "bodily eyes / Were utterly forgotten . . . what I saw / Appeared like something in myself, a dream, / A *prospect of the mind*" (*Prelude*, II, 349–352). This is why Keats, looking from the other side of the fence, could speak of Wordsworth's poems as "a kind of sketchy *intellectual landscape*" (to Bailey, October 1817) and why Shelley could describe Wordsworth's art as "Wakening a sort of thought in sense." Wordsworth's poetic experience seeks to recapture that condition of boyhood when, as he said, he was "unable to think of external things as having external existence, and I communed with all that I saw as something not apart from, but inherent in, my own immaterial nature."

It is notable that Wordsworth's major contemporaries—Coleridge, Keats, Hazlitt, De Quincey, and Shelley—all recognized that at the core of his thought and art is the tendency to assimilate the outer world to the mind, to absorb object into subject. Their vivid awareness of this suggests not only the epistemological center of Wordsworth's poetry but also the overriding importance to his contemporaries of the epistemological problem. . . .

[For] Keats, who is Wordsworth's exact antithesis, . . . significant experience absorbs the self into the essence of the object, and therefore he condemned Wordsworth's inversion of this relationship as the "egotistical sublime." The epistemological difference between the two is that . . . between the two eighteenth-century traditions from which they stem. Wordsworth derives mainly from the empirical and associative doctrines which speculated on how the imagination transmutes sensation into the stuff of the mind; Keats belongs to the tradition of sympathy, largely by way of Hazlitt, who protested against an art in which some sentiment is forever "moulding everything to itself." But however widely they differ, they obviously share a deep-rooted concern with how the subjective and objective worlds carry on their transactions. It is the question their culture had made of prime importance to the poetic act; and much of their poetry is the act of answering it.

Rejecting Wordsworth's "egotistical" assimilation of object to subject Keats assumed that everything has its own vital and immutable quintessence and that the fulfillment of experience is the absorption of the experiencing self into that essence through the intensity of the sensory enounter. The "Man of Genius," as opposed to the "Man of Power," has no "individuality," no "proper self," since he is "continually informing and filling some other Body" or, according to Hazlitt, losing his personal identity "in some object dearer to him than himself." When I am in a room full of people, Keats wrote, "then not myself goes home to myself: but the identity of every one in the room begins so to press upon me that I am in a very little time annihilated."

Consequently, whereas Wordsworth's major poetic process requires the dissolution of the object's sensory finitude, awakening "a sort of thought in sense," Keats's process requires that the self rise to increasingly more intense sensory ardor until it is of the order of the object's dynamic essence—just as his Porphyro must rise "Beyond a mortal man impassion'd far" in order to melt into his own immutable essence as it exists in Madeline's intense dream. For Keats the object becomes progressively sharper, richer, more vibrant—more, not less, itself—as the experiencing self is entangled, enthralled, destroyed, until, "Melting into its radiance, we blend, / Mingle, and so become a part of it" (*Endymion*, I, 798–811). Correspondingly, his images become symbols, not by becoming "sketchy intellectual landcapes," but by achieving their most intense sensory nature, since, as he wrote, everything becomes valued by the ardor with which it is pursued. The poet, capable of ecstatically entering the essences of objects, finds his way to the instincts of the eagle and knows the tiger's yell "like mother-tongue"; he can explore "all forms and substances / Straight homeward to their symbol-essences." The first three stanzas of the "Ode on a Grecian Urn" are a full enactment of this process of empathic absorption, as the observer is progressively drawn to the urn, to the frieze within it, and to the perdurably ecstatic life in the frieze—a life which he at last experiences by being assimilated into it. Endymion's detested moments, on the other hand, are those when, after absorption into essence, he makes "the journey homeward to habitual self," self-conscious instead of other-conscious. This epistemology Keats anchored in a private faith that we create our own post-mortal existence, since in our final absorption into the ultimate essence we shall experience hereafter in a "finer tone" and immutably our transient earthly absorptions into essences; and most of Keats's poetry is an exploration of the ramifications of this belief. But the form and quality his poetic materials take and the role they play are determined by his epistemology of empathy.

Since for Coleridge the goal of art is "to make Nature thought and thought Nature," neither the Wordsworthian nor the Keatsian position is adequate. Starting with the dualism of nature and the self, Coleridge made the purpose of his epistemology such a reconciliation of the two that they may be "coinstantaneous and one." Ultimate knowledge is self-knowledge, for only in this act are subject and object identical.* But in order to be an object the infinite subject must also be finite; and

* Cf. Charles Feidelson's *Symbolism and American Literature* (Chicago, 1953), espec. Ch. 2. See also Geoffrey Hartman's essay above.

therefore the act of self-knowledge, whereby "a subject . . . becomes a subject by the act of constructing itself objectively to itself," is the reconciliation and identity of the finite and infinite, nature and self. All higher knowledge must be a mode of this act, since "every object is, as an *object*, dead, fixed, incapable in itself of any action, and necessarily finite"; it is vital only insofar as the self is viewing itself in the object. Hence such Coleridgean carousels as this: "to make the object one with us, we must become one with the object—*ergo, an* object. *Ergo*, the object must be itself a subject—partially a favorite dog, principally a friend, wholly God, *the* Friend"—that is, either vehicles for the self or the total Selfhood. Consequently the Coleridgean imagination is the act of reconciling the phenomenal world of the understanding with the noumenal world of the reason. It incorporates "the reason in images of the sense" and organizes "the flux of the senses by the permanent and self-circulating energies of the reason" to give birth to symbols, which are both "harmonious in themselves, and consubstantial with the truths of which they are the conductors." Art, like the self-knowing subject, is "the middle quality between a thought and a thing, or . . . the union and reconciliation of that which is nature with that which is exclusively human"; and taste, a mode of imagination, "is the intermediate faculty which connects the active with the passive powers of our nature, the intellect with the senses; and its appointed function is to elevate the *images* of the latter [the Wordsworthian mode], while it realized the *ideas* of the former." Wordsworth occasionally wished to say something of the sort:

> . . . his spirit drank
> The spectacle. Sensation, soul, and form
> All melted into him. They swallowed up
> His animal being; in them did he live
> And by them did he live. They were his life.

But this is both more than the epistemology that motivated him and far less than Coleridge's purpose, which is not merely to dissolve self and nature into each other, but, starting with "I am" instead of "it is," to develop the noumenal potential in the phenomenal.

With a single sentence Coleridge has preserved from embarrassment the critic who would make the transition from his metaphysics and poetics to his poetry: "I freely own that I have no title to the name of poet, according to my own definition of poetry." Frankly, it is not readily conceivable how Coleridge's epistemology could be translated into the life of a poem by shaping its matter, imparting a special quality to its imagery, or providing a process for the transformation of images into symbols. In other words, it is difficult to conceive of a poetry in which his epistemology and his theories of imagination and symbolism would be recognizable as shaping forces. But in fact he was not proffering a program; he was defining the ideal nature and role of poetry. As a practicing poet, for example, he performs no special act to cause his symbols to render intelligible the reality of which they partake; he merely deposits images which we are expected to conceive of as significant. Occasionally it is true, we find him making poetic statements that approximate his conception of a self constituting itself by constructing and viewing itself as object. Thus, of Mont Blanc he wrote:

> Thou, the meantime, wast blending with my Thought,
> Yea with my Life, and Life's own secret joy:
> Till the dilating soul, enrapt, transfused,
> Into the mighty vision passing—there
> As in her natural form, swelled vast to Heaven.
>
> ("Hymn before Sunrise")

To the complaint of Wordsworth, expectedly unsympathetic on epistemological grounds, that this is the "Mock Sublime," Coleridge replied: "from my childhood I have been accustomed to *abstract* and as it were unrealize whatever of more than common interest my eyes dwelt on; and then by a sort of transference and transmission of my consciousness to identify myself with the object." And of course his epistemology is the necessary gloss on the Dejection ode to explain why the senses are inadequate and how the imagination develops subjective life in objects, which, as objects, are "dead, fixed":

> I may not hope from outward forms to win
> The passion and the life, whose fountains are within.
>
> O Lady! we receive but what we give,
> And in our life alone does Nature live:
> Ours is her wedding garment, ours her shroud!
>   And would we aught behold, of higher worth,
> Than that inanimate cold world allowed . . .
>   Ah! from the soul itself must issue forth
> A light, a glory, a fair luminous cloud
>   Enveloping the Earth—
> And from the soul itself must there be sent
>   A sweet and potent voice, of its own birth,
> Of all sweet sounds the life and element!

But the most important poetic role of Coleridge's epistemology is to provide the dramatic form for a group of poems which act out the principle that the self becomes a self by objectifying itself so as to identify finite and infinite. "This Lime-Tree Bower," which may be taken as typical, begins with the poet disconsolately imprisoned in the bower, isolated and unrelated to anything, like Keats detesting the journey homeward to habitual self, like Wordsworth unable to assert a claim on the Highland girl. Between him and his departing friend Charles Lamb is a dell, the divisive gulf separating the ego from the non-ego. In imagination he attends Lamb in his passage through the dell until the imagined friend emerges on the glowing plain with a freedom and joy that mock the gloom of the bower-shaded poet:

> So my friend
> Struck with deep joy may stand, as I have stood,
> Silent with swimming sense; yea, gazing round
> On the wide landscape, gaze till all doth seem
> Less gross than bodily. . . .

Escape from the prison of selfhood requires a union, through the imagination, with an object, an object that is itself a subject, a "friend," a Charles Lamb; and the self must "become one with the object" so that the poem ends with Coleridge watching the sunset and imagining Lamb watching the sunset as he himself had once watched it. The end is release from the prison, the freedom which is the ground of the willful act of imagination; and the end is the joy and vitality returned to the self by its evolving its own life in the object of experience.

Shelley's epistemology is so deeply embedded in an idiosyncratic ontology that it is difficult to disengage it, especially since he does not start with the usual distinction between autonomous subject and object. His grounds are two empirical axioms: "the mind cannot create, it can only perceive"; and "nothing exists but as it is perceived." The mental image results from perceiving something whose nature we cannot know, and consequently, with respect to the mind, the perception *is* the sole object. Shelley has cut the epistemological knot by putting aside an external world that stands against the self and by making the basic transaction one between the self and its mental impressions in all their combinations. The subject is what we are; the object, our percepts and feelings. But even this distinction is false, relevant only because of the whole falsity of our mortal condition. In childhood, Shelley writes, we "less habitually distinguished all that we saw and felt, from ourselves. They seemed, as it were, to constitute one mass." In the most vivid apprehension of being, men "feel as if their nature were dissolved into the surrounding universe, or as if the surrounding universe were absorbed into their being. They are conscious of no distinction" ("On Life"). Only subsequently are we misled into supposing a dualism of subject and object and a categorical difference between things and thoughts. What we call a "thing," he said, is merely "any thought upon which any other thought is employed with an apprehension of distinction"; and the division between "external" and "internal" is merely nominal, so that "when speaking of the objects of thought, we indeed only describe one of the forms of thought" and, "speaking of thought, we only apprehend one of the operations of the universal system of beings." True phenomenal knowledge, then, does not consist in bridging the gap between self and nature, but in withdrawing these illusory entities to their common source. Consequently it is considerably less than a figure of speech when Shelley commands the West Wind: "Be thou, Spirit fierce, / My spirit! Be thou me. . . ." Or when, in "Mont Blanc," he *pretends* a distinction betwen thoughts and things, he can define reality only as a continuous mental act, a vain striving by the mind to identify its shadowy images with the corresponding but unknowable external world that has cast them.

Hence the curiously insubstantial, unrealized quality of Shelley's poetic imagery. Clouds, winds, vapors, skylarks, and flowers hover between thing and thought because his experiential reality is neither subjective nor objective, an irrelevant distinction if our being and our perceptions "constitute one mass." Insofar as, limited by time and space, we perceive a mutable world external to ourselves, we perceive what "seems," not what "is." Shelley's real, nonillusory world, unlike Wordsworth's or Keats's, is symbolic in its very nature, since it is not categorically different from other thoughts—or, more properly, since what we call the world is constituted of the mass of our thoughts, including our own nature. The West Wind *is* Necessity, the summit of Mont Blanc *is* the residence of the Power, its ravine *is* the Mind, and life *is* like a dome of many-colored glass, not because things are like thoughts, but because one order of thought differs from another, as Shelley said, only in force.

The four romantics, it is clear, are sharply at odds with each other, in the terms I have been concerned with. But the very fact that their positions do clash so directly on these terms, instead of being merely unrelated, confirms that they all face the central need to find a significant relationship between the subjective and objective worlds.* We may conceive of poetry as made up superficially *of* features, such as nature images, melancholy, or lyricism; but it is made *by* purposes, and epistemology is poetically constitutive. All the romantics, it is true, give extraordinary value to a faculty they call the imagination because they must postulate an extraordinary faculty that bridges the gap between mind and the external world; but no two of them agree on a definition of this faculty, any more than they do on the mode of existence of the external nature they so commonly write about. Admittedly, all are symbolic poets, since the symbol is the marriage of the two worlds, but their kinds of symbolism are necessarily as widely diverse as the epistemologies that generate them.

BIBLIOGRAPHICAL NOTE: Other essays that deal with the romantic subject-object relationship are those by Albert Gérard, Northrop Frye, and M. H. Abrams in this collection; also R. A. Foakes, *The Romantic Assertion* (London, 1958) and Wasserman's *The Subtler Language* (Baltimore, 1959). For an attack on Wasserman's conception of the romantics' new "cosmic syntax" see E. E. Bostetter, *The Romantic Ventriloquists* (Seattle, 1963). See also the works cited in the bibliographical note to Geoffrey Hartman's essay above, p. 297.

* Like Wasserman, Ian Jack rejects the term "romanticism" and emphasizes the conflicts among the several romantic poets; but largely ignoring the issue of epistemology, he is unable to see the romantics all facing the same "central need." See his *English Literature: 1815–1832* (Oxford, 1963).

Na